Year of Fire, Year of Ash

The Soweto Revolt: Roots of a Revolution?

Baruch Hirson

Zed Press, 57 Caledonian Road, London N1 9DN.

This book is dedicated to all political prisoners
held in South Africa, and in particular to those
held at Pretoria Local Prison

Year of Fire, Year of Ash was first published
by Zed Press, 57 Caledonian Road, London
N1 9DN in June 1979.

Copyright © Baruch Hirson, 1979

ISBN Hb 0 905762 28 2
     Pb 0 905762 29 0

Printed in U. S. A.
Typeset by Dark Moon
Designed by Mayblin/Shaw
Cover photo by Peter Magubane, courtesy of International
    Defence and Aid Fund

U.S. Distributor
Lawrence Hill & Co., 520 Riverside Avenue, Westport,
Conn. 06880, U.S.A.

First reprint, February 1981

Contents

List of Tables

Maps

List of Abbreviations

AAC	All African Convention
AAC	Anglo-American Corporation
ABCFM	American Board of Commissioners for Foreign Missions
ACROM	Anti-CRC Committee
ADP	African Democratic Party
AEM	African Education Movement
AFRO	Anti-CRC Front
AICA	African Independent Churches Association
Anti-CAD	Anti-Coloured Affairs Department
ANC	African National Congress
ASSECA	Association for the Educational and Cultural Advancement of the African People
ATASA	African Teachers Association of South Africa
BAWU	Black Allied Workers Union
BCP	Black Community Programmes
BIC	Bantu Investment Corporation
BOSS	Bureau of State Security
BPA	Black Parents Association
BPC	Black Peoples Convention
BWC	Black Workers Council
BWP	Black Workers Project
BYCA	Black Youth Cultural Association
BYO	Border Youth Organization
CFS	Committee for Fairness in Sport
CI	Christian Institute
CIS	Counter Information Service
CNE	Christian National Education
CPRC	Coloured Persons Representative Council
CRC	See CPRC
CYL	Congress Youth League
FRELIMO	Front for the Liberation of Mozambique
IDAMASA	Inter-Denominational African Ministers Association

IIE	Institute for Industrial Education
JASCO	Junior African Students Congress
LAY	League of African Youth
LEARN	Let Every African Learn
MPLA	Popular Movement for the Liberation of Angola
NAYO	National Youth Organisation
NEUM	Non-European Unity Movement
NUSAS	National Union of South African Students
NYO	Natal Youth Organisation
OFS	Orange Free State
PAC	Pan-Africanist Congress
PUTCO	Public Utility Transport Corporation
SABRA	South African Bureau of Racial Affairs
SACP	South African Communist Party
SACTU	South African Congress of Trade Unions
SAD	Society for African Development
SAFO	South African Freedom Organisation
SAIC	South African Indian Congress
SAIC	South African Indian Council
SANA	South African News Agency
SAPPI	South African Pulp and Paper Industries
SASM	South African Students Movement
SASO	South African Students Organisation
SOYA	Society of Young Africa
SPROCAS	Study Project on Christianity in Apartheid Society
SRC	Students Representative Council
SRRSA	Survey of Race Relations in South Africa
SSRC	Soweto Students Representative Council
SWANLA	South West African Native Labour Association
SWAPO	South West African Peoples Organisation
TEACH	Teach Every African Child
TLSA	Teachers League of South Africa
TRYO	Transvaal Youth Organisation
TUCSA	Trade Union Council of South Africa
UBC	Urban Bantu Council
UBJ	Union of Black Journalists
UCT	University of Cape Town
UTP	Urban Training Project
UWC	University of the Western Cape
WCYO	Western Cape Youth Organisation
YARM	Young African Religious Movement
ZETA	Zulu Education and Teaching Assistance

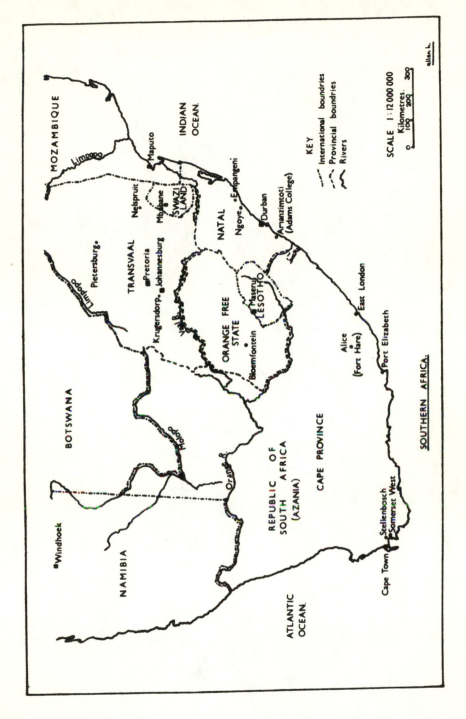

SOUTHERN AFRICA.

SCALE 1 : 12 000 000

Kilometres.
0   100   200   300

KEY
International boundries
Provincial boundries
Rivers

MOZAMBIQUE

INDIAN OCEAN.

Limpopo

Maputo

SWAZI LAND

Nelspruit

Mbabane

NATAL

Ngoye.

Empangeni

Durban

Amanzimtoti
(Adams College)

TRANSVAAL

Pietersburg.

Pretoria

Johannesburg

Krugersdorp

ORANGE FREE STATE

Maseru

LESOTHO

Bloemfontein

East London

Alice
(Fort Hare)

Port Elizabeth

BOTSWANA

Molopo

Orange

REPUBLIC OF SOUTH AFRICA
(AZANIA)

CAPE PROVINCE

Windhoek

NAMIBIA

Stellenbosch

Somerset West

Cape Town

ATLANTIC OCEAN.

ellen k.

Nineteen Seventy-Six

Go nineteen seventy-six
We need you no more
Never come again
We ache inside.
Good friends we have
Lost.
Nineteen seventy-six
You stand accused
of deaths
Imprisonments
Exiles
And detentions.
You lost the battle
You were not revolutionary
Enough
We do not boast about you
Year of fire, year of ash.

Oupa Thando Mthimkulu

Reprinted with permission from *Staffrider*,
Vol. 1, No. 1, 1978.

Foreword

The story of the Soweto Revolt has in the first instance to tell what happened, and how. And because all revolts have their origin in events, both remote and recent, I am indebted to the many sources from which I was able to borrow books, pamphlets and documents. There would have been little point in even commencing this study if it had not been for the International University Exchange Fund's distribution of documents, reprinted in Geneva after being banned in South Africa. Added to the material collected together in the annual *Survey of Race Relations in South Africa,* and the four annual *Black Review*s, from 1972 through to 1976, the events of the 1970s began to unfold.

Documents, manifestos, leaflets and copies of underground newsletters collected together in South Africa, and photocopied so that they became available in Britain, allowed me to cross-check some of the stories, and fill in some of the more obvious gaps. For these collections, I must thank the International Defence and Aid Fund, Counter Information Service, the Institute of Commonwealth Studies, London, and the Centre for Southern African Studies at the University of York. To Tom Lodge, Brian Willan, and others who willingly lent me copies of documents, I am equally grateful.

To tell the story, is little enough. Events do not occur fortuitously, nor are they preordained. Real live people have made the history recounted here, and even if events unfolded against their personal wishes, it is their actions which have to be understood. This was in many ways a most remarkable story. Youth at schools throughout the country, many of them young children, raised the banner of revolt and called on the workers, their parents, to disrupt the entire economy. And their parents listened. School children cannot, by themselves, topple a strong intransigent regime. But few would have dared to believe in June 1976 that the Revolt could last for more than a few weeks. Yet it did; it continued for well over a year and in the process altered the history of the country irrevocably.

Understanding these events was the task of the author, and I am more than aware of the shortcomings in the answers I give to many of the questions raised by the events of Soweto. The deficiencies in the book would have been far more serious if it had not been for the criticism of the earlier chapters by May Katzen, John Laredo, and Allen Hirson. The chapter on the actual events

1

in Soweto itself came to life after I had discussed the material with Nick Barker, and my ideas on Black Consciousness took final shape only after Shula Marks and her students at the School of Oriental and African Studies demanded more answers of me than I could provide at the time.

Eventually the task of editing this book rested on the never-tiring work of Robert Molteno. It is due to his critical appraisal that at least some of the grosser errors and oversimplifications were spotted and removed. It need hardly be added that I alone am responsible for some of the opinions that I obstinately held to despite the critical comments of all those who suggested further changes.

I am grateful to Thando Mthimkulu for permission to reprint his poem, and for the use of the last line as the title of this book. I must also thank Peter Magubane and the International Defence and Aid Fund for allowing me to use the picture that appears on the cover, Allen Hirson for drawing the maps for the book, and Bella Peters for typing the first draft of this study.

Finally it must be said that this book is by no means impartial. To write a book about South Africa, and in particular, a book about the Revolt of the 1970s, demands that the author take sides. That, indeed, is not difficult. There can be no doubt about the justice of the demands that lay behind the Revolt. But that does not mean that this book is a defence of one particular position. The telling of the story also discloses the forces at work in that society, and I have used the material available to me critically and without favour. The cause of the South African revolution requires no special pleading, no false argument, and no distortion of what was said or done. If in the process I have appeared to be harsh, and hyper-critical of some persons or organisations, it is because I believe that only a real understanding of 1976 will help the forces of socialism and liberation achieve the free Azania that the youth of Soweto so passionately called for in the days that followed 16 June, 1976.

Baruch Hirson
Bradford and London
1977-78.

Introduction

As I have told the South African public time and time again, race relations in this country have deteriorated to the extent that there will no longer be any possible reconciliation between black and white. What is happening is, in fact, a projection of black anger against the racist regime. This anger is directed at anything that is connected with the system and the government. It is not a question of the insistence on the Afrikaans language as the mode of instruction for black schoolchildren. The burning of the offices belonging to the government administration – the beerhalls, administration offices, post offices, administration-run buses and the like – should be enough for the people to realise this point. It has got nothing to do with vandalism . . . it is black anger against white domination. Winnie Mandela interviewed by Eric Abraham, after 16th June 1976.

Black anger against white domination has never been far below the surface in South Africa. In the countryside, on the farms, and in the towns, Africans have voiced their protests, organised campaigns, and used every means available to them in order to secure some concessions from the white ruling class. At every turn they were met by an intransigent minority which meant to maintain its control – by political hegemony, by economic subordination, by social segregation, by rules and regulations, and ultimately by brute force.

The anger has often been muted. The forms of protest have been 'peaceful'. The black population has shown a measure of self-control which belied the deep hatred of endless humiliation felt by every man, woman and child. In all the strikes, the boycotts, the demonstrations, and local and national campaigns, leaders urged restraint – and the police answered with baton charges, or with armoured cars, teargas and bullets.

The violence, all too often, turned inwards, and in the black townships that bordered the all-white towns, groups of *tsotsis* (as the delinquents were called)[1] terrorised the population. The seething anger, fostered by poverty and frustration, exacted its toll of injured, mutilated and murdered from the oppressed black population itself.

Soweto, a town that is not to be found on most maps, has been the focus of much violence for several decades now. Its population of 1.3 million serves the half million whites (who constitute the 'official' population of Johannesburg) as labourers in their homes, shops and factories. By all accounts this town that is not a town, this area known to the world by the

3

acronym Soweto (South West Township) is one of the most violent regions on earth. One year before Soweto erupted in revolt the newspaper of the students of the University of the Witwatersrand reported that:

> ... In the last year there was a 100 per cent increase in crimes of violence: 854 murders; 92 culpable homicides; 1,828 rapes; 7,682 assaults with intent to do grievous bodily harm.
>
> Four hundred thousand people in Soweto do not have homes. The streets and the eaves of the churches are their shelter. The faces and bodies of many Soweto people are scarred; the gun is quick and the knife is silent.[2]

The same black fury has been turned against whites. Not only in acts of 'crime' — the houses of white Johannesburg are renowned for their rose-bushes and for their burglar-proofing! — but through acts of violence directed against any individual seen to be harming members of the township population. There is a long history of rioting following motor, train or bus accidents in which Africans have been injured or killed. The fury of the crowd that collected was directed against persons who were present, or passing the scene. Voluble fury changed to stone throwing and the destruction of property. The crowd would metamorphose into a seething furious mass that sought revenge.

This violence was endemic in a country where local communities lived under intolerable conditions. There was always a deep sense of frustration and alienation inside the townships or segregated areas of the big urban conurbations. The riots served to bring a section of the community together; to fuse disparate individuals into a collectivity which rose up against long-standing wrongs.

When the riot was protracted — as it was in 1976 — the crowd was not static. Factions emerged and formulated new objectives. There was not one crowd, but an ever changing mass of people who formed and reformed themselves as they sought a way to change social conditions.

To describe the participants and their groups as being 'ethnic' or 'tribal' or 'racial', as many white South Africans do, does not help to explain the aspirations of such people or the causes of events. It only hides the glaring inequalities in the society and conceals the poverty of the rioters. Such descriptions, furthermore, distract attention from the *provocateurs* who egged the 'rioters' on, and from the prolonged campaigns of hatred in the local or national (white) press which often preceded African attacks on minority communities. An openly anti-Indian campaign in the press preceded the Durban riots of 1949. Direct police intervention and police direction accompanied the 'tribal' assaults during the Evaton bus boycott in 1956. Open police incitement led to attacks on Soweto residents by Zulu hostel dwellers in 1976.

When apologists for the system found that descriptions of the rioters in terms of 'race' or 'ethnicity' were not convincing, they tried another ruse.

They claimed that the events were due to 'criminal elements' and to township *tsotsis*. They ignored what has long been a marked feature of periods of high political activity in the townships of South Africa, namely a corresponding sharp drop in criminal activity. This decline in criminality was also a marked feature of the events of 1976 when the initial riots were transformed into a prolonged revolt against the white administration.[3]

It was necessary for the police and the regime to mask the new antagonisms that emerged in the townships. When the youth turned against members of the township advisory council (the Urban Bantu Council or UBC), or against African businessmen and some of the priests, the authorities blamed the *tsotsis*; when the youth destroyed the beerhalls and bottle stores, again it was the *tsotsis* who were to blame; and when plain clothes police shot at children, *tsotsis* were blamed again. Yet never once did any of these *tsotsis* shoot at the police, or indeed at any white. Not one of the slanderers, who glibly accused blacks of shooting their fellows in the townships, find it necessary to comment on this anomaly.

Race Riots or Class War?

The revolt, presented to the world by the media as a colour clash, was, in fact, far more than a 'race war'. The words used in the past had changed their meanings by 1976. The word 'black' was itself diluted and extended. During the 1970's the young men and women who formed the Black Consciousness Movement recruited not only Africans, but also Coloured and Indian[4] students and intellectuals. During the 1976 Revolt the Coloured students of Cape Town, both from the (Coloured) University of the Western Cape and from the secondary schools joined their African peers in demonstrations, and faced police terror together with them. In the African townships there were also indications that the Revolt transcended colour considerations. In Soweto there were black policemen who were as trigger-happy as their white counterparts; there were also government collaborators in the black townships who threatened the lives of leading members of the Black Parents Association; there were black informers who worked with the police; there were Chiefs who aimed to divert the struggle and stop the school boycott; and there was an alliance between members of the Urban Bantu Council, the police, and tribal leaders which was directed at suppressing the Revolt; and, ultimately, there was the use of migrant labourers against the youth. Armed, directed, and instructed by the police, these men were turned loose on the youth of Soweto, and in Cape Town, shebeen (pothouse) owners used migrant labourers to protect their premises. The result was widespread maiming, murder, and destruction of property.

Despite this evidence of co-operation by part of the African petty bourgeoisie and others with the government, there was one indubitable fact. The Revolt did express itself in terms of 'black anger' which *did* in fact express a basic truth about South African relationships. Capital and finance are almost exclusively under white control. Industry and commerce are almost entirely owned and managed by Whites. Parliament and all government institutions are reserved for Whites, and all the major bodies of the state are either exclusively manned by, or controlled by, white personnel. The conjunction of economic and political control and white domination does divide the population across the colour-line. Those Blacks who sought alliance with the Whites naturally moved away from their black compatriots and allied themselves to the ruling group. Certain others were cajoled or threatened, bribed, driven — or just duped — into buttressing the state structures and using their brawn-power to break black opposition.

Because most white workers, irrespective of their role in production, sided so overwhelmingly with the white ruling class, class divisions were concealed, and racial separation and division appeared as the predominant social problem. The economic crisis of 1975, in part a result of the depression in the West and the fall in the price of gold, and in part a manifestation of the crisis in South African capitalism, only cemented the alliance of white workers and the ruling class. The black communities found few friends amongst the Whites in the aftermath of the clash of June 16, 1976. Those Whites who demonstrated sympathy with the youth of Soweto were confined to a handful of intellectuals who came mainly from the middle class; or from a group of committed Christians who had established some ties with the groups that constituted the Black Consciousness Movement.

Capitalist production in South Africa owes its success to the availability of a regimented cheap labour force. In the vast rural slums, known as Reserves, the women and children, the aged, the sick and the disabled eke out a bare existence. All rely on the remittances of their menfolk in the towns. The accommodation in townships, in hostels, or in compounds (barracks) is likewise organised in order to depress African wage levels. At the same time, the vast urban slums, of which Soweto is by far the largest, were planned in order to ensure complete police and military control, were the administrative system ever to be challenged.

The government also sought to control more effectively the vast conurbations that grew up on the borders of the 'white' towns by dividing the townships, the hostels, the compounds and all the subsidiary institutions (like schools and colleges) into segmented 'tribal' regions. It also divided Africans from Coloureds, and both of these from Indians, by setting up residential 'Group Areas' (each being reserved for one 'race'). The map of South Africa was drawn and redrawn in order to seal off these communities, and ensure their separation from one another.

For much of the time the government has, in fact, been able to use its vast administrative machinery (reinforced by massive police surveillance) to keep opposition under control. Time and again small groups, organised by the movements in exile, were uncovered and smashed. Political organisations in the townships were not allowed to develop, following the shootings in Sharpeville and Langa in 1960, and the banning of the two national liberation movements (the African National Congress and the Pan-Africanist Congress).

It was only with great difficulty that political groups emerged at a later date, and it is some of these which will be discussed in this book.

The 1960s: from Quiescence to Resistance

Black anger seemed subdued through the sixties. Draconian legislation, constant police surveillance and the many political trials of the 1960's cowed the people.

Some found solace in drink, and it was the feeling that so many adults had surrendered the struggle for liberation and turned to the bottle that led to the onslaught on bottle stores and beerhalls in 1976.

Not all sought to escape. Although there were no effective open political organisations for them to join, and no industrial organisations to provide a lead, some workers were still determined to take action in order to secure higher wages. These working men and women participated in the widespread (largely illegal) strikes of the early seventies. This strike wave was the main indication of an end to nearly a decade of political inertia. No account of the Soweto Revolt can ignore the working class struggles of neighbouring Namibia or of Natal and the Witwatersrand. These too expressed 'black anger', but very different from the black anger which finally erupted in Soweto. It was the anger of a working class determined to secure better living conditions, and the workers needed no philosophy of 'blackness' to instruct them. They knew the price of discrimination, and they sought redress from those who could pay — the mine owners, the industrialists, and the business-men.

On to this scene of industrial stirring came the Black Consciousness Movement. Its leaders spoke of *black* awareness and of *black* identity, and this was a language which appealed particularly to students and intellectuals. There it might have rested — or in fact even been stilled — had it not been for two crucial factors. Firstly, the organisations were allowed to exist, and even encouraged, by members of the administration who were blinded by their own rhetoric into believing that this movement fitted into the framework of apartheid policy. The Black Peoples Convention (BPC), an umbrella organisation that embraced unions of journalists, students, artists, and a federation of black women, was more usually known as the Black Conscious-ness Movement, and given semi-official sanction. Secondly, the main constituent of the BPC was the South African Students Organisation (SASO), which was allowed to organise (or was tolerated initially) on the black campuses.

Students in Revolt

SASO was the latest of a series of organisations that set out to organise black university students. As such it was the inheritor of a long tradition of student struggles that started first in the boarding schools of the Eastern Cape, continued in boarding schools and colleges of education in the Cape Province and Natal, and eventually embraced the University colleges and every school in the country.

These struggles in the schools and colleges were not integrated into the activities of the national liberation movement before 1948. Their strikes were neither organised nor encouraged, and received scant attention. Although it is possible to trace the link between earlier struggles and the students' revolt in the 1970's, the continuity was barely recognised by the new leaders in SASO and in the townships. It is not even possible to find traces of any formal black students' organisation in the schools before the late sixties. Nonetheless, conflict situations developed year after year and erupted in periodic boycotts, strikes and arson. When, eventually, an independent *black* university organisation was formed in the late sixties, it immediately provided political direction and stepped into the vacuum left by the banning of the ANC and PAC in 1960. The new student body, SASO, provided the leading cadres for the BPC, and helped create the atmosphere which led to the 1976 confrontation in Soweto.

The Uprising of June 1976

Conflicts on the campuses in the seventies coincided with a contraction of the country's economy and with momentous events on the northern borders of the country. The fighting in Namibia, the collapse of the Portuguese army in Mozambique, the move to independence in Angola and the resumption of guerrilla warfare in Zimbabwe (Rhodesia) all influenced the youth of South Africa (or Azania, as they renamed the country). The BPC generally, and SASO groups in the universities, used more militant language. They now talked of liberation, and of independence; they defied a government ban on meetings, and when arrested were defiant in court.

When the government finally took steps to change the language of instruction of higher primary and secondary school students in 1975, the stage was set for a massive confrontation. The factors sketched above were by no means independent of each other. The strains in the South African economy, the wave of strikes, the new military situation, the resurgence of African political consciousness and the rapidly altering position in the black schools, were all interconnected.

The only non-tribal political organisation that was able to operate openly inside South Africa was the Black Peoples Convention. Yet from its inception in 1972 the difficulties it faced were insuperable. The South African state was powerful, its army undefeated and unshakably loyal to the regime. The police force was well trained and supported by a large body of informers in the townships – and it had infiltrated the new organisations. Above all, the regime had the support of the Western powers and even seemed to be essential to America and Great Britain in securing a 'peaceful' solution to the Zimbabwean conflict.

The young leaders of SASO and of the BPC were inexperienced. Their social base was confined (at least as of 1975) to the small groups of intellectuals in the universities, some clerics, journalists, artists, and the liberal professions. Furthermore, their philosophy of black consciousness turned them away from an analysis of the nature of the South African state. They seemed to respond with the heart rather than with the mind. They were able to reflect the black anger of the townships — but were unable to offer a viable political strategy.

At times, in the months and even weeks before June 16, the students in SASO seemed to be expecting a confrontation with the forces of the government. They spoke courageously of the coming struggle — but made no provision for the conflict. Even when their leaders were banned or arrested there did not seem to be an awareness of the tasks that faced them and when, finally, the police turned their guns on the pupils of Soweto schools and shot to kill, there were no plans, no ideas on what should be done. *Black anger* was all that was left; and in the absence of organisation, ideology or strategy, it was black anger which answered the machine guns with bricks and stones.

The people of Soweto had to learn with a minimum of guidance, and they responded with a heroism that has made *Soweto* an international symbol of resistance to tyranny. Young leaders appeared month after month to voice the aspirations of the school students — and if they were not able to formulate a full programme for their people, the fault was not theirs. A programme should have been formulated by the older leaders — and that they had failed to do. In the event, the youth fought on as best they could — and they surpassed all expectations.

Despite all the criticisms that can be levelled against the leaders of the school pupils, the revolt they led in 1976-77 has altered the nature of politics in South Africa. Firstly it brought to a precipitate end all attempts by the South African ruling class to establish friendly relations with the leaders of some African states, and it has made some Western powers reconsider the viability of the white National Party leaders as their best allies on the subcontinent. Secondly it marked the end of undisputed white rule, and demonstrated the ability of the black population to challenge the control of the ruling class.

In every major urban centre and in villages in the Reserves, the youth marched, demonstrated, closed schools, stopped transport and, on several occasions, brought the entire economy to a halt.

The youth showed an ingenuity that their parents had been unable to achieve. They occupied city centres, they closed alcohol outlets, they stopped Christmas festivities. At their command the schools were closed, the examinations were boycotted, and the teachers resigned. They forced the resignation of the Soweto Urban Bantu Council and the Bantu School Boards — both long castigated as puppets of the regime. They were even able to prevent the immediate implementation of a rent rise in 1977 and, in the many incidents that filled those crowded days that followed the first shootings of 16 June 1976, they were able to show South Africa and the world that there was the will and the determination to end the apartheid system.

9

References

Note: References to the Introduction have by and large not been provided. Evidence for all assertions will be found in the text when the events are described in greater detail.

1. See Glossary for words that are commonly used in South Africa.
2. This extract, taken from the *Wits Student*, 16 June 1975, was reprinted in an International University Exchange Fund bulletin after appearing in the *South African Outlook.*
3. The words used represent different phases in the struggle of an oppressed people. *Riots* are acts of violence against individuals or a community in order to redress some wrong. *Revolts* are risings against the local or national authority, usually to redress some wrong or secure some changes in the law. *Revolutions* occur when riots and revolts (or any other mass action) are aimed at changing the structure of a given society. The transition from riot or revolt to revolution can occur in the midst of a struggle, but such a transition usually involves a marked change in consciousness and the acceptance of an ideology.
4. The South African population in the mid-1970's consisted of approximately 4.3 million Whites, 2.4 million Coloureds, 0.75 million Indians, and over 18 million Africans.

10

PART 1
From School Strikes to Black Consciousness

1. The Black Schools: 1799-1954

Schools: Segregated and Unequal

In 1971, every white school child in the Transvaal was given an illustrated volume to 'commemorate the tenth anniversary of the Republic of South Africa'. On the subject of education the authors of the book declared:

> The cultural and spiritual developmental level of a nation can with a fair amount of certainty be ascertained from the measure of importance the nation concerned attaches to the education of its children . . .

> Only by developing the mental and spiritual resources of the nation to their maximum potential, can the need of the modern state for fully trained leaders, capable executives, industrialists with vision, dedicated teachers, scientists, engineers and skilled personnel be properly supplied.[1]

The subject of education was then explored in terms of facilities provided, buildings and equipment used:

> Not only has the equipment to be suitable with a view to efficient teaching, but the physical well being of the pupils must be taken into consideration.[2]

This was a state publication designed to instil patriotic fervour in the breast of every *white* child. It was the white child's well being that was being discussed, and the white child's future as leader, executive, industrialist or professional that was being described. It was also a self-congratulatory book; and the administration was satisfied with the role it played in providing facilities for the schools. Accompanied by lavish illustrations there were eulogistic descriptions of library facilities, school equipment and sports grounds, and also of teacher training, of psychological and guidance services, and of educational tours.

The claims made in this commemorative volume do not stand serious scrutiny. The educational system (for Whites) had serious defects which had been debated openly for many decades. The standards in many of the schools were low, the social sciences were designed to show the superiority of the Whites, and the natural science courses were antiquated in content. With all their blemishes, the white schools were however lavishly equipped, and the cost of educating each pupil was high.

If the commemorative volume had set out to describe the conditions of all sections of the population, a very different publication would have been necessary. In the realm of education alone, it would have had to be shown that the conditions of the vast majority of the youth were very different from those of the Whites. The Transvaal Province was responsible for financing and directing the education of all Whites below University level. And being the area of greatest population density, the Province catered for 52 per cent of the white youth of the country: that is, some 400,000.

The responsibility for African education, on the other hand, had been placed in the hands of the central Department of Bantu Administration and Education since 1954. Unlike the Whites, for whom education was compulsory, African youth had great difficulty in obtaining education, and what they were given was grossly inferior. Whereas every white child would complete primary school, and one quarter would complete the secondary school in 1969 (the date at about which the commemorative volume was being written),[3] 70 per cent of all African children who found a place in the schools would leave after four or less years of attendance. Less than four per cent would enter secondary school, and few of these would complete the five year course.

Some comparative statistics indicate the disparities in the schooling of Whites and Africans. In 1969 there were 810,490 white youth at school, and the total cost of their education was R241,600,000 (or £120.8 million). In the same year 2,400,000 African children were at school. The cost of their schooling, together with the cost of the infinitely more expensive University education, was R46,000,000 (£23 million).[4] In the Transvaal that year, when white primary and secondary education cost R88,000,000, the estimated cost per student for the year at school was: primary level — R175; secondary level — R234; vocational and agricultural high school — R350; and teacher training — R589.[5] The Minister of Bantu Education stated that the expenditure on each African child in 1969 was: primary level — R13.55; secondary level — R55.[6] African youth were not presented with the commemorative volume in 1971.

Since the mid-fifties African education has been directed by the Department of Bantu Affairs and Development (a department which changed its name, but not its function over the years). This has, however, not always been the case.

First Steps in the Cape

African education was not really required before the turn of the nineteenth century. The African people were still unconquered, and were not yet incorporated into the Cape economy and the schools were open to the children of freed slaves, or children of colour who had the opportunity of attending.

The first school built specifically for African children was established, in 1799, near the present site of Kingwilliamstown, by Dr. J.T. van der Kemp of the London Missionary Society. It was 21 years before other missionary bodies followed suit, and established schools for Africans in the Eastern Cape. Some missionaries moved further afield and built schools in the uncolonised interior, moving into Bechuanaland, Basutoland and the Transvaal.

The need for further educational facilities was apparently first felt after the freeing of the slaves in 1834. To cope with the children who were turned free with their parents more schools were required because of 'the need to extend social discipline over the new members of a free society'.[7] Through the nineteenth century and during the first quarter of the twentieth century African schooling was provided almost exclusively by the missionary societies. The missions were given land, but they provided the buildings, the teachers and most of the funds. Only a small portion of the expenses incurred, and usually only the salaries of staff, was provided by government grants (or after 1910, by Provincial Councils).

The first government grants to mission schools, of from £15 to £30 per year, were only provided after 1841, and were exclusively appropriated for the 'support of the teacher or teachers'.[8] It was only after that date that the number of schools increased considerably.

In one respect the colonial governments were bountiful. Land was available for the taking after the expulsion of the Africans, and mission stations were given extensive lands by the Governors on which to establish their schools, hospitals, colleges, as well as farms and orchards. The Glasgow Missionary Society, for example, received a grant of some 1,400 acres just inland from East London, and on this they eventually built the Lovedale school complex. The schools also needed state patronage and assistance which was to come with the appointment of Sir George Grey as Governor of the Cape from 1854 to 1861. Grey's task, as he conceived it, was to integrate the African peoples into the economy of the Cape, and he sought a solution by means of which:

> The Natives are to become useful servants, consumers of our goods, contributors to our revenue, in short, a source of strength and wealth to this Colony, such as Providence designed them to be.[9]

To assist Providence's design, Grey meant to break the power of the chiefs and educate a new class of Africans.

Grey brought with him the ideas on education then prevalent in Great Britain. Although he wanted an educated minority, he maintained that Cape schooling was too bookish, and proposed that the missionaries pay more attention to manual education. What was said by a Justice of the Peace in Britain in 1807 seemed apposite to the administration in the Cape in the 1850's:

It is doubtless desirable that the poor should be generally instructed in *reading*, if it were only for the best of purposes – that they may read the Scriptures. As to *writing* and *arithmetic*, it may be apprehended that such a degree of knowledge would produce in them a disrelish for the laborious occupations of life.[10]

Grey believed that the missionaries could provide the education he envisaged for the Blacks. He consequently met members of the Glasgow Missionary Society (later a branch of the Free Church of Scotland) who had already established an elementary school at Lovedale near Alice in the Eastern Cape.[11] As a result of these discussions the course of Cape educational policy for the nineteenth century was laid down: elementary instruction in literacy plus manual instruction for the majority of pupils, and a higher level of education for a small elite.

Lovedale opened an industrial department and tuition was also designed to:

give higher education to a portion of the native youths, to raise up among them what might be called an educated class, from which might be selected teachers of the young, catechists, evangelists and ultimately even fully-qualified preachers of the gospel.[12]

Grey also persuaded the Rev. John Ayliff to start an industrial school at Healdtown, near Lovedale, and undertook to support and subsidize missionary institutions that provided such training.[13] Henceforth the missionaries were to provide nearly all African education, but the government exercised overall control by virtue of its grant of funds. The government aimed in its policy at a disciplined population that would become an industrious workforce.

By 1865 there were 2,827 African pupils enrolled in the mission schools and by 1885 the number had increased to 15,568. Most of the schools however:

being short of funds, ill-equipped, with inadequately trained and paid teachers and children often under-fed, over-tired and staying too short a time to benefit – gave the mere smattering of elementary letters and touched only a fraction of the child population.[14]

Reports by successive Superintendents-General of Education in the Cape, on the standard of education in most of the schools, were scathing. In 1862 Dr. Langham Dale found that only five per cent of pupils in these schools could read, and few of the teachers had passed Standard 4. Dr. Dale's successor, Sir Thomas Muir found that 60 per cent of all African children at school did not reach Standard 1. In 1882, Donald Ross, the Inspector-General, said that half of the 420 schools in Kaffraria (Eastern Frontier area), Basutoland and the Cape could be closed without loss to education.[15]

Lovedale, Healdtown, St. Matthews (at Keiskama in the Ciskei) and a few other schools were exceptions in being able to produce trained craftsmen and youth who completed Standards 3, 4, and even 5. Many of the other institutions were little more than disciplinary centres where youth were kept occupied. Dr. Dale explained educational policy as follows:

the schools are hostages for peace, and if for that reason only £12,000 a year is given to schools in the Transkei, Tembuland and Griqualand, the amount is well spent; but that is not the only reason – to lift the Aborigines gradually, as circumstances permit, to the platform of civilised and industrial life is the great object of the educational vote.[16]

In 1865 the Cape Education Act made provision for three types of school: public schools, mission schools and Native schools. The Native schools were the only segregated institutions and few provided more than elementary classes. At the same time there was pressure on the mission schools to provide more manual instruction. In her book on the role of the missionaries Nosipho Majeka was scathing about government policy. She quotes Dr. Langham Dale in 1861: 'What the department (of Education) wants, is to make all the principal day-schools places of manual instruction.' Majeka continues, In the following year his successor, Dr. Muir is complaining that education for Africans is "too bookish and unpractical".'[17]

It is hard to conceive schools that do not succeed in training children to read as being 'bookish'. The education was certainly unpractical, but not in the sense that Dr. Muir meant. Manual training was, in most schools, menial labour and a source of much discontent. In 1920 Dr. D.D.T. Jabavu, a teacher in the mission schools, and later a professor at Fort Hare University College, explained the reasons behind the discontent in an article in which he contrasted the situation in South African schools with that at Booker T. Washington's Tuskagee Institute.

In our schools 'manual labour' consists of sweeping yards, repairing roads, cracking stones and so on, and is done by boys only as so much task force enforced by a time-keeper, and under threat of punishment. It is defended because 'it makes for character training.' The invariable result is that the boys grow to hate all manual work as humiliating . . .

Agriculture, where at all attempted at our schools, has suffered too, from being a motiveless task. It is the most important thing in native life, and therefore deserves a place in the school career of our boys, as it is practised in the Mariannhill native school in Natal . . .[18]

Dr. Jabavu spoke only about boys. In 1871 a girls' 'industrial department' was opened in which the girls were trained for domestic work.[19]

Progress in the schools was slow. They were starved of funds, and most of the African teachers were unable to offer advanced instruction. The only post-primary education available in the Cape was at Lovedale College, and at a few teacher training institutions. Under such circumstances, the fact that by 1907, 920 students were enrolled for training as teachers was extraordinary. In the nineteenth century the education provided by the handful of better endowed mission schools was on a par with any other school in the country. Between 1884 and 1886 it was reported that Lovedale had more passes in the Standards 3, 4 and 5 classes than any other of the 700 schools in the Cape.[20]

Many of the main missionary schools had no colour bar, and in some years the number of white pupils enrolled at Lovedale exceeded the Blacks. The pupils slept in segregated dormitories, ate at separate tables (and ate different food!), but they all attended the same classes. In 1885 when the total African enrolment in the Cape schools was 15,568, there were also 9,000 white pupils at the mission schools.[21]

There were, however, moves in the Cape towards segregation. The revenue that had flowed into the Cape, first with the discovery of diamonds at Kimberley in 1867, and then of gold on the Witwatersrand in 1886, led to a significant change in the Colony's economy. In order that the Whites might take their 'rightful place' in a racist society they would need an education that was different from that provided for Africans. In 1889 the Superintendent-General of Education in the Cape said:

> The first duty of the government has been assumed to be to recognise the position of the European colonists as holding the paramount influence, social and political; and to see that the sons and daughters of the colonists, and those who come hither to throw in their lot with them, should have at least such an education as their peers in Europe enjoy, with such local modifications as will fit them to maintain their unquestioned superiority, and supremacy in this land.[22]

The Superintendent-General was, it seems, making two broad assumptions. Firstly that the colonists needed an education that would maintain their paramount position (relative to Blacks) and, secondly, that in order to achieve this paramountcy they should be given an education 'such as their peers in Europe' received. But the Superintendent-General was not unaware of the nature of secondary education in Great Britain. This had been explored by the Taunton Commission (in Britain) in 1867. Three grades of schools had been envisaged which, said the Commission report, would 'correspond roughly, but by no means exactly, to the gradations of society'. The top grade was for the upper or upper-middle class, the next grade for the middle class, and the third grade was for the lower middle class. The boys (but presumably not girls) would stay at school till the ages of 18, 16 and 14 respectively and be trained for occupations suitable to their class origin. All in all, 10 children out of every 1,000 of the population would be in these schools, and eight of these would be in the third grade where they would be fitted for a living as 'small tenant farmers, small tradesmen, and superior artisans'.[23] Wherever possible, it was declared, sons of labourers might be enabled to enter secondary school. In 1851 the average duration of school attendance in England was two years; by 1861 the majority left school before the age of 11. Only in 1893 was the school leaving age raised to 11 years. There would obviously have to be much 'local modification' in Cape schools for the children of colonists who came from the lower middle class, or from the homes of labourers.

It also seemed that there would have to be a double process if the colonists were to receive the necessary education. The schooling offered to Whites would have to be upgraded relative to that provided for Blacks, and the schools would have to be more strictly segregated. Legislation to put this into effect was soon forthcoming. In 1893 a new law allowed the subsidising of mission schools that catered only for white children. Only one year previously, white students who had trained as teachers at Lovedale were not allowed to sit the examination.[24] By 1905 the Cape School Board Act established segregated state schools.[25]

Although attempts were made to introduce more manual instruction at Lovedale, in order to answer the accusations of 'bookishness', the staff worked to maintain the standard of education. Despite their efforts, however, Lovedale was bound to lose out. Although graduates of the college emerged with a relatively high standard of education, differentiation was achieved by pouring increasing resources into white schools, while African schools were always short of funds.

These changes took place at a time when the Cape no longer needed black school graduates to fill positions in the growing bureaucracy, and the only opportunities open to the young men who emerged from the schools were in the segregated schools and churches, and occasionally in one of the lower paid positions in a government office. Only a few Blacks were able to study overseas or, at a later date, gain entry into South African universities and so enter the liberal professions. They were the exceptions, not dissimilar from the sons of labourers in Great Britain who managed to surmount the barriers which kept them out of higher education.

Education in the Interior

White education in the Cape was some 200 years old when Sir George Grey offered assistance to the missionaries for the running of their schools, and conceived of education as an instrument for incorporating Africans into the colony's economy.

The situation in the two interior republics (now the provinces, Orange Free State and Transvaal) was obviously very different. The concerted movement of the Dutch frontiersmen into the interior did not take place on a large scale, and the 'trekkers' who moved across the Orange River in the 1830s had few resources, even for the education of their own children. They certainly had no intention of setting up schools for a people whom they meant to expropriate. Africans were only employed as servants or as farm labourers.

The first mission station was set up in 1842, and the first school built shortly thereafter. No grants were available from the government, and progress was necessarily slow. The most successful school, at Kilnerton, near Pretoria, was established by the Methodists in 1885. This institution trained Africans as teachers — the entrance qualification being Standard Three. After a two-year course they were posted to mission schools in the rural areas. The institution was closed during the war of 1899-1902, but reopened in 1903, when a government survey in the Transvaal showed that there were 201 mission schools, some of which must have provided the preliminary education for the students who entered Kilnerton. However, very few of these schools offered more than rudimentary instruction in reading and writing. The first Superintendent of Native Education in the Transvaal was appointed in 1904, and a special curriculum for African schools was issued up to the Standard 3 level. The first state grant of £4,342 was made for African education and shared by 121 schools, and in 1907 the first state school (for Blacks) was established. As for the OFS, it did provide token funds of £45 to £80 a year for mission schools in the 19th century. Only after 1902 were slightly bigger grants made and schools could enrol more pupils.

The fourth region of white settlement, Natal, developed a segregation policy to suit its requirements in the mid-19th century. Although the Zulus had been defeated, the settlers were too weak to absorb the majority of Africans as labourers in their society. The British government refused to provide the money which would have been required for any system of 'direct rule', and there was no possibility of restructuring African society with the resources available to the small settler community. Furthermore, the Natal government administered a territory in which there were as yet few signs of economic development. The land had been parcelled out indiscriminately, and absentee landowners exacted tribute from the Africans resident on their ill gotten estates. At the same time the whites believed they would be swamped by Zulu refugees, supposedly pouring into their newly settled areas.

The Natal government set up 19 mission reserves, each of which was under the exclusive control of one mission society. In these reserves, held in 'trust' for the Africans, the missionaries had the sole right to use of the labour available, and they also set up schools and churches.

In 1856 a government ordinance laid down guidelines for African education in Natal, which made provision for religious education, instruction in the English language and industrial training. Education was administered directly by the Governor and finances for the schools were provided by reserve funds.

One of the earliest colleges in Natal was the Amamzimtoti Institute, later to be known as Adams College. It was set up in 1853 by the American Board of Commissioners for Foreign Missions (ABCFM), and was to become one of Natal's premier African schools until vindictively expropriated only a century later. (This will be described in Chapter Two).

In 1869 Mary Edwards of the ABCFM set up a seminary for African girls at Inanda — the first African girls' school in the country. The object of the institution was to train the students to be Christian wives and mothers, and a special course was provided for girls who had run away from polygamous marriages.

Two other schools of particular note were set up in Natal. In 1882 Trappist monks set up a school at Mariannhill (between Durban and Pietermaritzburg) to train Catholic students. Graduates of this school (named St. Francis College), who were in later years to become political leaders or trade unionists, tended to be anti-communist and distinctly conservative in philosophy. In this they followed the main mentor of Mariannhill in the 1930's, Father Bernard Huss. The second college, which is unique in South Africa, was Ohlange Institute, initiated by the first president of the ANC, the Rev. John Dube, who had been sent by the ABCFM to America to further his education. John Dube had been deeply impressed by the work of the Tuskegee Institute founded by Booker T. Washington and, on his return to Natal, was determined to set up an independent industrial college controlled by Africans. The Natal government gave Dube the land he needed, and he was able to raise the funds for the school buildings.

By 1912 there were 18,000 African pupils in 232 primary schools, five industrial centres and three teacher-training institutes in Natal. In 1910 the two colonies (Cape and Natal), and the two former Boer republics (Orange Free State and Transvaal) became provinces within the Union of South Africa. At that time, the provision of African schooling in the country was very uneven, and the major schools established in the Cape and in Natal maintained their pre-eminent position. The pattern of mission control of African education also persisted. Until 1951 84.5 per cent of all African schools and training colleges were mission run and controlled.[26] It was only in the realm of finance that the Provinces (who had charge of all primary and secondary education until 1954) and the central government played an ever larger role.

Early African Criticisms

The problem of finance, and the paucity of state funds for African education had long occupied the minds of African men and women. In 1903 the South African Native Congress addressed a statement to Joseph Chamberlain at the British Colonial Office strongly protesting against the disparity in grants made to schools for white and black students. The grant for each white child in the 'first class public schools' was £3.87. In equivalent schools for Blacks the grant was 61p per child.[27]

Giving testimony before the South African Native Affairs Commission in 1904 Martin Lutuli of the Natal Native Congress asked that education be transferred from the missions to state control. Answering the Chairman's question on the changes he would prefer, Lutuli said:

I would prefer that the Government should build a Government school to

teach everything — to teach the knowledge in head and hands and everything, to know how to work at trades such as blacksmiths, carpentering,
mason work, and all those things.[28]

African parents, school pupils and the graduates of the mission schools
were caught in a double bind situation from which there was no real escape.
The only way in which they could hope to get full free and compulsory
education was through a state schooling system. Only the government had the
resources and the ability to provide the training they desired. They were,
however, also aware of the many difficulties they would face if the government did decide to take over the schools. They had heard or read the many
denigrating remarks made by officials of the education department, and they
resented the many statements on the futility of educating the African people.

In 1903 the South African Native Congress issued a statement condemning
the salaries paid by the Cape Government to African teachers as 'scandalously
illiberal' and was scathing about the comments of Dr. Langham Dale. The
Congress Executive rejected his statement to the effect that: 'I do not
consider it my business to enforce education on all the aborigines, it would
ruin South Africa. If I could produce 6,000 educated Tembus or Fingoes
tomorrow, what would you do with them? Their education must be gradual.'[29]

And, indeed, from the point of view of the needs of the Cape economy,
there would be no place for 6,000 educated Africans. This was an issue to
which Congress members did not address themselves, if only because this was
a problem with which they could not cope, and with which they had no
desire to cope. The task of providing employment rested with the government
and with the employers. But there was a more important reason for not
taking the matter any further. To have challenged the right to decide who
should be educated would have required a different set of Africans, and a
very different set of social attitudes. It would have required an organisation
that was prepared to challenge the state, and the priorities set by that state.
This was not possible in 1903, and it would be unreasonable to expect the
men who constituted the Congress Executive to have taken such a radical
stance.

In the one crucial stand they took, they were correct. The state had to
provide the schools, the teachers, and the finance. Meanwhile, the parents
clamoured to secure entrance to mission schools for their children. In so
doing, they preferred Lovedale, or Healdtown, or Adams, and if they were
Catholics they sought entrance at Mariannhill. Yet here too there was
dissatisfaction. There were cheers when J. Tengo Jabavu, editor of *Imvo
Zabantsundu*, addressed the South African Races Congress in April 1912, and
condemned mission schools where 'such is the rivalry of sects that schools are
placed with an utter disregard to efficiency.'[30] Jabavu spoke of the drop in
educational standards, and of the 'great failure of Native students at their
Missionary Institutions', and obviously expressed the concern of the audience,
many of whom had once attended mission schools.

Criticism of the missionaries became increasingly outspoken. Tengo

21

Jabavu's son, Professor D.D.T. Jabavu, addressed the Natal Missionary Conference in July 1920, and praised the early missionaries who 'faced opprobrium' for befriending Africans, but criticised the more recent arrivals at the mission stations. Jabavu claimed that the present incumbents weŕe socially distant, standoffish, and even 'lordly'. The missionaries were accused of maintaining a military discipline, and of treating Africans as masters would servants. Although these were doubtless a minority, said Jabavu, the many were apt to be judged by their behaviour.[31]

The pupils at the schools were not heard at conferences, but they too were dissatisfied with conditions in the mission schools. The way in which they voiced their protests will be discussed in the second part of this chapter. Their dilemma was even greater than that of their parents. The mission schools provided the only education available to Africans — and in the better schools it was but little inferior to that provided in white schools. For some, in fact, the extensive grounds, the wide fields, the country setting, and even the school equipment made them a very privileged group. Yet despite these privileges, which if anything made them more sensitive to any deficiencies, they were confronted by the attitudes that Professor Jabavu alluded to. They resented the heavy handed discipline, together with an inflexibility in the schoolroom which far too often bordered on the racism of the outer world. The process which led to changes in the schools in Britain, where these attitudes were once so prevalent, was not repeated in the South African context. On the contrary, the Act of Union of 1910 led to an increasing uniformity in educational practices in the four provinces, which worked against any liberalisation.

Discrimination After 1910

Initially, the four provinces had very different attitudes to African schooling, and standards differed appreciably. Finances were partly raised from 'Native taxes', and in 1922 this led the Transvaal to impose an additional direct tax on every African male; on the grounds that 'Native schooling' was too costly. The South African government intervened to stop such additional taxes, and furthermore introduced legislation which required local authorities to continue spending no less than the amount voted for education in 1921-22. Each province, therefore, pegged expenditure at the 1921-22 level, and this acted as a brake on further expansion.

After 1925, the finance made available for education was increased by new legislation. The fixed amount (which was calculated as £340,000) was henceforth to be supplemented by one-fifth of the general tax paid annually by Africans. The formula was changed in 1935 when seven-twentieths of the general tax was allocated to the education fund. By 1942 five-sixths of the tax and, in 1943, all the general tax was paid into the education account.

Finance contributed by the Provinces was considerably less than recurrent expenditure, and did not provide any of the capital needed for buildings and grounds. The additional monies were raised by donations — a considerable proportion being contributed by African parents, and the missionary societies provided part of the annual revenue.[32]

The growth of pupil enrolment, and estimated state grants, in the period 1855-1945, are shown in Table 1(a). The overall picture presented by the figures indicates continued growth. But a more detailed breakdown of expenditure over the depression years 1930-39, given in Table 1(b), shows that there was a long period of stagnation and indeed decline during that decade.

The number of African children receiving formal education was always small. Although the absolute number enrolled at school rose over the years, the percentage of school-age youth actually at school remained low. Uncertainty about census figures relating to the total African population makes all percentages uncertain, and those quoted in the literature are too high. Nevertheless, by 1936 it was thought that only 18.1 per cent of all African children were ever enrolled at a school. In 1946 the figure was 27.4 per cent, and only reached 30 per cent in 1951. Only in the 1960's did this figure rise appreciably to 40 per cent.

Attendance figures, however, can be deceptive. The overwhelming majority of children who entered school stayed for less than four years. By 1945 the number attending school for more than four years was only 24 per cent of the total school-going population (or seven per cent of children of school-going age). In 1962 only 30 per cent of those who entered school proceeded beyond the second standard.[34] Few of the youth who left at this early stage of schooling — many aged from 11 to 13 years — could be considered literate.

Many children were unable to obtain admission to schools because there was insufficient finance to allow the schools to expand. Even when enrolment did expand considerably, as it did between 1925 and 1935, state expenditure lagged far behind. In 1935 the position had deteriorated to such an extent that an Inter-Departmental Committee, consisting of the four Chief Inspectors of Native Education and the Director of the Bureau of Educational and Social Research, was appointed to examine and report on Native education.

During the 1920's the state increased its contribution to the schools, so that the amount paid for every student attending school had risen slowly from £1.84 to £2.14. Thereafter the state contribution per student dropped, and did not return to the 1930 level until 1939. Economies during this period were effected by cutting the salaries of black teachers and by stopping nearly all capital investment in buildings and equipment. Conditions, bad as they had been in the pre-Depression days, deteriorated further as the mission societies found that they were also deprived of the donations they had previously depended on from private sources, and from parents. The recession stopped the flow of donations from abroad, and local contributions were hard to secure.

The children came in increasing numbers to schools which had smaller, rather than larger resources, less books and equipment, and grossly overcrowded classrooms. Inevitably, the level of education declined considerably.

The situation, as the Inter-Departmental Committee found it, was

Table 1(a)*
African Schooling: Estimated Enrolment and State Expenditure, 1855-1945[33]

Year	CAPE		NATAL		TRANSVAAL		O.F.S.		TOTAL		
	Pupils	State Expenditure	Pupils	State Expenditure	Pupils	State Expenditure	Pupils	State Expenditure	Pupils	State Expenditure	Expenditure per pupil
1855	n a	n a	155	90	n a	nil	n a	nil	n a	n a	
1865	2,827	3,570	n a	n a	"	"	"	"	"	"	
1870	n a	n a	1,683	1,466	"	"	"	45	"	"	
1880	n a	n a	3,153	2,312	"	"	"	45	"	"	
1885	15,568	n a	n a	n a	"	"	"	nil	"	"	
1890	25,000	38,000	3,307	3,831	"	"	"	80	"	37,000	55p.
1900	n a	n a	10,618	6,028	"	nil	"	80	"	n a	
1905	45,000	25,000	n a	n a	9,800	7,000	9,296	1,300	73,900	49,000	67p.
1910	50,750	79,000	13,452	10,431	12,447	10,979	9,652	6,265	86,300	106,700	£1.25
1920	110,000	260,000	25,579	36,195	28,953	39,054	16,432	4,000	185,400	340,000	£1.82
1930	139,087	358,033	48,397	108,745	71,884	92,258	24,638	39,223	283,726	598,259	£2.10
1940	207,960	484,390	86,638	204,984	124,000	222,313	45,424	84,828	464,022	996,435	£2.20
1945	241,700	936,557	116,436	452,930	172,129	615,500	57,591	216,638	587,856	2,213,405	£3.90

* These figures are taken from a number of sources. These do not often coincide, but the numbers are usually of the same order of magnitude. Some figures are not available (n a), as indicated. All figures of expenditure in £ pounds.

Table 1(b)*
African Schooling: Details of Enrolment and Expenditure
During the Depression, 1930-39

Year	Pupils	NATIONAL TOTAL State Expenditure (£)	Expenditure per pupil (£)
1930	287,000	611,805	2.14
1931	296,500	612,293	2.07
1932	298,600	584,058	1.96
1933	318,000	586,029	1.84
1934	327,900	624,458	1.90
1935	355,500	684,232	1.93
1936	362,600	744,400	2.05
1937	398,700	835,883	2.10
1938	428,600	902,153	2.11
1939	444,000	953,363	2.15

* See Reference 33.

disastrous, and little that transpired in many of the classes they visited could pass for education. They suggested some amelioration, but fundamentally their task was to exonerate the system, and this they proceeded to do in the language that was becoming familiar from all government departments charged with providing facilities for Africans.

The Committee found that there was a divergence between the ultimate aim of education and actual practice in the schools. They claimed that the objective of education was the same for all people. There were, however, reasons for not providing the same schooling: 'Practically considered, the aim in the two cases is not the same because the two social orders for which education is preparing Whites and Blacks are not identical. . .' Being more explicit, the Committee declared:

> The education of the White child prepared him for life in a dominant society, and the education of the Black child for life in a subordinate society . . . The limits (of Native Education) form part of the social and economic structure of the country.

The Committee recommended that African education should be financed by the government. They suggested a grant of £3.65 per pupil. Grants paid at the time for white and coloured pupils were £23.85 and £5.20, respectively.[35]

The recommendation was not put into effect and the grant per pupil declined. Only in 1945 did the government increase its financial contribution to African education. (In addition a sum of £582,374 was voted for African school meals in 1943, in line with a general scheme that each school child should receive one meal a day.)[36] The number of primary schools in the Provinces in 1946 as compared with the number of secondary schools, and the slowly altering proportions of students enrolled in the sub-standard and primary classes are shown in Tables 2(a) and 2(b).

Table 2(a)
The Number of Primary and Secondary Schools in the Four Provinces, 1946[37]

Province	Primary Schools	Secondary Schools
Cape	2,042	30
Natal	864	108
Transvaal	1,030	31
O.F.S.	478	4
Total	4,414	173

Table 2(b)
Percentage of African Pupils Enrolled in Sub-standard and in Primary School Classes, 1924-1945[38]

Year	Number at school	% in sub-standards	% in primary classes	% in secondary schools
1924	183,862	62.5	99.9	0.1
1930	263,418	61.5	99.9	0.1
1935	353,134	58.0	99.4	0.6
1940	464,024	53.3	98.3	1.7
1945	587,128	51.2	97.8	2.2

When the war ended in 1945, an era had come to a close in South Africa. During the war there had been a large-scale influx of Africans into the main urban centres without concomitant increases in housing or transport facilities. There had also been no basic change in the nature of schooling offered to African children.

In one respect the missionaries had fulfilled everything that Sir George Grey had wanted from them. They had provided the teachers and the religious leaders. They had even provided a small group of doctors, lawyers, and nurses. The philosophy they had espoused was one of 'Christian trustee-ship', and they had all too successfully transmitted this philosophy to most of their pupils. The missionaries had, however, been criticised by both the Afrikaner nationalists and sections of the African people.

The Afrikaner critics accused the missionaries of 'liberalism', of propagating the idea of equality (of races) and of failing to inculcate the idea of segregation. The education provided in the schools came under attack in National-ist Party documents, and the mission schools were accused of not having sufficiently inculcated 'the habit of doing manual work'.[39]

Criticisms levelled by radical African groups started from very different premises. Nosipho Majeka, who presented one such anti-missionary approach, started with the basic presupposition that: 'From the very beginning the missionaries, who were the protagonists of capitalism, sought to implant the *ideas* of that system. . .'[40] Majeka claimed that the mission-schools trained the child to accept an inferior position in society, and maintained that the excessive concentration on religious and moral instruction was designed to inculcate 'humility, patience, fear, and passivity'. She continued: 'Missionary-controlled education, therefore, has played an important part in subjugating the minds of the people and in this way ensuring the continuance of White domination.'[41]

It would seem that, at least on occasion, the African pupils agreed with Majeka's standpoint.

The Students' Response

From 1920 through to the introduction of Bantu Education in 1954 and beyond, there were periodic outbursts in the schools. Students protested and demonstrated, boycotted chapel or classes and rioted.

Despite changes in the country — economically, socially and politically — the pattern of student protest in the schools remained remarkably constant. Almost all protest movements took place in schools situated in rural areas, and almost all action was spearheaded by pupils who boarded at the schools. Most occurred in secondary schools, or in teachers' training colleges, and the age of the pupils involved ranged from 15 to 20 years.

Life at the schools was not easy, and students resented the 'paternalism', and the demands that they work in the orchards and on the farms. They were not as enthusiastic as the members of the Native Economic Commission in 1932 when they noted that:

> The students [at school] were also taught gardening and other manual work; every student at Lovedale had to work two hours in the gardens or on the roads; this excellent practice continues to this day.[42]

The situation, as presented above by Professor Jabavu, was far nearer the truth and many protests and demonstrations followed orders from teachers that students carry out some unpleasant cleaning task.

The events that provoked students and led to some counter-actions were generally related to a restricted number of complaints. By far the commonest were about the severity of punishment, about assaults perpetrated by white staff on both pupils and black servants and about the quality and the quantity of food. The obvious disparity between the food served to staff and to students was a constant source of protest. The 'meat and veg' served at high table was contrasted by the students with their own fare. Over and above this unfavourable comparison, the disparities between food served to students who paid higher fees and those who paid less, created unending tensions.

A student-waiter at Lovedale in the Eastern Cape has described conditions in the dining room in the mid-thirties. At this most prestigious of all black colleges of the time, the white teachers sat apart from the few Africans who were also on the staff. This separation was maintained when casual travellers stopped at the college. The white passerby received a meal in the refectory. The itinerant black received bread and lard in the yard. Amongst the student body there was a division of another order:

> The students were divided into four categories and sat at separate tables: there were the £14 students, the £17, the £22 and the £27 per year students. The first category of students received meat once a week with their samp [crushed maize], the £17 students had meat twice a week, and so on up the scale. [43]

In the refectory it was obvious to all students that the pattern of South African discrimination was repeating itself. The distinctions across colour — and class — lines were at work in the school. Prefectships went in the main to the £27 students, they sat at separate tables (and got their superior food) and obtained leave of absence more readily than other students. They were considered by their peers to be the 'eyes and ears of the boarding master'. When eventually students at Lovedale rioted the prefects were the only Africans attacked by the student body.[44]

Nonetheless, over long periods of time students were quiescent and did not make their complaints known. Where discontent became known, impositions, extra duties, chastisement or threats of expulsion were usually enough to abort any move to collective action.

School students were particularly vulnerable and did not readily take action to redress perceived wrongs. People are not easily moved to open conflict and students, who had so much to lose, would tend to be even more restrained than most. The tiny minority in the secondary schools were set for careers which would allow them to avoid the menial jobs that awaited the less educated (or illiterate) African. A secondary education placed them amongst the top two per cent of their people, and prepared them for a number of jobs — of which teaching was one obvious choice. [45] Completion of secondary school could open the gates to the one existing University College for Africans, Fort Hare. A confrontation with the staff at school could lead to a precipitate end to these aspirations.

Despite these restraints, the students were in a unique position. They constituted the small elite of Africans who were literate and had access to books, journals and newspapers. They could (and did) conduct discussion and debating clubs, and life in boarding-schools was conducive to intensive discussions of current problems.

It was precisely this heightened awareness which led the staff to take steps against what they saw as an 'unnatural' interest in politics. Ezekiel

Mphahlele, who was at Adams College, records in his autobiography that at the beginning of the war:

> In a great number of their [missionary] schools, certain political journals were banned, topics for school debate were severely censored. . . As the world war raged on, the tempers of the students raged to the extent that certain school buildings were burnt down.

And the sanctions were severe, because: 'pupils expelled from our schools have not the slightest chance of entering another.' [46] It was one of the features of school strikes that they tended to coincide with disturbances outside the campus, and there were at least six strikes at mission schools at the beginning of the war. [47]

Although it is not always possible to find evidence linking student militancy in the schools and colleges with events in South Africa or abroad, there are many indications (for example, factors listed by the Smit Commission below), to show that the students were influenced by outside events. The outbreak of the second world war, the many strikes on the Witwatersrand during its course, the African mine workers' strike of 1946, events in Ghana in the 1950's, or in the Congo (Zaire) in 1960-63 and Mozambique in 1974, all contributed to increased political consciousness and helped to precipitate student clashes with school staffs.

Despite this response to events inside and outside the country there were few (if any) instances of school students joining forces with any of the national liberation movements prior to 1973. During a large part of the inter-war period and through to 1950, the existing political movements were barely viable; they were not capable of reaching pupils at school and would undoubtedly have rejected any suggestion that secondary school students be organised. The aspirations of the political leadership during that period would have made them unsympathetic to militant school action, and there was no likelihood that these elders would have deigned to 'talk politics' with 'children'.

It was only after the formation of the Congress Youth League as the youth section of the ANC in 1943, that attempts were made to win recruits at the University College of Fort Hare. School students, however, were not recruited, despite the fact that many students in the upper school forms were 18 years of age or more. They were mature and aware of events — but not yet considered fit for political activity. Although strikes at schools often followed in the wake of political or industrial action in the country, they were *not* organised, or even prompted, by political movements.

Evidence on the effect of external events comes from the unofficial Commission of Inquiry set up under Douglas Smit at the request of the Lovedale College authorities after the strike there in 1946. The commissioners were told that the students followed the press carefully, had copies of a call to support the African mine workers in their strike, and received circulars through the post. They were also said to have 'brought back the atmosphere of preparation' for the miners' strike when returning from their mid-year vacation. [48] This last statement, unfortunately, is not in accord with all the facts, and was undoubtedly added in order to strengthen the case for shifting the blame onto 'outside influences'. The African miners had been discontented over a long period, but it was only on 5 August that a specially summoned conference decided, for the first time, to strike. On 7 August, long before the students could have heard of the decision, they started their boycott of classes. Nevertheless, the evidence does show that the students were responsive to events outside the school walls.

If the interconnection between events in the country and abroad and those on campus played some part in fuelling student discontent, the direct causes of conflict were to be found inside the schools and, having started in the schools, the students restricted their actions to the campus. They did not move off the campus, and they did not appeal to the neighbouring communities for assistance. Such behaviour would have been inconceivable before the 1970's.

Nevertheless, all actions taken by Africans in South Africa are 'political', and all school strikes reflected the discontent in South Africa over discriminatory practices. As one witness said to the Lovedale Commission:

> The modern African boy is given access to the newspaper press and is born in an environment of complaint by the African against the colour bar. They identify the European staff in the institution as part of the Government machinery, and so when they go home we find that they are unhappy with the school authorities whereas in our time we worshipped the school authorities. [49]

Strikes in the Schools

Presumably, not all students of the earlier generation 'worshipped the school authorities'! The first recorded stoppages of lessons, (always called strikes in the South African newspapers), and the first riots in African schools occurred in 1920. In February, students at the Kilnerton training centre went on a hunger strike 'for more food'. A few months later theological students at Lovedale rioted and set fire to the buildings 'in protest against bad bread'. The damage was estimated at between £3,000 and £5,000. A large number of students must have been involved, because 198 students were brought to trial and received sentences ranging from three months imprisonment plus a fine of £50, to strokes with a light cane.[50]

There is little information about events in schools in the inter-war years. Short items in the African press did mention strikes in the late twenties, and there were reports of many more in the pre-war years. It would have been strange if pupils in the schools, starved of resources during the 1930's (as described on p.23), had not expressed their anger by striking, rioting, and burning the premises. There is, however, a dearth of information on these events, as the government of the day wished to avoid the adverse publicity which would have followed disclosure of such events in the schools. The two official Commissions of Inquiry, set up in 1940 and 1946 to report on grievances and disturbances at African schools, were never published. [51]

The investigations by the Commissions did not lead to better conditions in the schools. In the period 1943-45 there were more than 20 strikes and serious riots in schools. Each strike led to expulsions (and often court appearances) — and to renewed disturbances the following academic year. The most serious confrontation occurred on 7 August 1946, and in the months that followed at least six more strikes occurred in schools and colleges. [52]

Parents were very disturbed at the seemingly endless closures of colleges, and organised a delegation to meet the school principals. The Heads of the Association of Native Institutions (as the college principals styled themselves), appointed four of their members to meet the delegation in October 1945, and they obviously meant to 'teach' them a lesson. The parents got little sympathy and were read a prepared statement which criticised them for not exercising sufficient control over their children. They were also informed that no flouting of school rules would be tolerated, and that continued disturbances ('exclusively confined to Native students in the Union of South Africa' the parents were told), would lead to stricter control of admission, and closer supervision at schools. [53]

It was the Lovedale riot of August 1946 which attracted most attention — partly because this was the premier black school in the country, and partly because the 'independent' Commission of Inquiry set up by the Lovedale Governing Council did issue a report. [54] From this, it is apparent that the school had been in a state of unrest since 1945, that the students had their own unofficial organisation known as 'The Board' (borrowed, it appears, from 'The Board of Guardians' in Oliver Twist), and that there was a call for a student strike and the removal of the headmaster. The administration's response was to arrange for patrols of the school grounds by members of staff during the night and by a constable during the day. Those assumed to be ringleaders were pinpointed and threatened with exclusion if they failed the forthcoming examinations. None of the 17 so named were able to proceed to the University College of Fort Hare in 1946.

The school seemed to have been quiet during the first half of 1946 despite the introduction of new rules of conduct by the principal of the high school who had recently returned from military service. In the aftermath of the riots of 7 August, involving damage to school premises and attacks on prefects and white members of staff, the principal, Dr. R.H.W. Shepherd, wrote that the staff had no intimation of dissatisfaction — and this despite the events of the previous year! [55]

One hundred and fifty two students were arrested and charged with public violence. Most were fined (with the alternative of imprisonment); all were excluded from schools in the future. There was an obvious unanimity amongst principals on the need for 'stern measures'.

Lovedale was closed for nine weeks, and on reopening more than 80 students, said to have been guilty of violence, were debarred from the school,[56] and from every other college in the country. The college presumably returned to 'normal'. There were no further reports of student activity at Lovedale in the post-1946 period, and only a more intimate knowledge of conditions on the campus would provide information on the way the student body was now controlled, and how many individual students found continued schooling closed to them due to some transgression of the rules.

The spate of student demonstrations was not over, and continued in 1946 and subsequently. After the Lovedale strike there were at least five others in the Cape and the Transvaal in 1946, and in December these were followed by a sitdown strike at the Bethesda Bantu Training College near Pietersburg.[57] On through the late forties and the fifties students struck, boycotted and rioted. Each event had its own local causes, and in most cases students acted only after prolonged periods of discussion and representations to the responsible teachers. One columnist of the time summed up the mood when describing the situation:

At almost every African mission boarding school conditions for students are deplorable and this has been the root of all the minor revolts which have taken place from time to time at these institutions. Food and the Nazi-like control are usually the main causes for dissatisfaction. Last week the authorities were expecting some sort of explosion at Healdtown (Methodist) Missionary College . . . Police at five Eastern Cape towns were asked to stand by in case something should happen at the college.

Earlier, last week, 100 senior pupils were sent home after a passive resistance strike — escorted off the premises by 20 (armed) police . . .[58]

The University College of Fort Hare

The one university college for Blacks in the country prior to 1960 was situated in the Eastern Cape. Like so many other features of South Africa, the college reflects the superimposition of an advanced economy on a broken agricultural community. D. Gordon, a student at the college in 1949, described it as follows:

Fort Hare is situated on the East Bank of the Tyumie River, overlooking Lovedale Institution and the Victoria Hospital. The little town of Alice, a white man's paradise, serves both these institutions and is the centre of an area of African learning and native poverty. Of all the trading stores in the village not one is owned by an African though business would be impossible without their support. The Tyumie Valley is very fertile and it is startling to note how the European farmer has squeezed the African onto the barren and soil-eroded hillsides. It is amazing how these people manage to exist and propagate.

In the midst of all the racial and agricultural disparity we have the only non-European University [College], Fort Hare.[59]

Founded in 1916, and accepting Indians, Coloured and Africans, Fort Hare had given some 90 degrees in arts and science to its graduates by 1939.[60] It also gave diplomas to students who had not completed secondary school but wanted their higher teacher's certificate. Nearly half the student intake was made up of those who took this diploma course.

Most trained teachers came from one of the 26 colleges in South Africa which provided the necessary certificates or diplomas. At the outbreak of the second world war there were 3,500 pupils enrolled for such courses. Some had only completed primary school, others had some secondary schooling. After one or two years at the colleges they were certified as fit to teach.[61]

Both the colleges of education and the University College of Fort Hare were segregated institutions (although a few Whites had been enrolled at Fort Hare). For many Africans, the University College presented the only opportunity for receiving a higher education in South Africa, although the universities of the Witwatersrand, Cape Town and Natal allowed a limited number of Blacks to enter their faculties.

The number of degree and diploma students at Fort Hare was always small. In 1959 (the year the university structure of South Africa was altered), the enrolment was 319 Africans, 70 Coloureds, and 100 Indians. In the same year 300 Africans, 541 Coloureds, and 815 Indians were enrolled in the 'white' universities.

The black students constituted a tiny minority in the 'white' universities. In Durban they attended segregated extra mural classes at the university, or were enrolled at the medical school which was exclusively for Blacks. In Cape Town and Johannesburg (the 'open' universities) there was no segregation at lectures, but Blacks faced a number of restrictions which they resented, but were powerless to alter. It was the more radical white students who protested against the quota system for Africans at the Medical school, and the exclusion of Blacks from the Dental school. There were even more protests against the complete social segregation and the prohibition placed on Blacks using the swimming bath and many sporting facilities. But the small black groups could play little part in such agitation — and many of them found meaningful political activity only in the national liberation movements off the campus. Only a few played any prominent part in student politics. It was only in the period preceding the introduction of the 1959 Universities Bill that the black students joined their white peers in protesting against the closing of the open universities. Despite the many disabilities they encountered, the education offered at Cape Town and Johannesburg seemed worth fighting for.

The position at Fort Hare was different. The University College was isolated from the main centres of political activity, and although some students joined one or other of the political movements prevailing during the 1940's, they were isolated from the mainstream of political events. Students recently out of school tended to be even more out of contact with events in

the large cities. They had come to Fort Hare straight from rurally based
schools and had lived in small, closed, missionary institutions for the
preceding 12 or more years.[62]

Throughout the second world war there were strikes at Fort Hare almost
every year. There was a strike in 1941 because a teacher was alleged to have
brutally assaulted an African waitress in hall,[63] another in 1942 when the
boycotting of divine service led to the suspension of 59 students, and yet
another strike in 1943.[64] The precipitating factors were always the atrocious
food, unbending discipline, or even physical assaults. But the crucial factor
was deeply embedded in the system. Writing at the time a student stated:

> The whole matter revolves round the principle of whether or not
> University students are going to allow themselves to be bullied like
> kindergarten children. It is the old matter of white South Africa regarding
> the non-European as nothing better than a grown-up baby.[65]

Politics Comes to the Campus

There was a new political mood amongst Africans during the war years, and a
section of educated youth formed the Congress Youth League (CYL) in 1943.
This was the junior section of the African National Congress (ANC) formed
with some reluctance by the older body to stop a drift into other political
movements in the Transvaal. The central core was mainly drawn from
graduates of St. Peters, the Anglican secondary school in Johannesburg, and
of Lovedale, Healdtown, or Adams College. There were also some who had
been at Fort Hare and had graduated, or had been expelled after the strikes.

The Youth League did not seek recruits in the schools, but did make
contact with students at Fort Hare. It seems, however, that it was only
towards the end of 1948 that a small branch of the CYL was formed on the
campus.[66] The Cape based Non-European Unity Movement (NEUM) also
established a branch in the late forties. It seemed to be the predominant
political group during the early 1950's, but lost the initiative to the CYL
during the Defiance Campaign in 1952. By the mid-fifties the NEUM was
reduced to a small group.[67]

There is an impressionistic account of events at Fort Hare, written by
D. Gordon who arrived on the campus in 1949. In that year the Congress
Youth League-sponsored *Programme of Action* became official ANC policy.
This programme, more radical than previous ANC Conferences would have
accepted, espoused 'Africanism' — a philosophy which called upon Africans
to reject alliances with any other racial group. Gordon was a supporter of the
NEUM and opposed to the CYL and its avowed Africanism. Nevertheless, he
expressed admiration for their actions on the campus, while rejecting their
nationalistic philosophy.

His comments on the students at the college in 1949 give some picture of
events at the time:

> The African student is more politically conscious at Fort Hare than any non-European student at any South African university . . .
>
> The outstanding political contributors were the students who came from the Native territories of the Union [of South Africa], the large towns and the Transkei . . .
>
> For the African [as distinct from Coloured and Indian students], Fort Hare is a hive of political activity. He questions freely and openly every suggestion made by the European, whether lecturer or visitor . . . So tense is the atmosphere that politics is brought into every College activity whether it be a hostel meeting, a church service, a sports gathering, a college lecture or a social gathering.[68]

Gordon is scathing about both the coloured and Indian students at Fort Hare, and it does seem that unlike Coloureds and Indians at the 'open universities', those at Fort Hare mainly kept aloof from politics.

The CYL was undoubtedly the major force at Fort Hare. Gordon continues:

> I must express great admiration for the unity which existed in the African ranks and the Youth League. They had a feeling of one-ness and suspension and expulsion was not feared, while fighting the cause of the African. That is probably why they were reluctant to admit any other racial group into their organisation. The coloured and Indian students had no political programme . . .
>
> At a Completer's Social three Youth Leaguers addressed the students in the presence of the principal and the staff and turned a social gathering into a violent attack on the political and social conditions prevailing in the land. The slogan for the evening was 'Africa for the Africans' . . .[69]

One of the Youth Leaguers who spoke that evening was Robert Mangaliso Sobukwe, later leader of the Pan-Africanist Congress. (See Chapter 16.)

The students faced increasing restrictions and a hardening of attitudes in the aftermath of the Nationalist Party success at the polls in 1948. This was, no doubt, the crucial factor which led the students to come out in full in support of the 14 days sit-down strike called by nurses at the Victoria Hospital in 1949. Despite the failure of the strike this event did more than any other to strengthen the CYL's hold on the student body.[70]

The post-war years brought an increase in political activity and quickened the students' interest in events in other parts of the colonial world. They read all that could be found on Asia and Africa despite the unofficial censorship. Gordon continues his account: 'The book on Colonies by George Padmore *[Africa: Britain's Third Empire]* was extremely popular, but it disappeared from the shelves of the library.'

Despite this, only a minority of students were interested in politics and Gordon, near the end of his article, observes:

... there are those who feel that the African must build himself financially
so that Africans can become an economic unit. Several of the students,
especially those that had taught for many years, thought on these lines and
they had very little sympathy for the Youth League or any other political
organisation.[71]

In adopting this attitude the students were displaying class aspirations
which accorded with the status they already held as students of the University
College. Many of their colleagues, radical while they were on the campus,
would revert to the same attitude after they had graduated. Nevertheless, they
created a tradition which would be drawn upon in the coming years when the
colleges came into increasing conflict with the government.

References

1. *Transvaal 1961-1971*, (1971), (Voortrekkerpers), p.106.
2. *Ibid.*, p.113.
3. Muriel Horrell (Ed.), *Survey of Race Relations in South Africa*, 1969,
pp.205-6, (henceforth referred to as *SRRSA*).
4. For the changing value of the Rand, see Glossary.
5. These figures are all taken from the section on education in the
commemorative volume, pp.106-150.
6. *SRRSA*, 1969, pp.183-5.
7. P.A.W. Cook (1949), 'Non-European Education', in Ellen Hellman,
(Ed.), *Handbook of Race Relations in South Africa*, (OUP, Cape
Town), p.349.
8. Howard Rogers, (1949), *Native Administration in the Union of South
Africa*, (Government Printer, Pretoria). p.234.
9. Quoted in Nosipho Majeka (Dora Taylor), (1952), *The Role of the
Missionary in Conquest*, (Society of Young Africa, Cape Town), p.66.
10. Quoted in Raymond Williams, (1965), *The Long Revolution*, (Penguin),
p.156.
11. Muriel Horrell, (1963), *African Education: Some Origins, and Development Until 1953*, (South African Institute of Race Relations,
Johannesburg), pp.2-3.
12. N. Majeka, *op.cit.*, pp.68-9.
13. P.A.W. Cook, *op.cit.*, p.350.
14. Freda Troup, (1976), *Forbidden Pastures: Education Under Apartheid*,
(International Defence and Aid Fund, London), p.11.
15. M. Horrell, *op.cit.*, pp.11-2.
16. P.A.W. Cook, *op.cit.*, p.351.
17. N. Majeka, *op.cit.*, p.136.
18. D.D.T. Jabavu, (1920), 'Native educational needs', included in *The
Black Problem: Papers and Addresses on Various Native Problems*, by
Professor Jabavu, (Lovedale, n.d.), p.94. (For Mariannhill, see text
below.)

19. M. Horrell, *op.cit.*, p.12.
20. *Ibid.*, p.13.
21. *Ibid.*, p.7, and P.A.W. Cook, *op.cit.*, p.349.
22. Quoted by David Welsh, 'The growth of towns' in Monica Wilson and Leonard Thomson, (Eds.), (1971), *The Oxford History of South Africa*, Vol. II, (OUP), p.222.
23. R. Williams, *op.cit.*, p.159. All information on schools in Great Britain is taken from this book.
24. M. Horrell, *op.cit.*, p.13.
25. F. Troup, *op.cit.*, p.11.
26. Pablo Eisenberg, (1962), 'Education in South Africa' in Helen Kitchen, (Ed.), *The Educated African*, (Heinemann), p.268.
27. Statement of the Executive of the South African Native Congress, 1903 (?), reprinted in T. Karis and G. Carter (Eds.) (1972), *From Protest to Challenge*, Vol. I, (Hoover Institute Press), p.19.
28. Printed in *Ibid.*, p.31.
29. *Ibid.*, p.17.
30. *Ibid.*, p.75.
31. D.D.T. Jabavu, *op.cit.*, p.123.
32. M. Horrell, *op.cit.*, pp.33-5, provides some examples, but states that there is no exact account of all the contributions made by missionaries, overseas organisations and by Africans.
33. Table 1(a) is compiled from figures taken primarily from P.A.W. Cook, *op.cit.*, pp.351-4. Additional data was added from M. Horrell, *op.cit.*, F. Troup, *op.cit.*, and H. Rogers, *op.cit.* Some calculations of state expenditure or of expenditure per pupil are my own. Discrepancies in the sources used have led to totals that do not tally. Table 1(b) is taken from H. Rogers, *op.cit.*, p.248.
34. Sources from which these figures are taken include the following publications of the South African Institute of Race Relations, Johannesburg: a) Nathan Hurwitz, (1964), *The Economics of Bantu Education in South Africa;* b) Muriel Horrell, (1964), *A Decade of Bantu Education;* c) E.G. Malherbe, (1964), *Bantu Manpower and Education.* See also Pierre van den Berghe, (1967), *South Africa: a Study in Conflict*, (University of California Press), table XV, p.298.
35. For information about the Committee, see M. Horrell, (1963), *op.cit.*, p.32; F. Troup, *op.cit.*, p.15; and I.B. Tabata, (1960), *Education for Barbarism in South Africa*, (Pall Mall), p.8.
36. M. Horrell, (1963), *op.cit.*, pp.32, 57.
37. P.A.W. Cook, *op.cit.*, p.367.
38. *Ibid.*, p.366.
39. Quoted in F. Troup, *op.cit.*, p.21.
40. N. Majeka, *op.cit.*, p.139.
41. *Ibid.*, p.137.
42. *Report of Native Economic Commission, 1930-32* (U.G. 22, 1932), par. 584.
43. James Phillips, personal interviews, 1976-77.
44. *South African Outlook*, 1 January 1947. (See also ref. 28).
45. The majority of teachers at the time had only primary school education plus a further two years training. A secondary school graduate was

obviously well placed for a senior teaching post.

46. Ezekiel Mphahlele, (1962), *Down Second Avenue*, (Seven Seas), p.146.
47. *Inkundla ya Bantu*, September 1940.
48. *South African Outlook*, 1 January 1947.
49. *Ibid.*
50. *South African Outlook*, 1 February 1947. There is a short account in this issue of the 1920 Lovedale strike, but no reasons offered for the outbreak. E. Roux, (1949), *Time Longer Than Rope*, (Gollancz), p.164, states that both the riots at Kilnerton and Lovedale followed complaints about bad food.
51. *Inkundla ya Bantu*, September 1940, reports the setting up of the first commission by the Department of Education to report on a series of school strikes. The report is highly critical of the composition of the commission which consisted exclusively of white school inspectors. On 25 February 1943 the same paper reports a request to the government from the Transkeian Organised Bodies (the regional federal association) that the report be made available. It was never published. An official commission was appointed by Parliament to report on the Lovedale strike in 1946. The Smuts government refused to publish its findings.
52. The *Torch* carries reports (unfortunately very sparse) in two issues: 14 October 1946 and 9 December 1946.
53. *Inkundla ya Bantu*, 2 October 1945.
54. The college authorites asked D.L. Smit, former Secretary for Native Affairs, to head a Committee of Inquiry into the 1946 events. The report was printed in full in the *South African Outlook*, 1 January 1947.
55. *South African Outlook*, 2 September 1946. A statement issued by the Executive Committee of the United Cape African Teachers Association in *Inkundla ya Bantu*, 1 October 1946, said that Dr. Shepherd 'lacked imagination'. The position of the prefects, as described by the Smit Commission, is quoted above. Compare also a statement by C. Motsepe (1949) in an article 'Strikes in African Institutions' (a cutting found in the Fabian Colonial Bureau papers, Rhodes House, Oxford — origin unknown) which compared the prefect system to police (informers?) because they carried reports to the white headmasters.
56. R.H.W. Shepherd, (1971), *Lovedale, South Africa 1824-1955*, (Lovedale Press), p.130.
57. *Torch*, 14 October 1946 and 9 December 1946.
58. *Torch*, 3 November 1953. See also the report on the same event in the *Eastern Province Herald*, 30 October 1953. The *Herald* stated that a refusal of meals and a refusal to be seated in the dining hall were the causes of the expulsion.
59. D. Gordon, 'Some impressions of the African intellectual at Fort Hare'. This article, written by a coloured student about conditions on the campus in 1949, appeared in the journal *Discussion*, Vol. I, No. 2 (c.1951).
60. J. Burger (L. Marquard), (1943), *The Black Man's Burden*, (Gollancz), p.173.
61. *Ibid.*, p.172.
62. D. Gordon, *op.cit.*, makes a similar point in rather patronising terms

and also suggests that these pupils were intolerant of the Coloureds and Indians on the campus. He fails to note the equal intolerance (or patronising attitude) shown by Coloureds and Indians to the African students — and his article could be quoted in part as an example of such intolerance!

63. *Guardian*, 25 September 1941.
64. *Inkundla ya Bantu*, 25 February 1943.
65. *Guardian*, 1 October 1942.
66. Letters by A.P. Mda to G.M. Pitje, 24 August 1948 and 10 September 1948. These documents are reprinted in T. Karis and G. Carter, *op.cit.*, Vol. II, pp.319-22. A.P. Mda was one of the founding members of the CYL. Trained as a teacher, he later became a lawyer. Godfrey Pitje was on the Student Representative Council and later became a lawyer in the Transvaal.
67. In 1935 an All-African Convention (AAC) was convened in order to form an African united front against the Native Bills of 1936. The ANC withdrew from the AAC in 1938, and by 1940 it was almost extinct. In 1943 the AAC was revived in the Cape and soon won the support of the federal Transkeian Organised Bodies and the Cape African Teachers Association. In 1943 a group of coloured intellectuals in the Cape formed the anti-Coloured Affairs Department (anti-CAD) and this too was a federal body which included the (Coloured) Teachers League of South Africa. The AAC and Anti-CAD formed a united federal body known as the Non-European Unity Movement in December 1943. For the NEUM at Fort Hare, see D. Gordon, *op.cit.*
68. D. Gordon, *op.cit.*
69. *Ibid.*
70. *Ibid.* Gordon only gives a perfunctory description of the strike.
71. *Ibid.*

2. Bantu Education: 1954-1976

In the 1940s there was much criticism of the schooling provided for Africans from many different sources and the missionaries were castigated for providing inferior education. It was stated that the mission schools were poorly funded, that facilities were grossly inadequate, and that teachers were poorly paid and badly trained. The curricula in use were dull and overloaded with moral instruction, the teaching was unimaginative, and much that passed for education consisted of repetitive recitation, or of learning texts by rote.

Dr. O.D. Wollheim, an executive member of the South African Institute of Race Relations, wrote an article on the crisis of Native education in 1943, after inspecting some of the African rural schools. The conditions he found were deplorable:

> Native education has been in an appalling condition . . . Buildings in most cases consist of tin shanties or wattle and daub huts into which are crammed two or three times the number of pupils which the room should hold. The equipment is correspondingly pitiful . . . The salaries paid to teachers are likewise appalling . . . The teacher will occasionally be found to be teaching from eighty to a hundred pupils in two or three different standards all in the same room.[1]

African communities were equally discontented with the school system, and the extent of the dissatisfaction can be gauged from the account given by Muriel Horrell:

> . . . there was a growing antagonism among Africans to the mission control of schools. Opponents of this system wanted their schools to be administered in the same way as were those of the whites, and felt that Departmental schools were better off in regard to funds and supplies. Of 2,000 mission schools in the Transvaal, 800 had been transferred to the Department (of Education) by about 1949.[2]

The demands made in the 1940s, were little different from those made earlier in the century. The African wanted more schools, compulsory education and state responsibility for education. There were few who called for an end to 'Native education' and for integration of the school system, and few who connected the rotten school system with the entire apparatus of segregation in the country. Most criticism ended with calls for improvement, and except for the small groups on the left who demanded radical change, and condemned the message of humility in missionary education, there were few proposals for restructuring the educational system.

The Afrikaner nationalists saw the matter very differently. Not only did they claim that graduates of the schools were liberals and radicals, but they also contended that the doctrine of Christianity, as taught, was suspect. The only Christianity that could be accepted, they proclaimed, was that which followed the creed of the three Afrikaner churches.[3]

Christian National Education: the Afrikaner Ideal

The Afrikaner nationalist approach to education had been shaped in the course of a long struggle to have their rights recognised by the British in South Africa. In terms of their own struggle, which involved a long and bitter fight against the imperial presence, the demand for 'mother-tongue' (or Afrikaans) instruction, and for separate schools, was understandable. They were a fraction of the dominant white minority and were fighting for control of the economy and of the state, yet any move to apply these principles to the African people was inexcusable. The African people were in a position of subordination, and their overriding demand in the forties was *not* for mother-tongue instruction or separate schools, but for an education that would allow them to play their full part in commerce and industry.

The reality behind Afrikaner aspirations was put succinctly by a school inspector in 1943. His view was that:

> The Afrikaner teacher will show Afrikanerdom what a power they possess in their Teachers Associations to build up the country's youth for the future republic. I know of no more potent instrument . . . A nation is born by having its youth impregnated at school in the traditions, customs, ways and ultimate destiny of its people.[4]

This was obviously not what was intended for African youth at school. The only youth that had to be moulded for the 'future republic' were the Afrikaner youth.

In February 1948 a pamphlet was issued by prominent Afrikaner nationalists on Christian National Education (CNE). In a set of 15 articles, the authors of this work ('after ten years of silent labour') laid down the ideological basis of education for the youth of South Africa. The first thirteen of these articles were devoted to the problems of white education, and laid down the philosophical framework within which the authors were working:

All white children should be educated according to the views of life of their parents. Consequently all Afrikaans-speaking children should have a Christian-Nationalist education . . .

The key subject in school should be religion . . .

All teaching should also be nationalist . . .

Owing to the Fall, all children are born sinful, but the children of believers have inherited God's promise, through Christ, of redemption . . . the necessity for education lies in the fact that the child's soul is undeveloped . . .

Civics should teach the child to preserve the Christian and nationalist character of home, church, society and state.

Every nation is rooted in a country allotted to it by God.

Geography should aim at giving the pupil a thorough knowledge of his own country . . . he will love his own country, also when compared and contrasted with others, and be ready to defend it, preserve it from poverty and improve it for posterity.

History should be seen as the fulfilment of God's plan for humanity . . . Next to the mother tongue the history of the fatherland is the best channel for cultivating the love of one's own which is nationalism.

In normal circumstances, the church should not erect schools, but may be compelled to do so (a) if the existing schools are unchristian and unnationalistic and (b) in the heathen world.

Science should be expounded in a positively Christian light, and contrasted with non-Christian science.

All authority in school is borrowed from God . . .

Unless (the teacher) is a Christian, he is a deadly danger to us.[5]

Articles 14 and 15 were devoted to the issues of 'coloured' and 'native' education. The previous articles, where relevant, were obviously intended to be read together with these final propositions. The article on African education stated:

The white South African's duty to the native is to Christianise him and help him on culturally.

Native education should be based on the principles of trusteeship, non-equality and segregation; its aim should be to inculcate the white man's way of life, especially that of the Boer nation, which is the senior trustee.

The mother tongue should be the basis of native education but the two official languages should be learned as keys to the cultures from which the native will have to borrow in order to progress. Owing to the cultural infancy of the native, the state, in co-operation with the protestant churches should at present provide Native education. But the native should be fitted to undertake his own education as soon as possible, under control and guidance of the state. Native education should lead to the development of an independent, self supporting Christian-Nationalist Native community.

Native education should not be financed at the expense of the white.[6]

The CNE pamphlet appeared only three months before the Nationalist victory at the polls on 26 May 1948, and proponents of the manifesto moved that the programme be adopted by the government. One such attempt was made at the Transvaal provincial congress of the party in November but was blocked by the Minister of Education, Dr. A.J. Stals, on the grounds that the government only controlled higher education, and that school education was in the hands of Provincial Councils.[7]

African education, however, was controlled by the Department of Native Affairs, and in January 1949 the government appointed a Commission of Enquiry, headed by Dr. W.W.M. Eiselen, to propose ways in which this education could be altered to meet the needs of the Africans 'as an independent race'.

The Commission consisted of educationalists, rather than theologians, and their final report was not couched in the religious terminology of the CNE pamphlet. Nevertheless the substantive points in Article 15 (on African education) were all adopted by the commissioners. The guiding principle of education was conceived of as being Christian and, although it was proposed that the missionaries who had 'diligently acted as guardians of the Bantu' should be replaced, it was suggested that there was a place for them in extra-curricular activities.[8]

The Commission also endorsed the CNE suggestions that education be in the vernacular; that control be exercised by the state; and that the burden of finances be shifted to the African population. None of this was new, and the Commission did not offer anything that had not been repeated *ad nauseam* by Nationalist Party spokesmen in the past.

There was, however, one set of proposals that seemed at first sight to go well beyond the terms of reference of the Commission. In paragraphs 789 to 792 the Commission proposed the establishment of 'Bantu Local Authorities' in the Reserves and (white) urban areas. These bodies which, said the commissioners, should be composed of chiefs (if any), plus elected and nominated members, would carry out the functions usually delegated to local authorities, and also 'achieve the active participation of the Bantu in carrying out the educational plans.'[9] In the words of the commissioners:

> . . . a happy and prosperous Bantu population must have a social organisation with healthy and vigorous social institutions: a fitting religious, economic and political structure based on orderly family life and attuned to the demands of modern conditions.[10]

The social organisations that the Commission wished to promote were the proposed Bantu Local Authorities. These new bodies, it was said, would help the child find a bridge between his 'traditional' social setting and the new practices he acquired at school. The Commission report said, by way of example, that there was a disjunction between 'the virtues and merits of modern hygiene' as apparently taught at school and practices in the 'traditional family'. The Local Bantu Authorities would, in some unexplained fashion, restore the harmony between the 'hygienic child' and his seemingly unhygienic parents!

Even more important in the eyes of the commissioners was the social environment in which this restoration of harmony could be effected. This they claimed could happen only in the Reserves:

> It is particularly in the Reserves that the qualities of independence, self-reliance, initiative and responsibility could be developed; the development of these qualities demands life in social institutions unfettered by outside control.[11]

The Minister of Native Affairs, Dr. E.G. Jansen, addressing Parliament while the Commission was still sitting, made the same point:

> We are of the opinion that the solidarity of the tribes should be preserved and that they should develop along the lines of their own national character and tradition. For that purpose we want to rehabilitate the deserving tribal chiefs as far as possible and we would like to see their authority maintained over members of their tribes.[12]

Dr. Jansen took the matter further. The Eiselen Commission might believe in 'unfettered' institutions, but this was not the government's view. The chiefs had a role to play in controlling the labour force in the Reserves:

> The most effective way to arrest the influx of natives into the cities is to see to it that life within the reserves becomes more versatile. The idea is that we should see to it that the tribal chiefs in the reserves have contact with and exercise discipline over their fellow tribesmen in the urban areas.[13]

Bantu Authorities and Bantu Education

In 1951, the Bantu Authorities Act was passed by Parliament. The Act made provision for the establishment in the Reserves of tribal, regional and territorial authorities, and for the delegation of administrative and some executive powers to bodies composed of chiefs, headmen, and tribal councillors. In 1953 the Bantu Education Act was enacted, and the major provisions recommended by the Eiselen Commission became law. The two Acts were conceived as part of one overall plan, and Dr. Verwoerd, who replaced Dr. Jansen as Minister of Native Affairs, made this quite explicit:

> My department's policy is that education should stand with both feet in the Reserve and have its roots in the spirit and being of Bantu society . . . The basis of the provision and organisation of education in a Bantu community should, where possible, be the tribal organisation.[14]

The Bantu Education Act of 1953 was an administrative rather than a substantive measure. The control of African education was vested in the Department of Native Affairs, and the drafting of all regulations governing the content of education was left to the Minister of Native Affairs. All schools now came under the Minister's control, and no educational institution could be established or conducted without his permission. An amendment to the Act in 1954, aimed against mission institutions, stipulated that all teacher-training schools would have their subsidies terminated in 1955, and that subsidies paid to other schools would be reduced progressively until they ceased in 1957. Missions were offered the options of either renting or selling their schools to the government, or of continuing unaided. Those that chose the latter option found in many instances that other legislation made it impossible for them to continue in existing premises because that would contravene one or other of the apartheid laws.

The legislation of 1954 also fixed the state's contribution to African education at an amount equivalent to the 1953 expenditure. Henceforth the yearly contribution would be R13,000,000. Any expenditure in excess of this amount had to be met by African taxpayers.

There were two further administrative measures. Education in the junior classes was to be conducted in the vernacular, and the schools were to be under the supervision of boards or committees. In the Reserves these were to be partly or wholly nominated by tribal authorities. In the urban areas two-thirds of the members of the school boards were to be government (usually tribal) appointees, and the remaining third were to be elected by the parents.

It remained for Dr. Verwoerd to outline the philosophy that would guide his Department in the conduct of the schools. Speaking in the Senate in June 1954, the Minister made his intentions quite clear:

> When I have control of Native Education I will reform it so that the Natives will be taught from childhood to realise that equality with Europeans is not for them. . . People who believe in equality are not desirable teachers for Natives . . . When my department controls Native education it will know for what class of higher education a Native is fitted, and whether he will have a chance in life to use his knowledge . . . What is the use of teaching the Bantu child mathematics when it cannot use it in practice? That is quite absurd.

Schooling was, quite evidently, blatantly used as an instrument of social control. The child would be taught that equality was not for him or her — either in society or in the work place:

> The school must equip him to meet the demands which the economic life will impose on him . . . There is no place for him [or her, presumably!] above the level of certain forms of labour . . . For that reason it is of no avail for him to receive a training which has as its aim absorption in the European community.[15]

In practice this meant that even technical training would be inferior. Speaking about the training of African building workers, the Minister of Labour said in 1950:

> The standard of training is not the same as the standard given to the ordinary (*sic*) artisan who enrols under the Apprenticeship Act . . . Native builders will therefore not be artisans in the full sense of the word. They will only receive training which will enable them to erect houses and buildings for their own use.[16]

The schooling was inferior, as a matter of principle. The Africans only had to perform unskilled work for white employers; or, when they served their own community, it was presumed that the work should be inferior. From bricklayers through to nurses and teachers the training that was recommended by the government would ensure third class status. Nurses, said Dr. Eiselen, should only receive the training necessary to serve their own community. This differential training, he added, would also determine the rate of pay.[17]

The parsimony of the government was to have a debilitating effect on African education. The schools were bleak and dilapidated, overcrowded and ill-equipped. Lower primary schools were built by the state, and the capital costs recovered by raising rentals in the area. The parents who wanted schools at a higher level had to bear half the capital costs.

There were few books in the schools. Primary school pupils received a reader. Other textbooks had to be bought by the parents. The school library often consisted of no more than a dozen dog-eared volumes, and the maximum grant permissible for purchase of books was R20 per year for primary schools, and R50 for post-primary schools.[18] The yearly grant for scientific equipment for a school with approximately 1,000 pupils was R35! In 1966 it was reported that in four Soweto schools (with 3,080 pupils) in which 80 per cent of the pupils were taught science, the total equipment consisted of 13 bunsen burners, six balances, and three microscopes.[19]

In 1954 Dr. Verwoerd also announced that new salaries for teachers would be 'less favourable' than those in existing scales, and that in future it would be departmental policy to employ women in the primary schools in order to save money. As existing posts fell vacant all men would be replaced by women (at salaries approximately 25 per cent less).[20]

New measures followed in quick succession. School meals were restricted to primary schools — but only those which had participated in the scheme in previous years were included. The amount per child per meal was cut from 2.0d (1p.) to 1.2d. Finally, in 1956 parents were given the 'choice' of either continuing with the meals, in which case there would be no grants for buildings and equipment, or of forfeiting the meals in return for assistance with new accommodation. Within a few years all school feeding had stopped in African schools.

ANC Responds: the 'Resist Apartheid Campaign'

The publication of the CNE pamphlet had led to considerable agitation amongst white educationalists, and meetings of parents were summoned to protest against the obscurantist views in the 15 articles. Counter-pamphlets were written, the English-speaking press wrote editorials criticising the proposals, and church and mission leaders voiced their opposition. There was, however, little that these protests could achieve.

There were also angry reactions from African organisations. The Cape African Teachers Association (CATA), affiliated to the All African Convention and the Non-European Unity Movement, announced that they were calling a national conference to discuss the Bantu Education Act. They were warned that the government would not tolerate a discussion of educational policy by teachers, and they cancelled the conference.

The only campaign against the implementation of Bantu Education in the schools was initiated by the African National Congress. On 8 May 1954, the ANC and its associated organisations of the Congress Alliance (the South African Indian Congress, the South African Coloured People's Organisation, and the [white] Congress of Democrats), launched a campaign that was dubbed the 'Resist Apartheid Campaign'. The particular measures that Congress aimed to resist were: the Bantu Education Act; the Native Resettlement Act (which was designed to remove 60,000 Africans from the black townships of Sophiatown and neighbouring regions, and transfer them to Soweto); the pass laws; the Group Areas Act; the Suppression of Communism Act; and anti-trade union measures.[21]

Little more was heard of this campaign as a whole, and the first two issues alone occupied the ANC in 1954. In fact it over-extended the movement, and showed that the ANC did not have the resources to defeat the government on any one of the six discriminatory measures against which they had planned to campaign. In the case of both the Bantu Education and the Native Resettlement Act, the campaigns mounted by the ANC were heavily defeated. It is the former which concerns us here.

In view of the seriousness with which the ANC viewed the Bantu Education Act, the handling of the issue at the December 1954 conference was remarkably casual. The report of the National Executive Committee was brief. It said:

> The Bantu Education question has been handed over to the women and youth sections of the African National Congress working together with other organisations whose purpose is to fight against this Devil's piece of legislation. This means that they work under the supervision of the senior body, but specialise on this campaign.
>
> The plans have been drawn up which recommend a withdrawal of children at least for one week. A speaker on the subject will enlighten you more as to precisely what should be done.[22]

The resolution adopted by the conference called for the 'total rejection of Verwoerd's evil act' and further decided to call on parents 'to make preparations to withdraw their children from schools indefinitely as from 1 April 1955, until further directive from the National Executive Committee.'[23]

Nothing further was heard about the role of the women's section, nor of the 'plans' that had been drawn up. According to a report of the Cape ANC, there was no comprehensive programme of campaign, and it was left to the provincial and local branches to put the issue to the people and prepare for the boycott.[24] It seems, in fact, that there was little thought given to the campaign, and that the conference did not even check to see whether 1 April was a school day. The day had been chosen by the government for the commencement of the new system and fell in the Easter recess.

The provincial and local branches did very little to put the conference resolution to the people, and on 6 March the ANC National Executive stated that there had not been enough time to organise the boycott, and decided to postpone its start to 25 April. At this stage the National Executive also decided that the boycott should not proceed until arrangements had been made for children who were to be withdrawn from the schools.[25] In April a committee of individuals was set up under the chairmanship of Father Huddleston to provide alternative education. This committee was later transformed into the African Education Movement (AEM) and under its aegis a chain of Cultural Clubs was established to provide an outlet for children who were kept out of schools when the boycott commenced.

The setting up of the Huddleston committee, and the decision to postpone the boycott brought strains inside the ANC to the surface. Not everyone in Congress accepted the idea of 'alternative education', and at least one editorial in the Congress journal *Liberation* rejected it. Writing at a time when it was still hoped by some that the flagging boycott could be revived, it was stated:

> The idea that a boycott should be made conditional on providing 'alternative education' is, in fact, quite wrong in principle . . . It is not the aim of a political boycott of this sort to relieve the State of its obligation to provide proper education, but rather to compel the State to fulfil that obligation honourably.[26]

But the biggest issue was over the boycott itself. Members of the Congress Youth League were afraid that the National Executive decision to postpone the boycott signalled an attempt to revoke the Conference decision of December 1954. Despite the fact that there had not been adequate preparation for a large-scale campaign, members of the CYL called the boycott for 12 April (the first day of the new school term) in the Eastern Cape, and on the East Rand (that is, the Witwatersrand to the East of Johannesburg). On that day school entrances were picketed by members of the Youth League, and in some instances schools were entered and classes dismissed. Women and children marched through the streets of Benoni, Brakpan and Germiston carrying ANC banners and posters rejecting Bantu Education and large crowds congregated at street corners. They were, inevitably, dispersed by armed police.

In some towns in the Cape the election of parents' representatives to school committees was stopped by Youth Leaguers, and in the Eastern Cape children were withdrawn from schools in six districts – the only districts in which the ANC had done any preparatory work.

Early in April, Dr. Verwoerd warned that any children still boycotting schools on the 25th of the month (the date chosen by the National Executive to start the campaign!) would be permanently excluded from all schools. The National Executive was in disarray, and several prominent ANC leaders called on parents to end the boycott, and sent their own children to school. This all but ended the campaign. Only in Port Elizabeth was any attempt made to extend the school boycott, but this too was aborted when Dr. Verwoerd announced that a single day's absence (if shown to be part of a boytcott) would lead to immediate expulsion. The boycott was dead, although the ANC only formally recognised that the campaign was over in 1958!

Some 7,000 former school goers did not return to school on the 25th. Most of these young boys and girls, together with some 4,000 who had not been at school in 1955, were catered for by the Cultural Clubs.

The African Education Movement started in mid-1955, and continued through until 1960. Many of its committee members were banned, its club leaders in the townships harassed, and the children subjected to police raids (and in one case at least, had police guns levelled at them). They provided little formal education and served little political purpose (as the *Liberation* editorial had claimed), although they were an example of dogged perseverance. They also did provide some sheltered occupation for children who otherwise would have roamed the township streets.

The clubs could not legally provide any 'education' and had to resort to story-telling, quizzes, play-acting, and similar activities. The club leaders were unfortunately untrained in methods of informal teaching: they were mothers or teachers who had left (or been expelled by) the Bantu Affairs Department. They were often unpaid, or received a few pounds per month, contributed by the parents. Their accommodation often consisted of a clearing under a tree, and rain closed such clubs for the day.

The parents hoped that their children would receive instruction in reading and writing – even though that would have been illegal, and club leaders had instructions to avoid such activity. The children, consequently, were often sent to the clubs with slates, exercise books, and readers, and these were invariably seized by the police and used as evidence in court when the leaders were prosecuted.[27] AEM activity became, increasingly, the provision of money for bail, for fines, and for lawyers' fees. The Committee and the clubs finally collapsed in 1960 when many of the active club leaders and some of the committee were placed in detention in the post-Sharpeville state of emergency. They were not restarted after the detainees were released.

The boycott failed in 1955 and there was never any possibility of its succeeding. The state was far too strong, and the government too determined, while the opposition was weak and undecided. To suggest that errors were made is not, therefore, to contend that the school system could have been altered appreciably in 1955.

In March 1955, the ANC Executive had stated that not enough time had been set aside to organise the boycott although the editorial writer in *Liberation* maintained that:

> Three months (from January to April) could be enough to get a campaign going properly, provided that massive, well-organised work was done . . .

> The real fault with the decision about April 1st was that it assumed that all that was necessary was to issue an order and the people would hasten to obey . . .[28]

The problem was, however, not only organisational, but lay in the whole conception of the boycott. The initiative was to be left to *parents* to withdraw their children, and little consideration was given to the fact that parents of school-going youth relied on the schools, in fact depended on the schools, to occupy their children while they were away from home. Furthermore, the parents hoped that education would allow their children to advance up the economic ladder. To call on these parents to withdraw their children was not realistic, and only a small number could be expected to respond.

Secondly, and far more fundamentally, even a longer period of preparation would not have ensured a greater response to the boycott call in 1955. Campaigns, even on issues over which people are agitated, cannot be called unless there is already a readiness for action. There must be a potential for response, and this in turn depends on a tradition of struggle in the arena chosen for confrontation. There was, however, no open conflict in the schools in the *towns*, and no history of conflict in the *primary schools*. When the ANC decided on the campaign, it did not take cognizance of the fact that it was primary school children who would be involved, and that parents had always clamoured to get their seven or eight year olds into the schools. What might just have been feasible at Fort Hare, or even in the secondary schools, was not possible then in the primary schools.

The extension of Bantu Education to the secondary schools, and the legislation to alter the universities, only came four years later in 1959. There was, however, no attempt to call on older students to boycott the schools, the colleges or the universities on that occasion. Nothing had changed in Bantu Education since the time when Professor Z.K. Matthews had addressed the Cape ANC in his capacity as President on 18 June 1955. In a long address on education he had maintained that: 'As the years pass under the new dispensation even our deputation friends will come to realise that education for ignorance and for inferiority in Verwoerd's schools is worse than no education at all.'[29] In the circumstances the fact that seven and eight year olds were pulled out of schools while older youth were not called upon to resist the new measures only four years later, needs explanation. The ANC never offered reasons. Nor did any of the other political movements suggest an alternative lead. The NEUM youth sections, the Society of Young Africa (SOYA), only opted out in 1955 when they cursorily dismissed the ANC as cowards who: 'shifted the burden of the struggle on to the backs of our children.'[30]

Higher Education Under Attack

The missions and churches faced a government which was intent on expropriating all teacher training colleges and ensuring that all state-aided schools be transferred (after a short interval) to state controlled 'Bantu Community Organisations'. The teacher training colleges were to be taken over immediately but the schools would be given a 'choice'. The existing schools could continue to function under licence provided they found the funds, if they removed all white teachers, and adopted the new Bantu Education syllabus.

Most mission institutions were closed, or were appropriated by the state. Only a few churches (the Roman Catholics in particular) were prepared to continue, raise the necessary funds, and teach the new syllabus. There were also a few establishments, each comprising secondary school, industrial school and teacher training college, which meant to maintain their existence in some form. One such attempt by the staff of Adams College (Natal), aided by the ABCFM, was described by the principal, the Reverend G.C. Grant, in 1956.[31]

Adams College

Rev. Grant had been opposed to the Bantu Education Act from the date of its first publication, and his account describes the harassment to which he was subjected by the police because of his vocal objections. The College was visited by members of the Native Affairs Commission (the top advisory committee responsible only to Parliament), and the principal and his staff were subjected to lengthy questioning on their policy and their political attitudes. Rev. Grant likened the proceedings to an 'inquisition', and it was obvious from the meeting that Adams College would not be allowed to continue for much longer under private control.

In an attempt to save Adams College and the industrial school, the staff decided to close the teacher training college. This latter, however, the government had decided to take over immediately. Furthermore, in July 1956, the principal was informed that only the training college would be allowed to continue operating: the schools would be closed. By government decision the institution was renamed the Amamzimtoti Zulu Training College, and most of the staff replaced by government nominees. The students who stayed on had been opposed to the transfer of the college and through 1957 and 1958 the situation there was tense. Students objected to the extensive use of their fellows as 'informers', and the tension was exacerbated when the government threatened to expel any student who maintained an association with the liberal National Union of South African Students (NUSAS).[32]

In 1958, one of the black school servants inadvertently interchanged tea-cups belonging to white and black teachers, and a white teacher, enraged by this 'misdemeanour', struck the worker. The students then instituted a passive resistance campaign. Hymn books and chairs belonging to the white staff members disappeared at morning assembly; and these men stood, insulted, while their black colleagues sat! The pettiness of apartheid had turned full circle, but the situation was not allowed to rest there: twenty alleged ring-leaders were expelled, and 254 students then threatened a walk-out. The police were called in to 'restore order' and several students were arrested and charged, although none were convicted.[33] The discontent did not disappear, and in May 1960 50 students left after complaining about the standard of tuition.[34]

Fort Hare

The situation at Fort Hare was significantly different. There, the complaints about conditions on the campus were closely integrated with events in the rest of the country. The Congress Youth League competed with the Society of Young Africa for control of political life on the campus, and the growing militancy of these two groups led to a campaign against association with 'liberal' or white student bodies. In 1952 Fort Hare moved 'leftwards' and voted to secede from NUSAS. The students also boycotted a reception for the Nationalist-appointed Governor-General at the College in the same year, and several students were expelled, including Gatsha Buthelezi who later came to prominence in Bantustan politics.

During the next two years, members of the CYL were in the forefront of the agitation against the implementation of Bantu Education, and demanded that the schools be closed. It was due to their organisation, particularly in the Eastern Cape, that the boycott of schools got under way on 12 April 1955.

There were also serious complaints about conditions on the campus. A Commission of Inquiry was set up to investigate conditions at Fort Hare after the Students Representative Council resigned *en bloc* and the students boycotted the annual graduation ceremony in early May, 1955. It stated:

> members were shocked, they said, to realize how bad the atmosphere really was at Fort Hare . . . There had, on the part of the authorities, been a carry-over of the traditional paternal missionary approach. Some of the rules were impracticable and unenforceable. The authorities depended too much on 'informers' for information. The hostels were controlled by churches and wardens were church, not College, appointments, responsible for discipline as well as for certain teaching. Conditions in at least two of the hostels were unsatisfactory: living quarters were overcrowded and equipment inadequate. Requests from students did not receive proper attention.

The Commission called 'for a bold transition from the methods and atmosphere of the missionary high school from which Fort Hare sprang to those of a university'. They also suggested that academic facilities should be improved; that post-graduate classes and scholarships be provided, that religious services be made voluntary rather than compulsory; and that there be changes in the administration of discipline. At the same time both political movements (SOYA and CYL) were criticised in the report because: 'They imagined they were in the vanguard of "the struggle for liberation", and confused the issue of the maintenance of legitimate college discipline with the idea of *baaskap* (domination).'[35]

These political forces, said the Commission members, could not be eliminated — but their effectiveness might be reduced by the 'expulsive power of new affections' (*sic*). The principal, finally, was praised for his integrity, deep care for students, and unsparing hard work for the College. The government was already preparing legislation which would transform the College, remove the principal, and reduce the effectiveness of the political groups, so that the Commission report could have been of little worth even if its suggested reforms had been acceptable to the students.

The Extension of University Education Act

In 1959 the Extension of University Education Act was passed through parliament. The 'open universities'[36] would not be allowed to register any new black students (unless granted special permission by the Minister for Bantu Affairs in individual cases). Fort Hare would fall under the Minister of Bantu Education and be open only to Xhosa-speaking Africans. Two new tribally based university colleges would be established — the University College of the North at Turfloop to serve the Sotho, Pedi, Tswana and Venda, and the University College of Zululand at Ngoye, Natal, to serve the Zulus. Coloureds would all be directed to the new University College of the Western Cape in Bellville, and Indians to their own University College near Durban.

During the two years preceding the change the students and staff at Fort Hare expressed their disapproval, but there was *no* talk of taking militant action, nor were there any moves to boycott the College. In 1958 students on the campus passed a resolution condemning the dismissal of staff members and claimed that the atmosphere of insecurity made the 'normal pursuit of academic activities almost impossible'. They continued:

> But let it be noted, once and for all, that our stand as students of Fort Hare and as the future leaders of our country, upholding the principles of education as universally accepted, remains unchanged and uncompromising . . .
>
> We wish to warn the architects of white domination, the whole country and the world at large that we will not be held responsible for the

disastrous repercussions of this apartheid policy, which in the foreseeable future will destroy the entire social, political and economic structure of our country.[37]

The words of the resolution, defiant as they were, did not reflect the situation as the national leadership saw it at the time. The Congress movement had taken a number of knocks, and was considerably weakened by a long drawn out Treason Trial which had restricted the leadership and eaten deeply into the resources of the entire Congress movement. The leadership looked to the possibility of widespread opposition which would confront the government and remove fascism (as they were wont to describe the ruling party). The opposition to the University bill encouraged them, rather mistakenly, in the belief that a broad united front could be built. At the time this was expressed in an article by Nelson Mandela:

> The Bill has aroused extensive popular indignation, and opposition throughout the country as well as abroad. Students and lecturers, liberals and conservatives, progressives, democrats, public men and women of all races and with varying political affiliations have been stirred into action.[38]

and he argued that

> Fascism has become a living reality in our country and its defeat has become the principal task of the *entire people* of South Africa. But the fight against the fascist policies of the Government cannot be conducted on the basis of isolated struggles. It can only be conducted on the basis of the united fight of the *entire people* of South Africa against all attacks of the Nationalists . . .
>
> A *broad united front* of all the genuine opponents of the racial policies of the Government must be developed . . .[39]
> (my stress)

The students affiliated to SOYA, and those who were turning to the 'Africanists' inside the ANC (soon to become the Pan-Africanist Congress) rejected this appeal for a united front with 'liberals', 'progressives' or 'democrats', not to mention the 'conservatives'.

The campaign against the new Bill was no more effective than others during the previous decade, although there were more illusions aroused than previously. The names of former judges, academics and politicians opposed to the new legislation aroused hope that it would not be enacted. There were mass meetings, on and off the campuses; one-day boycotts of classes (at Cape Town, Witwatersrand and elsewhere); solemn processions of dons and students in academic garb in the main cities; yet the legislation was placed on the statute book. Symbolically, plaques proclaiming the idea of the 'open university' were unveiled at Cape Town and Witwatersrand, a yearly lecture on 'academic freedom' was instituted. The new 'closed' universities returned to 'normal'.

Fort Hare, however, was not to be allowed to forget the opposition of the past year. The principal and eight white members of staff were informed they would not be reappointed. Professor Z.K. Matthews, the senior African academic and vice-principal, rejected the government's demand that he leave the ANC and resigned. He was joined by four lecturers who left rather than stay in the new Bantu university college.

Students fared little better. When Fort Hare was reopened in 1960, 11 students were not readmitted on disciplinary grounds and the SRC was instructed to resign from NUSAS (which the students had rejoined in 1956). This led to a new wave of indignation amongst the student body:

> Next day there was a near-revolt at the college, meetings of protest being held and demonstrations staged in the dining halls. The students decided to dissolve the SRC pending the drawing up of a new constitution.[40]

The incipient revolt was stifled by the college authorities who demanded that every student sign a declaration reaffirming acceptance of the college regulations, or face dismissal. This was followed by the promulgation of new regulations which required students at Fort Hare to provide yearly testimonials of good conduct, and to sign yearly undertakings to comply with all college rules and regulations.[41]

At the boarding schools and colleges, and at Fort Hare, there were new administrations and new regulations. Inevitably there were new grievances added to the old, and, in the late 1950s and through the 1960s, there were reports of disturbances.

Schools Dismantled and the Struggle Continues

One of the lesser known features of the transference of schools to the Department of Bantu Administration was the displacement of students from schools after their structures had been altered. Part of the story was told by Phyllis Ntantala in an article in the journal *Africa South*.[42] Teacher-training for boys was discontinued at St. Matthews, and the school restricted to girls. Lovedale, which was once co-educational, was transformed into a single-sex school and its industrial department was closed down. All the displaced boys and girls were given five months in which to find alternative accommodation, and most found that there was no place for them in schools which already had long waiting lists of applicants: they were forced to abandon their education.

The reorganisation of the schools showed the government's determination to wipe out the old tradition. At Lovedale, said Ms. Ntantala, the Cuthbert Library, 'one of the biggest and best school libraries in the country' was dismantled, the books sold, and the library building converted into a storeroom for Departmental books. The campus sites were also allowed to deteriorate and most of the maintenance staffs were dismissed. All the chores were allocated to the pupils, and compulsory manual work was introduced both before and after school hours.

Ms. Ntantala lists some of the events which followed the inevitable student discontent and administrative repression. Thirty senior girls were expelled from Shawbury in the Transkei in 1957; 200 men sent home on the eve of the examinations at St. Johns College; over 300 students at Lovedale staged a walkout in February 1959 and went home.

The incidents continued, moving from one school to another. In 1960, 420 students were sent home from Tigerkloof School in the Cape. A carpentry block was subsequently burnt down, students were detained and eight were eventually sentenced.[43] A political dimension was added in 1961 when, in addition to demonstrations at schools over food and disciplinary issues, students protested against the official festivities held to celebrate the proclamation of the new Republic of South Africa. Once again there were riots and expulsions across the country. In the Transkei the demonstrations took a more serious turn because the territory was in a 'state of emergency' and all meetings were prohibited. At St. Johns College, the students refused to disperse and destroyed government vehicles before attempting to burn down the school library. Two hundred and seven students were arrested, and of these, 21 were fined (from £15 to £25) and 86 were sentenced to strokes.[44]

The disturbances never stopped, and the list of expulsions grew, but the reports became sparse in the aftermath of the banning of radical journals. It was only in the late 1960's, when events in the new university colleges became front page news in the national press, that reporting of school demonstrations and riots was renewed.

It could not have been otherwise: the educational system had to breed rebels, and the students had to react. The repression, whether overt or covert, had to lead the young men and women to confrontation situations: and the intransigence of the staff had to lead to periodic explosions. Rebellion was endemic in these colleges and schools, and could be hidden from public scrutiny only as long as they continued to be isolated from other events in the country. When the time came, as it did in 1976, that the revolts were too large to be concealed, and when, furthermore, they coincided with deep antagonisms in the country, such student disturbances were to take the country to the edge of revolution. At such a time the young men and women of the country would step right outside the classroom and enter the battleground.

References

1. O.D. Wollheim, (1943), 'Crisis in Native Education', *Race Relations Journal*, Vol. 10, No. 2, quoted in M. Horrell, (1963), *op.cit.*, p.54.
2. M. Horrell, (1963), *op.cit.*, p.37.
3. Christian National Education, Article 1. Abridged translation from the Afrikaans printed in *Blueprint for Blackout*, (Education League, Johannesburg, n.d.), p.17.
4. From the secret Silver Jubilee conference of the Broederbond, 1943. Quoted by J. Malherbe in 'Separation in schools', *Education for Isolation*, special issue of *Black Sash*, Vol. 4, No. 5, September 1960.
5. These statements, taken from the first 13 articles, are from *Blueprint for Blackout, op.cit.*, pp.17-22.
6. *Ibid.*, p.23.
7. *Ibid.*, p.15.
8. K.B. Hartshorne, (1953), *Native Education in the Union of South Africa: a Summary of the Report of the Commission on Native Education in South Africa – UG 53 – 1951,* (South African Institute of Race Relations), pp.44-5.
9. *Ibid.*, p.29.
10. *Ibid.*, p.24.
11. *Ibid.*, p.25.
12. House of Assembly, 20 April 1950. Quoted in A. Hepple, (1966), *South Africa*, (Pall Mall), pp.111-2.
13. *Loc.cit.*
14. Quoted in I.B. Tabata, (1960), *Education for Barbarism*, (Pall Mall), p.6. Mr. Tabata was the first author to stress the close relationship between the Bantu Authorities and Bantu Education Acts.
15. These extracts, taken from Dr. Verwoerd's policy statement, have been widely quoted. See A.N. Pelzer, (Ed.), (1966), *Verwoerd Speaks: Speeches 1948-1966*, (A.P.B., Johannesburg).
16. *Hansard*, Vol. 5, 1950, quoted in Tabata, *op.cit.*, p.21.
17. I.B. Tabata, *op.cit.*, p.26.
18. M. Horrell, (1964), *op.cit.*, pp.67-8.
19. *S.R.R.S.A.*, 1966, p.240.
20. A.N. Pelzer, *op.cit.*, pp.79-80.
21. ANC annual conference, 16-19 December 1954, Report of National Executive Committee, reprinted in Karis and Carter, *op.cit.*, Vol. III, p.152.
22. *Loc.cit.*
23. *Ibid.*, p.168.
24. Cape Provincial Secretarial Report, January-November 1955. (*Luthuli papers*, microfilm reel 1, available at Institute of Commonwealth Studies, London.)
25. *SRRSA*, 1954-55, p.184.
26. *Liberation*, December 1955. See also Karis and Carter, *op.cit.*, p.233, report to the ANC annual conference, December 1955 for the same point of view.
27. This account of the African Education Movement is taken from the unpublished manuscript 'The African Education Movement' by the

secretary, Myrtle Berman, (c.1959), 21pp., (available in the library,
School of Oriental and African Studies, London). Trevor Huddleston,
(1957), *Naught For Your Comfort* (Fontana), describes one of the Cultural Clubs in Chapter 9, 'Education for servitude'. A less sympathetic
account can be found in Edward Feit, (1962), *South Africa: the
Dynamics of the African National Congress*, (OUP).

28.   *Liberation*, December 1955.
29.   Karis and Carter, *op.cit.*, p.177.
30.   Quoted in Karis and Carter, *op.cit.*, p.34.
31.   A shortened version of the original report 'The liquidation of Adams
      College' was printed in David M. Paton, (Ed.), (1958), *Church and Race
      in South Africa*, (SCM Press), pp.51-93. See also *SRRSA*, 1954-55, for
      a description of the reactions of the different Churches to the Bantu
      Education Act.
32.   An account of NUSAS's role in student politics will be found in
      Chapter 3.
33.   Although this was the largest disturbance at an educational institution
      during the period, there are few press reports of the event. The account
      here is taken from M. Berman, *op.cit.*, and *Ikhwezi Lomso*, February
      1959 (available on microfilm, Centre for Southern African Studies,
      York University).
34.   It is not clear whether this was a continuation of the older discontent
      or a response to the tension in the country following the shooting at
      Sharpeville. In the same month, 240 of the older students at the
      Moroka Training Centre (Thaba N'chu, Orange Free State) were sent
      home after boycotting the dining hall and stoning the house of the
      Assistant Boarding Master. There were also reports of demonstrations in
      the secondary schools after several years of relative quiet.
35.   *SRRSA*, 1954-55, pp.193-5, contains in summary form some of the
      recommendations of the Commission under Professor J.P. Duminy.
36.   'Open Universities' only admitted black students in limited numbers
      and in a restricted set of faculties. No more than 5 to 6 per cent of
      student intake was black. At Durban, which was not 'open', 22 per cent
      of the total student number was black (mainly Indian), but there were
      parallel classes and white students met separately from their black
      peers. A limited number of Arts faculties were open to Blacks. There
      was a segregated black medical school attached to Natal University in
      Durban and a quota system for black students in the faculties of
      medicine at UCT and the Witwatersrand (no Africans, however were
      accepted at UCT!). No dentistry or physiotherapy courses were avail-
      able for Blacks and there were no African architectural students. Prior
      to 1959, only four Africans were accepted into the engineering faculty
      at Witwatersrand. There was complete social, residential and sports
      apartheid at all universities.
37.   Quoted in *SRRSA*, 1958-59, p.277.
38.   Nelson Mandela, 'Bantu Education goes to university', *Liberation*,
      June 1957.
39.   *Ibid.*
40.   *SRRSA*, 1959-60, p.237.
41.   *Ibid.*, pp.232-5, for a summary of the regulations.

42. Phyllis Ntantala, 'The abyss of Bantu Education', *Africa South*, Vol. 4, No. 2, Jan-March 1960.
43. *SRRSA*, 1959-60, pp.219-21.
44. *Ibid.*, 1961, pp.238-41.

3. The University Student Movements: 1960-1969

Bantu Education Implemented

From 1954 to 1958 mother-tongue or vernacular instruction was introduced in the African primary schools, and in 1959 vernacular instruction was extended to the first class of the secondary schools. The implementation of Bantu Education in the schools was nearing completion, and the government anticipated that within a few years the students' progress would be controlled by the Minister of Bantu Education from the first sub-standard of the primary school through to the fifth and final form of the secondary school.

A select few who continued their education in training colleges for teachers, or nurses and midwives, or in the university colleges would also be controlled by government regulations. By far the largest group receiving vocational training in 1975 were the 15,563 students enrolled at the 35 colleges which offered two year courses for teachers' certificates. These candidates had either completed the sixth standard or the third form at school before entering training colleges and were still governed by the regulations and syllabuses issued for Bantu Education. A further 476 students were enrolled at the black university colleges (373 for diplomas and 103 for degrees) in teaching courses.[1]

There were also 5,958 students at the black hospitals and 10 training colleges for African nurses in 1975. Although these women received the same training as their white peers, there had been pressures brought to bear since 1951 to alter their status. The original government proposals, in the Nursing Amendment Bill, contained clauses which would have excluded any of the 2,000 registered black nurses from being appointed or elected to the South African Nursing Council or to the Board of the South African Nursing Association. Considerable opposition led to the bill being withdrawn in 1951, but it was again presented to Parliament in 1954 and then sent to a Select Committee. Dr. Eiselen, one of the witnesses to give evidence, presented the case that had become commonplace since he had headed the Commission on Native Education. He stated:

> Our experience has been that . . . the professional Bantu is uprooted and is no longer tribe conscious. The longer it is possible for the Bantu nurse to

remain a member of the Nursing Association, the more difficult she would find it to forego such membership.[2]

It was not only membership of the Nursing Association that Dr. Eiselen objected to. He also believed, in line with his views on Bantu Education, that the course of study offered to African nurses should be different. This he explained as follows:

> The attitude of the Native towards bodily cleanliness is different from that of the European . . . He further sleeps with his head under the blanket, not because he finds it warmer that way, but because he feels safer. To counter that, it would not be of much use to try to drum into him that he must have more oxygen, but it should rather be pointed out to him that the *tokkeloshe* [imp or spirit] is not as dangerous as he thinks.[3]

Despite a determined campaign by African nurses to stop the bill, the government proceeded with the Nursing Act Amendment Bill in 1957. The terms of the new Act prevented blacks voting for, or being members of, the Board of the Association, or of the Nursing Council. In place of this, black nurses were offered Advisory Boards and Advisory Councils through which they could advise their all-white official counterparts on matters that concerned them. In addition the Nursing Council was empowered to introduce separate uniforms, and separate syllabuses and examinations for different racial groups. The black nurses were finally silenced in 1957 by a notice posted in every hospital which warned them that they were 'public servants' and that those who 'took part in political activities' would be dismissed.[4]

The threat of dismissal cut off the possibility of the nurses continuing their campaign against the new regulations, but did not end the resentment that was felt by both registered nurses and pupils. In March 1958 a hundred nurses came out on strike at the Lovedale Hospital after a staff nurse had been dismissed. The nurses demanded her reinstatement or a month's extension of the dismissal notice. When their demand was refused, they picketed the hospital. As in 1948, the students at Fort Hare helped organise the strike, negotiated on behalf of the nurses with the principal of Fort Hare and the Medical Superintendent of the hospital, and set aside a portion of all meals to provide the striking nurses with food.

The authorities were not prepared to make any concessions and the strike collapsed.[5] On later occasions the nurses and student-nurses were far more circumspect and, even in 1974, when the entire student body at Turfloop boycotted classes and organised a sit-in, the Students Representative Council excused all student nurses from participation.[6]

African teachers were also subjected to a severe disciplinary code. They could not claim annual salary increments as a right, could be deprived of annual leave, and could be dismissed without any reason being proferred. Under the thirteen points of 'misconduct', teachers could be punished if they 'treated with gross discourtesy a member of the public or any official'. Nor could any teacher:

> ... contribute to the Press by interview, or in any other manner, or
> publish letters or articles criticising or commenting on the Department of
> Native Affairs, or any other State Department, or school committee,
> school board, or any Bantu Authority, or any official connected with one
> or more of the above-mentioned bodies.[7]

In the aftermath of the introduction of Bantu Education, says Mr. Tabata:
'a reign of terror has been let loose on the teachers'.[8] Leading members of the
Cape African Teachers Association were dismissed; teachers were seized and
interrogated in front of their classes; pension rights were forfeited after lifetimes of service; and hundreds of teachers, who had conformed and never
dared criticise the Department, were arbitrarily replaced by young graduates
who qualified under the new syllabus after 1956.'[9]

In 1959 when the Extension of University Education Act was passed, the
government appeared to have completed their plans for controlling education
in South Africa. They had separated the races and the tribes, they had either
provided differential training or made provision for differentiation, and they
had written disciplinary codes into the schools, colleges, universities, and
even into the contracts of employment of most graduates of the educational
system.

Until the 1970's it even seemed that the government plan was successful.
Despite all opposition the legislation had been passed, and the schools and
colleges were producing graduates trained by teachers less inclined to criticise
the government. Nonetheless the entire edifice was built around a contra-
diction that could not be resolved. Those students who did manage to pass
through the educational mesh and reach the secondary schools, or perhaps
the universities, received sufficient instruction to inform them that they were
neither different nor inferior. They were both the products, and the living
refutation of the philosophy of Bantu Education.

Under the new system the number of students at schools and universities
had risen in absolute terms. There was, however, a constraint on the number
that could be accepted because of the ceiling placed on the state contribution
to finances. It was consequently cheaper to expand intake at the primary
school level; cheaper if there were two sessions daily for children in the sub-
standards; and cheaper still if women replaced men as teachers at three-
quarters of the salary.

The restricted expansion in secondary schools was partly a reflection of
state parsimony. It was also due to a calculated decision that secondary
education be restricted so that no more school graduates be produced than
were thought to be required by commerce and industry.

The increased enrolment in the schools from 1955 to 1969 is shown in
Table Three. In the first decade of Bantu Education the percentage of pupils
in the secondary schools dropped slightly relative to the total enrolment for
the year. In 1955 3.5 per cent of the total number of pupils were in the

Table 3
African Pupils in School, 1955-1969[10]

Type of School	1955	1960	1965	1969
Primary school	970,200	1,452,300	1,885,000	2,435,400
Junior secondary	32,900	45,000	62,620	82,630
Forms IV and V	2,100	2,700	4,230	6,110
Total	*1,005,200*	*1,500,000*	*1,951,850*	*2,524,140*

(The figures for 1969 exclude pupils at school in the Transkei.)

secondary school. By 1960 the figure had dropped to 3.2 per cent, and in 1965 was 3.4 per cent. Only by 1969 had the proportion returned to the 1955 level.

In the late 1960's there were signs of a significant change in official policy, and the number permitted to enter secondary schools was increased. By 1975 the proportion of pupils receiving secondary education had risen four-fold. The reasons that lay behind this change of policy, and the effects it had on school pupils, need fuller discussion which will be deferred to Chapter Five.

Despite the slow growth of the secondary schools, there was a more rapid development of higher education. The establishment of two new African university colleges, together with a Coloured and an Indian college, as a result of the Extension of University Education Act of 1959, led to a sudden expansion in student numbers. This is reflected in Table Four.

Table 4
Students at Black Universities[11]

University	1961	1965	1968	1970	1972
Fort Hare	335	263	451	610	942
Turfloop	129	276	613	810	1,164
Ngoye	51	161	368	591	837
Total (African)	515	700	1,432	2,011	2,943
U.W.C. (Coloured)	156	416	669	936	1,219
Durban-Westville (Indian)	120	1,008	1,407	1,654	2,004

The Black Campus Protest

Within a year of the passing of the University Act of 1959, the two national liberation movements, the ANC and PAC, were banned, and the students who entered the new tribal colleges in the early 1960's brought with them memories of Sharpeville and the march on Cape Town from Langa-Nyanga. In 1961 there was another stay-at-home called by an *ad hoc* committee headed by Nelson Mandela and, despite its limited success, the country seethed with rumours of massive police and army concentrations, of underground organisation, and of plans for new black action.

In fact, there was no peace or quiet in the country. In 1962 there were the first well publicised acts of sabotage. In 1963 the new organisations that appeared, carried out widespread acts of disruption, and the names of the clandestine movements, Umkhonto we Sizwe and Poqo (connected to the ANC and PAC respectively), and the newly established and much smaller National Committee of Liberation (NCL, later called ARM), appeared in the national newspapers. The arrest of the national High Command of Umkhonto, and the continued police pressure that led to the crippling or destruction of Poqo and the Committee of Liberation, continued to be front page news for over a year. All this was known to the university students, and many of them maintained an allegiance to one or other of the two main liberation organisations, even though the blanket ban on overt political discussions on the campus prevented open organisation.

During the first years numbers were low, except at Fort Hare, and there were no traditions of past activity on which the students could build new organisations. But each year brought increased enrolment, which facilitated the growth of informal groupings. Corporate identities were built up in halls of residence, and students felt increasingly able to voice complaints about conditions on the campuses.

The students had a lot to complain about: they were subjected to a tight disciplinary code; they were isolated on campuses that had been deliberately built in rural areas far from the mainstream of social or political activity; they were, furthermore, separated on tribal grounds (Fort Hare for Xhosa, Ngoye for Zulu, and Turfloop for Tswana-Sotho-Venda), and isolated from Coloureds and Indians, whom they came to welcome as fellow black oppressed. As the years went by they also became increasingly critical of the staff. They had always protested against the all-white control of the Councils and Senates of the universities, and against the preponderance of white professors and lecturers. They became even more indignant when they found that they were being offered a succession of 'introductory' courses, through to their final year of study, and were never allowed to proceed beyond an elementary level in most of their optional courses. When lecturer after lecturer demanded uncritical regurgitation of texts, they objected, but all protests were ignored or rejected.

The avenues available for formal protest were restricted, and only at Fort Hare were the students able to show their discontent openly in the early 1960's. As a first step they refused to vote for a Student Representative Council, claiming, correctly, that the constitution rendered the body impotent and, furthermore, that membership of the Council invited victimisation. The student body at Fort Hare, smarting under the need to produce 'good conduct' certificates, and sign their acceptance of the regulations before registration every year, organised a number of demonstrations. They boycotted visiting dignitaries (including cabinet ministers), and refused to attend graduation ceremonies, unless due to be capped themselves. They also, on rare occasions, sent delegations to meet the Rector and carry their collective complaints. The result was usually disastrous. In 1967, for example, they sent a deputation to protest against the presence of police informers on the campus. Fourteen of the students who went to see the Rector were arbitrarily refused admission the following year.[12]

It was only in 1967, when many students joined the University Christian Movement and two years later, when the South African Students Organisation (SASO) was formed, that the students on the different campuses were able to participate in organisations that were tolerated, to a greater or lesser degree. The evolution of these bodies, and some of the strains that followed in their wake will be discussed below. Before they could appear, however, the issue of organisation across the colour line dominated student discussion, and was seen as the major problem by the majority of black students. The government was determined that the racial groups be kept separate, and throughout the 1960s the issue of affiliation to the predominantly English-speaking National Union of South African Students (NUSAS) appeared to be the single most important political issue on the black campuses.

The NUSAS Issue

Throughout the 1960's black students campaigned for the right to affiliate to the National Union of South African Students — and just as steadfastly, the move was vetoed by the campus authorities. NUSAS was also keen to welcome the colleges into their fold. Not only would this make it the largest student organisation in the country, but it would also bring into the liberal fold all student opponents of the government's apartheid policy.

Despite this general clamour by leading members on the black campuses to affiliate, there had always been dissident voices which claimed that NUSAS was part of a 'white imperialist front'. The Non-European Unity Movement had always adopted this viewpoint, and between 1954 and 1957 had even managed to secure student support at Fort Hare for disaffiliation from NUSAS. In the late fifties, the Non-European Unity Movement body, the Progressive National Student Organisation, called for 'non-collaboration with the collaborators', and secured considerable student support. This attitude was later described by the South African Students Organisation (SASO) leaders, in one of their publications, as 'emotional'.[13] Yet, after nearly a decade of agitation in which students in the black colleges demanded the right to affiliate to NUSAS, and after witnessing some of the most militant action ever taken by the white students in 1968, the black student body, SASO, denounced NUSAS, in terms not dissimilar to those used by the Unity Movement.

This *volte face* changed the nature of black student politics and contributed, in part, to the launching of other black organisations in the early 1970's. To trace the events leading to this reversal, after a decade of agitation in favour of affiliation, it is necessary to look briefly at developments inside NUSAS.

NUSAS was formed in 1924 in order to unite all the university students of South Africa. At that stage the universities concerned were few in number, and were exclusively white in composition.[14] The attempt to unite English and Afrikaans-speaking students failed during the thirties. In the decade preceding the second world war, many students on the English-speaking campuses were inclined towards a programme of liberal democracy, although they thought primarily of a democracy that would embrace all whites. In 1933, when Fort Hare was proposed as a full member of NUSAS, a Commission was set up by the students, and as a result of their report the constitution was amended to read: 'NUSAS is a federation of the SRCs of European universities, and University Colleges, and of pro-NUSAS branches at European University Colleges.'[15]

The University Colleges of Potchefstroom and Pretoria, and Grey University College, Bloemfontein had already withdrawn in 1933. The latter College had already decided that NUSAS was:

> too English, too imperialistic, too negrophilistic in colour . . . [and displayed a] liberalistic tendency especially as a result of the strong influence of socialistic international-minded Jews who wish to effect a general world citizenship without founding it on genuine nationalism.[16]

When Stellenbosch left NUSAS in 1936, the National Union was confined to the English-speaking campuses until 1945 when Fort Hare again applied for admission and was accepted.

The Nationalist Party, the parliamentary opposition from 1933 until 1948, and since then the governing party, condemned NUSAS in terms not dissimilar to those used by the students of Grey University College in 1933. Through the years the stress of individual politicians altered, but NUSAS was always accused of being negrophilist, liberal, imperialist, socialist (and communist), cosmopolitan, English, Jewish and, obviously, subversive.

There were times when NUSAS policy was ahead of white opinion in the country, and also times when students at the black colleges believed that they could work with their white peers. But far too often it was only because of the activity of pressure groups (both black and white) that more radical statements were made by NUSAS leaders. There was, however, a pervading feeling of self-satisfaction amongst students on the liberal white campuses, and a former national student leader, Neville Curtis, commented on the lack of perception of these young men and women:

> After 1959 liberalism had established within itself a myth of moral impeccability that made it unable to see itself as an integral part of white racism, and of the white racist establishment. At the same time the myth of the common society precluded recognition of the real and actual divisions which apartheid was creating.[17]

Read out of context, the point made by Curtis seemed to coincide with the criticisms made by SOYA and the far left in the 1950's. But Curtis started from different premises. He was critical of the new 'ideological liberalism' and wanted a return to 'the open-ended, essentially tolerant [and presumably, pragmatic] liberalism of NUSAS'. He stated furthermore that English-speaking students saw the need to maintain contact with the black students, but that the lecturers 'feigned not to know that they existed'. The conclusion he reached was that '. . . ideology had warped the real concern which had existed with regard to black education'.[18] It was not a new radicalism that Curtis was espousing but a condemnation of 'the effort to cling to principle, and the elevation of 'idealism to adherence to fixed points'.[19]

NUSAS could neither move away from liberalism, nor could it become a radical organisation. The continued attack on the organisation and on its leaders by the government precluded any possibility of NUSAS altering its liberal stance. It was an organisation under siege, and short of abandoning the movement, the leadership had to maintain the tradition of opposition to apartheid. On the other hand the bulk of the white student body looked forward to the positions of leadership, and of affluence, that they were being trained for. There was no possibility of a large-scale radical movement growing out of the white student body. It was this realisation that led to the withdrawal of some of the more radical students from NUSAS in the late 1960's. Inspired in part by the world-wide student revolts, they were liber-tarian, anti-establishment, and also engulfed by the feeling that whites were irrelevant to the struggle they foresaw in South Africa. Some abandoned their studies, most refused to accept posts in NUSAS.

NUSAS was weakened by defections against radical Whites, and also by tentative moves by Blacks to form their own organisation, but they were given a lease of life in 1968 (and again in 1972) by sit-ins and demonstrations in Cape Town, Rhodes (Grahamstown), and Johannesburg. This only concealed the fragility of NUSAS, and the fact that conservative white opinion was being organised to oust it. After 1972 NUSAS was only a shell of its former self.

Action began at the University of Cape Town (UCT) when, early in 1968, Archie Mafeje, a former African student at UCT, was appointed senior lecturer in the School of African Studies.[20] The Minister of Education demanded that this appointment be rescinded, and the University Council complied, although it protested against government intervention.

Over 1,000 students and many lecturers protested, and gave their support to some 200 students who staged a sit-in for nine days. On the ninth evening the demonstrators were raided by right-wing students from UCT and from the University of Stellenbosch. The police said they could not guarantee the safety of the sit-in in future and the campaign came to an end.

Students at all other English-speaking universities also protested over the 'Mafeje affair' and at the University of Witwatersrand they planned a march through the city of Johannesburg. This was forbidden at the insistence of the Prime Minister, and the students formed a picket line inside the campus perimeter, bearing placards: 'We have had enough!' They were attacked and assaulted by campus conservatives and students from the neighbouring Rand Afrikaans University and the (Afrikaans) Goudstad (Goldtown) Teacher Training College. The police confiscated placards and took the names of students in the picket-line. When a deputation of Witwatersrand University students went to Pretoria, hoping to hand the Prime Minister a letter of protest, they were assaulted by students of Pretoria University.

The demonstrations in Cape Town and Johannesburg started on 14 August 1968. On Saturday 24 August the Prime Minister issued a warning that, if the student protests had not ended by Monday, police would move onto the campuses. The protests had already been called off, however, and the students were back at lectures by 26 August.

It was only one month later that students at Fort Hare were also involved in a sit-in. This action was precipitated by the growing resentment of the students against the ban on affiliation to NUSAS. The students boycotted a leading Cabinet Minister and painted slogans on campus walls. Police interrogated senior students which led to a build-up of tension culminating in a sit-in demonstration in September. This only ended when police moved in with dogs and teargas. The demonstrators were taken to the railway station and sent home. Twenty-one students were rusticated for the year, although they were allowed to take examinations off the campus. The rest of the student body were allowed to return, but only after they and their parents had signed declarations undertaking not to take part in any further demonstrations, and to refrain from any act of insubordination.

The SRCs at both Turfloop and Ngoye also claimed the right to affiliate to NUSAS, and students on both campuses gave their full support to the sit-in at Fort Hare. Although there is no evidence of any concerted student action, the college authorities banned all demonstrations. At Turfloop the Senate forbade a student statement of support for their fellows at Fort Hare, and the Minister of Bantu Education banned the application for affiliation to NUSAS. Those deemed to be behind the dissent were expelled.

Black Students Break with NUSAS

Through the period 1960-67 the black students fought the administration on the issue of affiliation to NUSAS. Every move by the Students' Representative Councils was vetoed by the universities. Student action was met by stern disciplinary counteraction, and a large number of students were expelled. In the light of Curtis's criticism (of student liberalism as being an integral part of white racism), and the even sharper criticism from the far left that coupled affiliation with 'collaborationism', this concentration on a campaign for membership of NUSAS needs explanation.

In seeking affiliation, the black students were demanding the right to associate with organisations of their own choice, and the more intransigent the government showed itself, the more determined the students seemed to become. There was, furthermore, little possibility of engaging in open politics, and the students, confronted by Rectors and staff who were determined to make the tribal colleges work, became engrossed in campus affairs. For a time it might even have seemed that there was an identity of interests between black and white English-speaking students. Nevertheless the disparities between the position of the two racial groups must have been obvious.

The white students were preoccupied with the whittling away of democratic rights: the Blacks' concern was to secure the most elementary of such rights. The white students did not often feel the need to take their political demands outside the campus: the Blacks were always conscious of the fact that they came from an oppressed majority, and they could not divorce the demand for national liberation from their own student demands. No matter how unpleasant the white students found apartheid, they could live outside the oppressive system; the African could never escape it.

Periodically the divergence of interest came to the surface. When NUSAS set up a Freedom in Society commission in 1969 to examine laws that infringed on human liberties, a black delegate asked pointedly: 'What is the use of an African talking about the erosion of freedom in South Africa? We have no freedom and one or two laws more or less make no difference to our situation.'[21] There were also indications that some Blacks resented the paternalistic attitudes that they perceived at conferences. One student leader expressed irritation at the way meetings were white-centred: 'It does not help us to see several black faces in a multi-racial gathering which ultimately concentrates on what the white students believe are the needs of black students.'[22]

The black university students were irritated; the pattern of South African discrimination was only too obviously being repeated at meetings. Nonetheless they continued to press for affiliation, because they too shared the liberal ideology of their white peers; and they too aspired to positions of (comparative) affluence after graduation. It was the realisation that they would not in fact get the posts they knew they deserved, that pushed them to more radical positions. They were demanding equality, and that drew them to NUSAS: the realisation that this equality could not be obtained in any alliance with NUSAS forced them to adopt new political solutions. The split was inevitable, but the reasons were 'felt', rather than understood.

'Black Man, You Are On Your Own.'

The most prominent slogan of the students, and of the student organisations in the 1970's was 'Black Man, you are on your own'. It acted as a rallying call on all the black campuses, and was incorporated into the language of those men and women, students and intellectuals, who espoused the philosophy of black consciousness. The slogan was an assertion of the right to independent organisation on the campuses, and was also a political statement of more general application. The young students were aware of the hiatus in their political lives following the banning of the ANC and the PAC, and they saw campus politics as only one part of the broader fight that had to be taken up by the African people. Apartheid on the campus was inseparable from the general division of the country on colour lines as envisaged by the government, and campus organisation was only the prelude to building a national organisation.

Nevertheless the first step towards independent organisation occurred under conditions which indicate that the black leaders were most undecided on the tactics they should adopt. The precipitating factor occurred at the annual conference of NUSAS, held at Rhodes University in July 1967. At the conference, the black delegates were informed that the Minister of Bantu Affairs had decreed that, under the Group Areas Act, they were required to sleep in the neighbouring township, and could not be accommodated at the university residence. The student body, both black and white, were furious. The situation was exacerbated when the university Vice-Chancellor stopped all racially mixed social gatherings, and even forbade Blacks the right to take meals in the residence.

Many white delegates boycotted the official meals, and conference decided, overwhelmingly, to work for the abolition of racial segregation on the campuses.[23] Despite the fact that NUSAS could not be held responsible for the Minister's decision, and despite the solidarity expressed by many whites, it was this event which led the black students to query the value of maintaining links with NUSAS.

A second conference was also scheduled for Rhodes University in July 1967. Some 90 delegates, more than half of them black, attended the founding conference of the ecumenical University Christian Movement. The new movement did mark a reversal from the now defunct Student Christian Association (disbanded in 1965), which had maintained a colour bar. Nevertheless, as at the NUSAS conference, the accommodation was segregated.[24]

Many of the accusations levelled against NUSAS in 1967 could equally hace been made against UCM. The Christian Movement was also subjected to segregatory requirements — and like NUSAS protested, but was forced to comply. UCM could not change the structure of the country. The Whites tended to dominate the proceedings at the conference and were no more able to decide what was good for the Blacks than the leaders of NUSAS.

There were, however, differences. The majority of delegates at the conference were black. The movement was Christian, and was furthermore allowed to exist on the black campuses, where it attracted a considerable membership. These factors, in varying degree, attracted the student leaders, as they explained in 1972:

The formation of the University Christian Movement in 1967 gave Black students a greater chance of coming together. Because of its more radical stance, and also because at that stage it had not developed a 'bad' complexion politically in the eyes of the Black campus authorities, UCM tended to attract more Black students to its conferences, and this opened channels of communications amongst the Black students.[25]

It is not at all clear what this 'more radical stance' consisted of, nor is there much evidence that students who were attracted to the UCM in 1967 wanted such a stance. Furthermore, if the students were satisfied with the programme and constitution of the UCM, it is not easy to follow the reasoning of the SASO authors of the 1972 document, when they continue:

Among the Black students, one of the most talked about topics is the position of the Black students in the open organisations like NUSAS and UCM. Concern was expressed that these were White dominated and paid little attention to problems peculiar to the Black student community . . . It was felt that a time had come when Blacks had to formulate their own thinking, unpolluted by ideas emanating from a group with lots at stake in the *status quo.*[26]

It would seem, in fact, that there was a far more cogent reason for the students to work in the UCM in 1967. NUSAS activity was banned on all black campuses in 1967[27] and the move into UCM was an act of adroit political opportunism on the part of the black students! This supposition is borne out by the history of UCM presented in *Black Review*, 1972. After mentioning the banning of NUSAS, the account continues:

It was not surprising, therefore, to find that the constituency at the 1968 UCM Conference at Stutterheim was very different from the one at Grahamstown the previous year. The majority . . . were those whose ties with their particular denominations were weakening and who were therefore far less conservative theologically.
It was at this conference that a black caucus was formed out of which grew SASO [the South African Students Organisation], the spearhead of Black Consciousness.[28]

The UCM proved to be less useful as a political cover than the students had hoped. The police kept the members under surveillance, halls of residence were raided periodically and leading members were held for interrogation. Attempts were made by the authorities to discredit the organisation, and in 1969 the UCM was banned on black campuses after only two years' activity.[29]

The black students had not broken sharply with NUSAS, and they sent delegates to the 1968 conference. Even when the Students Representative Councils of the black campuses met at Mariannhill in December 1968, and decided to form SASO, the NUSAS President was invited to attend the inaugural conference the following July. The President was unable to be present and the white students, seemingly unaware of the significance of the new movement, made little effort to prevent the split.

SASO is Born, 1969

The black students were by no means unanimous in their resolve to form a

separate organisation. In a communique issued at the end of the 1969
conference those opposed to separation were quoted as saying:

> Any move that tends to divide the student population into separate
> laagers [camps] on the basis of colour is in a way a tacit admission to
> defeat and seems apparently in agreement with apartheid.
> In a racially sensitive country like ours, provision for racially
> exclusive bodies tends to widen the gap that already exists between
> races and to heighten resentment, and the student community should
> resist all temptation to do this.[30]

The majority however maintained that apartheid had already separated the
communities, and that mixed organisations were farcical. They argued that an
independent organisation would be more effective, and that black students
owed their first allegiance to the black community. Even more crucially it
was argued that it was the students' task to raise the level of consciousness of
the black community 'by promoting awareness, pride, achievement and
capabilities.'[31]

Over and above the assertion that Blacks had to organise alone, the leaders
of SASO held that Coloureds and Indians were also black, and from the
inception the Executive of the student body included members drawn from
the Coloured and Indian campuses. Being black, as it was explained, was
associated with a way of viewing the world, and not with skin colour.

This formulation, as will be shown later, led to a number of strange
rationalisations. Many men of black skin were not considered black, particularly if they co-operated with the government. But Whites, irrespective of
their political sympathies, were always judged by skin colour, and could
never, despite their way of thinking, be 'black'.

The new way of thinking demanded by the students was called black
consciousness and was written into the preamble of the SASO constitution in
July 1970:

> Whereas, we the Black students of South Africa, having examined and
> assessed the role of Black Students in the struggle for the emancipation of
> the Black people in South Africa and the betterment of their social,
> political and economic lot, and having unconditionally declared our lack
> of faith in the genuineness and capability of multi-racial organisations and
> individual Whites in the country to effect rapid social changes . . . do
> commit ourselves to the realisation of the worth of the Black man, the
> assertion of his human dignity and to promoting consciousness and self-
> reliance of the black community.[32]

Some of the students who had opposed the formation of a new separate
organisation had done so on the grounds that the university administration
would not tolerate a black student federation, and in part their fears were
confirmed. Statements from the Departments of Indian Affairs and of

Coloured Relations declared that students under their control (at the Indian University and at the University of the Western Cape), would not be allowed to join SASO. Their statements asserted that the three black communities had nothing in common, either socially or culturally.[33]

But for reasons that still remain obscure, the administration at Turfloop gave SASO early recognition, and demanded only that the preamble to the constitution be altered. The Snyman Commission, appointed by the government to inquire into the disturbances at Turfloop in 1973, received evidence that the students had been urged by two former (white) rectors of the University to: '. . . shake off the yoke of NUSAS and to establish their own organisation'.[34] The government's intention, however, was not to replace one 'radical' organisation by another and, in the aftermath of confrontations between the students and the authorities, SASO was banned from all campuses except Ngoye in 1975.

The situation at Fort Hare was always difficult. SASO was discouraged from the beginning and student leaders were expelled because of the active role they played in the organisation. Here too, SASO was banned in 1975. The campus at Ngoye was the only centre at which SASO seemed to exist without friction between students and the Rector. In 1975 there was, however, a rival organisation which divided the students ideologically. For some time it looked as if SASO would be relegated to a subsidiary position, and it was only after the key opposition students graduated that the field was left open for SASO activists to re-establish their ascendancy. (This will be discussed in greater detail in Chapter Four.)

The UCM was banned on black campuses from 1969, but members of SASO retained individual membership and attended UCM annual conferences; but the differences widened between white and black delegates. There was a 'shift in focus' in the discussions, and the issues became increasingly social and political. Many white students left the organisation and the churches which had supported UCM were estranged. By 1970 SASO members were proposing literacy projects and were espousing the cause of Black Theology. This lay outside the perspective of the founding members of the UCM and, by 1971, the polarisation inside the organisation was formalised when it was converted into a federation of projects, or 'interest groups'. For the Whites there were White Consciousness and Women's Liberation sections, for the Blacks, Black Consciousness and literacy projects. The executive was converted into a consultative body for the four interest groups.[35]

In 1972 the UCM was dissolved and SASO took over responsibility for the literacy campaign. Black theology was an integral part of SASO's philosophy, and was accepted by all black consciousness groups as part of their overall world outlook. The UCM had helped shape an essential part of the programme of the movement which dominated black politics in the early 1970s, and the Christian world outlook continued to play an important part in SASO and its associated organisations.

References

1. *SRRSA*, 1967, pp.336-7.
2. Quoted by I.B. Tabata, *op.cit.*, p.28.
3. *Loc.cit.*
4. An account of the nurses' action — unfortunately rather sketchy — is in Martin Jarrett-Kerr, (1960), *African Pulse*, (The Faith Press), Chapter 4.
5. T.V.R. Beard, (1972), 'Background to student activities at the University College of Fort Hare', in Hendrik W. van der Merwe and David Welsh, (Eds.), *Student Perspectives on South Africa*, (David Philip, Cape Town), p.169.
6. Reprinted in J.G.E. Wolfson, (1976), *Turmoil at Turfloop: a Summary of the Snyman and Jackson Commissions of Inquiry into the University of the North*, (Institute of Race Relations, Johannesburg), p.72.
7. I.B. Tabata, *op.cit.*, pp.62-3.
8. *Loc.cit.*
9. *Ibid.*, p.64.
10. The figures are taken from M. Horrell, (1964), *op.cit.*, and relevant issues of the *SRRSA*. (The numbers are rounded.)
11. Extracted from issues of the *SSRSA*. There were always a large number of black students registered at the University of South Africa, which offered tuition through course notes. Students did not visit the campus, except for optional summer school courses — and these were always segregated. Students were not involved in any of the conflicts described in this work although some individuals were to become members of the South African Students Organisation (SASO) after 1968. Students at the University Colleges sat for the examinations of the University of South Africa until 1969. The colleges were given full university status thereafter and conducted their own examinations.
12. *SRRSA*, 1967, p.290.
13. Reprinted in J.G.E. Wolfson, *op.cit.*, p.12.
14. *SRRSA*, 1972, p.321.
15. Neville Curtis and Clive Keegan, (1972), 'The aspiration to a just society', in van der Merwe and Welsh, *op.cit.*, pp.98-9. Hereafter referred to as Curtis.
16. Quoted in *ibid.*, p.98.
17. *Ibid.*, p.115.
18. *Loc.cit.*
19. *Loc.cit.*
20. *SRRSA*, 1968, pp.263-6.
21. Clive Nettleton, (1972), 'Racial cleavage on the student left', in van der Merwe and Welsh, *op.cit.*, p.127.
22. Quoted in *SRRSA*, 1970, p.245.
23. *SRRSA*, 1967, pp.284-5.
24. *Ibid.*, p.13.
25. 'SASO 1972', reprinted as Annexure G, in J.G.E. Wolfson, *op.cit.*, pp.56-8.
26. *Loc.cit.*
27. B.A. Khoapa, (Ed.), *Black Review*, 1972, (Black Community Programmes, Lovedale), p.186.

28. *Ibid.*, p.187.
29. *SRRSA*, 1969, p.226.
30. C. Nettleton, *op.cit.*, pp.128-9.
31. *Loc.cit.*
32. J.G.E. Wolfson, *op.cit.*, p.12.
33. *SRRSA*, 1971, p.293.
34. J.G.E. Wolfson, *loc.cit.*
35. *Black Review*, 1972, *op.cit.*, pp.186-8.

4. Black Consciousness Politics: 1970-1974

SASO and the Black Consciousness Movement

When SASO emerged as a separate organisation, it addressed itself to both student problems and to the broader issues of black emancipation. In its aims SASO meant to achieve the unity of all black students in the country, and represent their interests. It also resolved to encourage students to become '. . . involved in the political, economic and social development of the Black people.'[1] While remaining predominantly a student organisation, SASO also claimed to be an instrument for changing society and sought allies outside the campus. There had always been a large number of African welfare, religious, sporting, and educational bodies in the townships of South Africa.[2] The student leaders were, however, searching for organisations which had 'a national outlook', and at that stage either had no contact with, or were not interested in, small township organisations.

In the late sixties the only African organisations that had nationwide memberships were sports federations and religious bodies. It was to the latter that SASO leaders turned, and organisations that could claim to have 'a national outlook' were invited to send delegates to a conference to be held on 24 April 1971, to consider launching a national political organisation.[3]

The April 1971 conference was the first of three held that year of which the proposals for a new body were discussed, and it was July 1972 before the Black Peoples Convention (BPC), as it was known, was formally launched. Ultimately, members of SASO were able to prevail and shape the national body in their own image, but in the process the delegates present at the first gathering in April left their imprint on the new political movement. Four organisations met with SASO in April, and some do need further scrutiny.

The organisations were: the Inter-Denominational African Ministers Association of South Africa (IDAMASA); the African Independent Church's Association (AICA); the Young Women's Christian Association (YWCA); and the Association for Educational and Cultural Advancement of Africans (ASSECA).[4] Three of these organisations were religious, and the only lay body was ASSECA. Many of the projects of the latter were similar to those taken up by SASO and the new BPC, and for that reason it will be examined first.

76

The Story of ASSECA
The Association for the Educational and Cultural Advancement of African people of South Africa was established in 1967 by P.Q. Vundla and Menassah T. Moerane.[5] Both had been members of the ANC. Mr. Vundla was a member of the National Executive Committee of the ANC in 1955 and took part in the decision to defer the boycott of the Bantu Education schools. He was furthermore strongly opposed to the Congress Youth League decision to start the boycott on April 12, and led a deputation to secure the reinstatement of the children that Dr. Verwoerd had decided to exclude from schools. He also told parents to send their children back to school until the National Executive called upon them to withdraw the children. Mr. Vundla was assaulted by Congress members and subsequently expelled from the ANC. He joined the Moral Rearmament Association shortly thereafter and played no further role in the then existing African political organisations. Mr. Moerane had also been in the ANC, and was particularly active during the second world war. He had participated in some of the discussions which led to the formation of the Congress Youth League, but in the early 1950's adopted a very conservative line in African politics. He was on the staff of the *Bantu World* which, during the 1950's and 1960's, was renowned as a right-wing paper. Mr. Moerane subsequently became editor of the paper (renamed the *World*). He also succeeded P.Q. Vundla as chairman of ASSECA in 1969.

ASSECA was started in the wake of the published matriculation (fifth form) examination results for 1967 which disclosed the fact that less than a quarter of the 2,034 candidates had secured university entrance passes, that a further 23 per cent had obtained school leaving passes, but that 52.5 per cent of the candidates had failed. This was, in fact, an improvement over the 1965 results when 61.7 per cent had failed, but insufficient to reassure the parents.[6]

ASSECA organised tuition for pupils who had failed the matriculation examination; arranged adult education classes; raised money to buy equipment for secondary schools. ASSECA also ventured into the political field when it sent a deputation to the Rector of Fort Hare to discuss 'the future of' students expelled after the 1968 demonstrations. Following their intervention it was decided that students would be granted certificates to enable them to register at the University of South Africa.[7]

ASSECA was perpetually short of funds for its projects and in 1970 Mr. Moerane first suggested, in an address to the National Conference, that R1,000,000 be raised by a voluntary levy on every African adult in the country. The scheme was not proceeded with, but was raised again in 1973 when a 10 cent levy on students was suggested. This led to an outcry from parents who claimed that despite expansion of the organisation, it had nothing to contribute, and there was a demand that ASSECA publish a statement of its finances.[8] By 1973 there was considerable doubt about the integrity of the organisation. Starting in 1971, ASSECA had received R10,500 from the Polaroid Corporation in the USA (following demands made by its black American workers) 'to promote change' in South Africa by financing projects with part of its local profits. ASSECA also received a donation (of unknown magnitude) from the American First National City Bank. The Polaroid money had been used to purchase a motor car, establish an office, buy equipment, and pay the salary of an organiser. Although ASSECA awarded some (small) scholarships after 1971 and provided some laboratory equipment, there seemed to be a discrepancy between receipts and expenditure. Its leaders always refused to release the accounts that had been demanded of them.[9]

Reports do indicate that ASSECA made some impact on communities, particularly in the Cape. There are, however, few details available, and no indication of whether SASO-BPC members worked in the actual projects that ASSECA had pioneered. Subsidiary organisations of the BPC did, however, undertake to promote literacy and educational projects in the Cape after 1972, and the development of community projects was in keeping with the ideas that motivated the founders of ASSECA.

The Religious Focus
The most important influences on the newly founded BPC were those of the religious bodies, and this was not accidental. Most of the SASO leaders had been in the UCM and, political considerations aside, the student leaders were deeply involved in propagating Black Theology inside the black church movement. Steve Biko, first President of SASO, and Nyameko Pityana, Secretary-General of SASO, both contributed essays to the volume *Black Theology*, first published in 1972.[10] Biko summed up the students' approach when he said that Black Theology:

> seeks to relate God and Christ once more to the black man and his daily problems. It wants to describe Christ as a fighting god, not a passive god who allows a lie to rest unchallenged . . . It seeks to bring back God to the black man and to the truth and reality of his situation . . .[11]

Pityana stated the case more fully. He maintained that religion permeated the life of Blacks, and that a study of Black Theology was a study of black consciousness. In order to express African needs he maintained that:

> . . . the Church . . . must go back to the roots of broken African civilisation, and examine the traditional African form of worship, marriage, sacrifice, etc., and discover why these things were meaningful and wholesome to the traditional African community.[12]

After quoting from the SASO resolution of July 1971, to the effect that Black Theology 'is an authentic and positive articulation of the black Christians' reflection on God in the light of their experience', and affirming the belief that this theology was 'a theology of liberation', Pityana stated: 'In a nutshell, then, Black Theology concerns itself with liberation, and liberation presupposes a search for humanity and for existence as a God-created being.'[13] It was, therefore, obvious that members of SASO would work closely with African Christian organisations, particularly if members of those bodies adopted Black Theology as a doctrine relevant to the 'liberation' of Blacks.

The South African Council of Churches and the Christian Institute

The body with which members of SASO found themselves in sympathy was the South African Council of Churches (better known under the name it used before 1968 – the Christian Council of South Africa). Twenty-seven churches and church organisations were members of the Council in 1968, and this included the Christian Institute of South Africa (CI), IDAMASA, YWCA, and the UCM.

The Christian Council comprised the major church groups in the country, with the exception of the Roman Catholic Church, and the three Afrikaner Churches (referred to loosely as the Dutch Reformed Churches – DRC). Besides these 'established' churches there were also the African Independent Churches, which catered for one-fifth of all African Christians. A section of these churches had, with the assistance of the CI, established the African Independent Churches Association (AICA) in 1965. By 1968 it represented more than 200 churches, was a member of the Christian Council, and was a religious movement of some importance.[14] Three years later AICA claimed to represent 358 of the churches, and although there were some 3,000 African independent churches in the country, it was the larger congregations which owed allegiance to AICA.

The close ties that the Christian Institute maintained with AICA marked the CI, with many prominent Whites in the leadership, as a movement with considerable influence amongst black Christians. It was also a body that obviously had considerable influence inside the newly formed BPC, and in a further subsidiary body that was to be formed, the Black Community Programmes (BCP).

The Christian Council was pre-eminently a religious body, and a large part of its activities were devoted to the propagation of the Christian faith. Its significance, for this book, lies firstly in its international association with the World Council of Churches, which took an increasingly radical stance in opposing apartheid in South Africa, and secondly in the many clashes between the Christian Council and both the DRC and the government on the issues of race. This inevitably led to the issues of race and of Christian orthodoxy being inextricably interconnected. The government retaliated over the years by banning churchmen born in the country, and deporting priests from abroad. The DRC expelled dissidents from amongst their ranks, and it was men such as Dr. C.F. Beyers Naudé, Dr. B. Engelbrecht, and Professor A.S. Geyser, once adherents of the DRC, who set up and directed the CI.

The clergy inside the Christian Council were by no means united in their stand, and some felt that their disputes with the authorities were mainly on questions of interpretation of the gospels. Others were more radical in their political approach, and were even prepared to take direct political action when they felt that some issues needed a wider public airing. Three examples, chosen from a large sample, are: Father Cosmas Desmond, who exposed the conditions of the men, women and children removed from the land they farmed and dumped unceremoniously on wasteland; the Rev. David Russell who organised a protest against the low grants given to indigent Africans and, together with sympathisers, lived for six months on the average old-age pension of R5 per month; and Beyers Naude who faced endless persecution at the hands of the Security Branch because he championed black conscious-ness projects. It was men like these that seemed to Africans to be keeping faith with their own aspirations.

The extent to which some of these clerics represented a radicalism that could lead to meaningful change in South Africa needs further discussion. At best they remained a tiny minority, and did not have the support of many priests, and still less that of the overwhelming majority of the white laity from member churches of the Christian Council. Nor, for that matter, did they have the support of most African Independent Churches! Writing in *Pro Veritate*, journal of the CI in May 1968, Rev. Danie van Zyl, said that the 'White churches had failed to communicate with the African people'. Writing in support of this, Archdeacon R.F. Yates of the Anglican Church stated that: '. . . Africans scorned Western churches that condemned racialism with their mouths but in fact practised it.'[15]

In September 1968 the Christian Council, responding to the growing radicalisation of black Christians, issued a Message to the people of South Africa, that brought it into headlong conflict with the government. The Message was issued by the Council, but was not binding on member churches and organisations — presumably because there was no way in which members of the churches could be expected to support the document. In a summary of the Council's Message, the central thesis, as reported in the Survey of Race Relations was:

> . . . that the doctrine of racial separation had become, for many South Africans, a false faith, a novel gospel. The measure of conformity to the practice of racial separation in the life of the Church itself was the measure of the Church's deviation from the purpose of Christ. The practice involved a rejection of the central beliefs of the Christian Gospel . . .[16]

The message demanded that every Christian face up to the question: 'To whom or what are you truly giving your first loyalty — to a sub-section of mankind, an ethnic group, a human tradition, a political idea — or to Christ?'[17] The Prime Minister was not moved. He warned them to stop their agitation: 'I want to say to them, cut it out: cut it out immediately, because the cloth you are wearing will not protect you if you try to do this in South Africa.' He also warned the church leaders not to 'turn your pulpits into political platforms . . . to do the work of the Progressive Party, the United Party, the Liberal Party.'[18]

Mr. Vorster sought a political confrontation with the churches but, no doubt partly for tactical reasons, and partly because the organisations concerned were not primarily political bodies, the members of the Christian Council claimed that their concern was with the 'social and ethical problems of the country',[19] and an editorial in *Pro Veritate* objected that the arguments against the Message to the people of South Africa had been political. What they wanted, said the editors, was a 'denial or rejection on genuinely Biblical grounds'.

Standing firm on theological principles had its advantages. It challenged the government on grounds that Mr. Vorster, for all his bluster, could not easily counter: he was not going to get involved in theological polemics. For the Christian Council, however, it was a pyrrhic victory. They won the battle of words, but they could not stop the government's implementation of apartheid measures, nor the sniping which removed one radical priest after another by means of the inevitable banning orders.

The relationship between the Christian Council of South Africa (and its constituent members), and SASO, was equivocal. In many respects SASO was attracted to the Council, and more particularly to the Christian Institute. Nonetheless they sought to be an African (or, more accurately, a black) organisation which would act independently of any white body. The students were searching for a radical solution (although they were far from defining the 'radical change' in 1971), and were attracted by the report of the Church Commission which stated:

> Our approach to change is gradualist while seeking to be radical, that is to go to the roots. As a Commission we do not propose violence as a means of change in South Africa just as we do not approve violence which is being used to prevent change for the better.[20]

There also seems to be little doubt that the more radical Christian Institute was the predominant external influence on SASO.[21] They gave more attention to Black Theology (although the CI always had reservations on this issue), and were also able to offer a number of facilities to SASO, to the BPC after it was formed, or to members of SASO-BPC. Their publishing house (later under the imprint of Ravan Press) produced many of the books that publicised black consciousness. The Black Community Programmes (BCP), which was jointly sponsored by the South African Council of Churches and the CI, published the annual *Black Review*, and in many respects was indistinguishable from the BPC.

The Christian Institute, as it was led by Whites, was not invited to the meeting in April 1971 when the Black Peoples Convention was first mooted. But the President of the YWCA, Mrs. Oshidi Phakathi, was the Transvaal regional director of the CI, and many delegates were also connected with it.

IDAMASA

The largest, and possibly oldest, African church movement present was the Inter-Denominational African Ministers Association of South Africa. In 1935 the body had been associated with the protest against the three Native Bills which demarcated the African Reserves and removed the franchise rights which African men in the Cape had up to then enjoyed. Members of IDAMASA had taken leading positions in both the ANC and the All-African Convention, and had been associated with many of the policy statements published by these organisations. The African ministers had not been renowned for their militancy and were bypassed by events in the 1950's, but they were not immune to the changes taking place amongst Africans in the towns, and during 1971 decided to exclude white ministers from their executive committee.

Their attitude had been shaped by discussions organised by the UCM. In the words of Bishop A.H. Zulu, in a diocesan newsletter:

> . . . young concerned Christians . . . are shocked by the drift from the Church of young educated blacks, especially in the cities. They find the reason for this withdrawal a challenge to Christian leaders to demonstrate the relevance of Jesus Christ for black persons in apartheid and discriminating South Africa. They want black theologians to reply to the charge that Jesus is Lord and saviour of the white people only.[22]

The April conference was inconclusive, and two further conferences took place, in mid-August, in Maritzburg, and then in Soweto in December 1971. Speakers who were called upon to address the conferences included Drake Koka, former member of the Liberal Party, Dr. Willie F. Nkomo, one time member of the Congress Youth League and then adherent of Moral Rearmament, Steve Biko of SASO, Mrs. Mabiletsa of ASSECA, and Chief Gatsha Buthelezi, Chief Executive Councillor of KwaZulu. Mr. Moerane of ASSECA acted as interim Chairman.

It was not until the third conference, in December 1971, that pressure from SASO delegates, led by Ranwedzi Nengwekhulu, persuaded the delegates to establish a political (rather than a cultural) organisation. This decision ended a division inside the nascent movement, opened the way for new leadership, and replaced the older, more conservative founding members. The new BPC *ad hoc* committee prepared the way for a conference in June 1972, at which the organisation was formally founded.[23]

Black Peoples Convention (BPC) Launched, July 1972

July was conference time in South Africa, and in July 1972 the black students had a heavy programme. SASO held their own conference at Hammanskraal; sent delegates to Pietermaritzburg to help launch the BPC; were present at the disbandment of the UCM; and sent a message to the NUSAS conference, re-affirming their policy of non-co-operation.[24] The black students were angry and determined, after emerging from the largest revolt ever experienced on the campuses. The 1972 revolt (which is described below) hardened them in their resolve to break all open contact with organisations led by Whites.

At the UCM conference, the President, Ms. Winkie Direko, explained the unanimous decision to disband. She stated that:

> ... the main reason [for disbanding] was the growth of Black Consciousness among the Black members, and their consequent unwillingness to work within a multi-racial organization. They no longer believed 'that multi-racialism is a viable strategy to bring about real change'.[25]

At the SASO conference a unanimous resolution instructed the Executive to boycott 'the so-called leadership of the White racist institutions' and to explain to black people the 'fraudulence and barrenness of the promise' of these institutions, which were extensions of the system of oppression.[26] The editor of *Black Review* summarised the position of the students' movement as follows:

> SASO has mainly been instrumental in the spreading of the philosophy of black consciousness ... The slogan 'black man you are on your own' expresses the attitude black students and indeed most black people have now adopted in fighting for survival in this country.[27]

SASO delegates, however, made by far their biggest impression at the BPC conference. The equivocations of the previous year were set aside and political objectives agreed upon. The aims decided at Conference were:

> to liberate and emancipate blacks from psychological and physical oppression;
> to create a humanitarian society where justice is meted out equally to all;
> to co-operate with existing agencies with the same ideals;
> to re-orientate the theological system with a view to making religion relevant to the aspirations of the black people;
> to formulate, apply and implement the principles and philosophies of Black Consciousness and Black Communalism;
> to formulate and implement an education policy of blacks, by blacks, for blacks.

Conference also pledged itself:

> to establish and promote black business on a co-operative basis including establishment of banks, co-operative buying and selling, flotation of relevant companies, all of which would be designed as agencies for economic self-reliance for black people as a corporate unit and not for individuals;
> [and] to apply itself fully behind attempts to fully establish trade unions for black people, particularly directed at co-ordinating and unifying all trade unions.[28]

The conference also set itself organisational objectives. These included: a drive to enrol one million members in three years, the establishment of branches throughout the country, the formation of vigilante committees of residents, and a resolve to 'operate openly as an overt people's movement'. [29] There was to be no co-operation with any government institution — in the Bantustans, or in the townships, or in the communities.

The aims set out at the Pietermaritzburg conference contained in essence all the main points that were to be found in statements of the 1970's on black consciousness: psychological emancipation, black theology, communalism, black community business enterprise, black studies, and a rejection of apartheid institutions.

Black Consciousness in Action

During 1972, and extending through to 1977, there was a proliferation of organisations in South Africa that were connected with SASO and BPC, and with the Black Community Programmes. Each organisation had its own specific programme, and the audiences they addressed were somewhat different. Nevertheless, there was an overlap in membership of the three bodies, and their campaigns were often indistinguishable. Any attempt, therefore, to separate out the activities of these organisations becomes artificial.

The five years in which they were allowed to exist were the most turbulent in the history of post-war South Africa and yet a survey of their activities does not provide many concrete cases of organised campaigning. A report on the BPC in 1972 could, with small variations, have been made in any other year. Thus it was recorded: 'The issues picked up by BPC have to date depended a lot on spontaneous reaction by black people to their various situations, e.g. bus strikes in Johannesburg and Durban and the dock workers' strike in Durban.' [30] BPC 'action' in these instances consisted of issuing statements.

There were in fact only two 'campaigns', ascribable to BPC or SASO, that could be characterised as political. The first was the 'May revolt' on the campuses in 1972, and the second was the calling of the 'Viva Frelimo' rallies in 1973. All the other activities engaged in — literacy campaigns, health projects (in which students assisted at clinics), the building of schools and clinics and community centres, home education schemes (tuition for examinations), co-operative bulk buying, the establishment of a factory and a boutique, or involvement with black theatre in the townships — had effects on local communities which are not easy to appraise.

Black theatre, and with it the proliferation of black poetry, did help generate the aggressive atmosphere that was witnessed later at the trials of black consciousness groups. This was, however, always confined to small groups of intellectuals. The community projects and the co-operatives, on the other hand, might well have been the first steps towards building roots in local communities. But they were only first steps, and the Black Consciousness

Movement was never allowed (by police interference) to get beyond the opening move. Consequently, little or none of the activity pursued in those few years affected the social structure of South Africa.

Nevertheless, in describing their activities, the BCP was presented as an organisation that was, somehow, to become an instrument for social transformation. Explaining the formation of the BCP, it was stated at the time that:

> In the seventies Black South Africans are seeking a more effective means of rallying their common aspirations round a quest for identification as blacks living within a reality of domination by a white supra-structure and anti-black manipulations through economic power and cultural alienation. Groups and organisations have emerged whose basic aim is to bring back to the black community a black identification and an articulation of the black experience.[31]

Or put more clearly and without the heavy philosophical jargon, the goals of the BCP were said to be:

> To help the black community become aware of its identity.
> To help the black community create a sense of its own power.
> To enable the black community to organise itself, analyse its needs and problems and also mobilise its resources to meet these needs.
> To develop black leadership capable of guiding the development of the black community.[32]

The same claim was made for SASO:

> To date SASO has come to be accepted as one of the most relevant organisations in this search for the Black man's real identity and of his liberation. The involvement of students with the community by way of community development projects remains a testimony of the oneness of the two both in plight and in efforts.[33]

What SASO, BPC and BCP did not disclose was where the finances were going to come from for this ambitious programme. There was no way in which (to quote again from the BCP goals) the black community could 'mobilise its resources to meet these needs'. When SASO started an orientation course for pre-university students, they estimated the cost at more than £40,000 and this they obtained from the liberation support movement, based in Geneva, the International University Exchange Fund (IUEF).[34] To finance their offices, their publications, their equipment, and to pay their organisers, they obtained money from the USA and from Europe, from governments, private enterprises and church bodies. To organise their projects they used the facilities of the CI and of white friends. To speak of 'using black resources', or of exclusive 'black identification', did not present an accurate picture of the way the organisations functioned. A similar pattern will be observed later, when members of BPC set out to form a black trade union.

The May Revolt, 1972

In 1972 SASO claimed a membership of between 4,000 and 6,000. Most of the members were students in the universities, and although there were contacts and obvious groups of sympathisers in the colleges of education, there is no indication of the extent of SASO influence amongst this large student body.

Although the membership was by no means large, students were concentrated on the campuses for a large part of the year and had joined the organisation as individuals who accepted its aims. As a consequence SASO was a body able to campaign for particular objectives, and to mobilize its supporters. In March 1972, there was a confrontation between SASO members and the authorities at Turfloop when students were ordered to remove copies of the SASO Manifesto and a Declaration of Students Rights. In retaliation the students made bonfires of official diaries. [35]

The next confrontation followed the speech given by Onkgopotse Ramothibi Tiro, a former SRC President, on behalf of the graduands of 1972, on 29 April. Onkgopotse Tiro, studying for the Education Diploma, strongly criticized white control of black universities, discrimination on the campus, and the entire apartheid system. In a call to the assembled students he said:

> . . . the challenge to every black graduate in this country lies in the fact that the guilt of all wrongful actions in South Africa, restrictions without trial, repugnant legislation, expulsion from schools rests on all those who do not actively dissociate themselves from and work for the system breeding such evils . . .
>   Of what use will your education be if you cannot help your country in her hour of need? If your education is not linked with the struggle on the whole continent of Africa it is meaningless. [36]

On 2 May the all-white disciplinary committee expelled Tiro. A student petition for his reinstatement was rejected and the students boycotted lectures. All 1,146 students were expelled, but refused to leave the premises they were occupying until all services were cut off. Thereafter the students decided to leave and the police sealed off the university. [37]

Students at other black universities expressed their solidarity with Turfloop by boycotting lectures. First the University of the Western Cape on 9 May, then the Natal Medical School (for three days), followed by an eight day boycott at Fort Hare. By 1 June every black university had boycotted lectures, and they were joined by the M. L. Sultan Technical College and two colleges of education.

The students of the University of the North were persuaded to return by the President of SASO, but when they discovered that 22 students — mainly members of the SRC or of the SASO local committee — had been refused permission to return, some 500 to 700 students again left Turfloop.

As a result of the wave of boycotts students were suspended, staff members resigned, bursaries were suspended, and hundreds of students just left the universities. The mood was summed up by the students' manifesto drawn up at Fort Hare. It declared:

> We, the students of Fort Hare, believe that all Black institutions of higher learning are founded upon an unjust political ideology of a White racist regime bent on annihilating all intellectual maturity of Black people in South Africa. [38]

The Fort Hare manifesto was issued on 7 June 1972, but by this stage events on the black campuses were no longer considered news-worthy. All attention was concentrated on the NUSAS Free Education campaign which had been launched on 22 May. On 2 June, in Cape Town, a student meeting on the steps of St. George's Cathedral was baton charged by police and by persons in plain clothes. Students were pursued into the cathedral and several passers-by were also beaten up. This led to marches by 800 students from the University of the Witwatersrand, pickets at Natal University, Pietermaritzburg, and marches at Rhodes University. Police used teargas and dogs, and a large number of students and onlookers were arrested.

These events did not bring the black and white students closer together. The attitude of the black students was expressed by the report in *Black Review*

> . . . the course of the black student revolts was largely affected by the decision by white student campuses to join the bandwagon. There was a drop in further publicity on the black student activity whilst newspapers concentrated on the protests by white campuses. [39]

During 1973 there were new disturbances on the black campuses. At the University of the Western Cape, which had a strong SASO following (despite the prohibition by the Minister for Coloured Affairs), there were student complaints that the rules and regulations were oppressive, that there was a disproportionate number of Whites on the staff, and that the coloured staff salary rates were too low. The discontent on the campus was furthermore exacerbated by constant raids on student residences by members of the Security Police, which in turn was associated with the harassment of SASO officials on all the campuses. Slogans carried by students read: 'Dialogue — no; confrontation — yes, yes, yes!' And the chant of one student song (to the tune of 'Glory, glory, hallaluja') was symbolic of the mood: 'Arson, rape and bloody murder [repeated three times] — when the Black revolution comes.' [40]

The University of the Western Cape was closed on 12 June, and the students were told to reapply for admission one month later. The students met and, by an overwhelming majority, decided that they would not reapply as individuals. They dispersed to organise large public meetings in Cape Town, Port Elizabeth, Oudtshoorn and Johannesburg. The coloured community gave the students wide support. The largest meeting was at Athlone (Cape Town) where some 12,000 attended a rally to hear Adam Small (who resigned from UWC in 1973), Chief Gatsha Buthelezi, Sonny Leon (leader of the coloured Labour Party and of the Coloured People's Representative Council), and other prominent community leaders. Representatives of the BPC joined the platform, despite their previous refusal to appear with individuals like Buthelezi and Leon who worked in government institutions.

The students were all accepted back on 15 July, but boycotted lectures to support their demand for an impartial Commission of Enquiry. The suspension of 18 leaders was followed by a walk-out of several hundred students in sympathy. These were rusticated; SASO was sorely depleted; and the students of UWC maintained an uneasy quiet for the rest of the year.

Disturbances also continued at Fort Hare duing 1973. The immediate cause of new outbreaks in August followed student attacks on an unpopular African hostel warden. In an attempt to force his resignation, students raided his residence and caused some damage. The police were called in and 159 students were rusticated. Only the threat of a mass walk-out secured the re-instatement of the 159.

For about a week all students at the Federal Theological Seminary boy-cotted lectures in sympathy with Fort Hare. It is reported that: 'They called off this action on being satisfied that the S. A. Council of Churches was show-ing deep concern over the situation at the university.' [41]

At most other universities the students were quiescent. This was at least partly due to the banning of eight leading officials of SASO, followed by the banning of seven students who had been elected to replace them. SASO as an organisation was also banned at Fort Hare, Turfloop, the Western Cape, and throughout BophuthaTswana.[42]

The 'Viva Frelimo' Rally

In the period January 1973 to June 1974, there were more than 300 strikes in the country, involving some 80,000 African workers. [43] This included rioting on the mines and clashes between the workers and the police. At least 132 miners were killed and more than 500 injured. It was these clashes on the mines which led to widespread indignation and widespread activity on the white English-speaking campuses.

On the night of 11 September 1973 there was widespread violence at the Carltonville compound, which left a trail of arson, and of killed and wounded. There was widespread indignation throughout the country. The first protest came from white students in Johannesburg and Cape Town. Approximately 80 students from the Witwatersrand University forced their way into the

Anglo-American Corporation (AAC) headquarters and demanded an open enquiry into the shooting. Cape Town students called on Harry Oppenheimer of the AAC to resign as Chancellor of the University if genuine trade unions were not permitted and wages not appreciably raised. This was followed by demonstrations, days of protest and confrontation with the police. At Durban-Westville 600 Indian students held a prayer meeting for the dead and started a collection for the dependents; SASO condemned the shootings; and at Turfloop the students voted to remove the SRC because it had not arranged a protest gathering.

The deep feeling over the shootings had affected the students, but these sentiments were not translated into any closer contact between black student and worker; not could there be any immediate contact. The campuses were not only by deliberate design situated in the rural areas, but also constituted a world apart from life in the compounds or in the townships. It would have needed a revolution in the lives of any student group to switch their attention from the lecture room to the factory bench. This gulf between political need and social reality; the distance between the workers' complaints and the students' theories could not be closed, and at no time in 1973 through to September 1976 was it even narrowed. Carltonville touched a sensitive nerve of the black student, but the full message never got home, and the students seemed unable to build a bridge to the one social force that could back their own demands for political change in the country.

Nevertheless the experiences of 1973 did create a new mood in the country and when, in April 1974, the Caetano government was overthrown in Portugal by the Armed Forces Movement, BPC and SASO leaders did not conceal their delight. When, later in the year, Mozambique was granted independence, BPC-SASO called for nationwide 'Viva Frelimo' rallies to be held on 25 September.

The Minister of Police banned all SASO and BPC meetings for one month. In Durban a crowd gathered despite the ban, and was forcibly dispersed by the police. This was followed by raids on the homes of BPC leaders and the detention of many of them. Twelve BPC-SASO leaders were subsequently charged, and most of them, together with witnesses (also held in custody by the police), were in detention throughout 1976. This sorely weakened the movement, and contributed to the absence of the organisation in the crucial period of the 1976 Revolt.

The students at Turfloop also responded to the call for a rally. They only heard of the ban on the meetings in a radio announcement and argued that, as their gathering had been called by the SRC, and not by SASO, it was not covered by the ban. Some of the black staff supported this contention and the demonstration was not cancelled. Overnight the campus walls were plastered with posters containing slogans which were a mixture of radicalism, adventurism, and student irresponsibility. A selection taken from the subsequent Commission of Enquiry and reprinted in *Turmoil at Turfloop* read:

Frelimo fought and regained our soil, our dignity. It is a story. Change the name and the story applies to you.
The dignity of the Black Man has been restored in Mozambique and so shall it be here.
Black must rule.
We shall drive them to the sea. Long live Azania.
Revolution!! Machel will help! Away with Vorster Ban! We are Afro Black Power!!!
Viva Frelimo. Azania is bored (sic) and from this boredom a Revolution shall erupt. Down with Vorster and his Dogs (Boers)!
Power!!! We shall overcome. [44]

Twelve hundred students gathered for the meeting, but were ordered to disperse by a force of 82 policemen, equipped with guns, gas pistols and police dogs. Assaults by the police and stone throwing by students, attacks on two white members of staff and two white technicians, and the arrest of two students ended the day. Two days later the college closed for the short autumn vacation, but on reopening (eight days late to avert a threatened student sit-in) the president of the SRC was arrested. The students organised a march and a petition to the police, and this led to a further arrest. The postponed sit-in was then organised.

The action lasted for over a week, but was ended just before the college authorities could issue an ultimatum. Students returned to preparations for the examinations which they were not prepared to forego, and their arrested comrades remained in police custody.

There was no news of further student activity in the universities over the next two years (late 1974 to mid 1976), and in that period there was a change in the composition of the student bodies as older students left or graduated and younger students entered. The resentments, however, were always present. In a press interview, Gessler Nkondo, a senior lecturer at Turfloop, gave an account of the bitterness felt by black staff and students alike. Both had to endure discrimination, and for those students who aspired to academic jobs, there seemed to be no end to the barriers placed in the way of their advancement. Doors were shut at every level. He had the following to say of the students' mood:

[they] felt 'savage' because they were isolated, shut out from the main currents of thought and activity in the country. What had happened in Mozambique had excited them: they were beginning to feel that change was possible — and in their lifetimes. [45]

Mr. Nkondo had in fact put his finger on the crucial issues. At Turfloop they *were* isolated, geographically, and from the needs of the towns and villages. They saw change coming from Mozambique and not from the struggles of the local population. Their slogans pointed to foreign events, and not local ills — and in most revealing fashion spoke of a 'boredom' which was peculiar to student isolation, and not to township life.

When, later in 1976, South African troops who had entered Angola were forced to withdraw, there can be little doubt that students responded jubilantly, and that, like the rest of black Africa, they saw this retreat as a defeat for the South African government. Turfloop students were among the first to demonstrate in sympathy with the Soweto students and there can be little doubt that many who had been involved in the 25 September pro-Frelimo rally, joined in the general black jubilation at the victory of the Popular Movement for the Liberation of Angola (MPLA).

References

1.   Quoted in J.G.E. Wolfson, *op. cit.*, p13.
2.   See, for example, report of a conference in August 1971 attended by 26 such bodies in *SRRSA*, 1971, p. 45.
3.   B.A. Khoapa, (Ed.), *Black Review*, 1972, p.8.
4.   *Loc. cit.*
5.   *SRRSA*, 1968, p.227. ASSECA did not achieve much in its early years. In 1967 its chairman died and Mr. Moerane took over.
6.   *Ibid.*, p.222.
7.   *SRRSA*, 1969, pp.194, 223-4.
8.   *SRRSA*, 1970, p.210; *Black Review*, 1972, p.124.
9.   *SRRSA*, 1971, p.107; and Thoko Mbanjwa, (Ed.), (1975), *Black Review*, 1974-75, (Black Community Programmes), p.123.
10. Steve Biko, 'Black consciousness and the quest for a true humanity', pp.36-47; Nyamelo Pityana, 'What is black consciousness', pp.58-63, in Basil Moore, (Ed.), (1973), *Black Theology: the South African Voice*, (Hurst).
11. *Ibid.*, p.43
12. *Ibid.*, p.62
13. *Ibid.*, p.63.
14. *SRRSA*, 1968, pp.25-6.
15. Reprinted in *ibid.*, pp.24-5.
16. *SRRSA*, 1968, p.22. A 'new summary of the Message' is included in *Apartheid and the Church*, Spro-Cas publication No.8, 1972, pp.77-81.
17. *Loc. cit.*
18. *Loc. cit.*
19. Open letter to the Prime Minister from twelve leading members of the Council of Churches and CI, summarised in *ibid.*, p.23.
20. *Apartheid and the Church, op.cit.*, p.3.
21. Cf. for example Allan Boesak, (1977), *Farewell to Innocence: a Social-ethical Study of Black Theology and Black Power*, (Ravan Press), p.57. Boesak claimed that only Blacks had the right to ask whether violence should be used in South Africa. He continued: 'Whites have lost that right, except those few who live like Beyers Naude.'
22. Quoted in *SRRSA*, 1971, p.44.

23. *Black Review*, 1972, pp.8-10.
24. Details of the conferences are taken from *SRRSA*, 1972, pp.31, 386 and 392; and *Black Review*, 1972, pp.11-13 and 18-21.
25. *SRRSA*, 1972, p.31.
26. *Ibid.*, p.386.
27. *Black Review*, 1972, p.21.
28. *Ibid.*, pp.12-13 (shortened slightly).
29. *Ibid.*, p.13.
30. *Black Review*, 1972, p.13.
31. Mafika Pascal Gwala, (Ed.), *Black Review*, 1973, (Black Community Programmes, Durban, 1974), p.164.
32. *Ibid.*, p.165.
33. 'SASO 1972' in J.G.E. Wolfson, *op. cit.*
34. Ranwedzi (Harry) Nengwekhulu, 'Black Consciousness Movement in South Africa', speech given to the Assembly of the IUEF, 22 November 1976.
35. *SRRSA*, 1972, p.387.
36. Quoted in *Sechaba*, August 1972. The statement, printed in full as an appendix to G.M. Nkondo, (Ed.), (1977), *Turfloop Testimony: the Dilemma of a Black University in South Africa*, (Ravan Press), has excluded a line of this passage which makes it unintelligible.
37. Details are taken from *SRRSA*, 1972, pp.387-92; and *Black Review*, 1972, pp.174-80.
38. *SRRSA*, 1972, p.391.
39. *Black Review*, 1972, pp.179-80.
40. For the events of 1973 see *SRRSA*, 1973, pp.335-41.
41. *SRRSA*, 1973, p.340.
42. *Ibid.*, p.344.
43. A discussion of the strikes and the trade unions is deferred to Chapter 7.
44. J.G.E. Wolfson, *op. cit.* The original reads 'We are not Afro Black Power', but that seems unlikely. The word 'not' should presumably be replaced by the word 'for'.
45. Quoted in *SRRSA*, 1974, p.373.

5. Secondary Schools and the African School Movement

Education for Black Labour?

> We should not give the natives an academic education, as some people are too prone to do. If we do this we shall later be burdened with a number of academically trained Europeans and Non-Europeans, and who is going to do the manual labour in the country? (Mr. J.N. Le Roux, later Minister of Agriculture, in Parliament, 1945.)

Mr. Le Roux, Nationalist member of parliament was no expert on education. He never claimed to be. In fact, he saw academically trained men and women as a 'burden'. But as a farmer, and as a leader of a party which had the support of the white farmers, he claimed to know something about labour. He wanted, and he knew his constituents wanted, a plentiful supply of cheap manual labour: and he knew that he must prevent the type of education which might leave him short of his precious commodity.

When eventually the Bantu Education Act was promulgated in 1954, it did seem as if the provision of Mr. Le Roux's 'manual labour' would be ensured, and that South Africa would not be burdened by an excess of 'academically trained' men and women. Nor did Mr. Le Roux's constituents on the farms suffer from the extension of farm schools. In 1954 Dr. Verwoerd assured his supporters that schools that were established on the farms would have curricula which included training 'in order to fit [the child] for farm work'. This was made more explicit by the Minister of Bantu Education in 1959. He said:

> We have made it compulsory that where the farmer wants these facilities, part of the school instruction of these children on the farm of the European farmer must be training in the normal activities of the farm, in order to encourage a feeling of industriousness on the part of those children and particularly, to sharpen in their minds the fact that education does not mean that you must not work with your hands, but to point out to them specifically that manual labour and also manual labour on a farm is just as good a formulative (*sic*) and development level (*sic*) as any other subject is. In order to do this, we create the opportunity so that if there is

any farmer who has a farm school on his farm, and who wishes to make use of the schoolchildren under the supervision of the teacher to assist with certain farm activities, this can be arranged in a proper manner to fit in with the curriculum . . .[1]

In 1975 there were 3,815 farm schools in the country. This amounted to approximately one-third of all African schools, and catered for approximately 10 per cent of all African schoolchildren.[2] They provided only primary education.

In fact Mr. Le Roux and his supporters had every cause for satisfaction. New legislation was put into operation to ensure that cheap labour would be forthcoming for the foreseeable future. Not only would the children be taught to accept servitude; but the system of Bantu Authorities would also remove all African hope of political advancement by tying their aspirations to the Reserves; Group Areas, furthermore, would separate out all racial groups and ensure that black unity would never be achieved. That, at least, was the plan.

The plan did seem to work. The new school system was not seriously challenged by the ANC boycott of schools in 1955. The races were separated out into their little compartments throughout the country. The African opposition to the Homelands policy was crushed, at least temporarily, in the late 1950's, and by 1960 political movements of opposition were contained and severely circumscribed.

New Labour Needs and School Expansion

The real national income grew throughout the 1950's at an average annual rate of five per cent. Through the 1960's this increased to six per cent.[3] And this growth depended above all on the supply and control of black manual labour. It was this labour which was used to open up the Orange Free State gold mines after 1946; and this labour which kept the farmlands, the factories, the transport system and construction works functioning. But as the economy expanded — and in the process allowed those in power to enrich themselves — the type of manpower needed changed perceptibly. More and more skilled personnel were required, and this was not easily obtainable from abroad.

During the 1960's industrialists and financiers had warned that South Africa would soon reach the stage where skilled labour would be in short supply, and during the rapid expansion of the economy, this prediction was more than borne out. By 1965 the shortage of skilled labour had become so severe that there was a rapid rise in (white) wage levels and, consequently, an an inflationary spiral which was never effectively controlled. By 1969 the position had worsened considerably, and Hobart Houghton stated that:

Serious labour shortage, especially in the skilled categories, led to irresistible demands for wage and salary increases and there was a decline

94

in productivity per man. Private consumption expenditure accelerated and private savings declined. Foreign funds still poured into the country . . .[4]

The government tried to bring down the level of inflation by means of import controls and by reducing public expenditure on capital works, but this had only limited success. One other way suggested itself — and that involved the introduction of skilled black labour. That, in turn, required more training, and more secondary school education.

The number of pupils in black schools had increased by over 250 per cent in the period 1955-69 (see Table Three), but the number of school leavers who were literate was low. A government estimate based on figures taken from the 1970 census, claimed that 49.5 per cent of Africans aged 15 years and over were literate according to the United Nations definition of the term. Even this figure is higher than would be expected from schools where the drop-out rate was 55 per cent in the first four years. Of the children enrolled in African schools in 1969, 25 per cent were in the first year (sub-standard A), and a further 45 per cent were enrolled in the next three standards (sub-standard B, and standards 1 and 2).

In 1969 only 4.33 per cent of pupils were in secondary school,[5] and very few completed the fifth (and final) form successfully. In 1969 only 869 obtained a passmark which would entitle them to proceed to a degree course at a university. Not all would proceed to higher education, but even if they did, 869 would represent only a tiny fraction of the total South African university enrolment of over 83,000 in 1970.[6]

Indications that there might be changes in the school system came from an unexpected source: Dr. P.J. Riekert, economic adviser to the Prime Minister, and chairman of the Economic Advisory Council. On 28 January 1970 he addressed the annual general meeting of the South African Institute of Race Relations on the economy of South Africa. He asserted, in the course of his speech, that to maintain the growth rate of the economy there would have to be a 'shift' of black workers into skilled occupations. He continued: 'This shift indicates the contribution that the non-whites will have to make to the solution of the skilled manpower shortage within the next one to three decades.'[7]

Despite this statement of intent, there was no obvious move by the government to make any alterations in the school system, and the Department of Bantu Education resolutely refused to allow any private corporation or individual to donate money or equipment for African education.

In November 1970 the Anglo-American Corporation, the largest mining and finance house in South Africa, offered a secondary school in Soweto R3,000 for the erection of extra classrooms. The Department of Bantu Education vetoed the offer, but did make a grudging concession. In a circular letter sent to all principals of schools, it was stipulated that all donations from private sources up to R50 could be accepted. Any donation larger than this amount had to be forwarded to the Department who would both decide whether the sum could be accepted, and where the money would be allocated.[8]

The government did not, however, intend increasing the contribution from general revenue to African schooling. The percentage of gross domestic product spent on African education stood at less than one half of one per cent in 1970, a smaller percentage than had been contributed by the state in 1954.[9]

Despite Dr. Riekert's assertion that there would have to be a shift in the training of Blacks, the Department of Bantu Administration seemed reluctant to make any further concessions. The first and most obvious place to start was to provide additional classrooms. It was estimated, for example, that there were 1,307 classrooms in Soweto in 1971, but that a further 2,016 rooms were needed immediately to cater for those who had applied for admission to the schools.[10] A survey of school facilities in 1970 showed:

Many of even the primary schools in urban areas are seriously over-crowded, with two classes of children sharing one room. . . There are still not enough desks: it is reported from many centres that children have to squat on the floor, using benches on which to write.[11]

The Minister of Bantu Education said in Parliament that in 1969:

double sessions were operating in 4,246 schools, involving 8,361 teachers and 750,428 pupils. Besides this, 17 schools used the platoon system in 1968, the classrooms being used by two sets of pupils a day, each with its own teacher.[12]

Even this did not reveal the full extent of overcrowding. A survey in the *Star* of 24 January 1973 stated that a quarter of all registered schools in Soweto had no buildings of their own, but congregated in church halls, tents, or classrooms borrowed from other schools in the afternoons. Furthermore it was estimated that 35,000 children could not enter school because of lack of accommodation.[13]

But changes had to come, and in 1971 a long standing offer by the Urban Bantu Council to make an annual levy of 38 cents upon every head of family in Soweto, for payment into the education account was accepted by the Department of Bantu Affairs. The shift in official attitude led to a spate of donations and appeals for money. In summary these included: a campaign launched by the Johannesburg City Council for R200,000 to build 1,000 new classrooms by the end of 1971; offers of R85,000 from the Anglo-American Corporation and of R32,000 by the Bantu Welfare Trust (administered by the South African Institute of Race Relations); and the launching of TEACH (Teach every African child) by the *Star* newspaper in October 1970 to provide funds for classrooms in Soweto.[14]

Public subscriptions poured into the *Star* office for TEACH and the R200,000 target was soon oversubscribed. There were also additional donations or money for the acquisition of desks, office equipment, chairs and gymnastic and sports equipment. Textbooks were also donated — but only those titles passed by the school inspectors as suitable could be accepted by the principals.

Major policy changes followed. In November 1972 the Minister of Bantu Education announced that schooling for Africans would be reduced from 13 years to 12 years in 1976. This change was prompted by the 1971 decision of the World Court, at the Hague, on Namibia. The Court found that the 13 year school programme for Blacks (in contrast to 12 years for Whites) was discriminatory. The South African government acted on this issue, according to *Black Review*, 1974-75, by dropping the extra, sixth standard, in both Namibia and South Africa. The Minister also announced that English and Afrikaans would be used as the mediums of instruction in standard 5 in 1976.[15]

Through 1973 and 1974 TEACH collected more money for classrooms. The half a million Rand this fund had collected by the end of 1973 provided accommodation for a further 15,00 pupils in Soweto alone. Other newspapers organised parallel funds: the *Natal Daily News* initiated LEARN (Let every African read now) to provide books; the Cape Town *Argus*, the *Pretoria News*, the Port Elizabeth *Evening Post* operated similar projects; and a group of Indians launched ZETA (Zulu education and teaching assistance) for building classrooms in Kwazulu.

Secondary School 'Explosion'

One final alteration of great importance became effective in 1974. Prior to this date, African students who wrote the standard 6 examination obtained a pass at the end of the year if their marks were over 40 per cent; but they could only enter secondary school if they achieved 50 per cent or more. Of the 134,377 Africans in the country who passed in 1973 (out of a total of 181,455 candidates), only 78,677 were eligible for secondary school entrance. In 1974 the 150,324 pupils who obtained over 40 per cent all became eligible for secondary school.[16] In 1975 the last students to enter standard 6, together with all students in standard 5, wrote examinations which would decide eligibility for secondary schools.

The changing structure of African schools in the 1970's (as compared to enrolment in 1965) is shown in Table Five. The increase of accommodation which made it possible to accept the larger secondary school intake was funded by TEACH, by private individuals and corporations, and by the parents of Soweto. The government provided no additional money.

In 1976 the Minister of Bantu Education told Parliament that school enrolment in African schools had topped the four million mark.[18] The most marked increases were in the first form of the secondary schools. This is shown in Table Six.

The increase in 1975 was due to the administrative change which permitted pupils with pass marks over 40 per cent to gain automatic entry into the secondary schools. This had led to a new crisis in accommodation, and a large number had had to be accommodated in temporary premises as near to

Table 5
Enrolment of African pupils[17]

Year	Total Numbers at School	In Secondary School	In Form V	Number Gaining a University Pass	Percentage of Pupils in Secondary Schools
1965	1,957,836	66,906	1,405	323	3.44
1970	2,741,087	122,489	2,938	1,009	4.48
1971	2,916,419	132,812	3,817	1,348	4.72
1972	3,079,507	157,786	4,814	1,801	5.03
1973	3,286,499	181,064	5,736	1,860	5.51
1974	3,456,261	209,519	6,732	2,058	6.00
1975	3,697,441	318,568	9,009	3,481	8.61
1976	4,000,000	na	na	—	est. 12-15

Table 6
Enrolment in Form I at African Schools[19]

Year	Number of Pupils	Form I Enrolment as % of Total
1970	49,504	1.80
1971	53,605	1.84
1972	63,733	2.07
1973	70,711	2.15
1974	82,351	2.36
1975	149,251	4.04
1976	na	—

the schools as possible. It was expected that, as pupils progressed up the school, the accommodation in each successive year would be unable to cope with the increased numbers.

The problem that was anticipated for 1976 was infinitely greater. The numbers in Form 1 could even exceed 300,000 because graduates of both standard 5 and standard 6 would enter secondary school in the same year. The expected shortage of classrooms in 1976 was 4,000, and plans were made for most Form I pupils to *be taught in the primary schools*, by primary school teachers (in classrooms no longer needed for standard 6). The Form I classes, furthermore, would have to be taught on a shift basis, with two classes sharing the same classroom.[20]

There is some evidence, unfortunately not verifiable, that BOSS (the Bureau of State Security) was aware of the possibility of the situation being explosive, and even giving rise to concerted student action. Looking at the position with hindsight, it must have been obvious to observers (and who in a better position to observe than BOSS?) that there were bound to be severe tensions.[21]

Pupils who were to enter the first form of secondary school would face severe overcrowding, and a two-shift system (already a nightmare in the Sub-A and Sub-B standards). They would be taught by primary school teachers (upgraded after special in-service training), and not even be able to enter secondary school buildings.

Furthermore, the pupils would inevitably include a higher percentage of youth who were markedly different from the usual secondary school entrant. The examination results marked those with 40 to 50 per cent pass marks as being possibly of lower academic standard — and many would have been, in previous years, part of the 'push-out' group in the township. It seems most likely that a large number came from poorer homes where there were fewer facilities for study. If that was indeed the case, the class composition of the secondary schools would have undergone a marked change after 1975 when the first form entry was twice as large as that of 1974.

The Language Bombshell

Over and above the tensions which were bound to follow in the wake of this massive increase in numbers, the Minister of Bantu Education announced that the proposed changes in the language of instruction would commence in 1976. One half of all subjects were to be taught in Afrikaans, the others in English, in standard 5 and Form One. It was also stipulated that arithmetic and mathematics (the subjects with the highest failure rate) together with social studies (history and geography) would in future be taught in Afrikaans.

There was an immediate protest from the teachers. All African teacher training colleges, bar one, were conducted in the English-language medium, and African teachers were not proficient in Afrikaans. They certainly could not teach in the Afrikaans medium. But the government made it clear that they would countenance no changes in the regulations, and that both social studies and mathematics had to be taught in Afrikaans.

No explanation was offered for this intransigence, and no explanation given for the need to teach mathematics (in particular) in Afrikaans. The only previous reference to this subject had been Dr. Verwoerd's 'What is the use of teaching the Bantu child mathematics when it cannot use it in practice? That is quite absurd.' Perhaps it was no longer absurd, and presumably in this period of labour shortage Afrikaans firms needed black workers with a knowledge of arithmetic. One document does show the connection between the new regulation and labour needs.

On 20 January 1976, the Board of the Meadowlands Tswana School was given an 'explanation' for the new language regulations by the school circuit inspector. After stating that all taxes contributed by Africans were used to pay for education in the homelands, the inspector was reported as saying:

In urban areas the education of a Black child is being paid for by the White population, that is English- and Afrikaans-speaking groups. Therefore, the Secretary for Bantu Education has the responsibility towards *satisfying* the English- and Afrikaans-speaking people.[22] (my stress)

The instructions indicated that schools could apply for exemptions for one year only, but reiterated that there would be no alteration to the list of subjects that had to be taught in Afrikaans. In effect few, if any, exemptions were to be granted: the needs of the white population (Afrikaans-speaking in this case) had to be satisfied.

School Students Organise

A study of the world-wide student revolt in 1968 by Barbara and John Ehrenreich led them to the conclusion that student disaffection with conditions in the colleges was raised to the point of revolt by the growing awareness of the iniquity of the war in Vietnam, and of the poverty and racism that permeated society. They concluded that:

Understanding what's happening to the schools is the key to understanding what's going on with their students . . .

The American student movement didn't begin as a *students'* movement. People may have had plenty of gripes as students, but these seemed trivial and personal compared to issues like Vietnam, racism and poverty.[23]

In South Africa, the interconnection between what was happening in the schools, and in society, was transparently obvious to black students. The poverty and racism that permeated society, stalked them in the schools. Unlike America, the 'gripes' felt by black students inside the schools of South Africa were not trivial and personal; the students understood only too well that what was happening in their schools, was happening in the country. In 1949, writing about the strikes in the schools at that time, C.A.R. Motsepe observed that black students were aware of their parents' agitation for: '. . . better conditions of life, higher wages, better housing, better judicial rights, etc.'[24] The parents, deeply concerned about their children, also knew that the discrimination they faced affected their children's schooling. In her autobiographical account Joyce Sikakane stated: 'I remember hearing our parents talking about it [Bantu Education], saying "The Boers were wanting to indoctrinate African children into being perpetual slaves of the white man".'[25]

African children were never allowed to forget that they were from a 'subordinate' people. At home and at school they met discrimination, and learned to hate the institutions that oppressed them. Joyce Sikakane recorded one of the incidents in her life that left her smouldering.

It was at boarding school in 1960 that I turned 16 — a 'doomsday' instead of a happy birthday because I had to carry a pass, a 'reference book' I had to carry every day of my life or else face a gaol sentence. I was at boarding school when the passbook was issued instantly to me and 300 other girls. We had not been informed, we were taken out in small groups for finger prints and instant photographing by the Bantu Affairs officials, who had set up a mobile station in the college grounds.[26]

Joyce Sikakane was upset, not only because she had to carry a pass, but also because 'We who were politically active failed to organise a protest. The government had adopted very stringent methods to see to it that African women above 15 years carried the passes. . .'[27] The government had taken stringent measures not only with respect to women's passes, but in 1960 had also banned the ANC and the PAC, and had declared a state of emergency after the shootings at Sharpeville and Langa. It would not be possible to organise protests in the schools for over a decade. It would also be difficult for students to organise any overt political groups in the years to come.

We have few accounts of secondary school students' extra-mural activities in the 1960's. In fact there are few accounts of such activities at any time in the history of the schools. There can be no reason to believe, however, that school students in the townships were any different to their peers elsewhere. They either established societies in which they could discuss their problems, or they created the organs through which they could meet. The activities of a Soweto school-based body, known as the Society for African Development (SAD), must have been repeated in many other centres. *Black Review* said of SAD that it:

. . . concerns itself with the development of social awareness among the African youth and the spreading of black consciousness. This they do by means of organising symposia, group discussions and 'conscientisation' picnics.[28]

The first reports of activities in African schools on a national basis appeared in the annual reports of *Black Review* after 1972. There are only reports (and brief reports at that) of a few organisations. There is no indication of how representative or how big they were at the time. Nor is it possible to deduce whether the groups mentioned constituted a majority of the formally organised student bodies. Some organisations were religious; others were devoted to the propagation of black consciousness, or the mobilisation of African youth for some educational or community project.

Provincial or regional bodies which aimed to unite youth on a local or national scale included: the Natal Youth Organisation (NYO), established by the BCP in August 1972 with Durban and Pietermaritzburg youth clubs; the Transvaal Youth Organisation (TRYO) launched by SASO and BCP (founder groups included SAD and the Black Youth Cultural Association); the League of African Youth (LAY), also founded in mid-1972 in Umtata, which aimed at becoming a nation-wide body; and the Junior African Students' Congress (JASCO), founded in mid-1971 at Inanda Seminary. (Banned by the principal, together with threats of expulsion, the society was not revived.)[29] Further regional organisations were launched in 1973: the Western Cape Youth Organisation (WCYO), many of whose affiliated clubs were religious, belonging to different denominations; and the Border Youth Organisation (BYO) in the Eastern Cape.[30]

In June 1973, the Provincial Youth Organisations were invited by the Black Community Programmes and SASO jointly to a seminar, and a National Youth Organisation (NAYO) was established. The aims of the organisation did not differ in any way from those already outlined for SASO or for BCP or BPC. The two central objectives were:

> To project the Black consciousness image culturally, socially, religiously, educationally, politically and otherwise.
> To commit itself to the elimination of psychological and physical oppression of Black people.[31]

The programme was, in its main points, similar to that adopted by the BCP: literacy campaigns, home education schemes, bursary fund, the establishment of creches, the propagation of black theology, and the organisation of theatre, drama and art workshops.[32]

University and school students also formed local student associations, three of which (at Pretoria, Springs and Sharpeville) are mentioned in *Black Review*. There were to organise symposia, games, picnics, and so on. Their aims were to 'promote togetherness and brotherhood', and to secure co-operation between students and their parents.[33] There were also religious youth groups, one of which might well have had an influence on events in 1976. This was The Light Bearers which aimed at 'promoting Black Theology and combating excessive drinking in the black community'.[34]

The South African Students Movement

Despite the proliferation of groups, few of them functioned, and they were never able to organise large numbers of students. In part this was because of continued police harassment, bannings, and arrests. School students are also notoriously hard to organise – and leave the organisations when they graduate. One of the groups which was originally formed in Soweto, and subsequently won adherents throughout the country was the South African Students Movement (SASM). It too was persecuted, by police and school principals alike, but it managed to survive – and that was its most important achievement. When finally the school students rose in protest against the imposition of Afrikaans as the language of instruction of three school subjects, it was the SASM which provided much of the leadership, SASM that called the crucial demonstration for 16 June 1976, and SASM which created the

Soweto Students Representative Council (SSRC) from which leaders of the Revolt were drawn.

In 1970, at least two years before SASO/BPC and BCP had organised any school pupils, senior students from three secondary schools in Soweto (Orlando West High, Diepkloof High, and Orlando High) had met to found the African Students Movement. They were able to establish contact with schools in the Eastern Cape and the Eastern Transvaal, and met with them in conference in March 1972. It was this new enlarged body that called itself the South African Students Movement (SASM).[35]

The students who participated in the SASM had, in many instances, belonged to youth clubs in the township, and discussions at those clubs had led them to the decision that a students movement was necessary. In an interview, Tebello Motapanyane, Secretary-General of the SASM in 1976, described the situation as the students saw it:

> We were, of course, very alive to the fact that we as black people were being oppressed. The students especially were quite sensitive to this and we were all the time trying to find a way of doing something about it. It was just unfortunate that we were not so clear about how to show our anger and resentment in a clear political way. But we certainly expressed ourselves indirectly in things like poetry reading and so on.[36]

But, said Motapanyane, the school students movement was not just an extension of the youth clubs. They were concerned primarily with the problem of Bantu Education which was designed to 'domesticate' and not to educate. They discussed the subjects they were being taught and concluded that the education they were receiving was inferior.

Answering a question about the connection between SASM and SASO, Motapanyane denied that SASM was an offshoot of SASO. He maintained that the students movement was formed independently and was autonomous, but that many ideas had been held in common by both bodies. In particular he mentioned black consciousness as a philosophy that both groups had propagated.

It seems, however, that although the SASM was autonomous, it did have direct links with the movements that formed part of the SASO-BPC-BCP organisation. *Black Review*, 1972, reported:

> The main aim of SASM is to co-ordinate activities of high school students. Their other main areas of operation are their informative programmes concerning injustice in society and in schools and their campaign to preach black consciousness. SASM is an affiliate of TRYO.[37]

It appears, furthermore, that the Secretary-General of SASM, Mathe Diseko, under whom the organisation expanded in 1972, was also the acknowledged leader of the National Youth Organisation.[38] The activities of SASM were in no way different from those of any of the many BCP sponsored

groups and consisted of projects to assist senior school students to: prepare
for fifth form examinations; improve study techniques; bridge the Junior
Certificate (third form)-matriculation gap; bridge the matriculation-university
gap; choose the right career or profession.[39]

These were hardly 'revolutionary' projects. Yet early in its existence SASM
came under surveillance, and its members were subjected to police harassment. Some of its leaders left the country in 1973 to escape the police, and in
1974 and 1975 members of the organisation were arrested and tried under the
Suppression of Communism Act and the Terrorism Act. Partly due to this
harassment, and partly because some members of the organisation were in
contact with clandestine groups of the ANC, several underground cells were
formed in order to protect the members.[40] At about the same date SASM
worked more independently of SASO-BPC, and there seems to have been a
strong ANC influence inside the movement. At a trial of SASM students from
Healdtown and Tembalabantu schools, (Alice and King William's Town), one
of the accused, Wilberforce Sinxo, told the court that: '. . . SASM stood for
equality and majority rule, and that only white people like Bram Fischer and
those banned or imprisoned becuase of their struggle for Black liberation were
respected.'[41] The reference to Bram Fischer, imprisoned chairman of the
South African Communist Party and close associate of the ANC, might have
been fortuitous. Nevertheless, reference to him generally came from those
who owed allegiance to the ANC.

SASM had at an earlier date resolved not to affiliate to either the ANC or
the PAC, but that did not act as a barrier to personal, or even group, attach-
ment to the underground movements. This statement in court, taken in conjunction with the *Sechaba* interview given by Motapanyane, suggests that
there were links between SASM and the ANC. This would indicate that SASM
was different and distinct from all the other organisations that espoused black
consciousness.[42]

SASM was not able to make much progress. Leading members were forced
to leave the country or face detention and arrest. In many schools the organisation was banned by the headmasters, and could not point to any real
successes. In an article printed in *Z*, organ of the Students for Social
Democracy group at the University of Cape Town, and devoted to the story
of the leaders of the 1976 Revolt in Soweto, it was claimed that:

> SASM had been in existence for seven years and it had never really taken
> off. By early 1976 its prestige stood at a low ebb. It was banned in many
> schools by the headmasters, and had no really striking achievements to its
> credit.[43]

The appraisal made by the journal was harsh, but probably correct. No
school movement could point to any 'striking achievement'. No school group
'really took off'. But it is not so certain that its 'prestige' was at a 'low ebb'.
And what was of supreme importance was the fact that it continued to exist,
openly or clandestinely, throughout the agitation against the new regulations

in the schools in 1976, and had the personnel to take the decision that led to the demonstration of June 16. In the months that followed the first confrontation with the police, it was the members of this movement that provided what leadership there seemed to be in Soweto.

References

1. *Senate Debates*, 2 June 1959, Col. 3463.
2. *SRRSA*, 1975, p.216.
3. D. Hobart Houghton, (1973), *The South African Economy*, (OUP, Cape Town), p.43.
4. *Ibid.*, p.222.
5. *SRRSA*, 1970, p.211.
6. This total includes 2,397 students registered at the University of South Africa (Unisa), out of a total of 4,578 black university students.
7. P.J. Riekert, (1970), 'The economy of the Republic of South Africa, with special reference to Homeland and Border industrial development and the economies of Southern Africa', reprinted in *Mercurius*, No. 10, (Unisa, Pretoria, June).
8. *SRRSA*, 1970, p.206.
9. W.G. McConkey, (1971), 'A close look at Bantu Education', *Reality*, September.
10. *SRRSA*, 1972, p.349.
11. *SRRSA*, 1970, p.207.
12. Report of the Bantu Education Department for 1968, quoted in *SRRSA*, 1970, p.208. The platoon system involved the sharing of classrooms by different teachers and classes, usually at morning and afternoon sessions. It could also involve two teachers sharing a room simultaneously.
13. Reported in *SRRSA*, 1973, p.296.
14. Details taken from *SRRSA*, 1971, pp.255-6.
15. *Star*, 11 November 1972.
16. *Black Review*, 1974-75, p.150.
17. Statistics from *SRRSA*, annual issues.
18. Asha Rumbally, (Ed.), (1977), *Black Review*, 1975-76, (Black Community Programmes, Lovedale), p.141.
19. *Bantu Education Journal*, August 1975, quoted in *SRRSA*, 1975, p.221.
20. *Loc.cit.*
21. It is unfortunately not possible to disclose the source of this information.
22. Quoted in *SRRSA*, 1976, p.52.
23. Barbara and John Ehrenreich, (1969), *Long March, Short Spring: the Student Uprising at Home and Abroad*, (Modern Reader, New York), pp.165 and 175.
24. C.A.R. Motsepe, (1949), *op.cit.*
25. Joyce Sikakane, (1977), *A Window on Soweto*, (International Defence and Aid Fund), p.41.

26. *Ibid.*, p.42.
27. *Loc.cit.*
28. *Black Review*, 1972, p.183.
29. *Ibid.*, pp.181-3.
30. *Black Review*, 1973, pp.63-4.
31. *Ibid.*, p.64.
32. *Ibid.*, p.65.
33. *Black Review*, 1972, p.183.
34. *Ibid.*, p.184.
35. Interview with Tebello Motapanyane, 'How June 16 demo was planned', *Sechaba*, Vol. II (2), 1971, p.49.
36. *Ibid.*, p.50.
37. *Black Review*, 1973, p. 182.
38. *Ibid.*, pp.63-5.
39. *Ibid.*, pp.62-3.
40. Motapanyane, *op.cit.*, pp.53-4.
41. *Black Review*, 1975-76, p.87.
42. The issue is clouded, unfortunately, by the existence of another body which also styled itself the Southern African Student Movement (SASM). In June 1973, members of black universities from South Africa, Botswana, Lesotho and Swaziland set up an organisation under the presidency of O.R. Tiro, and this body is referred to in *Black Review*, 1973, as SASM. The school students organisation is referred to in the same issue of the *Review* by the confusing appellation Junior SASM. (See *Black Review*, 1973, pp.62 and 66.)
43. *Z*, Vol. 2, No. 5.

6. The Black Consciousness Movement: Ideology and Action

One Million Members? An Impossible Goal

Today when we speak of the Black Consciousness movement, we immediately think of students in SASO and a few clerics. The rest of the people are not involved. (Bonganjalo Goba, 1971)[1]

Most of our people will agree that, thanks to SASO efforts, Black Consciousness has come to stay in South Africa. Because of the nature of its membership and composition, SASO only reached the educated and sophisticated segment of the population. Through its projects it is now gradually moving towards the grass roots . . . Relatively a small number of Blacks will join BPC . . . (Rev. Smangaliso P. Mkhatshwa, 1975)[2]

At its founding conference in 1972, the Black Peoples Convention set as one of its aims the recruiting of one million members in three years. The objective was unreal. It is doubtful whether the organisation on its own ever achieved a membership of 3,000 or, together with SASO, a total enrolment of 7,000 members. The BPC remained an organisation of students, a few clerics, and some professional men and women.

The target of one million members, accepted by the conference, reflected the hopes of the younger members who dreamt of sweeping South Africa and filling the black population with their own undoubted enthusiasm. A more sober view of the role of the organisation was presented by Drake Koka, who had played a leading role in convening the conferences that led to the formation of the BPC, and who was its first Secretary-General. In a statement to a news reporter in 1973 he said: 'We are aware they can shove us in gaol at any time . . . That is why we are not a movement of confrontation, but a movement of introspection — our aim is to awaken Black Consciousness.'[3]

Although there appears to be some disagreement on what the BPC aimed to achieve, the differences between those who wanted a million members, and Mr. Koka who envisaged a 'movement of introspection', were not great. The BPC and SASO aimed to reach the black population of South Africa. They wanted to reach out into every section of their people and spread the message of black awareness and self-reliance. But those who wanted a large membership in the organisation were not able to induce large numbers to join – and it was left to the members to spread its ideas amongst the restricted groups with whom they worked.

SASO had a three year headstart on most other black consciousness groups and were consequently well established before other groups were launched. Although they did face the problem of a turnover of membership as students graduated, their potential recruits were gathered together in the universities and training colleges. The total number of black students in universities in 1972 was estimated as 9,000,[4] and early that year SASO claimed to have secured the affiliation (mainly through the SRCs of colleges) of some 4,000 of them. But every attempt to expand outside the campuses failed. SASO did try to organise school pupils, and assisted in the formation of the National Youth Organisation (NAYO). Unlike SASM, however, NAYO did not survive.[5]

SASO also planned to work on rural projects, but they were not very successful. A report to the third annual conference of SASO at Hammanskraal in 1972 stated: 'It is to our regret that we report that our field work projects leave much to be desired. As yet we cannot claim one completely satisfactory project.'[6]

The BPC was not very much more successful. In a report in 1973, it was claimed that its first year of operation saw 41 branches spread throughout the country.[7] Despite this claim, Rev. Mkhatshwa, a member of the executive of the BPC, stated that:

> BPC, the only non-tribal political organisation, needs to treble its efforts before it can even begin to give a semblance of being a people's mass movement . . . There are undoubedly millions of Black people whose political frustrations have no organized outlet . . .[8]

The failure to recruit more members does need explanation, and it would appear that there were three main contributory factors which need consideration. There was, firstly, the police harassment which removed leaders, prevented activity, and frightened off potential recruits. Members were detained or raided, charged, banned, and assassinated. Meetings were prohibited, unpublished manuscripts confiscated, books banned, and every device used to circumscribe the activities of the organisations connected with SASO/BPC.

Secondly, and by no means less restrictive, were the barriers to organising in the Reserves. These areas, which housed 40 per cent of the African population, were controlled by regional (or tribal) authorities, and political movements (where they were allowed at all) had to operate inside the policy of 'separate development'. The uncompromising stand taken by BPC against any officially instituted body or organisation, meant effectively that there was little chance of their operating legally or openly in the nine 'Homeland' areas. The BPC also found that apartheid laws made it extremely difficult to operate inside the Coloured and the Indian communities. Their major success amongst the Coloureds was at the University of the Western Cape where a section of the students were affiliated to SASO. There were few other

108

Coloured or Indian converts — and when organisations emerged inside these communities which seemed to move in the same direction as the BPC, leading members were banned by the government.

Thirdly, and most importantly, the BPC did not have the leadership that could either withstand police harassment, or provide the ideas and programme that could have rallied the mass of the population — which alone could have ensured survival and even success in the struggle that was bound to eventuate. At its inception, the BPC was composed of students, of clerics, and of men who had, in many cases, been regarded by both the ANC and the PAC as 'sell-outs'. Drake Koka had always been a 'moderate' and had worked in the Liberal Party. Menassah Moerane of the *World* and of ASSECA was a conservative. Dr. Nkomo, a member of Moral Rearmament, had, after a short stay in the Congress Youth League, stood aloof from the ANC; he died in 1972. And L.B. Mehlomakhula and Mrs. Mabiletsa were leaders of ASSECA which, in 1972-73, was under a cloud because of the way in which the Polaroid funds were used. After 1972 some of these individuals ceased to be on the central directing committees of the BPC but occupied other key positions in affiliated organisations. M.T. Moerane and L.B. Mehlomakhula continued to administer ASSECA. These two men, neither of whom had any connection with the working class, were members of the consultative Planning Committee of the Black Allied Workers Union (BAWU), which was organised and controlled by Drake Koka until he was banned in 1973.[9] Mrs. Mabiletsa joined the Federation of Black Women as its Vice-President under Mrs. Fatima Meer.

The Myth of BPC Radicalism

The students were ostensibly more radical, and there was some friction inside the BPC. At the Black Renaissance Convention in December 1974 they would not give Mrs. Meer, leader of a sister organisation, a hearing. They also clashed with their university authorities, but there was little that was specifically radical in their ideas or their projects. Their educational, clinic and work projects were identical to those that NUSAS conducted.[10]

Nor was there anything very radical about the ideas (or organisational plans) of the younger leaders. Rev. Smangaliso Mkhatshwa, interviewed by James MacManus, in a series on apartheid for the *Guardian*, was at pains to make it clear that he was no revolutionary and no communist: 'I recognise that my church is the Number One enemy for Communism . . . We are not going to exchange one form of dictatorship for another.'[11] But while he was not a 'communist', it is hard to discern from the interview what Mkhatshwa did want. He said that the African wanted 'full rights in the country', and then he expanded: 'I know the quandary of the Afrikaner. I know his fears for survival. But when will he realise that his survival depends upon an accommodation with the people of this country and not their suppression?'[12]

It is difficult to believe that the BPC really wanted an 'accommodation'. But there are few documents which set out clearly what the BPC or SASO did want. The Secretary-General of SASO, Nyameko Pityana, contributed a paper entitled 'Power and social change in South Africa' to the collection of essays on *Student Perspectives on South Africa*. He took care to stress that he was no Marxist — a system which he dismissed as 'utopian', and it was clear from the way he envisaged change that he worked outside the Marxist tradition:

> The first step, therefore, is to make the Black man see himself, to pump life into his empty shell; to infuse him with pride and dignity, to remind him of his complicity in the crime of allowing himself to be misused and therefore letting evil reign supreme in the country of his birth. That is what we mean by an inward-looking process.[13]

It was hardly likely that the worker in the townships would accept this statement. His life was anything but an empty shell; he was not guilty of any complicity in the working of apartheid; and he had little need for an 'inward-looking process'. He might, however, (if we are allowed to speak for the men and women who did not have the benefit of a university education), ask precisely what it was that SASO expected him to do. Pityana did supply his answer:

> This means that Black people must build themselves into a position of non-dependence upon Whites. They must work towards a self-sufficient political, social and economic unit. In this manner they will help themselves towards a deeper realization of their potential and worth as self-respecting people. The confidence thus generated will give them a sense of pride and awareness. This is all we need in South Africa for a meaningful change to the *status quo*.[14]

If this was indeed what was needed for a meaningful change in the *status quo*, then 'liberation' was going to be a long time coming. Pityana did not expand, and it is left to the reader to interpret this passage, and to give meaning to the claim that Blacks could become 'self-sufficient' politically, socially and economically. The mind boggles at the idea of Africans setting up a new set of economic institutions that would free them from white control. Mines, factories, industries, farms, co-operatives, shops, or whatever Pityana conceived of, would always remain phantom projects of his imagination. Self-sufficient political and social institutions were equally unreal, and if these were essential steps towards some deeper realization, then there was little hope for the oppressed people of South Africa.

Other statements from SASO leaders were equally obscurantist. Steve Biko, one-time President of SASO and organiser for the BCP, also called for the restoration of the 'great stress we used to lay on the value of human relationships'.[15] This led him however to quite remarkable conclusions in his appraisal of education:

The attitude of some rural African folk who are against education is often misunderstood, not least by the African intellectual. Yet the reasons put forward by these people carry with them the realization of their inherent dignity and worth. They see education as the quickest way of destroying the substance of the African culture. They complain bitterly of the disruption of the life pattern, non-observation of customs, and constant derision from the non-conformists whenever any of them go through school . . . How can an African avoid losing respect for his tradition when in school his whole cultural background is summed up in one word: barbarism?[16]

Biko concluded that it was necessary '. . . to reduce the hold of technology over man and to reduce the materialistic element that is slowly creeping into the African character.'[17] The description of the educational system contained a mixture of truth (the destruction of African culture, the denigration of the past), with a romanticisation of the past that was unrealistic. His observation that 'lack of respect for the elders is . . . an unforgivable and cardinal sin', while traditionally correct, was absurd in 1972: and his call for a reduction of 'the hold of technology' militated against every demand of blacks for more and better education.

Biko also sought some growth of awareness through participation in a 'Buy Black' campaign, which would show the 'power' the Blacks wielded as a group.[18] There were no further suggestions in Biko's paper for methods of countering apartheid, of building an organisation, or even of raising 'awareness'. His concluding paragraph was defiant but of little use to any person in his audience who sought some way to act against the regime. What he stated was:

Thus, in this age and day, one cannot but welcome the evolution of a positive outlook in the Black world. The wounds that have been inflicted on the Black world and the accumulated insults of oppression over the years were bound to provoke reaction from the Black people. Now we can sit and laugh at the inhumanity of our powerful masters, knowing only too well that they destroy themselves and not us with their insolent cynicism . . . We have in us the will to live through these trying times; over the years we have attained moral superiority over the White man; we shall watch as Time destroys his paper castles and know that all these little pranks were but frantic attempts of frightened little people to convince each other that they can control the minds and bodies of indigenous peoples of Africa indefinitely.[19]

Read today, in the aftermath of the Soweto Revolt, and of the brutal murder of the author, these words of Steve Biko need appraisal. It obviously was not enough to talk about 'moral superiority', and it was wrong to believe that the Whites lived in 'paper castles'. A serious political leader can be excused for exhorting his audience to greater defiance, but he fails badly if he does not warn of the consequences of taking on a well armed government. It

111

was not going to be realistic to 'sit and laugh' at these 'powerful masters'. The organisations needed at that stage (1971-72) to prepare for a bitter fight, and individuals had to find means of protecting themselves from the police. The stage had been reached when black movements had to appraise the enemy and probe his strength. To dismiss the Whites as 'frightened little people' frantically convincing each other that they could control the African, was not realistic, and there were few if any indications, in the years that followed, that Biko, or indeed any other member of SASO/BPC, reconsidered the logistics of the political struggle in South Africa.

The Appeal to Fanon
Both Pityana and Biko quoted extensively from Fanon in their articles. They used his earlier work, *Black Skin, White Masks*, and it was obvious that Fanon had appealed to their assertion of the Africans' intrinsic worth. Pityana quoted the passage: 'I am not a potentiality of something, I am wholly what I am . . . My negro consciousness does not hold itself out as black, it IS. . . That is all that we blacks are after, TO BE . . .' But Fanon wanted something more than an existential assertion from Blacks; particularly from radical leaders. He reserved his most trenchant criticism for the many nationalist leaders in the Africa of the late 1950's in his *The Wretched of the Earth*. He was not impressed by these men who sang the praises of *'Negritude'*, or of the 'African personality', who spoke of negro (or black) consciousness, and who quoted his (Fanon's) writings to justify their middle class politics. He became deeply suspicious of the products of the universities where 'colonized intellectuals' learned to accept the 'eternal' (social and political) qualities of the western world.[20] He disliked the political parties they built, but was able to see the effect they were ultimately bound to have:

> In their speeches the political leaders give a name to the nation. In this way the native's demands are given shape.
>   There is however no definite subject-matter and no political or social programme. There is a vague outline or skeleton, which is nevertheless national in form . . . The politicians who make speeches and who write in the nationalist newspapers make the people dream dreams. They avoid the actual overthrowing of the State, but in fact they introduce into their readers' or hearers' consciousness the terrible ferment of subversion.[21]

Fanon knew that these weavers of dreams could play a catalytic role in the colonial societies he had observed. But he was perpetually wary of them. He continued:

> The national or tribal language is often used. Here once again, dreams are encouraged . . . these politicians speak of 'We Negroes, we Arabs', and these terms which are so profoundly ambivalent take on during the colonial epoch a sacramental significance . . .[22]

Fanon was impatient of such men. He condemned them as leaders 'anxious to make a show of force' so that they would not have to use any; who appealed to the radicals for calm while looking to the right; and whose role generally was to stifle political action.[23]

It would seem unfair to quote from Fanon's appraisal of African leaders in 1961 (the date in which his work was first published) in discussing the leaders of BPC and SASO. Indeed not all that he said then is applicable to these young men who did not lack bravery. In the final analysis, however, there was no campaigning and no direction. In place of real political activity, there were just words — and far too often the words were incomprehensible. A sample taken from an organisational document will illustrate the frustration the membership must have felt:

> The arduous task of self-emancipation presupposes student activism. What must we do, students keep on asking. It is not easy to know what to do. In other words essence precedes existence. Behaviour and action are always preceded by some thought and theory, otherwise, they become haphazard and confused.[24]

Nevertheless the leaders of the Black Consciousness Movement did make people 'dream dreams'. And in dreams, a touch of confusion did not matter overmuch. There was, however, a deep gulf between dreams and reality, and it is not certain that this gulf was ever bridged.

Non-collaboration? The BPC Dilemma

At an early stage in the history of SASO, leading members declared that they would never work with Blacks who belonged to any of the political institutions established by the South African government. They rejected completely the concept of 'Homelands', and declared that any person who entered the tribal or regional assemblies was a traitor to the cause of African liberation. They maintained the same stand against any person who entered the Coloured Representative or Indian Councils, the Urban Bantu Councils (the advisory bodies in the townships), or any other government boards or councils in townships or reserves.[25]

This commitment to non-collaboration was reaffirmed in July 1972 when the President of SASO was expelled at conference because he had suggested that the organisation had to be more flexible in its approach and had to learn to speak even to its opponents. It was reported that Temba Sono, in addressing the assembly, called for: '. . . open-mindedness towards Bantustan leaders, white liberals and even towards security police.'[26] The reference to the security police, if correct, was inexcusable. But the issue of 'white liberals' and 'Bantustan leaders' became a recurrent problem for members of the black consciousness movement.

The relationship between individual members of the black consciousness groups and white liberals was in fact never resolved. A number of prominent leaders of BPC and SASO maintained contact with, or established very close relations with, liberal Whites. Steve Biko was in constant close contact with Donald Woods, editor of the East London *Daily Dispatch*, and Woods was accepted as a champion of the Black Consciousness Movement by Biko's friends.[27] There were also obvious close contacts with leading members of the Christian Institute, and with one-time leaders of the dissolved Liberal Party.[28] Even SASO's break with NUSAS was more organisational than ideological. They declined to work with the white students on grounds of colour, and not because they disagreed with the activities of NUSAS, or found fault with the programme of the National Union of Students. Most of their own activities, on the campuses or in the communities, did not differ appreciably from parallel activities undertaken by the Whites.

Members of BPC and of SASO were able to secure the expulsion of delegates from conferences if they were associated with any of the apartheid councils. The Declaration of the Black Renaissance Convention, which met in December 1974, stated that:

One of the most dramatic highlights of the Convention was the vehement condemnation of the policy of separate development, its exponents and institutions. By an overwhelming vote, the delegates prevented a prominent homeland leader from addressing the Conference.[29]

The Convention also expelled Collins Ramusi of Lebowa, David Curry of the (coloured) Labour Party, and S.S. Mothapo of the BophuthaTswana opposition party.[30] What was left unsaid was that these men had originally been invited to attend by members of BPC! Despite these expulsions BPC/SASO continued to be equivocal in their attitude to some of the men and women who participated in apartheid institutions.

Buthelezi's Politics Pose a Problem

In the early stages of the BPC, the convenors of the preparatory conferences did not exclude men who were actively involved in Homelands' politics. At the gathering, in August 1971, which was summoned in order to launch the BPC, Chief Mongosuthu Gatsha Buthelezi, chief councillor of KwaZulu, was invited to address the meeting from the platform.[31] Thereafter, it would seem, relations between BPC and Buthelezi were broken off, and the black consciousness leaders condemned the Chief in terms which did not differ from those employed against Chief Kaizer Matanzima of the Transkei.

There had never been any accord between Matanzima and the students, and the Transkeian chief had always been accused of being the main collaborator with the South African goverment. Matanzima had, furthermore, never used the radical language that Buthelezi was apt to employ in addressing a popular audience. It had been easy, therefore, for BPC to condemn

Matanzima, and to reject the direction taken by the ruling Transkeian party as it moved towards so-called independence in October 1976. Buthelezi, on the other hand, did present a more radical stance in his dealings with the government, did have a populist appeal when he addressed mass meetings and was able to win the support of a large number of people who were opposed to the apartheid policy. As recently as February 1971 P.V.T. Mbatha, writing in the ANC organ *Sechaba*, referred to 'this great leader of the people, chief Mongosuthu (Gatsha) Buthelezi', and praised him for leading the Zulu people against apartheid.

Buthelezi's policy was more complex than P.V.T. Mbatha's statement would indicate. He worked inside the apartheid system and he attacked it, he co-operated with the government but criticised government instructions; he spoke in favour of a united South Africa, but also seemed to favour a federation of black states; he seemed to support militant action against apartheid, but claimed that he feared the growing alienation in the townships. In the many statements that he made publicly, he veered from left to right, aiming to please the authorities at Pretoria, the black leaders of the other Homelands' governments, his followers in KwaZulu, and the meetings he addressed in the townships. He took as many stances as needed to satisfy his different audiences, and was obviously able to build up a large black following throughout the country.

In 1972 his reply to his critics in SASO was: 'We are doing no more than attempting to exploit the limited political expression within the framework of [government] policy, for what it is worth . . . [and] I am working within the system without accepting it.'[32]

Although he claimed that he was only 'working the system', his main concern seemed to be to secure more land for KwaZulu,[33] and he made constant appeals (some in government propaganda statements) urging foreign investors to build industries in the Homelands. Buthelezi also accepted ethnic (and racial) division in the country, and in a series of meetings at the end of 1973 secured the co-operation of Homelands' leaders for a federation of black states – leaving it to an ecstatic Matanzima to declare: 'My dream has come true. This fascinating historic occasion . . . is the renaissance of the United Nations of black South Africa.'[34]

Together with the black leaders, Buthelezi then attended a conference on federalism convened by Donald Woods of the *Daily Dispatch*. Present at the conference were members of the Progressive Party, and some small groups which were conservative in policy. Buthelezi outlined a scheme in which 'non-black states' could join the proposed federation of black states in a 'Federal union of autonomous states of Southern Africa'.[35] Two months later, in January 1974, Buthelezi met Harry Schwartz, leader of the United Party in the Transvaal, and in a joint declaration the two men called for peaceful change, leading to a federation of ethnic states.[36]

The acceptance of a federal state went contrary to everything that members of the Black Consciousness Movement advocated, precisely because such a position accepted the government's division of the country into ethnic units. This was 'working within the system' as Buthelezi had said, but it was also accepting its basic premises, and thus negating his claim that he rejected the government's policy.

Buthelezi's political pronouncements are often difficult to interpret. He seemed to intersperse phrases which cancelled each other out. He was for a unified South Africa, and he was for a federal structure; he was against foreign investment, but he was in favour of such investment if it was in the Reserves; he was for violence, and he was against violence.

In August 1974 he addressed a meeting of IDAMASA, one of the founding members of the BPC, and spoke about violence. Initially he seemed to say that violence was inevitable. The situation in South Africa, he declared, was the 'direct result of our system which is structured in violence', and this 'institutionalized violence' gave rise to 'guerrilla violence'. This seemed unexceptionable, even if the listener did not agree that one form of violence necessarily gave rise to counter-violence. As Buthelezi saw the problem, the two were interconnected, and out of the one situation the obverse situation had to emerge. But the Chief was not a proponent of violence, and going against the logic of his own argument concluded by saying that violence could not be condoned.[37]

Other examples of such Janus arguments will be quoted in Part Three of this book, and will show that at least Buthelezi was consistent in his inconsistencies. Far more important than what was said were the actions of Buthelezi and the support group he built to take his message into the country. In practically every instance his actions were instrumental in damping the black struggle, or in turning it away from its original path. An example of the disruptive effect of Buthelezi's politics, when his supporters acted at a local level, can be traced in the events at the University of Zululand at Ngoye.

The clash between Buthelezi and SASO was particularly severe on the Ngoye campus. In 1974 John Vusumuzi Mchunu, one time minister in the United Congregational Church of Southern Africa, was a student at Ngoye. He formed a cultural organisation with a strong 'back to Africa' revivalist stress, which called amongst other things for church services 'to suit the African cultural background'. Initially, the new society obtained strong support, particularly from members of SASO. Mchunu, however, championed Buthelezi, lobbied against SASO, and claimed that students on the campus who came from the Transvaal were not Zulu and should go home. As tensions grew the Mchunu group threatened to use violence, and the SASO group made little headway.

There was a change in 1975 after Mchunu had graduated and when, in mid-year, Buthelezi attacked the morals of the students, and claimed that the students were living a loose life on the campus, and that the Rector was doing nothing to stop the immorality, the students and the University Council condemned Buthelezi. The Chief had called for the appointment of a black Rector who would uphold the cultural values of his society![38] This nationalist (or in fact tribal) chauvinism was too much for the students, and SASO once again became the undisputed leader of the Ngoye student body.

116

Inkatha Yenkululeko Yesizwe

In 1974 Gatsha Buthelezi decided to revive the Zulu cultural society started by King Solomon (of the Zulus) in 1928. The organisation was to serve a double purpose: it was to provide Buthelezi with a machinery in KwaZulu through which he could control events in the Legislative Assembly, and at the same time give him a platform from which he could organise a movement throughout the country.

Inevitably Buthelezi faced new contradictions by trying to 'work within the system' and also operating outside the apartheid framework. He was not permitted by law to organise people who were not citizens of KwaZulu, and he was forbidden to organise amongst other ethnic groups. Initially therefore, Inkatha was open to all Zulus over the age of 18, and also to organisations (like trade unions, nurses associations, and so on) that were eligible to affiliate. Only Inkatha members could stand as candidates for the Legislative Assembly, and only the President of Inkatha could be the Chief Minister of KwaZulu. That is, he would have to be a hereditary chief.[39]

The national aspect of Inkatha was explained by its Secretary-General, S.M. Bengu, Dean of Students at Ngoye:

> Inkatha can be seen as part of the cultural identity movement that is sweeping Africa today . . . Instead of Africans endeavouring to be carbon copies of others they want to be distinctly themselves . . .
> . . . national unity and models for development should be based on values extrapolated from the people's culture and adopted to present-day needs and situation.[40]

Professor Bengu also made the point that Inkatha did not aim to live in the past. He was careful to stress that the movement worked within the system, but was not confined to one tribal group. This was a departure from the initial constitution of the movement which restricted membership to Zulus:

> Inkatha is a national movement which is open to all . . .
> . . . Our movement purports to abolish all forms of colonialism, racism, intimidation, discrimination and segregation based on tribe, clan, sex, colour or creed . . .
> One of the main objectives of Inkatha is to fight for the liberation and unification of Southern Africa . . . The movement aims at fostering the spirit of unity among the people of KwaZulu throughout Southern Africa, and between them and all their brothers in Southern Africa, and to co-operate locally and internationally with all progressive African and other national movements that strive for the attainment of African unity.[41]

Inkatha grew rapidly — having a 'captive' constituency in KwaZulu — and by 1977 claimed a membership of over 100,000 and funds of R136,000. The entrance fee was high by South African standards, and stood at R3 for an individual, and at R20 for doctors, lawyers and social workers. Organisations were levied at R100 on joining. The annual subscription was R2 per individual, R20 for professional workers, and R100 for organisations. This made Inkatha the largest and best financed black organisation that had ever been built in South Africa.[42] Who was recruited, and the basis on which the recruits were drawn into Inkatha, is not known. It is doubtful, however, whether any but Zulu joined and in 1976 Buthelezi was speaking about forming a set of Inkathas to cater for other communities if they did not wish to join his organisation. (See p.170.) When asked in an interview what Inkatha would do when they had organised, the answer from two leading members, Dr. Nyembezi and Mr. Mavuso, was: 'I'd rather not say'. When asked, further, how they recruited people 'without having any clear policy', the answer given was: 'You have a fine leader in Buthelezi. You must support him. You must work for the Zulu first and then attract all the good of the black community.'[43]

Zulu Consciousness, or Black Consciousness?
Frantz Fanon, in the passage quoted above, drew attention to the fact that 'tribal language is often used. Here once again, dreams are encouraged . . .' Buthelezi, at least in some of his pronouncements, claimed to transcend tribalism. In one statement he declared:

> Among the so-called homeland leaders there are some like myself who believe in Black consciousness, and who believe that they have done more in promoting the concept of Black consciousness than those who arrogantly dismiss them as 'irrelevant'. Although there is much talk today about Black consciousness as such, this concept was born long ago when Black people realised that their political salvation depended on their socio-political concept of one African people, whose destiny could only be reached beyond the limits of ethnic groupings.[44]

But basically Buthelezi's movement attracted the middle-aged, and rallied the population in the KwaZulu reserves. In the towns, it was the migrant Zulu worker who followed his lead. The youth, and the more permanent urban population were not attracted. It is not possible to see what was being offered to the recruits, nor was it obvious how Inkatha meant to break the apartheid system. When stripped of rhetoric, neither side could offer any means of breaking the apartheid system. All answers to questions on this matter were turned aside. In the case of Inkatha, the interview of Nyembezi and Mavuso produced the following *non sequitur:*

> *Question:* If you feel it is impossible for you to treat with the Nats [Nationalist Party] and if it is going to be impossible to get the Nats out of power by any peaceful means, how do you see Inkatha achieving its aim?
> *Answer:* People go into the separate development laager because the government says the Nats are the only people who can protect them. The issues are not even looked at.[45]

When pressed further, the two members of Inkatha maintained that talks with white groups, including presumably the government party, would provide a solution. They furthermore declared that Inkatha would 'overcome those people who will not sit down with other people'. They added: 'We want to avoid a Rhodesian situation. We want Buthelezi to talk now.'[46] Members of SASO used more radical language, but they too (as quoted above) could offer no answers to the urgent questioning of the students who asked 'what must we do?', except to pursue some mythical self-sufficiency.

When eventually the black population erupted in revolt, BPC and SASO had no direct hand in leading the townships; and only a few were able to participate, as individuals, outside the campuses. Personal initiative allowed members of these organisations to play a role — but the organisations as such were not in evidence. To a certain degree this was the consequence of police action. The BPC and SASO were severely damaged by harassment, arrests, bannings, and the precipitate flight of many leaders to avoid possible detention. But it was also the consequence of a failure to organise, the failure to expand out of the elite circles the students frequented, and the failure to work out a stategy by means of which the apartheid system could be undermined and then destroyed.

Inkatha played a more ominous role. Buthelezi condemned the 'violence', and sounded ominously like government ministers when he called on the township population to take a stand against the destruction wrought by the youth. His role during the Revolt will be fully described in Chapter Thirteen.

References

1. Basil Moore, *op.cit.*, p.73.
2. 'Putting the Black Renaissance Convention into correct perspective', *Reality*, May 1975.
3. Quoted in *Sechaba*, Vol. 7, No. 4, March 1973.
4. 'SASO 1972', in J.G.E. Wolfson, *op.cit.*, p.59.
5. R.H. Nengwekhulu, *op.cit.*, p.3.
6. Quoted in *Sechaba*, Vol. 6, No. 10, October 1972.
7. *Black Review*, 1973, p.74.
8. *Reality*, May 1975, *op.cit.*
9. *Black Review*, 1972, p.124.
10. In 1967, students at the University of the Witwatersrand started the South African Voluntary Service with the 'aim of involving students in the building of classrooms and clinics in Black rural areas'. (mimeographed information sheet of SAVS, c.1977).
11. *Guardian*, 25 March 1977.
12. *Ibid.*
13. N. Pityana, *op.cit.*, p.180. This passage first appeared in a SASO newsletter entitled *We Blacks*.
14. *Ibid.*, p.189.

15. Steve Biko, (1972), 'White racism and black consciousness' in H. van der Merwe and D. Welsh, *op.cit.*, p.200.
16. *Ibid.*, p.199.
17. *Loc.cit.*
18. *Ibid.*, p.201.
19. *Ibid.*, p.202.
20. Frantz Fanon, (1973), *Wretched of the Earth*, (Penguin), p.36.
21. *Ibid.*, p.53.
22. *Loc.cit.*
23. *Ibid.*, p.54.
24. 'Black universities — the hard road to freedom', reprinted in J.G.E. Wolfson, *op.cit.*, p.54.
25. See *Black Review*, 1974-75, pp.118-9.
26. *Black Review*, 1972, pp.24-5.
27. Donald Woods, (1978), *Biko*, (Paddington Press), passim.
28. *Black Review*, 1973, pp.180-1, claimed that *Pro Veritate*, journal of the CI, *The South African Outlook*, a journal of the Lovedale Mission, and *Reality*, whose contributors were largely former members of the Liberal Party, 'understood and supported' black consciousness.
29. Thoahlane Thoahlane (Ed.), (1975), *Black Renaissance: Papers from the Black Renaissance Convention*, (Ravan Press, Johannesburg), p.74.
30. *Black Review*, 1974-75, p.134.
31. See Chapter 4.
32. *SRRSA*, 1972, quoting from statements made in July and August, p.38.
33. *SRRSA*, 1971, p.33.
34. *SRRSA*, 1973, p.165.
35. *Ibid.*, p.47.
36. *SRRSA*, 1974, p.3.
37. *Reality*, November 1974.
38. *Black Review*, 1974, pp.178-9.
39. *SRRSA*, 1975, pp.131-2, and David Welsh, 'Inkatha', *Reality*, March 1976.
40. S.M. Bengu, 'The national cultural liberation movement', *Reality*, September 1975.
41. *Ibid.*
42. *Race Relations News*, December 1977, and Jill Wentzel, interview with Dr. Nyembezi and Mr. Mavuso, *Reality*, July 1977.
43. Jill Wentzel, *op.cit.*
44. Foreword to D.A. Kotze, (1975), *African Politics in South Africa 1964-1974: Parties and Issues*, (Hurst), p.ix.
45. Jill Wentzel, *op.cit.*
46. *Ibid.*

PART 2
Workers and Students on the Road to Revolt

7. Black Workers Set the Pace

Black workers in South Africa were obviously discontented in the early 1970's. The long period of industrial peace of 1962-68, when the number of Africans involved in officially reported strikes did not rise above 2,000 a year, came to an end in April 1969 when some two thousand Durban dockers came out on strike. The strike failed and a large proportion of the work force was expelled from the Durban municipal area and replaced by newly recruited workers. The old rate of pay remained, unaltered.[1]

Just over two years later, in September 1971, there was a new threat of industrial action by the Durban stevedores. Demands were made anonymously and no leaders were announced. A wage increase was granted from 1 October, although it was maintained that the management had been considering the rise since May, and had not been influenced by the threat to strike. The stevedores were far from satisfied and, in July 1972, appeared before a Wage Board and asked that the existing minimum weekly wage of R8.50 (£5.50) be raised to at least the poverty datum line of R18. The spokesmen for the workers stated that, if their demands were not met, they would appeal for assistance to their homeland governments.

In October 1972 the Durban dockworkers brought the harbour to a standstill and refused to negotiate. When asked to appoint spokesmen they only replied 'We will be fired'. They did however let it be known that their working hours were too long, their food unfit to eat, their barracks unhygienic, their beer diluted, and that they often worked a seven day week and received no sick pay.

The workers, being predominantly Zulu, appealed to Chief Gatsha Buthelezi for assistance. The KwaZulu government, however, was not prepared to offer any help, and following an ultimatum the stevedores returned to work on 23 October, pending the outcome of the Wage Board's determination.

The following day on 24 October, without any prior warning, African and coloured stevedores at the Cape Town docks stopped work at 5.0 p.m., three hours ahead of time. The stop-at-five strike continued for over a month, and built up a big backlog of cargo waiting to be loaded and unloaded. The men's leaders stated that the action would continue until there were considerable improvements in wages and hours of work.

The Wage Board decisions were made known in November, and minimum wages were raised by approximately 40 per cent. This government body, empowered to recommend minimum wages in occupations not covered by existing wage agreements, had granted one of the highest increases since its inception nearly forty years previously.

The Economic Paradox

This concession to workers who had struck work for at least a brief period, marked a reversal of South Africa's labour relations. Strike action in the past had usually been followed by arrests and deportations, or court appearances. In the 1972 strike, fifteen Durban workers were ultimately dismissed; but the outcome of the strike was seen as a victory and the wage increases, although insufficient, were significant. This was a new departure, and it reflected the ever increasing importance of black labour in the South African economy. Paradoxically, at a time when there was an ever increasing need for more semi-skilled black operatives in industry and commerce, there was a massive growth in the number of black unemployed. The number estimated to have been without work in 1962 had been just over half a million. This had grown to one million by 1970, a million and a half in 1974, and would exceed two million by 1976.[2]

The labour shortage in the docks reflected the position in the country. The staff shortages at the end of 1971, according to the Minister of Transport, included: 1,026 Whites in Durban; 456 Whites and 50 Blacks in Cape Town; 208 Whites and 64 Blacks in Port Elizabeth; and 42 Whites and 24 Blacks in East London.[3] By 'white' vacancies the Minister meant semi-skilled, skilled or supervisory posts; 'black' vacancies, in South African parlance, meant unskilled and some semi-skilled occupations. By 1970 it was becoming obvious that there was very little hope of the 'white' vacancies being filled unless Blacks were allowed to fill them and were trained to do so.

There are few indications that the government knew how to solve the problems of labour shortage at the time. They had, very tentatively, taken steps to alter the school system in order to provide some of the skilled personnel they needed. But even there, the changes were badly planned and inefficiently applied. The more basic changes needed in labour policies – and needed immediately – if the economy were to continue expanding, were not effected. We still lack information on the various solutions that were discussed by the government at the time, but those records that are available suggest that there was considerable confusion over the problems of economic expansion.

The plans that were discussed in the early seventies were based on the supposition that the economy could continue to grow at a rate equal to that achieved in the 1960's when capital poured into the country. Economists spoke of a growth rate in the gross national income of five to seven per cent, and no calculations ever considered the possibility of a recession, or even of a severe cut in the growth rate.

Over and above the failure to consider such possibilities, economic thinking was also predicated on the need, posed in the fifties by the Nationalist Party, for the ratio of Africans to Whites in the towns to be reduced after some fixed date (set at one time as 1978), and that thereafter the number of urban Africans would continue to diminish in absolute terms.

Dr. P.J. Riekert, economic advisor to the Prime Minister, seemed to base his entire plan for the future of South Africa on estimates of jobs that had to be created in and around the Reserves in order to stop the flow of blacks to the 'white' towns.[4] He made elaborate calculations of capital investment needed for job creation to reverse the movement of the black work force. Integral to his master-plan was the proposition that future development of industries in the towns should be capital-intensive, and that all industries built near or in the Reserves be labour-intensive. This, said Dr. Riekert, would simultaneously solve the shortage of skilled (white) personnel and the surplus of unskilled (black) labour.

The government did introduce legislation aimed at reducing the number of unskilled workers that any industry in the urban areas could employ. But Dr. Riekert's plan for labour-intensive industries in the rural areas was rejected because commodities produced under such conditions would not be competitive in the market. New economic developments were delayed by shortages of skilled labour, and vacancies in existing plant could not be filled. It was under these conditions that the government had to find some strategy to overcome the 'shortage' of labour — and in the ensuing period of indecision it became possible for black workers to press their wage demands.

Inflation

There was one other factor which made it possible for workers to press their demands successfully. In 1971 it seemed to many economists that the South African economy was entering an era in which it would expand at a rate which might even exceed the average yearly growth rate of the 1960's. This new optimism followed the decision of the United States to suspend the convertibility of the dollar into gold. The official price of gold was raised from $35 to $46.5 per fine ounce, and governments would henceforth be allowed to sell gold on the open market. Private buyers had always paid a considerably higher price than governments and, from 1971 through to 1974, the price soared to an all time high of $200 per fine ounce. Although the price thereafter was not anywhere near that peak value in 1971, it was rising continuously, and increased state revenue led to an expansionist programme. This in turn led to increased inflation, and the African standard of living declined as a result.

From 1963 to 1971 there was an estimated decline in the value of the Rand of some 24 per cent. This figure, taken from the officially calculated index of retail prices,[5] was based on the expenditure of the 'average white family', and did not reflect the increased cost of living of black families who spent a far higher proportion of income on food. Professor G. Trotter, head of the School of Economics at the University of Natal, reported that, between 1959 and 1971, the household costs of an average African family in Durban increased at almost twice the rate of those of a white family because of rapid increases in food prices. It was no different in the other major urban centres.[6] Black workers therefore had every reason to complain, but had to find effective means whereby they could express their demands.

Workers' Organisations: Old and New

By 1970, however, there were few trade unions to which black workers could turn. The unions which had once existed had been largely destroyed by the government during the mid-sixties. By banning the organisers and secretaries of any trade union which would not collaborate with the government, or appeared to be too militant in its demands, the Minister of Labour bled the unions dry. In 1963 it was reported that many of the black unions affiliated to the South African Congress of Trade Unions (SACTU), one time member of the ANC-dominated Congress Alliance, were being forced out of existence by the banning of their officials, and by the detention of some 35 of their leading members.[7] In 1964 the pressure on the unions was increased. Fifty-two officials and members had been banned by April; offices had been raided and files removed; members had been arrested on a variety of charges, and the journal *Forward* claimed that the government seemed intent on destroying SACTU without formally declaring it an unlawful organisation.[8]

The few unions which were able to survive had broken from SACTU. The National Union of Clothing Workers, the largest of the existing black unions, had left by 1957, and had a long history of collaboration with the government. Its secretary, Lucy Mvubelo, had allowed the government to use her name in appeals for investments in South Africa, and her avowed anti-communism made it easier for her to continue working in her union. Nonetheless the union had no official status, and was able to secure benefits for its members only because of the 'protection' afforded it in negotiations by its 'mother' union — the Garment Workers Union. In the wake of the strike wave of 1973, garment workers were eventually involved in work-stoppages, but the union could not take a lead in pressing members' demands, and the only role it could play was to bring the strikes to a speedy close.[9] When Department of Labour officials intervened in some of the disputes, union officials were (in several cases) pointedly excluded from the negotiations.[10]

Five small African unions had also been established by the African Affairs Section of the all-white Trade Union Council of South Africa (TUCSA), which operated from 1962-68. By 1968 strong internal dissension and government pressure led to the closing of the African Section, and all funds were withdrawn from the five unions. One of these, the Engineering and Allied Workers Union, managed to survive. It was short of funds, lost most of its full-time officials, and was barely able to pay the salaries of the two organisers who remained. Workers' subscriptions covered only the office rental and a funeral-insurance benefit premium. It was only after the union appealed for and obtained the support of the International Metalworkers Federation, that the continued existence of the organisation was assured. [11]

With most formal organisation broken by government action, the workers had to fall back on their own resources, or look to two small groups, the Urban Training Project (UTP) and the Institute for Industrial Education (IIE), which had been set up in 1970 and 1971, and offered some advice and assistance to working-class groups. The crucial factor was that the workers were able to build 'some degree of informal but effective organization', according to Foszia Fisher. In making this claim, she relied on the

> . . . observation of two graduates who have recently worked on construction sites in Natal, who both independently report that there is a relatively tight organisation which controls work pace, informal 'disciplining' of unpleasant supervisors, and also the recruitment process, largely by leaning heavily on unwanted fellow workers. Similarly the experience of union organisers [after 1973] is that it is a question of convincing key individuals in the factory of the importance of the union. [12]

These workers were influenced, or perhaps assisted, by the Industrial Wage and Economic Commissions set up by NUSAS together with the SRCs on some of the campuses, or by the Urban Training Project that was formed by personnel from the former African Affairs Section of TUCSA after 1968.[13] These groups, often consisting of no more than a dozen students, publicised black workers' rights under existing legislation, offered some training in organisational work, or helped groups of workers prepare evidence for meetings of the Wage Boards. [14]

Fozia Fisher denied that the strikes in 1973 were organised by any group from outside the working class, and although she was correct in stressing that the initiative in the strike wave came from the workers inside the factories, it is possible that she underestimated the effect on the workers of the evidence presented by students at Wage Board enquiries. The *Financial Mail* of 28 July 1972 was reported as stating that the student wage commissions:
'. . . represent a "new voice, highly articulate and backed by comprehensive research" '. [15]

The students in the Durban based Wages Commission also broke new ground in September 1972 when they established the General Factory Workers Benefit Fund with the assistance of Harriet Bolton, secretary of the Garment Workers Union in Natal. [16] Amongst the attractions offered by the Benefit Fund were death benefits and medical services for members, and a large number of Africans heard of the Fund when members of the Wages Commission visited factories and distributed their paper *Isisibenzi*. They joined the Benefit Fund and paid monthly contributions.

The Benefit Fund soon widened its scope. Workers started coming to the offices (provided by the Garment Workers Union) on Saturday mornings with grievances about workmen's compensation, unemployment insurance, victimisations, and wage rates. In many respects, the Benefit Fund provided the services of a general workers union, and, in the immediate aftermath of the first strikes in 1973, workers associated with the Fund formed the first African trade unions in Natal since the mid-sixties.[17]

A number of trade unions were also established in Johannesburg with the assistance of the UTP. The influence of this group was evident in the aftermath of a highly successful strike of bus drivers who were employed by the Public Utility Transport Corporation (PUTCO) which operated between the townships and adjacent towns in the Transvaal. In June 1972, some 300 of the strikers in Johannesburg were gaoled — some after demanding that they be taken into custody with those who had previously been arrested. The Attorney-General refused to prosecute the arrested men although they had been charged with participating in an illegal strike, and the employers offered a pay increase of $33^1/_3$ per cent which brought the strike to an end. The defence committee, set up by the drivers during the strike, was converted on the advice of members of the UTP into the Transport Workers and Allied Union.[18] The workers specifically rejected the use of the word 'black' in the name of their union.

Black Consciousness and the Workers

The rejection of the word 'black' by the PUTCO drivers was not altogether typical. Many unions indicated in their names that they were black (or more specifically African). But there were few cases in which the workers seem to have been won to the Black Consciousness Movement. Foszia Fisher, in appraising the groups that influenced the workers, stated that: 'SASO is much less likely [than NUSAS] to have been an influence, since it showed no awareness of specifically worker issues, and had no influence among workers.'[19] Ms. Fisher was in a position to know the attitude of members of the Black Consciousness Movement. She had been a delegate at the Black Renaissance Convention in December 1974 and, together with Harold Nxasana of the Institute for Industrial Education, presented a paper entitled 'The Labour Situation in South Africa'. In it they stated:

> We believe that the growth of 'Black Consciousness' among the black middle classes indicates a growing awareness of the extent to which they have up till now been used as functionaries to keep the system running. They are beginning to realise that the 'Western culture' to which they have been given access is nothing but a set of tools for domination. But 'Black Consciousness' does not as yet seem to have got beyond a simple rejection. And it does not seem to have made a clear analysis of the relation between conquest, discrimination and exploitation.[20]

There were very few members of the BPC who had any connection with trade unionism. Drake Koka, who was employed as an organiser by the Urban

Training Project, described himself as a trade unionist. Bokwe Mafuna, who had once been employed by the TUCSA African Affairs Section, and had been the secretary of the Engineering and Allied Workers Union until TUCSA withdrew and stopped all financial assistance, had resigned from the union 'bitterly disillusioned with broken promises',[21] and later became an organiser for the Black Community Programmes. But organised contact with the working class was slight.

When Koka's involvement in establishing the BPC became known to the Urban Training Project, the project's executive — containing both black and white members — decided unanimously that politics should be kept out of the organisation. The executive of the UTP had obviously brought from TUCSA a strong bias against politicisation of trade unions together with the belief that funding of the project (both in South Africa and from abroad) would be made difficult if political interests were displayed by its employees.

L. Douwes Dekker, one of the authors of a long review on the new trade unions and the strike wave of the early 1970's, had been employed by TUCSA as its assistant general secretary, and had left after the closing of the African Section.[22] In this review article it was claimed that the new awareness of the value of unions possibly lay 'in the stirrings of a "black consciousness" movement . . . which emphasises the need for independent black organisations.'[23] Quite inconsistently, however, the authors then said that the eventual failure of Koka's union and the government's action in banning him, '. . . reflected both the dangers inherent in black militancy and the fact that militants do not command a great deal of support from among African trade unionists, if partly for tactical reasons.'[24]

There may have been faults in the projects undertaken by Drake Koka, but nothing that he proposed or organised could be described as 'militant'. Nor was there any indication that the workers (as distinct from trade unionists or members of the Urban Training Project) were averse to militants or to militancy.

In June 1971, Koka and members of the BPC announced the formation of the Sales and Allied Workers Union, which aimed at organising salesmen and hawkers. It is not certain what services they offered their members, but they did not seem to make much progress. Koka, however, was able to use a meeting, summoned in the name of his union, to launch a general workers union in August 1972. This body, known as the Black Allied Workers' Union (BAWU), was henceforth to be the centre of BPC trade union activity until Koka was banned some seven months later. The Sales and Allied Workers Union seems to have continued (at least in name) although there is no indication of any trade union activity on behalf of its members.[25]

In a report in *Black Review* 1972, it appears as if the decision to form BAWU was a spontaneous outcome of the meeting called that day,[26] but there are indications that it had been planned beforehand. A decision to form some general workers body was approved by a SASO conference the preceding month, and the objects of that organisation, which was called a Black Workers Council (BWC), were almost identical in wording with the resolution accepted by the newly launched BAWU. The Black Workers Council's objects were:

> to act as a co-ordinating body to serve the needs and aspirations of black workers;
> to unite and bring about solidarity of black workers;
> to conscientise them about their role and obligation toward black development;
> to run clinics for leadership, in-service training and imbue them with pride and self-confidence as people and about their potential as workers.[27]

The BAWU had as its aims:

> to organise and unite all black workers into a powerful labour force that would earn the respect and de facto recognition by both employers and government;
> to consult existing trade unions to effect the calling of a Black Workers Conference where the Black Workers Council shall be elected;
> to improve the workers' knowledge through general and specialised (occupational) educational programmes, thus bettering workers' skills and know-how by conducting: (a) leadership courses; (b) labour seminars; (c) lectures and specialised commercial courses.[28]

The BAWU, furthermore, estimated that it would need the sum of R30,000 per year for 'sound administration'. SASO also estimated that it would require just over R30,000 per year for five years to set up the Black Workers Council and an associated Black Workers Project which would work towards the Council, by organising African workers into committees and unions. The details of the Project and of the Council, together with the budget and an outline of the aims, were sent to a number of bodies including the IUEF, and it is from the latter source that details are available.[29]

Besides acting as a trade union, the BWC was to train black workers in the skills of their jobs 'in consultation with the management' (*sic*); to offer literacy classes; and 'facilities and amenities for relaxation and creative occupation'. Far from being 'militant' as suggested by Douwes Dekker *et al.*, the programme was reformist and even collaborationist. The programme suggested for migrant workers would have pleased the most hardened employer:

> The absence of family life is very depressing. Recreational programmes will then be arranged to employ the workers creatively in their leisure time. Representations can be made about workers' problems about housing, transportation etc, which all affect the productivity of the black worker.[30]

Even literacy classes could be interpreted as being of value to the employer:

[Workers] are preparing to acquire school certificates which will put them in good stead for promotion. Arrangements can be made with volunteer students to assist with tuition and arrange vacation classes. Improvement in learning will imbue them with self-confidence and ambition.[31]

The Black Workers Project and BAWU were unable to persuade existing unions to join them in their attempted Black Workers Conference, and BAWU did not recruit many workers to a broad general workers union. Despite the claim that 'western elements of trade unionism . . . had to be modified' in order to handle the problems of housing, transport, pass and curfew laws, and illiteracy,[32] there was no indication of how the general workers union was going to act as both a trade union and as a social and political organisation. The workers did not seem to believe that there was any benefit to be derived from joining BAWU.

Foszia Fisher seems to have been correct: SASO 'had no influence among workers'. But Gatsha Buthelezi did!

Although Buthelezi has been received with a certain amount of suspicion among the black intelligentsia, he has enjoyed large, but perhaps varying popularity among the mass of Zulu workers. The fact that he has been attacking government policy was widely known, and probably improved the morale of workers.[33]

Nonetheless, Ms. Fisher reiterated her point, made earlier, that these influences only affected the strikes, but cannot explain their occurrence.

The Strike in Namibia, 1971

In December 1971 in Namibia (South West Africa), the Ovambo workers, followed by other black workers, struck work and brought the economic life of the territory to a standstill. This action undoubtedly influenced South African workers. Events in Namibia were prominently featured in the South African press, and the strike was the talking point of workers in townships, hostels and factories.

The situation in Namibia had been explosive for many years. Pressure from the United Nations had seemingly been brushed aside by the South African government, and plans to divide the country into 'Homelands' had been relentlessly pursued. The struggle for independence, led by the South West African Peoples Organisation (SWAPO), also seemed to have been contained after the first armed attack, launched in 1966, had been repulsed. But beneath the apparent calm, there was widespread discontent. The 'Homelands' policy, the educational system, low wages, and the contract system run by the South West African Native Labour Association (SWANLA), all caused resentment.

During the last half of 1971 there were widespread protests and

130

demonstrations in Namibia sparked off by the advisory opinion of the
International Court of Justice. On 21 June 1971, the Court declared that:
'. . . the continued presence of South Africa in Namibia being illegal, South
Africa is under obligation to withdraw its administration from Namibia
immediately and thus put an end to its occupation of the territory.'[34] In the
wake of the Court decision churchmen wrote letters to Prime Minister Vorster
and pastoral letters to their congregations, calling on South Africa to withdraw her administration. There were protest meetings addressed by local
leaders, demonstrations in schools and training colleges, and boycotts of some
school assemblies. There were anti-government demonstrations at the
Ougwediva Training Institution for Teachers and Trades, leading to a closure
of the college and the expulsion of a large number of the students. At other
schools there were demonstrations against the use of Afrikaans as a medium
of instruction, followed by the inevitable expulsions.[35]

One of the major sources of complaint in Namibia was the contract
labour system. Workers were recruited in the Reserves for fixed periods of
time (usually 12 or 18 months), at rates of pay that ranged from R10 per
month for mine labourers, R9.75 for farm labourers, to R3.75 for *picannins*
(children under 18). It was reported that some employers paid more than the
minimum prescribed rate, but the average wage was some R20 per month.
Only males were recruited and they were housed in 'bachelor' quarters in the
townships, or in compounds near the mines. They could not take their
dependents with them, and an ordinance of January 1970 prohibited wives
residing with their husbands in Katatura outside the capital, Windhoek, unless
they had been born there or had lived in the township for at least 10 years
and been in continuous employment. The contracts expressly prohibited
strike action, and made the breaking of the contract a punishable offence.
The worker, however, was not free to choose his employer, and was assigned
to his place of work by SWANLA after being graded according to physical
fitness and age.[36]

Discontent was also endemic in the townships. In June 1971, the men in
Katatura had been angered when riot police raided the township in a search
for illegal residents and arrested more than 500 men. In November, the
workers rioted against the proposed erection of guard towers.[37]

Towards the end of the year church leaders met the Commissioner-General
of the Native People of South West Africa, Jan M. de Wet, and drew his
attention to the mounting resentment against the contract labour system.
De Wet denied allegations that the system was akin to slavery, and claimed
that the Ovambo people accepted the system voluntarily and did not have to
sign the contracts. In early December, more than 3,000 Ovambo workers met
in Walvis Bay (Namibia's only port) and demanded an end to the system,
freedom of travel, higher pay, and the right to choose employment. If their
demands were not met they wished to be repatriated, or they would strike
from 14 December. They also decided to write to workers in other townships.
In the letter to Katatura they said:

We are having problems with the white man J. de Wet. You are having
similar problems. He said we ourselves want to be on contract, because
we come to work. But we must talk about ending the system. We in Walvis
Bay discussed it. We wrote a letter to the government of Ovamboland and
to SWANLA. We will not come back. We will leave Walvis Bay and the
contract, and will stay at home as the Boer J. de Wet said.[38]

The men in Walvis Bay formed a committee and their first step was to
demonstrate their rejection of the contracts. They handed in their papers, and
police who had been moved into the town rounded them up and repatriated
them to Owambo. News of the impending strike had been widely publicised
in the press, and the men at Katatura met on Sunday 12 December and
resolved to strike the following day. On the Monday 5,500 workers refused to
leave the township which was then sealed off by the police. When the workers
rejected appeals by headmen, specially flown in from Owambo to speak to them,
they too were repatriated – at their own request.[39] Within a week all work
had stopped at the Klein Aub and Oamites copper mines, the Berg Aukas lead
and vanadium mines, the Uis tin mines and the copper, lead, and zinc mines at
Tsumeb.

By 20 December 12,000 workers were out on strike in a dozen centres,
and most were repatriated. This did not bring the campaign to an end, and by
mid-January 1972 there were over 13,00 men out on strike. Early in January
the strikers elected a committee with Johannes Nangutuula as chairman, and
it was this committee that formulated a set of demands and issued strike leaflets. The committee rejected the government plan to refurbish the contract
system by handing over its operation to the headmen, and in its stead
demanded: freedom to choose their jobs; the right to have their families with
them; the rate for the job, irrespective of colour; an end to the pass-book;
removal of the police post at the Owambo boundary; and mutual respect
between bosses and workers.[40]

The strike lasted for over a month, and the workers returned on the understanding that the contract system had been scrapped, the SWANLA disbanded
and that workers would be free to leave employers and find new positions
without first being repatriated. The workers even achieved marginally better
wages in many cases. It was soon found, however, that controls on movements of workers had not been relaxed and that there were few possibilities
of changing employers or of moving from one form of employment to
another.

Despite this reverse for the Ovambo people, in South Africa the strike was
seen as a success for the workers and a blow for the authorities. One commentator said of its effect that:

What [the strike] has done is to show South Africa and the white
residents in Namibia that action against them is not confined to guerrilla
actions in Caprivi and Kavongo, or to paper opposition at the UN.
    The contract labourers too have shown a voice and a will . . . they too

will seek to express the will of Namibia as the next stage on the long road to nationhood is reached.[41]

The Ovambo strike had also shown the South African workers that strike action was possible and that concessions could be forced out of the ruling class. The widespread publicity that the strike achieved in the South African press took this message home to workers in the townships and hostels. Despite themselves the newspapers acted as carriers of a message that was bound to be discussed and thought about in the coming year and, when finally workers did decide on strike action, information about the events in Namibia could only strengthen them in their resolve to take action.

Natal Workers on Strike, 1973

From January 1973 to mid-1976, over 200,000 black workers struck work in South Africa. The overwhelming majority were African, but sizeable numbers of Coloureds and Indians were also involved. This was the most extensive strike wave since the early days of the second world war, and affected most of the main urban centres. The strikes started in Durban and for most of the period continued to affect industries in this region. In the first three months of the strikes, workers walked out of 146 establishments on 160 occasions in the Durban-Pinetown-Hammarsdale complex. More comprehensive figures released by the Minister of Labour showed that between June 1972 and June 1974 there were 22 work stoppages involving 78,216 workers in Natal, and that in the next nine months there were a further 68 stoppages in the Province involving 12,051 workers.[42]

Durban-Pinetown is the second largest industrial area in South Africa, and is surpassed only by the Witwatersrand complex. It has an African population of nearly 1,000,000, and some 200,000 are employed in industry. The workers live in segregated townships outside Durban and the nearby Pinetown/New Germany area. Hammarsdale is about 25 miles west of Durban and is adjacent to a Reserve. There were some 14 clothing and textile firms in the town, and workers employed there were paid less than their fellows in the main urban centres.[43]

There was large-scale unemployment in the region as men streamed from the Reserves into the urban areas in the hopes of obtaining work. In the circumstances, many firms paid wages that were well below the officially calculated Poverty Datum Line. In 1970 the Natal University Social Research Department had found that 85 per cent of all African families in the industrial complex were living in poverty.[44] Since that survey the cost of living had risen sharply without a corresponding rise in wages, and by the close of 1972 many families were in dire straits. Nonetheless most observers noted that in 1973 wages in Durban-Pinetown were no worse than those paid in other areas, and were appreciably better than some.

Workers in the area had been restless for some time, and the dockers had

struck work in 1969 and in 1972. They were equally restless in other industries. Officials of registered (non-African) trade unions in both the textile and
garment industries had warned managers in mills and factories over several
months that the workers were discontented and that strikes were in the
offing. Officials of the Garment Workers Union were in contact with the
General Factory Workers Benefit Fund, and fully aware of the extent of
workers' dissatisfaction. The employers were, however, uncompromising and
trade union officials were rebuffed.[45] There was obviously good reason for
the workers to take action in Durban-Pinetown, but no more so than in the
rest of the country and, in the first instance, the question that must be asked,
is not why the strikes took place, but why they started in Durban rather than
elsewhere.

The question 'Why Durban?' was posed by Gerhard Maré in a paper
presented at a symposium on *Labour organisation and the Africans*, in March
1974. Maré had been one of the main contributors, together with Foszia
Fisher, to the Institute for Industrial Education (IIE) publication *The Durban
Strikes, 1973*, and his answer to the problem was:

> The first factor was the initial strike at Coronation Brick and Tile
> [Company]. The second factor was the existence in Durban, strategically
> placed in each of the industrial areas, of a number of factories belonging
> to one organisation [the Frame Textile group] characterised by particularly
> low wages and bad labour relations. The third factor was the rise in
> transport costs and then the rumoured train boycott. The first rumour
> was only heard on the 27th January but it was only after that that the
> strikes really picked up.[46]

The three factors detailed by Maré affected the workers in entirely different
ways, and each needs to be examined in some detail. The first, relating to the
initial strike on 9 January 1973 at the Coronation Brick and Tile Company,
involved some features which were unique to Natal and will be considered
first.

The Strike at Coronation Brick and Tile
In the booklet, *The Durban Strikes, 1973*, it was asserted that the strike at
Coronation Brick '. . . seems to have been connected in some way with the
visit of Prince Goodwill to the factory.'[47] Two other claims were made.
Firstly, that the strike received widespread publicity because the work force
was so large; because workers marched through the streets to attend a
meeting; and because they did gain a wage increase. Secondly, that there
would have been no major strike in the textile plants if it had not been for
the Coronation Brick and Tile strike.[48]

The reasons for the strike are fairly clearcut. The workers demanded an
increase in the minimum wage rate from R8.97 to R20.00 per week. Some of
the workers were also aware of the fact that an enquiry into the industry had
been conducted nearly a year earlier by the Wage Board, and that the Durban

Students' Wages Commission had presented evidence at the hearing. The long delay in announcing an increase made those workers decide on direct action.[49]

The one additional factor which set Coronation Brick and Tile apart from other establishments lay in the fact that the Paramount Chief (or King) of the AmaZulu, Goodwill Zwelithini ka Bhekuzulu had visited the factory in the latter part of 1972 and delivered an address to the assembled workers. It was reported that there was some ambivalence in the King's message, and it was not clear whether he had indicated that the management had agreed to raise wages, or whether he had expressed a willingness to negotiate on their behalf.[50] Although there was nothing exceptional in the King addressing meetings of workers, there was no precedent for a direct intervention on matters pertaining to wages or working conditions.

Gatsha Buthelezi, Chief Executive Officer of KwaZulu, had made a number of pronouncements on wages and on the need for African trade unions, but had pointedly refused to come to the dockworkers' assistance in 1972, despite their appeal to him for assistance.[51] The appearance of King Goodwill at the Coronation Brick and Tile Company, and his intervention on the wage front, was perhaps not as disinterested as it appeared, and must be seen in the light of the deep conflict between some of the traditional leaders and the Chief Executive Officer.

Gatsha Buthelezi and his supporters had not willingly accepted the government's 'Homelands' policy, and he had been in open conflict with the then recently installed Regent Paramount Chief, Israel Mcwayizeni, who in 1969 had declared that he planned to set up a territorial authority in terms of the Bantu Authorities Act (i.e. that he was taking the first step towards accepting the apartheid plan for the Zulu).[52]

Buthelezi was unable to stop the Regent, and in April 1970 a Territorial Authority was established. On 9 June Buthelezi was elected Chief Executive Officer by a meeting of his peers.[53] It was traditional for the head of the Buthelezi tribe to inherit the role of Prime Minister to the Zulu king, and Buthelezi accepted office. He then called for the implementation of government policy with all possible speed.[54] Nevertheless, Buthelezi remained an outspoken critic of the government, and there were continued attempts to replace him by a chief more amenable to official policy. The Regent had been the centre of opposition to Buthelezi and had the support of the South African government. Consequently, when Prince Goodwill was installed as Paramount Chief in December 1971, the chiefs sought to neutralize him politically. In future, the King was told, he should hold himself aloof from party politics, and he should be represented in the Legislative Assembly by a personal nominee.[55]

Under the new constitution of KwaZulu, the chiefs retained traditional powers in ceremonial and tribal matters, and the Paramount Chief would 'personify the unity of the Zulu nation'. He also took precedence over the Chief Executive Officer on all matters except those dealt with by the Legislative Assembly.[56] The King also had the services of the traditional Royal Council. This created two centres of power in KwaZulu — one grouped around l the Royal House and the Royal Council and given legitimacy by tradition; the other situated in the Legislative Assembly which had yet to establish its authority. Furthermore, the South African government hoped to merge the two power centres and place the King's men in control of the Legislative Assembly. In these circumstances, every move of the King was seen by Buthelezi to be part of the struggle for power.

On 8 January 1973, the management of the Coronation Brick and Tile Company heard that there was an impending strike. They issued a statement accusing 'communists' of fomenting the strike, and threatening 'ringleaders' with 'severe punishment'.[57] The management's attitude swung even the doubters behind the existing informal organisation and, on 9 January, almost the entire workforce of 2,000 assembled at the football stadium. When told by the management to elect a committee, one worker responded: 'Our terms are quite clear. We don't need a committee. We need R30.00 a week'.[58]

There was deadlock, and it was only the intervention of King Goodwill on the 10th that persuaded the workers — albeit reluctantly — to allow him to negotiate with the management on their behalf.[59]

The workers had only agreed to the King's proposal after his representative, Prince Sithela Zulu, stated '. . . that if they could not trust in the Chief's word, this would "lower the dignity" '.[60] This was little other than a reprimand and the workers, who had earlier expressed their fear that they might lose the initiative if they agreed to negotiate, were forced to retreat. Buthelezi, on the other hand, seized on the appeal not to 'lower the dignity', and he was said to have 'advised' the King not to become embroiled in controversial issues which could tarnish the image of the Royal House. The King gave way to this pressure and did not meet the management as arranged. As the workers had feared, they had lost the initiative, and some talks were held between one of the men's leaders and management. Eventually the workers returned to work after grudgingly accepting a R2.07 rise in the weekly wage.[61]

The workers had not gained very much from the intervention of the KwaZulu leaders. It could even be asserted that the King had undermined the solidarity and determination of the workers, and that Buthelezi had turned his back on the strikers. The King and Buthelezi had been locked in a power struggle, and the workers' claims had been used by one of the tribal contenders for his own purposes. When Buthelezi demanded that the King withdraw, the workers were abandoned.

It is not clear, however, whether the workers in Durban-Pinetown were aware of the motives surrounding the King's actions. For many of them the crucial factor consisted of the King's intervention, and the possibility that the KwaZulu leaders would back their claim to wage increases. Irrespective of any other considerations, the workers at Coronation Brick and Tile *had* won higher wages.

Only further research will reveal the full impact of the KwaZulu dignitaries on subsequent events. This will have to unravel the effects of the recent inauguration of the King and the celebration of King Shaka Day as a national holiday in KwaZulu on 24 September (following an enactment in Parliament).

In like manner it will be necessary to discover the full effects of Buthelezi's outspoken criticism of the South African government's policies. Nevertheless there is some evidence which shows that the workers (or at least a large proportion of them) were responding to an incipient Zulu nationalism. The main slogan chanted by the workers as they marched or gathered at meetings was the traditional Zulu warcry *Usuthu*. Once a warcry associated with the Zulu King, it had become a chant that was associated with Zulu loyalty.[62]

The warcry, *Usuthu*, used throughout the strikes in Durban was also accompanied by other slogans which seem to indicate that the Durban workers associated themselves with the leaders of KwaZulu. It was reported in *Black Review* that, in the very next large strike, at four textile works in Natal, the workers were also chanting: 'We are now a united nation'.[63] The implication in *Black Review* was that this referred to a united African nation; but, coupled with the use of *Usuthu*, it seems more likely that the reference was to a united Zulu nation. The king, however, took no further part in the strikes and KwaZulu Councillors stayed in the background. When one of them, Barney Dladla, intervened in mid-March 1973, he introduced a new and significant element into the strikes. By then the strike wave had spread and involved thousands of workers.

The Textile Workers Strike

It was events in the textile industry which transformed the entire industrial scene, and it was in one firm in particular that the struggle turned out to be particularly bitter. Starting at the Frame Group of textile factories on 25 January, and initially involving 7,000 workers, the strikes spread throughout Natal, and were extended into the other provinces bringing out thousands of Africans, and with them Coloureds and Indians, in the Transvaal and the Eastern Cape.

Always starting at a factory or group of plants inside an industry, the workers poured into the streets and there influenced their fellows in what can be described as a 'multiplier effect'. This was graphically described as follows by L. Douwes Dekker, *et al*:

> The first factories to be affected were those with the worst conditions, but once the step had been taken by one group of African workers, the strikes spread by force of example. Whole streets would be affected . . . start[ing] in the lowest paying factory on the street, engulfing in the process a firm . . . where wages were considerably higher . . . Picketing and incitement is illegal in South Africa but much the same effect was gained by the presence of thousands of workers pouring out of factories and moving *en masse* down past neighbouring concerns chanting the old war cry of the Zulu armies, *Usuthu*.[64]

In hostels, compounds, buses and trains, in beer halls and in the townships, the workers discussed the strikes. Lacking formal trade union structures, they developed an inter-firm, inter-industry solidarity. They were conscious of their strength in the precincts of the factories, and even during the most bitter strikes they never stayed at home. They also turned their weakness into a source of strength. They refused to appoint spokesmen and would not elect committees, and thus avoided the possibility of victimisation. Faced by an acephalous body of strikers the police made random arrests, but the informal organisation remained intact.

On 25 January 1973, just two weeks after the Coronation Brick and Tile strike, textile workers employed in the giant Frame Group walked out at the Frametex factory in New Germany, near Pinetown. They claimed that they were being paid an average of R5.00 to R 9.00 per week, and they demanded R20.00. They were joined by workers of all the Frame Group factories in the area, and some 6,000 Africans were affected, as well as Indian workers.[65]

At this stage the workers were unintentionally assisted by the media and the employers. On 27 January there were widespread rumours of a boycott of all transport, and this received extensive press coverage. Firms made pre-parations for workers to sleep on the premises, and Durban Corporation waived curfew regulations and allowed all Africans to be in the 'white' areas between 11.30 p.m. and 4.0 a.m. The police moved heavy reserves into the townships in a show of strength. But there was no boycott and the workers had no intention of staying away from the factories.

The strikes had, in the process, been well publicised. On 29 January some 2,000 workers stopped work and demanded higher wages in four industrial areas in the Durban-Pinetown region. Another 3,000 workers came out the following day in three factories. And in the next three days over 35 more factories experienced stoppages, mostly in Durban, but also in Newcastle, East London (where some Coloured workers joined the Africans in their strike) and Boksburg in the Transvaal.

The strikes now covered a large number of industries, including sugar mills, canvas works, concrete pipes, transport, rubber works, engineering, construc-tion, clothes, food and plastics. But the largest and the most extended strikes were in the textile factories.[66] There were 41 textile units in Natal, and each one experienced one or more work stoppages. In some factories, as for example the Consolidated Textile Mills in Durban, the entire staff of 2,600 were dismissed. Workers of adjoining textile plants immediately joined the strikers.[67]

The textile workers in East London had demanded wage increases before their Durban colleagues and some 50 workers had stopped work at the Consolidated Fine Spinners and Weavers on 19 January. This rose to 1,000 four days later and to 2,000 by the end of the month.[68]

One further factor marked the textile workers' action as different from that of most other strikers. The registered union that represented the interests of Indian and Coloured workers, the Textile Workers Industrial Union, inter-vened and played a part in negotiations with the employers. They persuaded the workers to accept wage increases which were as low as R1.75 to R2.50 per week. Thereafter, however, the management bypassed and ignored the union officials.[69]

There were few other cases of workers having support from trade unions or their officials — neither from the few African unions, nor from the registered unions which organised white, Coloured, or Indian workers. Most of them were on their own, and the strength they drew on was the solidarity in the factory and the action of surrounding factories. Some workers, however, were isolated and dispersed by the nature of their employment. For example, on 5 February it was reported that a go-slow organised by 145 bus drivers employed by the Johannesburg City Council since 24 January would be converted into an all out strike, and this led to a compromise agreement. On 6 February a strike of some 3,000 black workers employed by the Durban Corporation brought public work to a halt. Very soon, some 16,000 municipal workers were out. The abattoirs were closed; food was handled by volunteers and drafted policemen; gravediggers decamped; rubbish piled up on the sidewalks. It seemed as if a general strike in Durban was in the offing when the workers accepted a 15 per cent pay rise on 9 February.

By 5 February 30,000 workers were on strike in Durban-Pinetown, 7,000 were out in Hammarsdale, and smaller numbers in other centres. But the workers could not stay out. There were no personal savings and no organisation to provide strike pay. Many stoppages only lasted a few hours; some lasted a day or two; and few were sustained for longer periods. Only in the textile industry were they more protracted. One lasted seven days; five lasted six days; three lasted four days; others were of shorter duration.

Indian workers joined in the strike, and although they were generally permitted by legislation to partake in strikes, in this instance they broke the ban on industrial action in municipal corporations.[70] In general Indian workers joined or encouraged African workers in their action and needed little persuasion to stop work whenever strikes were called.

There were over 60 strikes in February. By the end of this short period over 40,000 workers had been involved in stoppages or strikes, most of which had taken place in the Durban complex. There was, however, no discernible pattern, other than the obvious fact that in some districts groups of factories came out together. In Johannesburg the strikes were apparently disconnected and affected only small firms. The randomness of the action was a clear indication of the total lack of organisation and direction, and a clear sign that subterranean dissatisfaction had risen to the surface and overflowed. Nevertheless, the press publicity and the growing knowledge that workers were on the move throughout the country led to increasingly militant action. One strike near Mandini in Zululand reflected this growing determination of men (and in this case their families) to gain improvements. In the process members of the KwaZulu government were brought into the strikes and this raised afresh the relationship between the leaders of the 'Homelands' and the workers. It also brought internal struggles in the KwaZulu cabinet to the fore, and this affected, and was in turn affected by, the workers' struggles.

The Intervention of Barney Dladla

On 12 March 1973 a thousand workers stopped work at the giant Tugela mills of the South African Pulp and Paper Industries Ltd (SAPPI). The state had a substantial financial interest in SAPPI and this made any potential confrontation different from preceding strikes. The striking workers, encouraged by chanting women, set up roadblocks in Mandini and smashed the windows of buses in the township. Then thousands of men and women gathered on the outskirts of the township and started bushfires at the approaches to the mill. By the end of the first day, all 2,000 workers were on strike and police in armoured cars stood by.

On 14 March the strike came to a precipitate end after Barney Dladla, Executive Councillor for Community Affairs in KwaZulu, addressed the workers, and said that after meeting the mill management there had been an offer of an extra R2.44 per week. There was tumultuous applause and the workers returned to work.[71]

For a period of just over a year Barney Dladla figured prominently in news reports on the strikes. He intervened at a strike in Richards Bay and warned the employers that he would cut off their labour supply. He was reported as having said on 30 March:

> This is now a challenge to prove whether KwaZulu is a government or not.
> If these people are employed by this firm without my approval, it would be clear that we are not a government at all.[72]

The 500 workers at the Alusaf aluminium smelting plant, who had refused to accept a R2.00 per week wage increase, rejected an ultimatum to return to work and claimed that they wanted Dladla to represent them. But the management, which had used army trainees as scab labour, was immovable. They refused at first to meet Dladla on the grounds that the issue concerned labour matters in South Africa and not KwaZulu, and when they did grant him an interview, dismissed his appeal. On 2 April, after being out for just over a week, the workers accepted the R2.00.[73]

For a while Dladla was quiescent, but his reappearance was only a matter of time. It was stated in *Black Review*, 1973, that Dladla was a member of the Institute for Industrial Education, and it was also quite certain that he had the support of Buthelezi in his stand at Richards Bay.[74] His opportunity for intervening again seemed most propitious at the end of January 1974. A strike at Pinetex Mill (a member of the Frame Group at New Germany) involving 1,200 workers spread to 10 textile factories in the area. On the second day of the strike, Dladla marched at the head of between 5,000 and 10,000 striking workers to the main Frame Group textile mill in New Germany, and then conducted negotiations on their behalf. Together with Halton Cheadle, a trade unionist who was to be banned the following week, he addressed the workers and announced a wage increase.[75]

During this period, events had been moving fast in KwaZulu. Chief C. Hlengwa, formerly chairman of the Legislative Assembly, had resigned that post in order to launch a new movement known as Umkhonto ka Shaka (Shaka's Spear) at the end of October 1973. The movement, which had the backing of the South African government, was formed in order to restore political executive powers to the Zulu king.[76] Buthelezi was able to secure the dismissal of Hlengwa from the Legislative Assembly, and the King disowned the new movement.

There were also warnings from government officials and ministers against meddling in labour matters outside KwaZulu. Senator Owen Horwood (a member of the Cabinet) had issued a warning to Buthelezi in 1973,[77] and this was repeated in the months that followed. In September 1974 a pointed communique from the Secretary for Bantu Administration again warned the KwaZulu government against interceding on behalf of Zulu workers in labour disputes in 'white' South Africa. The reply from the KwaZulu government was defiant:

> We cannot see ourselves turning a deaf ear to any pleas from our people for intercession as our people have no proper machinery for negotiation and we cannot be insensitive to any alleged exploitation of our people.[78]

Dladla meanwhile had been silenced. He was accused of not having consulted the cabinet before intervening in the strikes. The Legislative Assembly said that he had exceeded his prerogatives and that it was the task of the KwaZulu urban representative to represent the workers. Dladla was first moved to the Justice portfolio and then removed from the Legislative Assembly in August 1974.[79]

The debate between Buthelezi and Dladla had been bitter. When he was still a member of the executive Dladla was reported to have said that Buthelezi was a dictator; that he did not communicate with his people; and that, furthermore, he was trying to attract overseas investors by claiming, falsely, that the country's labour force was stable.[80]

Buthelezi's attitude to trade unions was made explicit in an article in September 1974. He maintained there that his government was embarrassed from time to time by its involvement in labour disputes: the KwaZulu government, however, could not abandon its people. Two statements in the report summed up the Chief's attitude to the unions and to strikes:

> Even though we do not share adequately the fruits of the economy, we are the last people to want to destroy the economy of South Africa.
> I do not believe for a moment that the trade unions are instruments for organising strikes. I regard them as machinery for negotiation.[81]

In the light of this it seems that the earlier reply to the government expressed the frustration felt by Buthelezi's government. They had no desire to support strikes, but they also had to have an answer for the workers who appealed to them. They asserted their right to intervene, if and when they desired. By dismissing Barney Dladla they assured the government that they did not so desire.

The Organisation of Trade Unions

In the aftermath of the first strikes in January and February 1973, African trade unions were re-established in Natal. Branches of the Metal and Allied Workers Union were organised in May in Pietermaritzburg, and in June in Durban. In August the National Union of Textile Workers was launched, and shortly thereafter the Union of Clothing and Allied Workers was established.

> In the initial periods all the unions received financial and material support from the Garment Workers Union, the Benefit Fund and NUSAS. The unions in turn strengthened the Fund by their affiliation and their members were covered by the benefits of the Fund. Rent-free offices for the unions were provided in the Garment Workers Union building as well as office equipment and the free use of telephones.[82]

Organising the trade unions was far from easy. The government was determined to render all attempts at organisation ineffective, and leading young organisers were removed by banning. On 2 February 1974 Halton Cheadle, organiser for the South African Textile Workers Industrial Union; David Davis, administrative officer for the General Factory Workers Benefit Fund; David Hemson, the Textile Workers Industrial Union research officer; and Jeannette Cunningham Brown, assistant secretary of the Union in Durban, were banned. In 1976 a further 18 persons connected with the Urban Training Project, the Institute for Industrial Education, the university students' Wages Commissions, and officials of African trade unions were banned.[83]

It was claimed that 22 unions had been started by mid-1974 and that over 30,000 workers had been enrolled. Most of the workers in the unions also belonged to the Benefit Fund.[84]

One consequence of union formation was the appearance of disputes with management over recognition. In March 1974 the workers were in dispute at the Mobeni plant over the demand that the Metal and Allied Workers Union be recognised. A two day strike was followed by the dismissal of the work force of 220 Africans. The management then re-employed 155 of the old staff, and agreed to consult union representatives, provided they were employed at the plant. Inevitably, there was further victimisation five months later when the management again dismissed men deemed to be too militant.[85]

Nonetheless, very few workers joined trade unions, and in 1974 no more than eight per cent of the Durban African work force had been enrolled.[86] In other areas it was appreciably less. This reflected in part the fact that workers had found a means for conducting struggles and felt no need to join a formal organisation in order to take collective action. This represented a high degree of awareness on their part — as was shown by their consistent refusal to elect representatives, their statements that no negotiations were necessary and all that was required was that the wages be increased, and their complete solidarity in all action that was undertaken. At a later stage, however, the lack of formal organisation was to be a weakness, and the need to alter course and transform their economic struggle into a political struggle could not be met. In fact, political strikes were later called by the youth of Soweto, in August and September 1976, but for reasons not directly connected with the demands of workers. The disjunction of purpose by youth and workers when those political stoppages were proposed meant that the struggle could not advance to a higher level. It is just feasible that a well organised working class would have joined the calls to stay at home in 1976, but there was little organisation and the workers of Natal remained outside the orbit of the Revolt.

References

1. See Institute for Industrial Education (1976), *The Durban Strikes, 1973,* (Ravan Press, Johannesburg), p.5. Accounts of the strikes and action that followed are taken from *SRRSA*, 1971, p.247; and *SRRSA*, 1972, pp.325-8.
2. Estimates in *Financial Mail*, 16 July 1976.
3. *SRRSA*, 1972, p.318.
4. P.J. Riekert, *op.cit.*
5. D. Hobart Houghton, *op.cit.*, p.278.
6. Reported in the *Star*, 6 September 1975. See also F.P. Spooner, (1960), *South African Predicament*, (Cape), p.282.
7. *SRRSA*, 1963, p.215.
8. Quoted in *SRRSA*, 1964, p.265.
9. L. Douwes Dekker, D. Hemson, J.S. Kane-Berman, J. Lever, and L. Schlemmer, (1975), 'Case studies in African labour action in South Africa and Namibia', in R. Sandbrook and R. Cohen, (Eds.), *The Development of an African Working Class*, (Longmans), p.218.
10. *Loc.cit.*
11. Jane Hlongwane, (1976), 'Emergence of African unions in Johannesburg with reference to the Engineering Union', in J.A. Grey Coetzee, *Industrial Relations in South Africa*, (Juta, Cape Town), pp.206-7.
12. Foszia Fisher, (1974), 'Class consciousness among colonized workers in South Africa', reprinted in T. Adler, (Ed.), (1977), *Perspectives on South Africa*, (University of the Witwatersrand, Johannesburg), p.333.
13. *SRRSA*, 1972, pp.243-6.
14. Dekker *et al.*, *op.cit.*, p.218, and *SRRSA*, 1972, pp.243-6.
15. *SRRSA*, 1972, p.245.
16. David Davis, 'How black workers are organising', *Anti-Apartheid News*,

October 1974.

17.   *Loc.cit.*
18.   Dekker, *et.al.*, *op.cit.*, pp.219-20.
19.   F. Fisher, *op.cit.*, p.331.
20.   In Thoahlane Thoahlane, (1975), *Black Renaissance: Papers from the Black Renaissance Convention, December 1974*, (Ravan Press), pp.55-6.
21.   J. Hlongwane, *op.cit.*, p.206.
22.   See brief biography of L. Douwes Dekker in Grey Coetzee, *op.cit.*, p.204.
23.   Dekker *et al.*, *op.cit.*, p.218.
24.   *Ibid.*, p.219.
25.   *Black Review*, 1972, pp.122-3.
26.   *Loc.cit.*
27.   *Ibid.*, p.27.
28.   *Ibid.*, p.123.
29.   'SASO, Black Workers Project', reproduced by World University Service, dated 4 May 1973, (mimeo).
30.   *Loc.cit.*
31.   *Loc.cit.*
32.   *Black Review*, 1972, p.45. This point of view is, surprisingly, quoted with apparent approval by L. Douwes Dekker, *et al.*, *op.cit.*, p.234.
33.   F. Fisher, *op.cit.*, p.331.
34.   Quoted in *Namibia News*, Vol. 4, Nos. 11-12, November-December 1971.
35.   These details are taken from *Namibia News*, Vol. 4, Nos. 11-12. The journal carried both a news survey of the strike, and an address by Sam Nujoma, president of SWAPO, to the UN Security Council on 5 October 1971, on conditions in the territory.
36.   See Ruth First, (1963), *South West Africa*, (Penguin), pp.130-9, for the history of SWANLA. An up to date summary is provided in *Black Review*, 1972, pp.212-3. (The summary unfortunately contains some errors of fact which I have tried to avoid.)
37.   Dekker, *et al.*, *op.cit.*, p.228.
38.   From the strike diary kept by Leonard Nghipandulua, and produced as evidence in the trial of strike leaders in Windhoek. Quoted by Randolph Vigne, (1973), *A dwelling place of our own: the story of the Namibian nation*, (International Defence and Aid Fund), p.43.
39.   Details of the strike from Dekker, *et al.*, *op.cit.*, pp.226-32; *SRRSA*, 1972, pp.432-37; *Sechaba*, Vol. 6, No. 4, April 1972.
40.   *Sechaba*, *op.cit.*
41.   R. Vigne, *op.cit.*, p.44.
42.   *SRRSA*, 1974, p.326, and *SRRSA*, 1975, p.210. It is not always possible to determine what was meant in official statements. The term 'work stoppage' was used ambiguously. If workers stopped work but did not formulate demands, they had not legally struck work — but were engaged in a work stoppage. On other occasions the legal niceties were dropped, and stoppages and strikes were grouped together. Both were illegal.
43.   *The Durban Strikes*, *op.cit.*, pp.8-9.
44.   *African Digest*, Vol. XX, No. 2, April 1973, p.28.
45.   Dekker, *et al.*, *op.cit.*, p.221.

46. Gerhard Maré (1974), 'The strikes in February 1973 – insights from a research project just completed.', in D.B. Horner, (Ed.), (1975), *Labour Organisation and the African*, (S.A. Institute of Race Relations), p.25. (Note: Rail fares had just been increased by 16 per cent.)
47. *The Durban Strikes, op.cit.,* p.99.
48. *Loc.cit.*
49. *Ibid.,* pp.9-10.
50. *Loc.cit.*
51. Dekker, *et al., op.cit.,* p.226.
52. *SRRSA,* 1969, p.131.
53. *SRRSA,* 1970, pp.142-3.
54. *Loc.cit.*
55. *SRRSA,* 1971, p.182.
56. *Ibid.*
57. *The Durban Strikes, op.cit.,* p.10-11.
58. *Loc.cit.*
59. *Ibid.,* p.12.
60. *Loc.cit.*
61. *Ibid.,* p.13.
62. *Ibid.,* p.96.
63. *Black Review,* 1973, p.132.
64. Dekker, *et al., op.cit.,* p.221.
65. *The Durban Strikes, op.cit.,* p.16.
66. See *ibid.,* p.29.
67. *Ibid* , p.17.
68. *A View of the 1973 Strikes,* South African Institute of Race Relations, RR 151/73, 20 November 1973, (mimeo.), Table A. It is not clear from the table whether there were one or two firms involved in this strike.
69. *The Durban Strikes, op.cit.,* p.35-8.
70. *Ibid.,* pp.18-9.
71. *Black Review,* 1973, p.148.
72. Quoted in Barbara Rogers (1976), *Divide and Rule: South Africa's Bantustans,* International Defence and Aid Fund, p.44.
73. *Black Review,* 1973, p.153, and S.A. Institute of Race Relations, RR 151/73, *op.cit.*
74. *Black Review,* 1973, p.24.
75. *SRRSA,* 1974, p.328.
76. *Black Review,* 1973, pp.24-5, and *SRRSA,* 1973, pp.160-1.
77. Dekker, *et al., op.cit.,* p.226.
78. *SRRSA,* 1974, p.327.
79. *SRRSA,* 1974, p.194.
80. *Rand Daily Mail,* 24 June 1974, quoted in Barbara Rogers, *op.cit.*
81. *Race Relations News,* Vol. 36, No. 9, September 1974.
82. D. Davis, *op.cit.*
83. *SRRSA,* 1976, pp.103-4.
84. D. Davis, *op.cit.,* states that union membership was about 40,000, and Benefit Fund membership was 18,000. I have quoted figures as given by Foszia Fisher, *op.cit.,* p.342.
85. SRRSA,1974, p.328.
86. Eddie Webster, (n.d.) 'Consciousness and the problem of organisation – a case study of a sample of African workers in Durban', (mimeo.), p.17.

8. The Strike Wave Spreads

In the first months of the strike wave in 1973, the press, and in particular the English-medium press, were fulsome in their praise of the low profile maintained by the police. Despite the illegality of the strikes there were no mass arrests. The usual strike-breaking tactics employed by the police were not in evidence.

This did indicate some indecision on the part of the government, despite the inevitable statement by the Minister of Labour on 2 February 1973 that the strike was the work of agitators with hidden motives. The language used by some police chiefs was unusual. On 6 February, in the midst of the work stoppage by municipal workers, the officer in charge, Brigadier T.M. Bisschoff, said: 'The police have nothing whatsoever against people demanding higher wages − provided they do not break the law.'[1] He also stressed that the police would use force only if absolutely necessary, and then only the minimum required by the circumstances.

Other statements, made in the same vein, were widely quoted at the time and, in the South African context, came as a surprise. On the other hand, the massive police presence showed that the 'minimum force necessary' would be employed if and when it was thought to be required. There was a massive show of force when the rumoured transport boycott was expected on 1 February, and there was a baton charge followed by 106 arrests on the very day that Brigadier Bisschoff made his statement.

Compared to the large number of Blacks arrested every day, police action during the strikes appeared mild, but by any other standards the police were not benign onlookers during the strikes. In 1973 the number of arrests following strikes in the country was 353, and 207 of those arrested were charged with participating in strikes or stoppages. In the first six months of 1974, 542 were arrested and 439 charged.[2] An unknown number of workers were dismissed and not re-engaged following strike action, and many of these were then forced to leave the towns. It does, however, seem that other than injuries following baton charges, or discomfort following the release of tear gas, there were no serious casualties in Durban-Pinetown. The press, could, therefore, congratulate the police!

146

Black Miners Shake the Country

On 11 September 1973 workers at the Western Deep Levels mine at Carltonville came out on strike. In the events that followed, a detachment of 21
policemen, led by a major, arrived at the compound and were confronted by
an infuriated group of miners brandishing sticks. The police were unable to
disperse the miners and after using tear gas resorted to arms. In the shooting
that ensued, at least 11 miners were killed. A twelfth miner was said to have
died at the hands of the rioters. The beerhall and the kitchen of the
compound were wrecked.[3]

Strikes and riots affected mines on 54 occasions between 25 February
1973 and 15 April 1975. At least 140 miners were killed and 1,881 injured.[4]
Thousands of miners were repatriated. The number arrested and the number
charged do not seem to be readily available, although each event was usually
followed by arrests and by court sentences.

There were some factors in the mines which were not dissimilar to those in
industry generally. The miners wanted higher pay, and in one case it seems
that machine operators and other semi-skilled workers demanded that pay
differentials given them in the past be maintained after lower paid workers
had received increases. The difference between this and other industries (on
this issue) lay in the huge wage differentials between Blacks and Whites, and
the control which white workers maintained over black advancement. In
1972 the average wage paid to Africans on all mines was R24 per month
exclusive of the cost of housing and feeding the workers. White miners, who
constituted some 10 per cent of the total labour (or – to be more accurate –
supervisory) force, earned an average of R391 per month. When adjustments
are made for estimated benefits, the ratio of white to black wages was in the
region of 15:1.

In 1973, when the free market price of gold topped $100 per fine ounce
(and reached $126 by June), the federation of goldmining houses (the
Chamber of Mines) entered into negotiations with the white miners. In
exchange for handsome wage increases of R80 per month and increased
holiday leave allowances, the Mine Workers Union at last conceded the right
of the mines to train Africans for vacancies which could not be filled by
Whites. Just prior to this agreement the Chamber had raised the wages of
Africans in the gold mines to an average of R32 per month. When the new
categories of work were opened to Africans, a small number of workers could
expect substantially higher remuneration – but the implementation of the
scheme would take several months.[5]

The obvious injustice in the new agreements caused considerable discontent, but the white workers demanded even more and, in August, engine
drivers and reduction workers demanded a further 20 per cent increase and
backed this with the threat of a work to rule. They were offered, and
accepted, a 15 per cent increase.[6] On 4 August, the African machine
operators complained about their wages and demanded more. Between 70 to
100 of these men formed the hard core of the disaffected work force at

Carltonville on 11 September.

There were few strikes or riots on the mines that did not include dissatisfaction over pay, and even where the riots seemed to involve inter-tribal fighting, workers interviewed by the labour editor of the *Financial Mail* complained about exaggerations in the press. A group drawn from several ethnic groups said: 'Why do they always blame everything on this so-called faction-fighting? Why don't they look instead at the conditions under which we work and the pay we get?'[7] The complaints of the black miners related mainly to pay. Wages were too low; even the new pay scales were insufficient to allow them to make any financial progress; and there was an almost total lack of communication between management and workers over wage levels.[8]

The absence of any trade union on the mines left the workers without overt formal organisation, but there was ample evidence of informal organisation. Tribal and district contacts were maintained by the workers on the mines, and these were reinforced by the management's organisation of labour on tribal lines inside the compounds. Leadership was moulded inside national and tribal groups which responded to the problems faced by the workers inside the mines, and also to issues in the Reserves or countries of origin. Those workers from outside the Republic that faced unacceptable demands made by their national governments, were able to use their organisations inside the compounds to negotiate with cabinet ministers at home and to promote militant activity on the mines to back their own demands.

In January 1974 the Lesotho government demanded that 60 per cent of all their citizens' wages be compulsorily deferred and paid into the Lesotho National Bank. Many Basotho miners maintained that they preferred South African banks to those of Chief Jonathan (the Prime Minister). At one mine they were able to organise a petition signed by 700 miners against the deferred pay scheme. At Western Deep Levels, a 26 man delegation was elected by Basotho workers and flown to Lesotho by the mine management for talks with the Minister of Commerce, Industry and Mines. This led to the retraction of the scheme — at least temporarily.[9]

This concerted action against the pay scheme got support in many of the mines and reflected, at least in part, opposition to the government of Chief Leabua Jonathan, and support for the opposition party. It was this political stance which brought the mineworkers out on strike at Vaal Reefs on 5 January 1975. They also tried to close the mine by bringing all the workers out. This led to clashes with other bodies of miners who stood aloof from a dispute that involved Basotho workers and their government. Nonetheless it seems that the Basotho were able to win some sections of the mine workers to their side, and that press reports about 'tribal' or 'faction' fights obscured the real issue — the attempt by one section of the work force to secure inter-tribal solidarity.[10]

The existence of such sectional organisation within the mines did not always lead to working-class solidarity. In some cases it led to partial strikes involving workers of only one tribe (or at least mainly of that tribe). But in many of the strikes in 1974 working class solidarity was achieved. There was

obvious solidarity in the wages strikes at Lorraine-Harmony-Merriespruit
mines in May and June and again in Carltonville and Hartebeesfontein in
October 1974. At the latter mine,

> . . . the so-called ring leaders who were arrested were identified as
> representatives of the three main tribal groups on the mine. It was clear
> that cross-tribal solidarity was deliberately fostered by the strike leaders.
> On this, as on many occasions when informal leaders of Black miners
> have been arrested, the press carried no reports of subsequent court
> hearings.[11]

There were incidents however where the informal tribal organisations were
used to further sectional interests. From February through to April 1974
inter-tribal clashes appear to have been largely concerned with issues such as
access to women in the neighbouring townships. Debarred from heterosexual
relations by the recruiting system and all-male compounds, frustration was
diverted into internecine tribal conflict. But it also seems as if there were a
number of complicating factors, including the fact that Basotho workers
apparently taunted their Xhosa-speaking colleagues with the claim that the
latter's Bantustan territory (the Transkei) did not have real independence![12]

The struggle on the mines in 1974 was marked by continued violence. The
apparent mildness of the police in the Durban strikes was not repeated on the
mines. The authorities had no intention of allowing the miners to take any
concerted action, and from the inception the police assumed their usual role.
They shot, and they shot to kill. The miners, and in particular the Basotho,
retaliated in kind. Before a strike at Vaal Reef one press report stated:
'Basuto miners threatened to go on strike and start rioting at the South Vaal
gold mine . . .'[13] Commenting on this, Kirkwood said:

> It may well be that other *spontaneous* outbreaks of violence have been
> more deliberate than press reports make them seem, but one might draw
> a distinction between deliberate *expression* and deliberate bargaining
> through violence. It was this latter that was new in January.[14]

The threats, the strikes, and the violence, had a profound effect on the
country. The shootings at Carltonville initiated a set of demonstrations on
the university campuses; the governments of Lesotho and Botswana as well as
the cabinets of the Transkeian and KwaZulu Bantustans expressed criticism
of events on the mines; thousands of Basotho and (at a later date)
Mozambicans and Malawians were repatriated — and in the case of Malawi all
recruitment was eventually halted by President Banda for reasons that are still
not clear. The Chamber of Mines increased African wages by a further 10 per
cent on 1 December 1973, and after further riots the Anglo-American
Corporation seemed on the point of granting Africans the right to form trade
unions. They retracted after the Minister of Labour issued a statement
denouncing any such action.[15]

In 1974 it seemed that the mines faced an unprecedented shortage of African labour. Thousands of Basotho and Mozambican workers had been repatriated. Malawi had suspended all further recruitment, and there was a large deficit in the overall supply of mine labourers. The Chamber of Mines also required a sizeable number of trainees for the newly created semi-skilled jobs. At the end of November the president of the Chamber of Mines spoke of the need to think in terms of a black labour force that would adopt mining as a career.[16] Recruiting stations for the first time were opened in urban areas like Soweto, Germiston and Benoni to obtain labour, and there was a relaxation of the regulation that required all recruits to return to the Reserves on completion of their contract.[17]

An indicator of the urgency with which the labour situation was viewed was the donation in August 1974 of R186,000 by Consolidated Gold Fields Ltd. to TEACH, for the erection of four junior secondary schools in Soweto.[18] The mines' interest in building schoolrooms was discussed in Chapter Five; the amount they contributed to TEACH underlined their perception of the need to extend secondary education.

Strikes Become Endemic

News of the strikes and riots on the mines received wide publicity and it seemed that industrial disturbances had come to stay. The immediate impact on the African workers is hard to determine because workers do not usually start their own newspapers to publicise their ideas. The workers of the Orange Free State were strangely quiescent during 1973, but strikes spread to the Transvaal.

Between February and mid-September there were at least 14 strikes in Johannesburg and five on the Witwatersrand. Most of the stoppages had been of limited duration and involved small numbers of workers. But two strikes (on 2 April and 5 May 1973) were of work forces of more than 1,000, and in March 500 dairy workers struck work and won a R1 per week increase.[19]

One factor which had been so important in most Durban strikes was absent in the mine strikes. The mine compounds were closed to the outside and were far from the main industrial areas. The multiplier effect which arose from the mingling of workers in the streets around factories could not be replicated in the case of the mine strikes. The effects on the workers were consequently more indirect. When industrial strikes occurred in the Orange Free State in 1974, the fact that most were centred in Welkom — the main mining area in the Province — might not have been accidental, even though five months had passed since the big disturbances on the mines.

The distribution of strikes in 1974, according to the Minister of Labour in the Assembly on 7 February 1975, is shown in Table 7. There was no more discernible pattern in the 1974 strikes than in those of the previous year. In January there was a major stoppage in the dairy industry on the Witwatersrand; in February there was a riot in the Boksburg mine; in April

Table 7
Strikes by Africans in 1974[20]

Province	Number of Stoppages/Strikes	Number Involved
Transvaal	203	22,552
OFS	25	2,386
Natal	96	18,993
Cape	50	13,725
Total	*374*	*57,656*

there were disturbances again at Western Deep Levels in Carltonville. In July there was a strike at Rand Refinery, Germiston. In July the multiplier effect was noticeable when workers at engineering firms in Durban, Welkom and the East Rand stopped work. Some 3,000 workers were involved in 11 firms. Within a week workers at 15 other establishments were on strike.[21] Strikes and stoppages had become such common occurrences that few received publicity, and others were accorded only brief press reports. Some 1,400 workers were arrested and a large proportion were charged.[22]

East London: Bantustan Leaders as Strike-Breakers

The 1974 strike wave in East London did not initially seem to be different from any other in the country. In fact, there was a remarkable similarity to events in Durban in 1973. The impetus for the strikes came from an initial work stoppage at Car Distributor Assemblies on 22 July 1974. Soon workers in 21 firms in East London (involving some 5,000 workers) and one firm with 3,500 workers in neighbouring Kingwilliamstown came out on strike.[23]

The strikes lasted longer than in Durban. Most workers stayed out for three or four days, and some did not return for a week. In many of the strikes there were fairly lengthy negotiations with management — the workers' representatives having been delegated or elected by the work force. Most of the strikes were peaceful although there were three instances of violent action or threats of violence against scabs. The police intervened to disperse the workers with tear gas or batons, but there were no arrests and no serious injuries.[24]

Also, as in Durban, some strikes ended without any gains for the workers. In some instances they were all dismissed and invited to re-apply; other workers managed to get small wage increases amounting to 10 to 15 per cent.

In one other respect East London was similar to Durban. The town was on the edge of a 'Homeland' and the Chief Minister intervened in one of the crucial strikes. But the Ciskei, which borders East London and in which the township Mdantsane is situated, is very unlike KwaZulu. The average wage paid in East London was only 66 per cent of that paid to Africans in Durban, and a larger proportion of African workers in East London were in lower job categories than elsewhere in the country. Comparative figures are shown in Table Eight.

Table 8
African Wage Levels in the Principal Industrial Areas, 1974[25]

Town	Average Weekly Wage (in Rands)	Percentage of Africans in lowest category
Port Elizabeth	12.31	39.8
Johannesburg	10.53	30.7
Durban	10.45	26.6
East London	6.57	45.2

The Ciskei itself was impoverished, but probably not more than other Reserves. Its political structure was, however, simpler than that of KwaZulu. Its Chief Minister, Lennox Sebe, was a commoner and there was an open political fight about the acceptance of the government's apartheid policy for the 'Homelands'; unlike that in KwaZulu, the opposition came from intellectuals. This group was socially weak and the tensions were different in kind from those witnessed in KwaZulu, where Buthelezi faced the opposition of some of the chiefs.[26]

From the outset Sebe worked with the Chamber of Commerce, industrialists, and Brigadier Prinsloo (the head of the local police force) to end the strikes. On 30 July the bus drivers struck work, and this threatened to paralyse East London. Almost the entire work force lived in Mdantsane, which was 12 miles from the city and, without transport, industry and commerce would have closed down. Brigadier Prinsloo rounded up the drivers and took them to the police station. There they found Sebe waiting to meet them — and he 'persuaded' them to go back to work pending negotiations. The police were fulsome in their praise: 'Brigadier Prinsloo said after the meeting that Mr. Sebe and his ministers were the only people who could bring the wave of strikes on the Border to an end.'[27]

Thereafter Sebe met the Mayor of East London and leading dignitaries in commerce and industry, together with Prinsloo and senior police officers. This led to a tour of factories, at which there were strikes, by Sebe, leaders of the Ciskei Legislative Assembly and members of the Mdantsane town council; and the workers were advised to return to work. Despite some opposition, the intervention was effective and the strikes ended.

Sebe was caustic and read the industrialists a lesson he thought they should have known (!):

The calling of the police when things are very ugly does not solve the problem at all. In fact the industrialists make the police indirectly the enemy of the law-abiding workers. These situations could be saved if industrialists contact homeland governments immediately.[28]

The propensity for 'settling' strikes was taken a step further in December when residents of Mdantsane imposed a boycott on the buses as a protest against increased fares and the operation of the season ticket system. They complained that they could get no rebate on the weekly ticket for the occasions on which they had not used the buses, and demanded an alteration in the conditions of sale. Although the bus fares were reduced to the original price after the boycott had been in progress for some six weeks, the buses remained empty because there had been no change in the season ticket system. The bus company offered to sell its buses and the Ciskeian government indicated its interest in securing the stock. They were, however, unable to raise the capital!

New proposals made provision for the Xhosa Development Corporation to take the service over when the bus company's contract expired in June 1976. A black company would also be formed to run an auxiliary service inside the township and shares would be made available for purchase by the Ciskei government. At this stage the Ciskeian ruling party appealed to its supporters to use the buses. They did, and then proceeded to assault all commuters who persisted in using the taxi service or accepted lifts to work in cars. Prominent businessmen made provision for buying blocks of shares when the new company was formed and one was reported as stating in an interview: 'Perhaps we can say this has been the most important development brought about by the strike.'[29] In the light of such cynicism, any further comment would be superfluous.

Strikes Without End

In 1973, after the first wave of strikes had rocked industry and commerce, the government amended the labour laws and gave the African worker the legal right to strike, for the first time in the history of the country. However, as in so much of the legislation introduced to regulate the activities of Africans, the government framed the legislation to remove as many of the new 'rights' as it seemed to grant. A large number of workers were excluded from the legislation, and were under no condition allowed to stop work. This included agricultural workers, domestic servants, workers employed by local authorities and all workers employed in 'essential' services. The position of mine workers and other 'contract' workers was not clearly defined, but it seems as if they too were to be excluded from the right to strike.

Conditions under which workers could legally strike were also circumscribed by the elaborate process that was required before they could stop work. The dispute had to be referred to a works committee or to a Bantu Labour Officer, and 30 days had to elapse after notice of a dispute had been given. Over and above these requirements, no dispute could be declared if there was a wage agreement that was less than one year old, or if the wage rate was being attended to by a Wage Board. In short, the legislation was meant to bring the strike wave under control, and not to allow the workers the right to take precipitate action. The effect of the legislation on the stoppages was, consequently, minimal.

The strikes continued through 1974 and on through 1975. In the latter year it was reported that there had been 119 strikes, but this apparently excluded work stoppages and work disputes, because the Minister of Labour also referred to 175 'disputes' dealt with by labour officers during the year.[30] Over 500 workers appeared on charges following the stoppages. In 1976 there were at least 105 strikes, over and above work stoppages and excluding the stay-at-homes called by the youth to support the struggles in Soweto, Cape Town and elsewhere. Over 16,000 workers were involved in these industrial disputes in chrome, coal and gold mines; in the Pretoria municipal department; at meat suppliers in Johannesburg; and at a large variety of works in all four Provinces.[31]

In 1976 there were two strikes, in particular, which received large-scale publicity, and which attracted the sympathy of the township population. The first occurred at Elandsfontein near Germiston on the Witwatersrand in March 1976. The struggle in the plant revolved around the workers' demand that their membership of the Metal and Allied Workers Union be recognised by the management. Some 480 workers (80 per cent of the African work force) sent a petition to the firm, rejecting the company's liaison and works committees, and demanding recognition of their own trade union. After a month of continued agitation 20 workers were retrenched, ostensibly because of a recession in the building industry. This immediately led to a demand that the workers be reinstated and to a refusal to resume work, on 26 March. The entire work force was dismissed and told that they could re-apply for work, provided that they accepted the liaison and works committees. The workers claimed that this was a lock-out and also claimed that the company's statement about retrenchment was shown to be false by the pattern of re-hiring after the dismissals. When the workers assembled outside the factory in order to hear the secretary of their union, they were ordered by the police to disperse within 30 minutes. The union officials urged them to go home, and to the strains of the anthem *Nkosi Sikelel'i-Afrika* (God save Africa), they moved away.

Although the half-hour had not elapsed, police turned on the workers with batons and with dogs. Some were seen to wield pick handles. Men and women were savaged (including a woman who was seven months pregnant). Two trade union officials and a number of workers were arrested and later charged under the Riotous Assemblies Act, but were found guilty on lesser charges.[32]

The second strike, at the Armourplate Safety Glass factory in Springs (on the Witwatersrand), was unique in several respects. It was the first 'legal' African strike; and it was the longest strike in the history of labour disputes involving Africans. Furthermore, it took place during the Soweto Revolt, at a time when political strikes were taking place, without any noticeable interconnection between this industrial action and the political struggles of 1976!

Armourplate Safety Glass was a member of the British owned Pilkington Glass Group and accorded no recognition to the workers' union. In July the firm announced that in view of the depression the plant would only work a four-day week. Ten days later three workers were dismissed as part of the general policy of retrenchment. The African works committee demanded the workers' reinstatement and, when this was refused, gave warning of a dispute. After the statutory 30 days' cooling off period the workers struck work.

Although the strike was not illegal, the workers who formed a picket line were arrested for participating in an illegal gathering, and charged under the Riotous Assemblies Act. Although the sentences they received were quashed on appeal, the right to form picket lines was not established, and the case throws doubt on the future right of workers to stop scabs entering a factory even if their strike is deemed 'legal'. The strike lasted ten weeks, and all attempts at negotiation with the firm failed. Eventually, a large number of the workers decided to seek alternative employment because they feared that when the strike ended they would face victimisation.[33] This brought the industrial action to an end.

The Strikes and the Political Struggle

The strikes undertaken by workers without formal organisation showed at one and the same time the strength of workers in such a situation and their inevitable weakness. By having no formal structures, they were relatively immune from police action. There were no offices to be raided and closed by the police, no officials to be arrested and so removed from the scene, no weakening of the struggle because the 'head' had been removed. Using informal structures that had been built up amongst their fellows, the workers relied on their own resources, and the random arrests left the body of workers intact.

The realisation, in the very first week, that staying in the vicinity of the factory constituted their greatest safeguard was important. Dispersal would have weakened the workers and isolated them from their colleagues. On the other hand, pouring into the streets and walking (or marching) together pro- duced a multiplier effect and brought out the workers in the vicinity. Finally, the refusal to appoint negotiators saved them the frustration of division (over offers that might be made) and protected them from premature victimisation.

On the other hand, the lack of formal organisation eventually exposed their weakness. They had no strike funds and could not afford to stay out. In the case of Pilkington, the workers were fortunate in that workers from neighbouring plants collected money on their behalf, but this would have been impossible for large numbers of workers or for extended periods of time. There was also no planning of the strikes, no attempt to bring out workers in associated industries, and no plan to co-ordinate the stoppages, either locally or nationally.

The greatest weakness, however, lay in the fact that there was no political group that could offer a lead and make the strikes part of the political struggle against the government. The strikes of 1973 to 1976 helped create the atmosphere of revolt and showed that the Blacks were not powerless. It was by the multitude of strikes, small and large, that the example of resistance was taken into the townships. The ability to resist the terror of government action was demonstrated repeatedly. Although they have received little attention since the Soweto Revolt, these strikes must be seen as constituting the beginning of the Revolt, and as having affected a far wider section of the population than was ever reached by members of SASO-BPC.

As already indicated above, the BPC had little influence on the working class, and the one trade union they controlled had little effect on events in the strikes of 1973-76. The Black Allied Workers Union did not operate at shopfloor or industry level. During all the strikes there was only one instance in which their offices were used. When the sweet workers of Johannesburg struck work in 1974, they insisted that officials of BAWU represent them in negotiations. Only when they were called upon did this body intervene — and they only seem to have been required on this one occasion. Their policy was one of non-confrontation, and in many ways they held to a statement reported in the *Rand Daily Mail* on 9 December 1972, and widely quoted:

[The black unions are] not limited to the achieving of physical and material benefits such as good working conditions, increased wages, social fringe benefits, etc. Our concern and priority is the formation of a people and the development of a sense of responsibility in them.

This was a misunderstanding of the mechanisms by which a 'people' was 'formed' and a misunderstnading of the needs of the working class for 'material benefits'.

Even in terms of the requirements of the Black Consciousness Movement, it was only by helping the workers to achieve higher wages through strike action that political consciousness could be raised in the first instance. Particularly when the strikes came near to generating a general strike, the opportunity to raise consciousness was present and the existence of an organisation could have assisted in bringing general political demands to the fore. While BPC-SASO were concerned with establishing personal identities, the black workers were forging ahead in building a group identity that took them far beyond the black consciousness that was being propagated by the students and clerics of the BPC.

The economic struggle had to become political and the political struggle had to bolster the economic struggle. Rosa Luxemburg, drawing on the experiences of the mass strikes in Russia in 1905, tried to spell out the lessons for the workers. Her observations still have a freshness and a validity for workers today.

Political and economic strikes, mass strikes and partial strikes, demonstrative strikes and fighting strikes, general strikes of individual branches of industry and general strikes in individual towns, peaceful wage struggles and street massacres, barricade fighting — all these run together, run side by side, cross one another, flow in and over one another . . .

Every new onset and every fresh victory of the political struggle is transformed into a powerful impetus for the economic struggle, extending at the same time its external possibilities and intensifying the inner urge of the workers to better their position, and their desire to struggle . . . And conversely, the workers' condition of ceaseless economic struggle with the capitalists keeps their fighting energy alive in every political interval . . .

In a word: the economic struggle is the transmitter from one political centre to another; the political struggle is the periodic fertilization of the soil for the economic struggle.[34]

When, in August and September 1976, the students called for stay-at-homes, they were in fact politicising the strikes. But in part, they were too late, and in part they were unable to produce the slogans which could extend the economic struggle. The struggle in the factories produced the climate which led to Soweto, but there was no reciprocal action. The workers' struggle did not gain appreciably from the calls for two or three day political strikes. Also, as mentioned above, the Pilkington strike did not indicate that there was any connection between this important working-class action and the stay-at-home called at the same time by the school students. This failure to link the two struggles inevitably weakened both sectors of the fights that overlapped in time, but were light-years apart in orientation.

References

1. Quoted in *The Durban Strikes, op.cit.*, p.30.
2. *SRRSA*, 1974, pp.326, 329.
3. *SRRSA*, 1973, pp.242-3.
4. Report of Inter-departmental Committee of Inquiry into Riots on Mines in the Republic of South Africa, pp. 5, 49.
5. *SRRSA*, 1973, p.241.
6. *Ibid.*, p.242.
7. Quoted in Mike Kirkwood, 'The mine workers struggle', *South African Labour Bulletin*, Vol. 1, No. 8, January-February 1975, p.30.
8. *Ibid.*
9. *Ibid.*, p.39.
10. *Ibid.*, p.32.
11. *Ibid.*, p.34.
12. Mike Kirkwood, 'Conflict on the mines, 1974', *South African Labour Bulletin*, Vol. 1, No. 7, November-December, 1974, pp.35-6.
13. M. Kirkwood (1975), *op.cit.*, p.38.
14. *Ibid.*, p.39.
15. *SRRSA*, 1974, p.291.

16. Quoted in M. Kirkwood, (1975), *op.cit.*, p.29.
17. David Davis, *Anti-Apartheid News*, February 1975.
18. *SRRSA*, 1974, p.292.
19. *A View of the 1973 Strikes, op.cit.*
20. *SRRSA*, 1975, p.210. These figures were supplied in the Houses of Parliament. Other sources indicate that actual numbers were far higher.
21. *SRRSA*, 1974, pp.328-9.
22. In the first six months 552 were arrested and 439 charged (*SRRSA*, 1974, p.326). In the last six months 841 were reported arrested (*SRRSA*, 1975, p.211).
23. G. Maré, 'The East London Strikes', *South African Labour Bulletin*, Vol. I, No. 5, 1974. See also *SRRSA*, 1974, pp.329-30.
24. G. Maré, *op.cit.*, p.16.
25. *Ibid.*, p.27.
26. The political infighting in the Ciskei is described in *Black Review*, 1974-75, pp.41-8.
27. Reported in *East London Dispatch* and quoted in G. Maré, *op.cit.*
28. G. Maré, *op.cit.*
29. An account of the events, including details of the interference with the judiciary when government supporters were charged with violence against bus boycotters, is given in *Black Review*, 1974-5, pp.43-50.
30. *SRRSA*, 1976, pp.316-7.
31. *SRRSA*, 1977, pp.305-6.
32. *Black Review*, 1975-6, pp.173-4.
33. Steve Friedman, writing in *Race Relations News*, December 1976.
34. Rosa Luxemburg, 'The mass strike, the political party and the trade unions, printed in the collection of her works edited by Mary-Allice Watson, *Rosa Luxemburg speaks*, (Pathfinder, 1970), pp.181-2, 185.

9. State Repression and Political Revival: 1974-1976

The Schlebusch Commission Reports

The government in the mid-seventies took steps to circumscribe the activities of two other very different kinds of opposition movement — NUSAS and the Christian Institute. The activities of these two organisations, as well as those of the South African Institute of Race Relations, had been investigated by the Commission of Inquiry into Certain Organisations, set up by Parliament in 1973 under the chairmanship of A.L. Schlebusch, M.P.[1]

The Commission's report on NUSAS was published in August 1974. It claimed that the organisation had been run by a small clique which propagated 'anti-South African views' and promoted 'anti-South African' actions. NUSAS, furthermore, was accused of promoting black consciousness and of favouring a course which would lead to a confrontation between Blacks and Whites. The Commission described the NUSAS wages campaign as:

> ... really a means to another end, and that is political change to overthrow the existing order in South Africa and to replace it with an anti-capitalistic system which has sometimes been described as 'Black socialism'. This has to be brought about by stirring up industrial and labour unrest and by inciting Black and White against each other, by polarising them against each other, and eventually by inciting them to conflict, even violent conflict.[2]

There was little correlation between the aims of NUSAS as described by the Commission and the actual aims and actions of the organisation. Individual members may have had views similar to those imputed to them by the Commission, but there was no evidence that the activities of the Wages Commissions, or any other NUSAS committee, corresponded with the verdict of Schlebusch.

The tabling of the report in Parliament led to NUSAS and its subsidiary bodies being declared 'affected organisations' in September 1974. The effect of this measure was to stop the organisation receiving any financial aid from foreign sources. In 1973 the NUSAS budget had been approximately R100,000, and some 70 per cent of the money had been donated by overseas bodies. The immediate effect of the new regulation was, therefore, to curtail NUSAS activities, particularly in literacy training, prison education (for political prisoners), and community development projects.[3]

On 28 May 1975 a subcommittee of the Schlebusch Commission tabled its report on the Christian Institute. The CI and its associated projects — which included SPROCAS (Study Project on Christianity in Apartheid Society), Programme for Social Change, and the BCP — were accused of conditioning public opinion to accept violent change leading to a black dominated socialist state.[4] The CI rebutted the charges and claimed that they had consistently advocated Christian change by non-violent means and justice through reconciliation. It followed the gospel of Christ and never supported the violent overthrow of the government.[5]

On 30 May the CI was nevertheless declared an 'affected organisation', and consequently debarred from receiving foreign aid. For a movement that had previously worked on an annual budget of approximately R500,000, this was bound to have serious effects. A large portion of the money had been collected abroad and the declaration was bound to lead to a serious curtailment of activities.

Detentions and Arrests

While the government awaited the report of the Schlebusch Commission, the police continued their harassment of all organisations that seemed able to provide opposition to the apartheid system.

The calling of the Viva Frelimo rallies by SASO and BPC for September 1974, to celebrate the liberation of Mozambique, provided the pretext for widespread raids, arrests and detentions — crippling both BPC and SASO well before the Revolt of 1976.

The list of detainees grew in the months that followed, and by March 1975 there were 50 persons known to be in detention, all but 15 having been taken into custody in 1974.[6] Another 50 leading members of these organisations were also reputed to have fled the country, and throughout 1975 the activities of SASO/BPC, on and off the campuses, were restrained. The National Youth Organisation (NAYO), which organised in the schools, was also severely hit by police raids in August and September 1975 and many of their most prominent activists were detained.[7]

Throughout 1975 the harassment of the political movements continued. In June, Raymond Suttner, senior lecturer in law at the University of Natal, was arrested together with two associates. He was later charged with activities on behalf of the ANC and the Communist Party.[8] During August and September there were widespread raids on the homes of students, academics, and members of the Christian Institute. Many of the students were in NUSAS, and some were on the executive, and there was a wave of protests from members of the academic staff at the Universities of Cape Town and the Witwatersrand. Shortly after the first detentions it transpired that the raids were associated with the arrest of Breyten Breytenbach, the renowned Afrikaans poet. He was eventually sentenced to nine years imprisonment for trying to establish a movement amongst Whites, known as Okhela (the Spark), which was said to be associated with the ANC. The other Okhela-related detainees were released, but the arrests put an end to most of their political involvement.[9]

Impact of the Trials: 1976-76

The Okhela Trial

It was the government's intention that all radical opposition be silenced and that all political activists who advocated social or economic changes be banned, detained or imprisoned. The trials that took place in the mid-seventies were not very different from those that had been staged since the mid-fifties. Ultimately the intention was that the prisoners be found guilty and given severe sentences. In the process, those before the courts were to be discredited and the (white) electorate assured that everything was under control.

At the close of the Breytenbach trial an observer for the International Commission of Jurists, Professor Charles Albert Morand, observed that:

> . . . the cross-examination of the defendant amounted in reality to an attack by the Attorney-General upon those institutions in South Africa which oppose apartheid and which have not yet been declared illegal, in particular NUSAS, . . . the Christian Institute and the trade unions.[10]

In his report on the trial he stated:

> The results of the trial are difficult to evaluate. Nevertheless it may be ventured that they are very unfavourable to the struggle against apartheid. The attitude of the defendant and the passivity of the defence mean that numerous people and organisations find themselves compromised, at least in the eyes of public opinion.
> The Breytenbach trial constitutes a remarkable success for the government. It has helped to impress upon the white community the image of a vast subversive conspiracy . . . [The] trial, like many of those which preceded it, is to be seen as a lever which enables the white government to legitimate and reinforce its dictatorial powers and to pursue its policy of apartheid. It is the whole institutionalized system of exploitation of the Black majority which is reinforced.[11]

The Breytenbach trial was a fiasco for the overall liberation movement. Breytenbach apologised for his actions and offered no defence for his activities on behalf of Okhela. The poet, his friends and the organisation he had helped launch were completely compromised. The trial, as Professor Morand had stated, was a 'remarkable success for the government'.

The SASO/BPC Nine
There were other trials in 1975 that were different, and each one of them
played a part in rekindling the spirit of resistance. The biggest, longest and
most important trial took place in Pretoria, where thirteen (subsequently
reduced to nine) leading members of SASO/BPC were arraigned on charges
under the Terrorism Act. The State argued that these organisations, together
with the Peoples Experimental Theatre, the Theatre Council of Natal, and the
Turfloop SRC, inculcated anti-white feeling and encouraged racial polarisation and hostility in order to prepare for violent revolution. The defence's
case was that racial animosity was prevalent in the country, that there was no
need to encourage a reaction to white racism; and that the Black Consciousness Movement had the right to seek redress of their grievances by peaceful
methods.[12]

Neither the accused, nor those called as witnesses for the defence, made
any concessions on principled political issues. They used the courtroom to
present their programme and their philosophy of black awareness.

The accused also used the courtroom for public demonstrations. *Black
Review*, 1974-75, gave the following graphic accounts of a few of the many
incidents:

. . . February 7 . . . the accused started singing from the cells below the
court-room, up the stairs until they got into the court-room. At the end
of the song they bellowed 'POWER — AMANDLA'.

. . . April 21 . . . a fracas developed between the 13 trialists and the
police, in which some blows were exchanged. The accused were leaning
over the dock, to kiss, hug, shake hands or even touch relatives and friends
from the public gallery. The police were in turn trying to force the trialists
down the stairs . . . In the course of the mêlée, there was general shouting
and yelling by both the trialists and the swarming black crowd.

. . . April 25 . . . the trialists, clad in black T-shirts with letters BPC on the
chests, and black skull-caps came into the court with their customary
singing until they ended with the clenched fist Black Solidarity salute,
accompanied by a roar of 'Power'. Black spectators from the public gallery
responded to the salute.[13]

On 23 June, two of the accused were discharged and the case of two men
separated from the remaining nine. The nine pushed aside the police, stood
with the audience singing *Nkosi Sikelel'i-Afrika* (God Save Africa), and
embraced their former co-accused. The two freed men, surrounded by a
cheering crowd, then left the court at the head of relatives and supporters, all
giving the clenched fist salute.[14]

The trial extended through 1975 and 1976, and sentences of six years (for
six of the defendants) and five years (for three) were handed down by the
judge. In the judgment it was conceded that neither SASO nor BPC had the
characteristics of a revolutionary group and that there was no move to bring

about a revolutionary change, politically or economically, by unconstitutional or violent means. The accused were found guilty of committing acts capable of endangering the maintenance of law and order, and seven were held guilty of organising the Viva Frelimo rallies.[15]

The accused were imprisoned after more than two years on trial. During this long period their organisations were in a state of disarray and many leading members were in custody or had fled. By this time the main thrust of the 1976 Revolt was over and the state had ensured that these young leaders were out of commission.

An ANC/CP Trial

The trial of Raymond Suttner was shorter and the state's case was much simpler. The prosecution claimed that the accused had produced and distributed copies of *Inkululeko* (Freedom) and *Vukani* (Awake), the journals of the Communist Party and the ANC respectively. He had also recruited members and formed an underground cell of the ANC. The issue was never in doubt and Suttner received a seven-and-half year sentence. He made a statement from the dock affirming his convictions and beliefs, and concluded with the words:

> For this I will go to prison. But I cannot ever accept that it is wrong to act, as I have done, for freedom and equality, for an end to racial discrimination and poverty. I have acted in the interests of the overwhelming majority of our people. I am confident I have their support.[16]

Suttner then saluted the gallery with the clenched fist and the crowd responded by returning the salute and singing *Nkosi Sikelel'i-Afrika*.[17]

The NAYO Seven

The trial of the NAYO Seven, which only began in March 1976 in Johannesburg, was the centre of continued demonstrations. When the accused appeared on 1 March they were 'wearing colourful Afro-shirts'. They joined the public gallery in singing *Nkosi Sikelel'i-Afrika* and *Umzima Lomthwalo* (The burden is heavy).[18] After a two-week adjournment the court sat again on 15 March. For the next two days crowds of 400 spectators, swelling at times to just under a thousand, gathered outside the back of the court, singing freedom songs and giving the Black Power salute.

On 18 March the demonstrations continued, with the crowd again chanting freedom songs. The police moved in with dogs to disperse the gathering and questioned a man distributing pamphlets advertising a 'Hero's Day' meeting in Soweto to commemorate Sharpeville. Subsequent events were described in *Detention and Detente* as follows:

> The police, allegedly on a complaint from a white man, arrested a black youth allegedly for pickpocketing. In the confusion the youth ran towards the station [some quarter-mile distant] and the crowd surged after the

police who followed him. As the youth was arrested at the station, the crowd, whose ranks had been increased to about 2,000 [by] homeward bound commuters . . . started stoning the police. As police reinforcements moved in the rioters spilled out of the station into surrounding streets where a further clash occurred when some whites overlooking the station from a nearby railway building began to throw objects down . . . evoking extreme anger in the crowd.[19]

The crowd was eventually dispersed at about 7.0 p.m. when the police arrived with dogs. Subsequent reports showed that this was not an anti-white riot, and that the crowd turned against an African accused of being a police informer. A young white woman reporter was shielded and led to safety by a number of people in the crowd.[20]

The trial was moved to Pretoria because of the demonstrations, and proceedings continued well into May. It was apparent long before the end that few of the charges would be upheld and that the trial was designed to smash NAYO. In late May two of the accused were found guilty of 'inciting' two persons to undergo military training, and given the mandatory minimum sentence of five years.[21] Some of the detainees required to give state evidence were arrested and charged with perjury, and one of the released prisoners was immediately re-detained. The net upshot of the trial was to weaken NAYO and, because there had been dual membership, to weaken the South African Student Movement (SASM) in the crucial months before 16 June.

The arrests never stopped, and the trials were a constant feature of South African life. The accounts presented in this chapter were selected because they reflect the change of political mood in the townships. Other trials that were staged throughout the country were proof of continued police activity in unearthing small groups, dedicated to fighting apartheid, which sprang to life in communities up and down the country. Each trial told some story of local initiative, of plans for getting abroad or for organising local groups. Their story needs to be told, but would add little to the account already presented. Also excluded here, have been the harrowing accounts of torture in the prisons and of the deaths of detainees at the hands of the police. What was remarkable was the ability of prisoners to appear in the dock, able to join with their supporters in songs and defiant salutes, in the sure knowledge that their captors would retaliate in the darkness of the prison cells.

The spectators at the trials were also aware of the risks they ran in participating in the demonstrations of solidarity in full public gaze. On at least one occasion, at the trial of the SASO/BPC nine, the doors of the court were locked and police took the names and addresses of some forty of the spectators. They had allegedly participated in court-room singing and saluting.[22]

The Bus Boycotts in 1975-76

Throughout 1975 strikes in factories and shops continued, as mentioned in Chapter Eight. But the strike wave had decreased in intensity. There were a large number of incidents, but the work force involved in strikes was said to have been only 12,451.[23] When provision is made for the artificial distinction between 'strikes' and 'work stoppages', the total number of African workers who 'stopped work' in 1975 was 23,295.[24] This was small compared to the number of workers on strike in 1973, and the average duration of stoppages was only a fraction of that in 1973.

Police action had become tougher, and the concessions that were won were negligible. In the circumstances, the propensity to strike dropped and the workers sought other means to protect themselves from declining standards of living. Incensed by the steep rise in transport costs, workers at a number of centres organised boycotts of the buses, the largest and most protracted being at Newcastle (Northern Natal) in October 1975.

Newcastle was the centre of the second government steel works (Iscor) and the site of a growing industrial centre. There were large clothing companies, steel works, construction works and other industries. The black workers who staffed these firms were housed in KwaZulu in the townships of Madadeni and Osizweni, some eight and fourteen miles from Newcastle. The single fare to town from Madadeni had risen in a series of jumps from 8c (roughly 4p) at the beginning of 1973, to 25c in early 1975, and was scheduled to rise to 30c in October 1975. It was estimated that workers from Madadeni spent 13.6 per cent of their wages on transport. Osizweni fares were higher and equalled 20 per cent of the workers' wages.[25]

Residents of Madadeni organised a boycott of the buses, which were owned by the Bantu Investment Corporation (BIC), and demanded that the buses be taken over by either the rival bus company, PUTCO, or the KwaZulu government. Available sources give no information on the boycott committee, and it is not certain how far this demand was supported in the township, but the committee had the full support of the residents for boycott action. Every day some 20 to 40 thousand residents walked, cycled, or rode to work in private transport, and the 180 buses cruised along the roads virtually empty. Several thousand also walked the longer distance from Osizweni and the buses there were also almost empty.

The police tried to break the boycott by stopping cars carrying township residents and ordering them off the road. The workers, who had previously been goodnatured, retaliated by stoning buses, looting bottlestores and wrecking two beerhalls. For a time, four white officials were held as hostages in a compound and, in clashes with the police, two Africans were shot dead and many injured.

Ultimately, the KwaZulu government acquired a 50 per cent share in all transport companies operating in the Zulu Reserves and formed a holding company together with the BIC. Events followed a similar pattern to that already described in the Ciskei bus boycott and, four weeks after the commencement of the dispute, the boycott petered out. The residents of the townships had gained little, but the BIC had protected its investments and the KwaZulu government had been provided with a new source of income.

Bus fares were increased everywhere in 1976. In March they went up 50 per cent in KwaThema, near Springs. In fact, the total increase since PUTCO took over the service in 1975 was 250 per cent (from 6c to 15c for a single fare). Thousands of residents chose to walk the six miles to work and back and withstood the usual police intimidation. Nevertheless, after seven weeks, the boycott started crumbling and only a small number continued to walk during May. The increased fares remained unaltered. In mid-June bus fares throughout the Witwatersrand, the Vaal area and Pretoria were raised by 10 per cent.[26]

The increased bus fares coincided with rises — sometimes very steep — in the prices of staple foods. In May the price of maize, the staple diet of many families, went up by 18 per cent and milk prices rose by eight per cent. Other price increases during the preceding few months included those for: tea, instant coffee, tinned foods, rice, cooking oil, margarine, clothing, toiletries, soaps, detergents, coal (the only fuel available for heating in most black homes), cigarettes and liquor.[27] The only price rise that could have been fought was that in bus fares — and that increase was announced in the press on the morning of 16 June. By the end of that same afternoon the Revolt had begun, and at that stage resentment against increased fares was overtaken by events. Burnt-out buses were seen in every township, but that was part of a deeper resentment against any object that could be identified with the oppressor, and was not necessarily associated with higher fares. Those who felt aggrieved at the increased bus fares undoubtedly welcomed the sight of the burning buses.

'The Revolt Is Already Under Way'

In early 1976 Leslie Sehume, General Secretary of the Committee for Fairness in Sport (CFS), told an audience of white women in Pretoria that:

> . . . the black revolt in South Africa is already under way as was evident in a spate of strikes, boycotts, crime, unrest among students, agitation over urban home ownership and freehold rights, and protest over the medium of instruction in schools . . .
> It is destructive to one's own interests to fasten the bastions on the borders when right within the country 18 million people wallow in the mud of job reservation, inadequate educational facilities, the obnoxious pass laws, influx control, migrant labour, curfew regulations and abject discrimination all round.[28]

This statement, emanating from an official of a pro-government organisation which aimed to promote international participation in sport in South Africa, reflected the difficulties Mr. Sehume faced in selling South African apartheid sport to the outside world. The maladies he listed were real enough and they were all symptoms of the deep discontents in the townships, but the listing of crime and demands for home ownership, together with strikes, boycotts and student unrest, indicated a general breakdown of local controls rather than a revolt. Nevertheless Leslie Sehume had perceived something that many of the politicians failed to see and all the conflicts that he observed, affecting different classes inside the townships, were to merge into and become part of the conflagration after 16 June. The way in which some demands were bypassed or brought to the fore in the months to come provides an indication of the relative strengths of class groupings in Soweto and other regions. At this juncture, Sehume saw only black revolt against white authority and against 'abject discrimination all round'. As an official of the CFS he was not likely to expand on the one talking point that dominated South Africa at the time: the debacle that had followed South Africa's movement of troops into Angola. He bypassed this by referring only to the fastening of 'bastions on the borders', although the army's venture into Angola was the dominant factor that changed the mood of the black townships.

South Africa Invades Angola

Units of the South African army crossed the Namibian borders into Angola in August 1975, ostensibly to protect the Kunene hydro-electric scheme installations. By September it was reported that the troops were 10 miles inside Angola, and in October there were government statements that mentioned only raids on SWAPO military bases. The government persistently denied reports that the army would thrust into the interior of the country.

On 23 October the army advanced, with the covert aid of the United States, and moved rapidly to within 170 miles of Luanda (and over 400 miles from Namibia). The South Africans were halted by troops of the Luanda government, newly equipped with Soviet weapons and stiffened by Cuban advisers and troops.

Open US involvement in the conflict was stopped in December when the Senate voted against an expropriation bill to finance counter-revolution in Angola. Black African governments condemned the South African presence in Angola, and Nigeria and Tanzania, in particular, called on the OAU to recognise the MPLA government. The South African army had become an embarrassment to the US and, after particularly fierce fighting on 21 January 1976, the troops (who were reported to have suffered a defeat) were withdrawn, but stayed inside Southern Angola for a time.

South African Blacks rejoiced at the news of the army's retreat and welcomed the pictures of white prisoners in the hands of an African army. Callinicos and Rogers write that an eye-witness described the situation in Cape Town as follows: '. . . huge black audiences would watch the television news in coloured hotels and cheer every report of South African casualties in "the operational zone".'[29] A report from the *World* also stated that a poll taken during the invasion found that 203 out of 244 of its readers were not prepared to join the Whites in defending South Africa.[30]

Nonetheless there were few public statements by Blacks of support for the MPLA, and a seeming reluctance to discuss the issues in print. This

167

circumspection was, in part, a reflection of the fear of the Security Police. SASO and BPC had suffered severe losses after organising rallies to support Frelimo, and open support for the MPLA government in Angola could produce the same reaction. The BPC had passed a resolution at their conference in December 1975 recognising the MPLA as the legitimate government of Angola,[31] but do not appear to have given this much subsequent publicity. *Black Review*, 1975-76, contains no reference to Angola, nor to the resolutions of the BPC.

Conservative Blacks, aware of the feelings in their communities, did make statements. Most of them were oblique, and were couched in negative terms because these dignitaries could not support a movement (or government) that was condemned as Marxist. But they could not avoid the topic. Colin Legum quotes extracts from comments made at the time:

> 'Many blacks do not see themselves threatened as they are victims of other ideologies in South Africa.' Bishop Desmond Tutu (to a mainly white congregation at St Mary's Anglican Cathedral)

> 'People are saying "The devil we don't know cannot be worse than the devil we now know".' Professor Ntsanwisi (Chief Minister of Gazankulu)

> 'If the blacks don't have a stake in the country they cannot give it their full loyalty.' Dr. Phatudi (Chief Minister of Lebowa)[32]

Buthelezi's Road to Liberation

It was left to Mangosuthu Gatsha Buthelezi to make the most forthright public statement at a mass rally of between 16 and 18 thousand people on 14 March 1976. Buthelezi avoided mentioning the MPLA, but he proclaimed the collapse of the South African attempt to win allies in Africa (the so-called policy of detente) and maintained that the 'wind of change' was no longer distant, but was blowing on the borders of South Africa itself.

Buthelezi did not shy off the invasion of Angola, and he linked the strategic defeat of the South African army with events which were bound to follow in Namibia:

> Prime Minister Vorster's detente policy has not succeeded. Not only has it not succeeded but White South Africa has burnt her fingers in Angola. The pace of events and the struggle for liberation in Southern Africa is gaining momentum, to the extent that the country's all-White Parliament cannot dictate events in Namibia for very much longer . . .
> Every hour of the day, the time is drawing nearer, when we will see White South Africa's enemies encamped on South Africa's border.[33]

In his speech, which was enthusiastically received, Buthelezi spoke of the revolution that was coming and challenged the Whites to decide whether the revolution which was unfolding would be peaceful or bloody. He went further:

> It is still not too late for a white change of heart. I believe this not because I think that Whites are going to have a sudden spasm of benevolence towards Blacks. I believe that now the Whites can see the writing on the wall and can realise that the country must move towards majority rule.

The 'revolution' Buthelezi was calling for, he claimed, could be peaceful and compassionate. In the process of liberation, the church had a role to play which they had previously failed to fulfil:

> The Church must take active steps towards reconciliation in this country before it is too late. There will be no true reconciliation until the Blacks are liberated. The Churches must act with conviction and what is more they must act in public.

It is not clear how the church was supposed to assist the black liberation struggle nor, in fact, how Buthelezi saw this liberation being effected. He said that he wanted 'to go beyond negative criticism' and 'provide alternative policies'. To this end he proposed the holding of 'a series of representative National Conventions representing all shades of black opinion'. One was to be on economic matters, one on the 'Homeland Independence issue', and one on South Africa's foreign policy. He proposed that the first convention be summoned for August; that international speakers be invited; and that thereafter a black caucus deliberate on the problem themselves.

The role that Buthelezi saw for the black population at large was not stated, but they could hardly be other than observers at conventions. Their role in the liberation of the country was to do as they were told. In the first instance Buthelezi said: 'I am offering a Black hand of friendship [his own, presumably] to the Whites of South Africa, probably for the last time. Yes, it is a Black hand, but it is still a hand of friendship.' He returned to this theme later in his speech:

> I have in the past called upon the Whites to come to their senses. The Whites are politically underdeveloped and they need assistance. The federal formula I offered them was a compromise proposal and I must say with considerable emphasis that such reconciliatory offers will be increasingly difficult to offer in the South Africa that is now emerging.

Having stressed his own role in offering to make the 'Homelands' system work — albeit concealed in the phrase about a 'federal formula', the speaker turned to his audience:

> My brothers and sisters, when I lie awake, thinking about you and your

suffering, I know that thousands of you get on crowded buses and trains to go to a menial job for a pittance. Most of you work without security and social benefits, and are denied real trade unions. I know you are exploited. I know you feel anger because there seems to be no hope of improving your circumstances.

My message to you is that history has overtaken apartheid. There *is* hope for the future. Justice *will* prevail, and you *will* be given the opportunity of participating in the building of a better South Africa.

Buthelezi seemed to have begged the question. He had moved from exploitation to a better society without explaining how justice would be made to prevail. He therefore moved to fill this lacuna:

My message to you, however, is that there is no magic formula to change the present Racist Regime into a garden of Eden overnight. The sweat of the Blackman built the economic wealth of South Africa which is denied to the Sons and Daughters of South Africa. It will be by the sweat of the Blackman's brow that a new future will be built.

I appeal to your sense of realism to act constructively. We do not build a better South Africa by doing something in the future. We build a better South Africa in what we do *now*. (Buthelezi's stress throughout)

It is hard to believe that Buthelezi's audience grasped the full implications of what had been said. Even at this distance it is difficult to see how he could have spoken to an audience in Soweto and told them that liberation would come by means of hard work, or how they could respond to an appeal to 'act constructively'.

Buthelezi's appeal was to quietism, and it was not insignificant that he did not raise a single real issue. The agitation at the time over the rising price of food, the cost of transport, the language issue in the schools, the increasing arrests under the pass laws, the ever rising number of unemployed, went unmentioned. Even his call to join Inkatha (or a set of.Inkathas which would join in a national movement for liberation) was shrouded in mysticism. He promised his audience that: 'As this movement gains momentum we will produce a ground swell which will bring about change in South Africa.' But obviously his audience had to take it on trust that the speaker would ensure that there would be a ground swell and that change would follow.

Although the Chief's words seemed at times to offer a new lead, there were peculiar gaps in his pronouncements. He did not call for radical changes in the country and he did not inveigh against foreign investment. Yet, only four days before, in a statement signed jointly by Buthelezi and Dr. C.F. Beyers Naudé, both these issues featured prominently, alongside a call for a National Convention on foreign investment in South Africa.

In many respects the joint statement, which would not have been widely distributed in Soweto, if at all, was far more militant in tone than the text of the Soweto speech. It commenced with the demand for: 'A radical redistribution of wealth, land and political power . . . [and] . . . the establishment of a stable and moral society in South Africa.' The document then claimed that:

> In South Africa for over a century capitalistic paternalism has produced the conclusive evidence which makes us reject government by minority elite. Men have been consistently dehumanised, the many blatantly crushed to reproduce wealth for the few, and the whole of society designed to protect and intensify the naked exploitation of man by man.[34]

The formulation is open to objection. The crushing of many to produce wealth for the few can hardly be described as 'capitalistic paternalism', but there is no need to quibble here on a relatively minor point. What does need explanation from Buthelezi is the compatibility of this statement with a call to workers to continue as before and provide their sweat to extend this wealth.

The statement of 10 March was not very instructive on the question of political and economic change. The authors said that the Blacks would 'require for themselves the liberation they witness amongst their brothers in neighbouring states'. But apparently this would be achieved without great effort by the workers: 'We are convinced that this capitalistic endeavour is doomed. It will fail because the selfishness of South Africa's white elite is already unrealistic and cannot survive in today's world . . .'

Having made these assertions the two authors came to the nub of their document. They condemned government statements which relegated the 'homelands' economies to a subsidiary position in the greater South African economy. Under these conditions they maintained: 'Foreign investment in the central economy is devoid of all morality.'

It is not possible to discuss here all the implications of this statement — that must be done elsewhere. It must be noted, however, that it scrupulously avoided any mention of investments in the Reserves. Buthelezi had been an active advocate of the need to attract foreign capital to KwaZulu, and he had travelled abroad to win such investment. This apparently was not to be described as 'devoid of morality', and raises many questions also about the role of Dr. Beyers Naudé, erstwhile ally of SASO/BPC, and the latter's condemnation of Buthelezi for encouraging such investment. These issues, presumably, could be discussed at another National Convention.

The March supplement to *Pro Veritate*, besides carrying the text of Buthelezi's speech, also carried a statement signed by Timothy Bavin (Anglican Bishop of Johannesburg), Denis Hurley (Roman Catholic Archbishop of Natal) and Dr. C.F. Beyers Naudé. The three churchmen welcomed the speech as a 'courageous and reconciliatory call to a revolution in attitudes. . .' and praised it in glowing terms:

> The Chief's astute call is the true recognition by a Christian layman that God summons Christians to a new involvement and commitment in these

171

days of portent. God is calling his people to Christian liberation, that is, to an acceptance of the law of love, not only between individuals in limited communities, but also between communities themselves, between races, nations and classes. Black liberation, and the consequent liberation of whites, which blacks fervently desire, are fundamentally activities of this law of love.[35]

Concluding that the leaders of Southern Africa needed the 'true insights of the Christian gospel', they urged that black Christians take the initiative and call a National Convention on Christian concern.

The multiplicity of National Conventions that were proposed must have seemed irrelevant to the bulk of the population, and certainly had no effect on the students. There were clear indications that the latter would have nothing to do with any project mooted by Buthelezi when some 200 students demonstrated against him and stoned his car at the graduation ceremony at Ngoye in May when he was awarded an honorary doctorate. The SRC, furthermore, refused to apologise to the KwaZulu government for the incident.[36] With the students opposed to him, and undoubtedly most of the clerics attached to the BPC likewise, the only persons that would have attended the proposed Conventions would have been men and women who were prepared to collaborate with the government. These were indeed precisely the people that Buthelezi brought into his Black United Front later that year. By that time the townships were in revolt and in Soweto National Conventions were irrelevant.

References

1. The Commission was the successor to a Parliamentary Select Committee established in 1972. The Commission was also required to investigate the activities of the already disbanded UCM.
2. Quoted in *SRRSA*, 1974, p.33.
3. An extract from the NUSAS press statement is quoted in *SRRSA*, 1974, p.36.
4. *SRRSA*, 1975, p.34.
5. Extracts from the rebuttal, quoted in *ibid.*, pp.34-5.
6. *Black Review*, 1974-75, provides a list of known detainees, p.91.
7. *SRRSA*, 1975, p.63.
8. *Ibid.*, pp.62-3.
9. *Ibid.*, pp.64-5.
10. Christian Institute, (1976), *Detention and Detente in Southern Africa*, Johannesburg, p.24.
11. *Loc.cit.*
12. See Donald Woods, *op.cit.*, p.114; and IUEF, (1976), *The new terrorists: documents from the SASO/BPC trial*, Geneva, indictment, pp.1-11.
13. *Black Review*, 1974-75, pp.84, 85, 87.
14. *Ibid.*, p.90.

15. *SRRSA*, 1977, p.132.
16. Raymond Suttner, (1976), 'Why I will go to prison', UN Centre Against Apartheid, *Notes and documents*, No. 1/76.
17. *Detention and Detente, op.cit.,* p.22.
18. *Ibid.,* p.6.
19. *Loc.cit.*
20. *Loc.cit.*
21. *SRRSA*, 1976, pp.129-30.
22. *Black Review*, 1974-75, p.88.
23. The Minister of Labour, quoted in *SRRSA*, 1977, p.306.
24. David Hemson, 'Black trade unionism, industrial strikes, and mass struggles in South Africa', (mimeo), quoting from Bulletin of Statistics, September 1976.
25. Details of the boycott are taken from *SRRSA*, 1975, pp.88-9, and *Anti-Apartheid News*, November 1975.
26. *SRRSA*, 1976, p.180.
27. The *Star*, 8 May 1976 and *Rand Daily Mail*, 27 May 1976.
28. Quoted in Colin Legum, (1976), *Vorster's Gamble for Africa: How the Search for Peace Failed*, (Collings), p.45.
29. Alex Callinicos and John Rogers, (1977), *Southern Africa after Soweto*, (Pluto), p.157.
30. Quoted in C. Legum, *op.cit.,* p.45.
31. *SRRSA*, 1976, p.23.
32. C. Legum, *op.cit.,* p.45.
33. Mangosuthu G. Buthelezi, (1976), 'A message to South Africa from black South Africa', printed as a supplement to *Pro Veritate*, March 1976. All quotations from this speech are taken from this source.
34. 'Foreign investments in South Africa', a statement signed by Chief Gatsha Buthelezi and Dr. C.F. Beyers Naudé, 10 March 1976.
35. Timothy Bavin, Denis E. Hurley and Dr. C.F. Beyers Naudé, (1976), 'A National Convention on Christian Concern for Southern Africa' printed in supplement to *Pro Veritate*, March 1976.
36. *Black Review*, 1975-76, pp.156-7.

10. The Soweto Revolt: June 1976

Chaos in the African Schools

The reorganisation of the African schools in the wake of the changes governing secondary school entrance led to conditions bordering on chaos. The first step was scheduled for December 1974 when all pupils in the sixth standard who obtained over 40 per cent would qualify for entrance to secondary school. This, it was estimated, would double the number of candidates for the first form. In one instance that has been reported, the full impact of the change proved to be disastrous.

KwaMashu, the township just north of Durban, had an official population of 22,000 families. The entire area contained only one secondary school and it was already overcrowded. After the examination results were announced in December 1974, parents were informed that: '. . . hundreds of standard six pupils who passed their final examination in 1974 were required to repeat the standard in 1975 because of the shortage of schools.'[1] Parents were told that 'there would be confusion' if only a small number of the successful candidates entered Form One. At the end of 1975 the number of candidates requiring positions in the secondary schools would again be doubled when the sixth standard in primary school was phased out.

The situation did not, however, lead to any student action. At a time when everyone was clamouring to get into a school, there was little opportunity for any group to suggest a boycott, a demonstration, or a strike. Any such proposal would have run counter to the incessant demand for a place in the schools.

The apparent quiescence in the urban (township) schools contrasted markedly with the position in the rural areas. Since 1972 there had been reports in the press and Parliament of widespread dissatisfaction and student action. In 1972 there were reports of violence and damage to property in at least five schools. It was also reported that 296 pupils had been arrested and 37 convicted in the courts.[2] In 1973 there were signs of widespread strikes and demonstrations, not much below the level of action in the immediate post-war years. At least six schools or training colleges in Lebowa in the northern Transvaal, two schools in the Transkei, and one each in the Ciskei and in KwaZulu experienced strikes, arson, or other student action. Over 600

174

pupils were arrested, and at least 472 convicted by the courts.[3] In one case, at Cofimvaba High School in the Transkei, pupils stoned the principal's house, overturned a police car, and looted the school shop. One hundred and thirty were arrested and 116 found guilty and either fined or sentenced to cuts with the light cane.[4]

There was little relaxation in 1975. Nine schools in the Transkei, including five primary schools, Mariannhill near Durban, Hammanskraal near Pretoria, the Moroka High School at Thaba'Nchu in the OFS, and a school in the Ciskei were all reported to have been the scenes of violence. Over 2,000 pupils were sent home, (some being told that they could re-apply for admission), hundreds were expelled, and the police made large-scale arrests.[5] The discontents were not dissimilar to those registered in the forties and fifties. There were complaints about the food, about unnecessary restrictions on freedom in the dormitories, and general hostel conditions. The one difference in 1972-75 was that the principals and teachers were now all black and were operating a state controlled system.

The Campaign to Stop Afrikaans Medium Lessons

The instructions issued from the office of the Minister of Bantu Education that half the subjects taught in standard five and in the first form be in Afrikaans, was immediately opposed by parents, teachers and pupils. This opposition grew during the closing months of 1975, and by early 1976 there were demonstrations in some schools against the introduction of lessons in Afrikaans. As the protests increased, school after school, at least in the Soweto region, joined forces and eventually marched together in the demonstration of 16 June that sparked off the Revolt.

The widespread opposition to the new regulation, which brought together conservatives and radicals, teachers and taught, indicated that the many strands of opposition — based on very different premises — were uniting against something more than an instruction over language. In 1976 the united stand against Afrikaans, was only the external manifestation of the deep resentment inside the townships against the entire administration. Moreover the language predominantly used by police, prison warders, pass-office officials, township administrators and, indeed, the entire bureaucracy, was Afrikaans.

There were reasons for opposing Afrikaans, and there were reasons for preferring English. From the point of view of the educationalist, a switch to instruction in Afrikaans would be disastrous. Time and again both teachers and pupils stressed the fact that their education was inferior to that of the Whites. The view of a young African, reported in the *Natal Mercury* in February 1975, was not atypical: 'The education given to Africans is so low that a Junior Certificate [that is, third form pass] with us is equivalent to a standard 6 in the other racial groups.'[6] There were no easy solutions to the problem and little chance of improvement in a system which was designed to

175

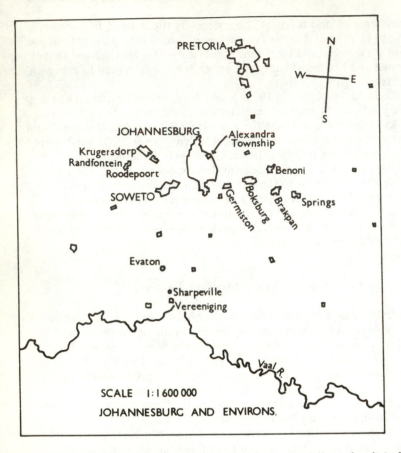

SCALE 1:1 600 000

JOHANNESBURG AND ENVIRONS.

fit youth for a subservient position, economically, socially and politically. Yet it was perceived that education conducted in Afrikaans would lead to a definite deterioration in standards. African teachers had received instruction almost exclusively in English, and many were barely able to converse in Afrikaans. They could not possibly have conducted a course of instruction in that language, and it was inconceivable that they could ever master the technical language required for the classroom in a language they did not speak — more especially for arithmetic or mathematics.

The secretary of the African Teachers Association of South Africa (ATASA) stated the teachers' case in measured terms:

> To say that the Blacks are opposed to the study of Afrikaans is a gross understatement . . . In strict terms what we oppose now is the manner in which this is being done without regard to the interests of the children concerned. And if this trend continues without being checked then the education of the Black child will be seriously threatened . . .[7]

Parents and their children and, undoubtedly, many teachers objected to the new regulations for a number of reasons which included the widely held contentions that: English was the main language of industry and commerce, and was essential for any youth who wanted to find a place inside the economy of South Africa; it was an international language and the medium through which contact could be maintained with the rest of Africa; and it was the one lingua franca which bound Blacks, at least in the urban areas, together.

For the school pupils, or at least for that section which sought to organise opposition to the system of Bantu Education, the language issue assumed importance because it bound together pupils in the primary and the secondary schools on a single issue and offered a theme around which a campaign could be built.

The first vocal protests seem to have come from the School Boards in Soweto. These were bodies set up under the Bantu Education Act to administer Community Schools, and were considered by all anti-government groups to be instruments of the Department of Bantu Education. Nonetheless the first recorded opposition came from the Meadowlands Tswana School Board early in 1976. The Board issued a circular, under the names of Abner Letlape and Joseph Peele, countermanding the instruction that Afrikaans be used as a medium of instruction in the schools.[8] The two men were dismissed and the dispute, between School Boards and parents and the Department, was openly acknowledged.

Active student opposition seems to have commenced with an altercation between third form pupils of the Thomas Mofolo Secondary School and their principal over the introduction of Afrikaans on 24 February 1976.[9] Motapanyane, recalling the confrontation in 1977 stated:

> As early as March 1976, Thomas Mofolo was the first school to have Afrikaans imposed on it, and immediately there was a student protest. In March 1976, the principal called in the police to cool the students and force them to accept Afrikaans. Some students from my school, Naledi High School, went there to investigate their problems. We also visited schools in Meadowlands. We found that these students also felt bitter about what the government was doing. They immediately stopped attending classes because they felt as we did that what was needed was a positive reaction.[10]

The parents' committee then intervened and approached the school inspectors. But they were rebuffed. Motapanyane continued his account:

> The Naledi High SASM branch also went to Orlando West Junior Secondary. . . . The students there agreed with us and started destroying their books and refused to attend classes. And this was the first effective protest started in Soweto . . . because the students there were quite clear about what they wanted. Despite the threat by the Bantu Education inspector that the schools would be closed . . . they remained very

firm . . . We went on to other schools . . . By May 1976, the protest
actions were quite general in many schools.[11]

By now a large number of schools in Soweto were in an uproar. Normal
lessons were replaced by debates on current affairs or on the shape of things
to come. Essays were attempted on the shape of South Africa twenty-five
years hence. Teachers joined pupils in these discussions and there were few
signs of the supposed age gap between the generations. The students discussed
the US, the role of the Black Power movement, and Martin Luther King (a
much admired figure). They spoke of orderly change in the country leading
eventually to majority rule and there was, it appears, little talk of revolutionary activity. Some schools were more aware politically than others, and the
extent to which such discussions took place varied from school to school.
Naledi and Orlando West (amongst others) were developing a very conscious
student leadership and were to provide many of the leaders in the months to
come.

Young men and women were drawn into the vortex of politics and learnt,
within the space of weeks, what might otherwise have remained outside their
experience. Daniel Sechaba Montsitsi, fourth president of SASM, told the
World in an interview on 27 February 1977 that, until he joined SASM, he
knew nothing of the ANC or the PAC. Thousands of other could undoubtedly
have made similar remarks.

By May 17, 1,600 pupils had withdrawn from Orlando West Junior
Secondary School[12] and over 500 pupils at the Phefeni Junior Secondary
School refused to attend classes and stoned the principal's office.[13] The
following day two further schools closed and the children congregated in the
school grounds, playing and skipping, while teachers stood by unwilling to
interfere.[14]

At this stage there was no clear direction from any organisation; children
left the classrooms and in many cases drifted back. None of them, however,
took any heed of threats — either of expulsion or that schools would be
closed down and teachers transferred.[15]

The first overt violence was reported on 27 May, when a teacher of
Afrikaans at Pimville Higher Primary School was stabbed with a screwdriver.
The police who arrived to arrest the offending pupil were stoned.[16] The
stonings were henceforth a regular feature of the violence that was evident
everywhere. On 5 June, pupils at the Belle Higher Primary School stoned
children who had returned to classes during an apparent lull in the boycotts.[17]
Motopanyane adds from his own recollections:

> Early in June the police sent their men to collect one of our colleagues
> . . . They arrested one student but he was later released. Then on the 8th
> they came again. Hey, it was unfortunate for them to be seen by the
> students. They were beaten and their car was burnt. On that day they were
> coming to arrest our local secretary of SASM at our school . . . in connec-
> tion with the student protests . . .[18]

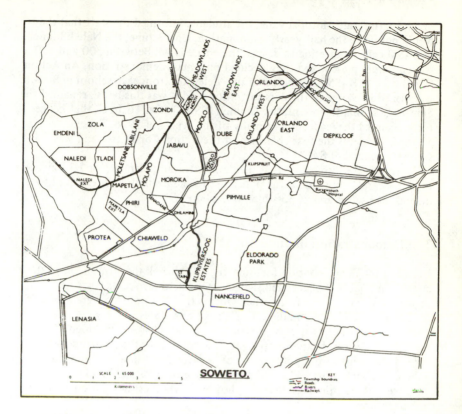

Thereafter, said Motopanyane, the students informed the staff that they would not write the half yearly examination. On 13 June, the Naledi branch of SASM called a meeting to discuss the entire issue. Between 300 and 400 students were present and they decided on a mass demonstration. An Action Committee of SASM, composed of two delegates from each school in Soweto, was placed in charge of the demonstration, and it was this body, renamed the Soweto Students Representative Council (SSRC) after 16 June, that henceforth assumed the leadership of many of the events of 1976. Tebello Motopanyane was the first chairman of the Action Committee and was secretary-general of SASM.[19]

Motopanyane also stated that the demonstration, planned for 16 June, was to be peaceful — but that if the police used violence they were resolved to defend themselves and, if possible, to retaliate.

The Demonstration of June 16, 1976

In calling the demonstration for June 16, SASM took the struggle on to the streets, and publicly challenged the government to revoke its language regulations. It is evident from other sources that the students were aware of the need for solidarity and discipline. Pupils at schools which were not thought to be wholeheartedly against the regulations were excluded.[20] It is not clear, however, from Motopanyane's account how the students meant to defend themselves from police violence or how they thought they would be able to 'hit back'. The realisation that their demonstration could lead to violence was realistic. It is doubtful, however, whether they anticipated what was to follow.

The nature of such demonstrations generally was discussed in a seminal essay written by John Berger in 1968. People, he said, congregated in an announced public place. 'They are more or less unarmed . . . They present themselves as a target to the forces of repression serving the state authority against whose policies they are protesting.'[21] Demonstrations, said Berger, are a trial of strength. They indicate the extent of popular support for the protesters and they reveal the intentions of the authorities. Yet presumably both these factors are known beforehand. As Berger stated:

If the state authority is open to democratic influence, the demonstration will hardly be necessary; if it is not, it is unlikely to be influenced by an empty show of force containing no real threat.

Demonstrations took place before the principle of democracy was ever nominally admitted. [The Chartist demonstrations, and the presenting of the petition to the Czar in 1905, were appeals to authority for an extension of democracy] . . . In the event — as on so many hundreds of other occasions all over Europe — they were shot down.[22]

If, then, the state, and particularly the state which is not amenable to

democratic practices, will not make any significant concessions, the demonstrations 'are rehearsals for revolution' or, more explicitly, 'rehearsals of
revolutionary awareness'.[23] But, '. . . any demonstration which lacks this
element of rehearsal is better described as an officially encouraged public
spectacle.'[24]

Few, if any, of the pupils gathered together on 13 June could have
envisaged their proposed demonstration as a 'rehearsal for revolution'. It was
nevertheless a rehearsal of revolutionary awareness that had grown out of the
increasing tempo of clashes in the preceding months. The number of youth
that gathered for the demonstration at 7.0 a.m. on the morning of the 16th
was an indication of the intensity of feeling in the schools, centred emotion-
ally on the issue of Afrikaans.

Fifteen thousand youth, ranging in age from 10 to 20 years, were ready to
march off, bearing slogans written on cardboard torn from packing cases or
on the stiff covers of old exercise books. The banners were all makeshift and
bore signs of rapid construction. The slogans were simple and to the point:

Down with Afrikaans
Afrikaans is oppressors language
Abolish Afrikaans
Blacks are not dustbins — Afrikaans stinks

The plan was for the columns to converge at the Orlando West Junior
Secondary School, and from there march to the Orlando stadium — one of
the few large open spaces in Soweto. The column that wound its way through
the streets of Orlando was, by all reports, carefree and jovial. The youth
greeted car drivers with raised clenched fists and shouts of *Amandla* (Power).

Then, apparently, a message got to the leader of the column that the police
were coming. Sophie Tema, veteran reporter, in recalling the event as she saw
it, said that one of the leaders stopped the column and addressed the
students:

Please brothers and sisters I plead with you, remain cool and calm. A
report has just been received to say the police are coming. We do not
know what they are after, after all we are not fighting. All we want is that
the department and officials must listen to the grievances of our brothers
and sisters in the lower schools.[25]

Ms. Tema recorded her apprehension as she watched the police arriving: 'I
had seen at Turfloop on 25th September 1974, how the students were
attacked with batons and teargas by the police even before they showed signs
of hostility.'[26]

What happened next is not altogether certain. Ms. Tema saw a policeman
throw what she thought was a tear gas canister into the crowd; Willie Bokala,
another journalist, said he saw a white police officer pick up a stone and hurl

it into the crowd. The children in the front rank turned and scattered. Some reporters stated that the children retaliated by hurling stones at the police — others say that the police opened fire first. A reporter of the *Rand Daily Mail* wrote:

> I did not hear the police give any order to disperse before they threw tear gas canisters into the crowd of singing school children. The children scattered in all directions . . . The pupils then regrouped and when the police charged again, they threw stones at the police. The police then fired a few shots, some in the air, the others into the crowd. I saw four school children fall to the ground.[27]

On June 16, the school students stayed firm and threw stones. It was an unequal battle — stones against bullets. Some fled, others fell, but those behind stepped in and closed the ranks. Observers commented on the fact that the youth seemed oblivious of the danger. They kept advancing on the police and pelting them with any object at hand.

The Youth Take Revenge

By 10.00 a.m. youth were surging through Soweto, taking what revenge they could for the massacre of their fellows. They stoned passing cars, set up barricades and stopped delivery vans and buses, burnt down the major administrative buildings, and attacked beerhalls, bottlestores and some shops. The beerhalls were gutted, the bottlestores destroyed, and slogans attacking drink appeared on the walls. Two white officials, one caught in the administrative centre, were killed.

There could be little doubt that the object of the attacks was to destroy all symbols of state control. The demonstrators had moved beyond the stage of congregation and had taken the next logical step — they had shown that they could occupy the area, even if they were still far from having the power to maintain that occupancy. They could destroy the symbols of power despite their obvious inability to install their own power.

In his essay, Berger explored this aspect of mass action. Demonstrations, he said, were essentially urban phenomena, and were usually planned to take place near the symbolic centre. The action involved the 'symbolic capturing of the city', where the 'regular life of the streets' was disrupted. Berger continued: 'They "cut off" these areas and, not yet having the power to occupy them permanently, they transform them into a temporary stage on which they dramatise the power they still lack.'[28]

The demonstration in Soweto was somewhat different. The life of Soweto was disrupted or, at least, the region of Orlando was. But the demonstration was not in an urban centre such as Berger was describing. In fact, in the months to come, the youth showed their realisation of the weakness of their position and tried to enter the centre of the 'white' city. But on June 16 they operated inside the township. They certainly lacked the power to take over the area permanently, but they dramatised their situation by destroying the existing symbols of power.

There was some similarity between the separated housing areas of Johannesburg and Soweto, and the divisions between Catholic and Protestant housing in Northern Ireland; and the experience of militants in that country proved to be apposite to Soweto that day. One participant in the fighting in Ireland in the seventies stated:

> We were to learn in time that when organising a march towards confrontation it is essential to begin in 'home' territory and march out, so that there is somewhere for people to stream back to if this proves necessary.[29]

To move out of Soweto there would have had to be a different type of organisation and a different kind of demonstration. The fact was that the demonstration was in the heart of Soweto and, when police reinforcements were brought in, there was nowhere to 'stream back to'. Furthermore, when the residents returned that night, unaware of the events of the day, they were met by rows of police who confronted them with canisters of tear gas and drawn batons. Because the demonstration had not, indeed could not, move out of home territory, the returning workers found themselves in the midst of a battleground.

The police attack on tired commuters was an indication of the state's determination to intimidate and destroy the student movement, and poses the question of whether the earlier shooting that day was accidental; or a deliberate act by the police, in the belief that one salvo would end the entire protest. The police failed that morning because they had not understood the depth of frustration and anger in the township. They miscalculated again that evening and the workers, instead of turning tail, responded as the youth had in the morning. They hurled bricks and stones at the police and joined the youth in the streets. When buses returned from the city with full loads, they were commandeered and destroyed. Soweto shops, beerhalls, liquor stores and official buildings burnt through the night leaving only charred walls and scribbled slogans.

Police Terror

The police action in Soweto on 16 June (and subsequently) also indicated the weakness of fighting in that particular kind of 'home territory'. Regulations governing the layout of townships, in force over many decades, were designed to provide the police with the maximum manoeuvrability and control in the event of any disturbance. Townships were always designed with provision for the marshalling of armoured cars at convenient vantage points, and houses were always placed in low lying areas where they could be kept under surveillance.

In an interview with the city engineer of Durban in 1957, a group of young (white) architects were told that a number of conditions had to be observed in the layout of an African township. Three provisions which particularly struck one of the architects, Alan Lipman, at the time, were:

> The width of the roadways would have to be sufficient to allow a Saracen [tank] to execute a U-turn.
>
> . . . the distance between houses had to be kept above a given minimum, and the houses had to be aligned so that firing between houses would not be impeded, and so that there would be no shelter for a fugitive.
>
> The distance between the boundaries of a township and the main highways had to be beyond the range of a .303 rifle.[30]

When the para-military police poured into Soweto on June 16, their effectiveness was ensured by the ease with which they could move through the main roads in their Hippo armoured cars and the ability to direct their firepower between the houses. They shot at random and they shot to kill. Any person suspected of being a 'leader' was pursued and shots often found a target. Other youth were considered fair game and if sighted on the streets were instant targets.

The number that died on 16 June, or in the days to come, is not known. Some sources said that the death toll on the first day was 25; others placed it at nearer 100. Nobody knew, and the police took every step to prevent a full list being compiled. Journalists were warned to keep away from piles of bodies, on the grounds that it was none of their business! Baragwanath hospital was closed to the public. Lorries arrived and took away corpses, and many were never accounted for then, or later.

Deaths at the hands of the police had become commonplace in the country. Figures of casualties due to police action in the 'normal course of their duties', as supplied by the Minister of Police in Parliament, are given in Table Nine.

The ever rising toll of persons killed due to police action (as supplied officially) excluded fatalities in the prisons. The numbers were alarming and increasing complaints were voiced about the trigger-happy police. In 1976, exclusive of casualties sustained as a result of the Revolt in the country, the police killed 195 persons and injured 410. Most of the fatalities were adults, and very few juveniles had ever been injured. When, on that first day, the number of children shot dead was well over 20, and possibly even 100, there was universal black fury, and in townships throughout the country there were calls to revolt.

The Response of a People

This widespread reaction had obviously not been anticipated by the government. It had also not been anticipated by SASM and, after the first shootings,

184

Table 9
Persons Killed and Injured by Police in the 'normal course of duty' 1971-76[31]

| | | *Number Killed* | | | *Number Injured* | |
Year	Total	African	Coloured	Total	African	Coloured
1971	54	42	11	223	165	53
1972	94	77	14	299	237	52
1973	117	98	16	352	278	60
1974	102	88	11	354	288	57
1975	134	106	25	382	299	79
1976*	195	165	28	410	345	53

Note: The total includes a few Whites and/or Indians who are not listed
separately.
* Excluding any persons killed or injured as a direct result of the Revolt.

they worked on an *ad hoc* basis, sending some of their fellows to nearby
townships to inform people of events and urge them to spread the revolt. In
some regions there were SASM branches or other groups that took the
initiative and organised some action. In general, however, there was no central
co-ordinating body. This was, in some respects, an advantage. There was no
head that could be lopped off, and each region acquired its own momentum.
Local groupings (some of which will be discussed below) were content to
observe events elsewhere and then call their own supporting actions. The
same pattern had been observed earlier during the strike wave. But once again
it was found that an initial strength turned to weakness and, in many centres,
the local leadership was found by the police and snuffed out. Without some
central body to assist areas that had been silenced, the townships in question
took little part in subsequent events.

It was in the nature of the segregatory pattern of the country that some
groups would always be isolated, and that was the fate of the small band of
radical students at the University of the Witwatersrand. The very next day,
Tuesday 17 June, 400 white students expressed their solidarity with the
pupils of Soweto in a march near the campus. They were joined by black
spectators who marched with them. Police and a group of Whites (said later
to be plain clothes police) wielding chains and staves broke up the demonstration. When the students regrouped later they were again attacked by
police. This was the only overt action attempted by white students in the
north and, after this initial action (for which they were severely castigated by
the university authorities), they played no further part in the Revolt.

In Soweto the Action Committee, which was soon to style itself the
Soweto Students Representative Council (SSRC), still had the support of the
school pupils and was able to offer some lead. But after June 16 there ceased
to be a leadership in overall control of events in the township; henceforth
these were often decided by individual initiative, or by small groupings

assuming local leadership. The SSRC only regained the initiative in late July.

On June 17, PUTCO suspended its bus service and a large number of residents were forced to stay in the township. They joined the youth who were back in the streets and erected road blocks. In the 'no-go' areas controlled by the residents, police patrols faced the possibility of ambushes from stone-throwing youngsters, and visibility was reduced by smoke from burning buildings, and from cars, vans and trucks which had been overturned and set alight.

Police vans and armoured cars patrolled the streets, and the crack of FN rifles was heard all day. Shooting was directed at groups of youth in the streets. A car driver who was careless enough to be seen giving the Black Power salute was killed by police. Often in plain clothes, the police were also seen cruising down the streets in cars, shooting down any child in sight. Other patrol cars lobbed gas canisters into houses in random fashion. The police aimed to terrorise and to kill — there were no initial attempts at arrest or detention.

Groups of youth infiltrated Dube, the more prosperous region of Soweto, and burnt down Barclays Bank. There were also reports that the homes of 'collaborators' and some of the more prosperous were set alight. Some of the richer inhabitants and some of the clergy left Soweto and sought refuge in Johannesburg; they did not return for many months, and a few were accommodated at the international hotel adjoining Jan Smuts Airport.

On the 17th there was news that the Revolt had spread beyond the borders of Soweto. At Kagiso (adjoining Krugersdorp) some schools were deserted and at least one was burnt, and at Thembisa (adjoining Kempton Park and near the airport) the schools were also emptied. There was intense fighting at Alexandra Township, a small black enclave of some 40,000 residents in northern Johannesburg. The youth poured out of the schools with banners pledging support to their fellows in Soweto. They set fire to the entire administration block and business centre, burnt vehicles and buses and, armed with stones, faced the police in their mine-proof Hippo vehicles.

The Alexandra region was sealed off by police blocks, and for the first time the Whites felt the direct impact of the Revolt. The roads to Pretoria and the North, and much of the traffic to Jan Smuts Airport, was halted by this police action. Residents in the neighbourhood organised the first white vigilante groups, and these were to patrol the surrounding white suburbs in the weeks to come.

On Friday 18 June, the third day of the Revolt, the pattern of events was repeated. Beerhalls and bottlestores were looted and burnt (if they had managed to escape the initial outbursts), passing cars faced stone-throwing youth, and burnt-out vehicles blocked the roads inside the township. Youth were now being detained by the police, and Mateu Nonyane, a reporter on the *Rand Daily Mail*, said that he heard people screaming and saw students being tortured in the courtyard of the Orlando police station. Outside the police station, bodies were piled up, and the heaps grew through the night of the 17th and on into the 18th.[32] The situation was unchanged at Alexandra and the reports filtering out spoke of intense fighting. In other townships along the Witwatersrand there were angry confrontations between the youth and police and, at Thembisa, more reports of attacks on administration buildings.

On Thursday the Minister closed the schools and on Friday the working week was over. At the weekend, the pattern of life in the township invariably changed, but the weekend after the Soweto shootings was unlike all others. Most shops were closed and the delivery of food stopped. The bottlestores stood gutted and the beerhalls closed (if not destroyed). Many homes were in mourning and the police admitted that 96 had died and over 1,000 had been injured in the three days. Many parents were unable to secure access to the mortuaries and no visitors were allowed at Baragwanath hospital. Those who were brought in were first checked by police before being given treatment, and relatives were refused entry.

For Soweto, as for Alexandra, Thembisa, Kagiso, and along the Witwatersrand there was a temporary lull, and reports of only sporadic action in some areas. There were reports of student activities from further afield when the news of 16 June became known. There had been a large demonstration at Turfloop and a Soweto solidarity boycott of lectures, and the University was closed on the 18th. Later, 176 students were detained. On 18 June the students at Ngoye burnt down the library, the administration building, and the DRC chapel. Several university vehicles were destroyed and two (white) staff members badly injured. Many students were arrested and the university was closed for the year.[33]

In Durban, the library of the University of Natal (black) Medical School was burnt down and 200 students organised a march down Umbilo Road on the way to the centre of the town. They were stopped by police and 87 were taken into custody; the others managed to slip away. The medical students were subsequently charged under the Riotous Assembly Act and were fined R50 each.[34]

The African university students in Natal played no further part in the events of 1976 as a corporate body and the students at Turfloop also seem to have been silenced. Students who later reappeared in the townships might have played some role as advisers, but most were known to the police and few could operate openly without fear of being detained.

There were also reports of disturbances in schools in the Orange Free State, and in Cape Town the police were on the alert and were patrolling the townships.

Revolt in the Northern Transvaal

In the early days of the Revolt, a large number of events in outlying districts were ferreted out by journalists. Many of them went over the telex and some were printed in the papers. Others never became known outside the small local (black) communities. But even those initial outbursts, once reported, received no further mention as the news of ever new incidents indicated that a national revolt was about to break out in South Africa. The Southern African News Agency (SANA), a 'loose association of free-lance journalists' (as they described themselves), sent out news of some of the early incidents. On 21 June they telexed: '. . . unrest has broken out in Basutho-Qwa-Qwa Homeland where student teachers attempted to burn down a training college. In the BophutaTswana Homeland all hostels and schools have been closed to avoid possible unrest.' On 23 June they telexed:

> . . . Jouberton Township, near Klerksdorp — 90 miles from Johannesburg . . . Police fired warning shots over the heads of high school students there who had attempted to hold a meeting. The meeting allegedly dissolved in uproar and soon afterwards cars and bottlestores were stoned, beerhalls raided and petrol pumps at the local Administration Board's Works Department were set on fire. . . . Police used a helicopter to disperse the crowds.
>
> Trouble broke out for the first time in the Lowveld [northern Transvaal] when the Teachers Training College (Ngwenya) at Lekazi Township near Nelspruit was set on fire. Damage estimated at R50,000.
>
> There were other incidents of arson in East Rand when a bottlestore and cinema were set on fire.[35]

These reports gave an insight into the depth of hatred throughout the country and the extent to which local groups responded to the events in Soweto. The two components that made up each incident — local resentment and response to national events — cannot be found in the terse telex communications. Nor is there any indication of what group, or groups of people, were involved in the local outbreaks. The gap between news item and social analysis in any locality will only be unravelled by close investigations of some of these regions. Writing from afar, there is no way of undertaking this detailed investigation and, at most, it will be possible to present some picture of unfolding events in a few of the major regions of revolt.

There are more reports from Pretoria than most other areas in the Transvaal outside Soweto. Although it is still not possible to provide more than an impressionistic picture, it is clear that events there were significantly different from those elsewhere in the country.

There were two townships on the borders of Pretoria, Atteridgeville which had an (official) population of 65,900 and Mamelodi with a population of 103,758.[36] It was declared government policy that the populations of these townships should be, as far as possible, confined to 'single' persons. That is, there was an embargo on erecting family houses, and it was planned to build only single-sex hostels in future. In the early seventies hundreds of families who were classified as Tswana had been removed to two towns in Bophuta-Tswana, GaRankuwa and Mabopane. The removal of the Tswana families was supposed to relieve the pressure on housing, separate out the 'ethnic' groups, and also provide a work force for industries on the borders of the Reserves — the so-called Border Industries. In effect, the housing shortage became even more severe because no new houses were built and there was no accommodation for the growing population in the two townships; the 'ethnic' composition of the Pretoria townships was not appreciably altered. The two townships in BophutaTswana, furthermore, attracted large numbers of Ndebele, Shangaan and Pedi and were hopelessly overcrowded. GaRankuwa had an official population of 81,241 in mid-1977 and over 20,000 squatters living in its outskirts; Mabopane's population was (officially) 86,900, and there were an estimated 350,000 squatters in the nearby Winterveld area.[37]

Both the Reserve townships were approximately 20 miles from Pretoria, and residents worked at Babelegi (inside BophutaTswana), Rosslyn (officially a Border area, but actually on the outskirts of Pretoria), and in Pretoria itself. In periods of tension these residents were affected by events in either BophutaTswana or Pretoria, or both!

On Monday 21 June, residents of both Pretoria and Mabopane entered the Revolt. At Mabopane two events coincided that day. One hundred and seventy workers at the Klipgat Waterworks struck work for higher wages and, according to the police, that precipitated the trouble.[38] At the local high school, students at assembly refused to leave for classrooms and the police were called in. There was shooting and at least one boy of 13 was killed. Students left the school and burnt buses which normally transported workers to Pretoria or Babelegi. They also closed the road to Pretoria, blocking any attempts to get to the city. Those that managed to slip through were turned back by police, uncertain of what the workers might do if they got to the factories!

In Attridgeville there was a mass march of pupils, confrontation with police and, after shootings, buses and beerhalls were burnt and bottlestores gutted. Students at Mamelodi were also out and the pattern of events was repeated. By mid-day both Pretoria townships were engulfed in the smoke of burning buildings, and at least 10 youth had been killed.

On 22 June, the Pretoria work force took further action. Over 1,000 stopped work at Chrysler Park car factory, claiming that they were concerned for the safety of their homes and families in Mamelodi. Although they appeared to make no demands, the matter was treated as a strike and the police were summoned. There were also reports that students were demonstrating in GaRankuwa and that they were stoning buses and burning buildings.

There are no indications of any co-ordination of events in Pretoria and Soweto, nor of events in the Pretoria townships of GaRankuwa or Mabopane. Each region, and each township, seemed to have responded to events in neighbouring towns and then acted largely independently of the other. There were occasional signs that activity initiated in one region was followed by another — but whether this was a reaction to press reports, or actual liaison between areas, has yet to be disclosed.

The BophutaTswana Reserve (or Reserves — there being 19 disconnected regions) had a total population estimated at just under 900,000. Of this, nearly one-third (284,000) were non-Tswana. Affairs in the Reserve parodied relations in South Africa and the minorities were treated as second-class citizens of BophutaTswana. Lucas Mangope, the Chief Minister, assisted the South African government in its policies and supported the removal of non-Tswana from the areas under his jurisdiction on the grounds that there were insufficient land and jobs for Tswanas.[39] The local administration also discriminated against non-Tswana who sought trading rights, and connived at the removal of Ndebele from Temba Township in Hammanskraal.[40]

One of the most contentious issues was the instruction from the Bophuta-Tswana Department of Education that Tswana be used as the medium of instruction in all schools.[41] This instruction was immediately challenged by Chiefs of the Ndebele, who had four tribal authorities under their control, but who were split geographically and existed under the suzerainty of BophutaTswana and Lebowa. These chiefs demanded their own 'Homeland' and the right to have their children taught in Pedi, their home language. At one stage the dispute over language-medium led to the closing of schools accommodating 4,000 youth. Although the South African government claimed that alternative schooling would be provided, the dispute extended through 1976, when Chieftainess Esther Kekane withdrew the Southern Ndebele representatives from the Legislative Assembly.[42]

The Lebowa authorities exacerbated an already tense situation when they demanded that GaRankuwa, Mabopane and Winterveld be removed from Tswana jurisdiction and declared international territory![43]

The struggle for land, jobs and privileges inside the Reserves was intimately connected with the struggle over the nature of education and the language of instruction. In the process the school pupils were left unsettled and their progress impeded.

It is not known how this protracted, if mainly verbal, fight influenced the youth of GaRankuwa, Mabopane or BophutaTswana. Their actions after 21 June indicated that they were thoroughly disenchanted with schools and with all tribal authorities. From 6 to 8 August schools were burnt down in GaRankuwa and Hammanskraal (home of Chieftainess Esther Kekane), and on 8 August students marched through Montshiwa township, near Mafeking, and burnt down the Legislative Assembly of BophutaTswana. The homes of Mangope and other cabinet ministers were placed under heavy police guard, and hundreds of men, women and youth detained.

There was no concerted move by pupils in Pretoria to coincide with events in the Reserves and, from both Atteridgeville and Mamelodi, there were sporadic reports throughout the rest of the year of buses being stoned, or of schools and other buildings being burnt. There were occasions when the events in Mamelodi (where the activity was most intense) seemed to coincide with campaigns in Soweto. But generally, those groups that offered leadership acted in response to local needs, in the schools, and in the community, and did not seem to act in concert with Soweto.

Leaders of the Revolt

Speaking in the immediate aftermath of the demonstration and shootings of 16 June, Hlaku Rachidi, president of the Black People's Convention, maintained that the old order would not easily be restored. He was reported in the press as saying:

> . . . The authorities, the parents and the teachers are going to be faced with a new child. The kids have learned a whole political lesson during the last week . . . They are rejecting the imposition of the whole White establishment and system plus the norms and values of Whites . . . The BPC interprets this as Black Consciousness in the kids. It is gut reaction, not lofty philosophy, and it reflects and articulates the feelings of the people.[44]

Rachidi's comments were themselves part of a 'gut reaction' to the revolt in Soweto. His assertion that a 'new child' was emerging and that the 'norms and values of Whites' were being rejected was part of BPC rhetoric and will be discussed in Part Three of this book. What is central to the issue of leadership, is that Rachidi did not then, or indeed later, claim that the BPC had either initiated the events of 16 June, or provided leadership for the events that followed. There was a strong thread of libertarianism in SASO/BPC: 'gut reaction' for them was more important than 'lofty philosophy' and more important than organisation and leadership.

The Action Committee/Soweto Students Representative Council

The Action Committee of SASM could not be satisfied with 'gut reactions' and did take some steps to widen the base of their revolt. Motapanyane, in his account of events, said:

> Immediately after [the shootings and stoning] . . . we told our students to do what they could to spread the actions to other locations. The struggle went on for some days immediately after June at the same pace because at that time the Action Committee was meeting everywhere in an attempt to intensify the struggle so that it should really be felt by the Government.
> *Question:* The struggle spread throughout the country within a short while. Was the spread of the struggle all organised by any centralised body, or did it have a spontaneous element to it?
> *Answer:* SASM is a national organisation and has regional and local branches. If a certain member of a team is doing something that is right, the rest of the team will join him to do it; it was not always a matter of having to instigate the others to do it.[45]

Where branches of SASM existed and were able to function, they might have followed the Soweto example and called on the student body to demonstrate. There were, however, few functioning branches because of continued police harassment.

In the absence of such branch initiative, or of other groups to call on the youth, there were cases in which school pupils did hear accounts from boys or girls who left Soweto soon after the initial shooting and returned to their home towns. One such recorded instance came from a student at UCT who interviewed pupils in the Cape Town townships. A girl at Guguletu High School stated that she and her classmates had heard a full account of events in Soweto from youth who had returned to Cape Town. In her opinion, it was this personal account which precipitated the local revolt.[46] Cape Town, in turn, provided a focus for events in the rest of the Western Cape. Local dissatisfaction fused with national revolt, each centre reinforcing the others and in turn receiving fresh impetus. Local organisation, growing out of groups that had existed before 16 June, issued leaflets, called for specific actions, or secured some influence amongst sections of the community. Some regions had committees that were acknowledged by at least part of the local community, and consequently initiated campaigns. There were other areas in which individuals, sometimes involved in local political groups, acted on their own initiative and organised some local action. That was the pattern of events in Kagiso (to be discussed below), where individuals who were members of a PAC cover-organisation, took it upon themselves to set buildings alight on 18 June.

It was only in Soweto that there existed a formal, non-clandestine organisation able to initiate a number of events over an extended period of time. That organisation was SASM, acting through an Action Committee and known to the public as the SSRC.

Since its inception in 1971 SASM had always functioned inside the schools and, prior to May 1976, had not engaged in public political affairs. After the introduction of Afrikaans language instruction it was thrust forward, first in the schools, and after the 'June 16 demo', in public, as an initiator of political activity. Also, before May, it had as an organisation faced a certain amount of harassment: after June 16 of course, its members were actively hunted down by the police. Before June its activities were partly shielded behind school walls; after the demonstration the schools were closed down and the membership scattered (literally) in the streets of Soweto. This body of school students, and in particular its leadership, unseasoned in political activity, had nonetheless to take the initiative in extending their struggle into the wider community and summonsing the entire population of Soweto to demonstrations against the apartheid system.

The transition from classroom discussion to strike and then revolt was far from simple. The members of the SSRC faced decisions that would have taxed a mature political organisation. More than that, the students had to define, and redefine, their position in society, and establish a relationship with the non-school-going youth, with their own parents, and with the wider working class community. There were severe shortcomings that had to be overcome in their understanding of (black) social forces. They had to appreciate the need to keep contact with the migrant workers who lived in the hostels and whose problems were so very different from those of householders, and they had to face confrontations with the 'push-outs' whose social aspirations were so different from their own.

In the course of time these youth would also have to face advances from members of both open and clandestine movements, and take decisions on proposals that they work with (or even under) the aegis of the BPC or the ANC. They had to decide on public statements and press interviews; make pronouncements on violence and non-violence; on strikes and boycotts; and more prosaically, on whether to return to schools, and whether pupils should write examinations.

The Perils of Leadership

The matter might have been simpler if the SSRC had been able to retain its leading cadres and had had a period of stability in which to consolidate its gains. This was a luxury it never found and, even though its leaders learned fast, the large losses to police action led to a continuous turnover in the leadership. Tsietsi Mashinini, the second president of the SSRC, was in office for only five weeks. On 23 August he left South Africa with the police hunting him and a price of R500 on his head. Khotso Seathlolo, president at the age of eighteen, lasted longer, but was shot and wounded in a car chase, in mid-January 1977, and escaped to Botswana. A number of his executive had been arrested earlier and one commentator said that at this stage '. . . this was the fourth time in as many months that the SSRC appeared to be dead.'[47] The SSRC was not dead, but it had to restart and gather together a new leadership. This repeated itself, although never under such difficult circumstances as in June 1977 when it was said of the new president that: 'Trofomo Sono, the new leader, was not picked because he had special leadership qualities. Only because he was one of only two executive members left to pick from.'[48]

The discontinuities in leadership, and the loss of membership due to deaths and detentions or flight, led to changes in tactics, altered orientations, and above all to indecision and uncertainty. This makes any generalisation about the SSRC, and any statement about the attitude of the students very difficult. Nevertheless some tentative analysis must be attempted if the events of 1976-77 are to appear as something more than a series of 'gut reactions' to events in the country.

In the days following the demonstration of 16 June, the students had the support of large sections of the township. Eric Abraham who interviewed Mrs. Nomzamo Winnie Mandela on 18 June for SANA telexed the following:

Abraham: . . . from the workers and adults I spoke to in Soweto yesterday it would seem that [the students] have the support of the black population at large and that the base of the confrontation has broadened beyond that of the Afrikaans language issue. Would you agree?
Mandela: Precisely. We warned the government that this would happen if they continue compelling the children to learn [Afrikaans] . . . and if they demonstrated their hatred against the language they have our full support. But as such, the Afrikaans issue was merely a unifying factor — it could have been anything.[49]

The extent of SSRC control of events in those first days is open to question. Very few people in the township had ever heard of SASM or of the Action Committee. In fact it did not seem to be until 1 August that Mashinini was able to address a meeting that had been called by the Urban Bantu Council — after a six-week interval in which all gatherings had been prohibited — and announce the existence of the SSRC.[50] Prior to that date the SSRC was known only by a small circle of persons who were not students.

It would have required a remarkable organisation to maintain control of the situation once the fighting began. The youth that fought were not all students, and there was no reason to believe that the 'push-outs' would, at that stage, have accepted instructions from students.

Soweto's population must have consisted of over half a million youth under 20 years (if it was similar in structure to other townships).[51] Of this number, those registered at school in 1976 were approximately 170,000. Not all these were known to support the SSRC, although eventually they could be expected to respond to SSRC instructions. However, there was no reason to suppose that those rejected by the school system had any particular regard for those receiving education. Although there was no assurance that Blacks who succeeded at school in South Africa would find lucrative careers waiting for them, the overwhelming drive by parents (and their children) to acquire education, was based on the supposition that at the end of a successful school career there would be enhanced economic opportunities. Those that fell by the wayside could only envy and, even possibly, hate the small group that achieved the necessary grades.

A number of push-outs — unemployed and with little hope of getting jobs — gathered daily in the streets of Soweto and of most urban townships. They were not in the demonstration on 16 June, but there is little doubt that they collected after the shooting and many must have been involved in the riots that followed. Some joined the students as fellow victims of apartheid. The cause for anger might have differed, but the anger itself was present in all. Perhaps the unemployed were more daring — but that is mere supposition. They struck together. There were others, however, who used the opportunity to loot; and in one report, dated 20 June, from SANA, it was said that:

> The inhabitants of the townships have formed themselves into vigilante groups to protect themselves from looters and vandals . . . and yesterday two looters were killed by such a vigilante group in the township of Alexandra.

After the first bout of rioting and looting, and more particularly when some authoritative voices were raised and there was some measure of leadership, the level of criminal activity dropped in the townships. All talk about the Revolt being the work of *tsotsis*, so prevalent in the white press in June, disappeared as the year progressed.

A drop in the crime rate is not, however, equivalent to acceptance of the students as leaders. The SSRC did not always secure the support of the student body in its instructions regarding returns to school or to writing examinations. There is even less reason to believe that youth not at school would accept SSRC instructions unless they were seen to satisfy their own special needs. The slogans used by the students were also not often designed to attract this element of the population, and it is difficult to see how demands relating to education could be designed to appeal to those who had already abandoned hope of further education. The origin of the Revolt had established a barrier that was not easy to transcend – and there is little evidence that any group was even aware of the difficulty.

One further comment on the students' organisation must suffice at this stage. The change of name after 16 June was primarily tactical in order to protect the membership from the police. But the choice of the new name, the Soweto Students Representative Council, was indicative of a change in direction. The students no longer claimed to represent all schools in South Africa, and this was a concession to reality. The new committee encompassed the schools of Soweto, and other localities owed no formal loyalty to it. Despite this, leaders of the SSRC still issued statements at times that were addressed to a national audience and claimed to come from a national leadership. The committee, furthermore, was marked as a students council, and this too was realistic. Because they had a confined constituency and a definite set of common aims, the students had a basis for organisation, for membership, and for the recruitment of leadership. The question of whether they were 'representative' was raised,[52] but under the conditions at that time, when the police were making every effort to destroy the body, the issue of democratic procedure in constituting the committee or in electing the officials was less important than the problem of survival.

A student council, fighting for student rights, is inevitably something different from a council that is directing the population in revolt, and this factor escaped the young men – there were few women in the leadership – who claimed on occasion to be the 'national leaders'.[53] Appearing openly, as they did, when there were no other functioning non-clandestine bodies prepared to take the initiative, the SSRC filled the gap and summoned the people of Soweto to participate in several important events. This seemed to have blinded the committee to the fact that they were *not* representative of the wider community and did not have the resources or the experience to extend and so deepen the Revolt. As an SSRC, the committee was more than sufficient to fight the school issues and also to obtain adult support for their cause. To extend the Revolt and secure basic social change, as their activities and statements implied at a later stage, was beyond the scope of an all-student body.

The Parents Play Their Part

Myths grow easily in periods of turbulence, and the belief that the SSRC alone was responsible for organising the township and for securing victories (limited as they were) has been widely accepted. In one respect this also led to acceptance of a second myth: that the Black Consciousness Movement (or more explicitly SASO/BPC) had organised, or led, the Revolt.

The connection, or supposed connection, between the Soweto Revolt and black consciousness was proclaimed from the beginning. And from the beginning it was denied. In the interview with Winnie Mandela, Eric Abraham recorded this exchange:

> *Abraham:* Would you agree then that black consciousness should be viewed as a strategy for change in this country?
>
> *Mandela:* Precisely. There is no other solution. Black has to speak for black, black has to develop self-reliance, self-pride and there is no other solution.
>
> *Abraham:* Winnie Mandela, would you agree that the confrontations which began in Soweto and have since escalated and spread to other parts of the Witwatersrand, and indeed other parts of South Africa, is a culmination or outcome of the Black Consciousness Movement?
>
> *Mandela:* Black consciousness is not a thing of today, it is not new. In fact it is not necessarily a culmination. What is happening is just ordinary black anger at the white racist regime. But it cannot necessarily be attributed to black consciousness as such. The issue is more that of a Black nation versus a white minority.[54]

Some opinions expressed by Mrs. Mandela are open to question, and will be discussed in Part Three, but her major contention, that the Revolt was not the outcome of the Black Consciousness Movement, accords with the evidence that has been presented above.

It is also obvious that the students' committee could not have proceeded unaided and the leaders were aware of this from the inception. Some resources were available in the community, and these the students obtained directly, or through the assistance of the Black Parents Association (BPA), formed a few days after the shootings began. Private transport was needed and, at a later stage, all public transport had to be stopped. The bus service was halted by direct action and the train service by sabotage, but private transport (both when required and at the time of the stay-at-homes) could only be regulated with the co-operation of the taxi drivers. This the students obtained, and taximen stood behind the SSRC. The doctors on the panel of one taxi association also supplied their services and this protected many victims of police firing from falling into the hands of the state.

The families, rather than the youth, required assistance for funerals, and through the BPA the services of undertakers, together with grants of money for the funeral services, were obtained. The co-operation of undertakers also led to the provision of free coffins, and the help that families received made it easier for them to accept the supreme burden they carried.[55] Assistance received by parents, whether spiritual or financial, also made it easier for the students to maintain cordial relations with the adults, and this contributed to the development of the Revolt.

196

Other associations in Soweto, some formal, some informal, rendered assistance in the course of the Revolt. The teachers, nurses, priests, and shop-keepers, and groups of mothers, and many others helped in a hundred little ways. They counselled, they tended the injured, they extended credit, or they brought water to douse tear gas; the many services usually found in a community were extended as the inhabitants of this beleaguered region came closer together in the face of police terror.

The full extent of community support to the students has still to be uncovered, although many of the significant acts of individuals will linger on only in the memory of persons directly involved. It is only when a community closes ranks and is prepared to assist, as Soweto inhabitants assisted, that a Revolt can be extended over a protracted period. It is only when householders are prepared to hide people on the run, and incur all the risks involved in defying the police, that a leadership can maintain itself — even if sorely depleted. These things the inhabitants of Soweto were called upon to do — some more, some less — and they responded magnificently despite the hardships involved.

There was surprisingly little formal organisation available to co-ordinate this vast supportive operation and, as in other cases discussed above, this did have advantages. The police were not able to decapitate and so remove this support.

The one organisation that was established was the Black Parents Association (BPA). Its origin was described by its first chairman, Dr. Manas Buthelezi, and then issued in 1976 as a confidential report by Horst Kleinschmidt of the Christian Institute. Dr. (later Bishop) Buthelezi said:

A few days after the outbreak of the large-scale disturbances in Soweto and other parts of South Africa, a meeting was called by black parents whose children had become the victims of police shooting, mass arrests and the many consequent hardships which would ensue. At this meeting which was supported by a vast number of influential Black organisations a committee was elected which was to attend to the needs which had thus arisen.[56]

The BPA, said the Bishop, was initially constituted in Soweto because it was there that the first shootings took place, and the meeting was called to take care of those victims. It soon had connections along the Witwatersrand and in Pretoria, and also contacts with legal firms in Durban and Cape Town who sought its help.[57]

The SSRC saw the BPA in a somewhat different light. Motapanyane's appraisal of the Parents Association was:

The main activity of the Black Parents Association was to get figures of how many people died. It was also there to give material assistance to people who were injured in the police shootings. It also had meetings with the authorities. We felt it was impossible for us as SSRC to meet Vorster and the so-called Minister of Bantu Education, M.C. Botha. We felt that they knew what we wanted and it was pointless for us to meet them.[58]

The BPA never did get to see the Minister because the government refused to meet their deputation, but in many respects the BPA did operate as the external mouthpiece of the student committee. The adult body was prepared to submit grievances supplied by the students to the authorities and was careful not to go beyond that mandate.[59]

The BPA's achievements were in the field of legal, medical and financial assistance, and in the arrangement of funerals, of which more will be said below. But their political role was very restricted. There was never any possibility of the BPA assuming a leading role in the Revolt, or providing the means for setting up a council which could play such a role.

The BPA committee was headed by Dr. Manus Buthelezi and included Nomzamo Winnie Mandela of the Black Women's Federation (and obvious links with the banned ANC), Mrs. Phakathi of the CI and the YWCA, Dr. Aaron Mathlare and Dr. Nthato Motlana — two medical officers, Thomas Manthatha and Aubrey Makoena of the BPC, and others. Yet despite the political affiliations of members of the committee, there was strong criticism of the BPA from the Black Peoples Convention because it was felt that the Association should have taken a stronger political lead.[60] They also faced criticisms from parents in the township on the grounds that they were not representative, because few of them were parents of school-going children. This matter was not however resolved, in part because the entire committee, with the exception of the Bishop, was detained in mid-August. Dr. Buthelezi had also been arrested, but was released after world-wide protests, and worked with a reconstituted committee which confined itself to providing aid for victims of the Revolt, and to detainees' families.[61]

The BPA also faced bitter attacks from members of the puppet Urban Bantu Councils, who did not hesitate to show their hostility to the SSRC or to persons who supported the students. An aspect of the bitterness with which this fight was being conducted surfaced when Winnie Mandela and Dr. Motlana made an urgent application to the courts on 15 August to restrain members of the UBC from interfering with their property and the lives of themselves and their children. The court was informed that at a meeting at the house of T. Makhaya, chairman of the UBC, Councillor Lucas Shabangu urged that the houses of Mandela and Mathlare be attacked, and that the children who tried to prevent workers going to work should be killed.[62]

Shabangu and Makhaya went into hiding after the court hearing and the UBC stood even more discredited than before. The two who made the court application disappeared into the gaols where they stayed in detention until their release in December 1976. Thereafter Winnie Mandela was banned and placed under house arrest, and five months later removed and placed under restriction in Brandfort, a remote town in the OFS.

The Underground Organisations

The ANC

A number of the organisations banned since 1951 and 1960 have claimed
that they continued operating inside South Africa clandestinely, and indeed
periodic reports of raids, detentions and arrests have indicated that cells of
the ANC, the PAC, and the South African Communist Party (SACP) still
functioned in the country. The raids had obviously disrupted work in the
ANC and the SACP during 1975, and a further set of arrests in mid-March
1976 dealt the ANC a particularly hard blow.

The ANC was known to some students and the fact that there were
underground groups became known from the newspaper reports of arrests and
trials, and also from pamphlets and journals that circulated in the townships.[63]
Some of the students were also persuaded to form cells of the ANC.
Motapanyane claimed that these were first formed in 1974 and that:

> They were formed by the ANC. We in SASM did not actually think of
> forming such things. We were operating legally and tried to keep SASM
> as a broad legal organisation. But some of us listened to our elders from
> the ANC when they said we needed more than just mass legal organisation.
> Hence we founded these underground cells.[64]

Nonetheless, because of poor organisation or bad communications, the
ANC did not seem to be aware of the extent of agitation and conflict over the
language issue, or the explosiveness of the situation in Soweto until the
conflict was far advanced.

The internal newsletter of the ANC, *Amandla-Matla*, issued in South Africa
in 1976, but before June, listed a number of issues on which it urged people
to campaign. The complaints that were mentioned covered everything from
rising prices to transport costs, rents, and workers' rights. They urged campaigns against the Bantustans, support for Angola and Mozambique, and
opposition to the 'border wars' against the people of Namibia, Zimbabwe and
the new government in Angola. For the youth, they suggested:

> Organise the youth and students against Bantu Education, separate
> colleges, and their right to demand in what medium they must be taught,
> by whom, how, where and what to be taught, and to demand free, com-
> pulsory and proper education.[65]

The list of demands was comprehensive, but was too wide and nonspecific to
indicate where attention should be focussed. The ANC, having members on
the executive of SASM, should, moreover, have been aware that the students
were being organised. They should also have been more specific in their
demands if they were to assist the student struggle.

The same issue of the newsletter did address a section to the youth, and
criticised the Black Consciousness Movement on two fronts. Firstly, the ANC

199

maintained that the black consciousness leaders had erred in not 'laying down . . . a firm basis of principle on which it will co-operate with all other anti-racist groups, irrespective of colour'. Secondly, the ANC took a strong line in opposing the community projects that the BCP and SASO/BPC sponsored.

> We . . . oppose such efforts as the building of clinics, work camps and home industries no matter how well meant. That energy and enthusiasm of the youth must be directed in efforts to destroy the one and only source of our misery and oppression, namely white domination.

The ANC counterposed the need to reach all youth, in all classes of life, organise them, and take them

> . . . out into the streets in demand of their day-to-day needs like higher wages, an end to victimisation, subsidies in bus fares, free, compulsory and proper education, integrated sports at lowest levels etc. [66]

There is unfortunately no information on whether students in SASM read this issue of *Amandla-Matla*, whether they agreed with the point of view expressed, or whether they were prepared to direct attention to the problems of working class (and of unemployed) youth. There was no indication in the slogans of 16 June, or subsequently, that the students paid much attention to these ideas. And yet, it is precisely at times of approaching conflict that readers of pamphlets (or even of ephemeral leaflets) might be expected to pay greater attention to proposals such as those in ANC literature.

There were expressions of anger and abhorrence in leaflets that appeared under the name of the ANC in the days that followed the first shootings. [67] In their leaflets, the ANC called for mass protests, demonstrations and action 'against Bantu Education, Bantustans, the pass laws and all the hated policies of Apartheid'.

The first appraisal of June 16 appeared in another underground news-sheet, *Vukani-Awake*, issued by the ANC in July 1976. After referring to the shootings of Sharpeville and the events of 1960-61, which, it was said, ended a decade of 'peaceful protest', the publication continued:

> The reaction of the racist state then proved to our people that protest was not enough and opened a new stage of struggle in which the liberation movement prepared to seize power by force. Our youth understood that their protest would be met by massive police violence but were not intimidated. They have won a great political victory — the Vorster government has been compelled to drop the use of Afrikaans in schools. More important, they have demonstrated the power of the people and shown that mass protest remains an important part of the liberation struggle.

The article then turned to the 'valuable lessons' that had been learnt in 'solidarity actions' in townships and campuses across the country. There were, however, shortcomings and the authors urged that:

> because the protests were largely confined to the locations [townships],
> damage to the economy, the heart of white power, was limited — the
> struggle must be taken into the cities, the factories, the mines; the youth
> mobilised on the burning issue of forced Afrikaans — to maintain the mili-
> tancy and keep the initiative, demands that unite and draw in the broadest
> mass of the people, (Abolish passes! Down with Bantustans and Group
> Areas!) must be advanced.

The ANC had responded rapidly to the events of June and their call to
take the struggle into the cities either coincided with, or helped shape, part of
the strategy of the SSRC in the coming period. The struggle was, however,
not taken into the factories or the mines because this was beyond the capabilities of school pupils, and there was no other organisation capable of undertaking such tasks.

The issue of *Amandla-Matla* (Vol. 5, No. 2), that appeared in late June,
proclaimed: ' . . . this is not the time to weep over our fallen heroes. It is time
to hit back at the enemy with everything we have got . . . ,' The publication
set the events of Soweto against the unfolding events in the country — the
strikes at Heinemann electric company and the gold mines in the OFS, the
bus boycott at KwaThema, the demand for free trade unions, and the
protests against the Bantustans.

There was also an article on the school pupils which seems to have been
written before 16 June. The authors refer to the boycotting of classes, but
not yet to the shootings, and consequently some of the suggested demands
were dated by the time the issue appeared: as was the call for pickets 'in front
of all places administering Bantu Education'. On the other hand, the
suggestion that student-parent committees be elected to co-ordinate the
campaign was apposite both before and after the shooting. [68]

ANC leaflets were distributed by means of pamphlet bombs, exploded in
the centre of cities, and by other forms of delivery. Cell members also
received copies and there must have been a large number circulating in townships. Nevertheless the ANC as an organisation was not able to act directly
in Soweto and, in recognition of the pre-eminent position of the SSRC, it
made several attempts to persuade its leaders to work with its clandestine
organisation. These were rejected by the student leaders — or at least by the
president at the time, and the ANC operated separately. At an informal level
members of the SSRC executive, some of whom were, as remarked above,
members of the ANC, sought advice from or worked with cell members.
There were also occasions when the President of the SSRC apparently
journeyed to a neighbouring territory to meet one of the exiled leaders. It is
yet too early to ascertain the extent of the contact or the effect this contact
had on the direction of events in Soweto or the rest of the country. [69]

The PAC

There is little information about PAC involvement in the revolt, and few or
no examples of PAC literature distributed inside the townships. But this
organisation was active in Kagiso, the township outside Krugersdorp,
according to evidence which has become available following the trial of youth
accused of having been in the PAC.

Despite reluctance to use material produced at a trial, because of the
general unreliability of evidence given by state witnesses against former
friends, the short account below does tell of events that could have occurred
in any of South Africa's townships. If the story as told in the witness box
was false -- as some stories undoubtedly were -- there was still an essential
truth in it that can be accepted.

Some time in 1975 (it was stated in court), a religious movement was
launched in Kagiso ' . . . to teach youngsters the correct interpretation of the
Bible to enable them to "liberate themselves from the oppression" in South
Africa.' [70] The group was first known as the Young African Christian Move-
ment, but in December 1975 changed its name to the Young African
Religious Movement (YARM) because one of the leading members was of the
Islamic faith.

The group had been formed by persons who belonged to the PAC and one
of its leading personalities, Michael Matsobane, was said to have served a
sentence on Robben Island for PAC activities. The aims of YARM were to
unite black youth, provide a fresh interpretation of what was said in the
Bible, and ultimately recruit students for military training in camps outside
South Africa.

The activities of YARM did not differ appreciably from those of other
youth groups in Soweto schools. They went on picnics (for which purpose
they recruited women in order to avoid suspicion), organised discussions and
sports, and were to offer bursaries for youth interested in military training.

After 16 June, members of YARM formed or helped start a Kagiso
Students Representative Council and a Kagiso African Parents Association.
Both these organisations, although restricted to members of YARM, were
obviously based on the Soweto example. It was claimed that Matsobane
had said that the function of the SRC was to obtain information on those
arrested and those who were being sought by the police. The function of the
Parents Association was to assist students to cross the border and escape
arrest.

Evidence from a state witness, who had been on the SRC, alleged that a
fellow-member on the SRC had burnt the school and a bottlestore on 18
June. In September members of YARM were said to have been responsible
for burning the Kagiso administration buildings.

The abbreviated account that became available from the court-room
contained many of the elements that have appeared earlier in this book. The
use of church or religious group in the early stages of discussion or organisation, the search for new religious meaning, recruitment in the schools, and
ultimately the formation of an SRC and of a parents association. In this

instance a small political group tried to keep all activity in its own hands, and dominated both the students' and parents' organisation. These bodies were not used to mobilise large sections of the community and individuals on the committees seem to have arrogated to themselves even the task of burning down some buildings. If this is true, then the PAC made a mockery of political mobilisation and sought only to build their own organisation while neglecting the need to involve larger sections of the population in the events of 1976.

References

1. *Black Review*, 1974-5, p.143.
2. *SRRSA*, 1973, p.308.
3. *Loc. cit.*
4. F. Troup, *op. cit.*, p.47 and *SRRSA*, 1974, p.351.
5. F. Troup, *loc. cit.* and *SRRSA*, 1975, p.308.
6. Quoted in *Black Review*, 1975-6, p.144.
7. Interview in *Weekend World*, 25 May 1975, quoted in *Black Review*, 1974-5, p.97.
8. *SRRSA*, 1976, p.54.
9. *Loc. cit.*
10. T. Motapanyane, *op. cit.*, p.55.
11. *Loc. cit.*
12. Counter Information Service (CIS), (1977), *Black South Africa Explodes*, p.7.
13. *Black Review*, 1975-6, p.98.
14. CIS, *op. cit.*, p.7.
15. *Black Review*, 1975-6, p.98 and *SRRSA*, 1976, p.55.
16. *Rand Daily Mail*, 28 May, quoted in *SRRSA*, 1976, p.55.
17. *SRRSA*, 1976, *loc. cit.*
18. T. Motapanyane, *op.cit.*, p.56.
19. *Ibid.*, pp.51 and 56.
20. See Joan Hoffman, (1977), 'Fragments of a view', in *Quarry '77: new South African writing*; Pupils of Jabulani High School 'had been deliberately left out because it had been thought that our school would give "too much trouble".'
21. John Berger, (1971), 'The nature of mass demonstrations', in *Selected Essays and Articles*, (Penguin), p.246.
22. *Loc. cit.*
23. *Loc. cit.*
24. *Loc. cit.*
25. *Bulletin of the UBJ* (Union of Black Journalists), No.2, n.d.
26. *Loc. cit.*
27. Quoted in *Black Review*, 1975-6, p.99.
28. J. Berger, *op. cit.*, p.248.
29. Eamonn McCann, (1974), *War and an Irish Town*, (Penguin), p.41.
30. Interview with Professor Alan Lipman, 1978.

31. This information was compiled from figures quoted in issues of
    SRRSA: 1972, p.92; 1973, pp.74-5; 1974, p.89; 1975, pp.56-7; 1976,
    p.94; 1977, p.108.
32. CIS, *op. cit.*, p.13.
33. *Black Review*, 1975-6, p.101.
34. Details from *Black Review*, 1975-76, p.101 and 'Diary of urban black
    revolt', *X-Ray*, July-August, 1977.
35. The Southern African News Agency (SANA) Bulletin was declared an
    'undesirable publication' in South Africa. That is, it was banned. Copies
    of the Bulletin were reproduced and distributed externally by the IUEF.
36. *SRRSA*, 1976, p.192.
37. Information from *SRRSA*: 1973, p.192; 1974, p.167; 1976, p.251;
    and 1977, p.420. See also Cosmas Desmond, (1971), *The Discarded
    People*, (Penguin), pp.125-8 for descriptions of Mabopane and
    GaRankuwa.
38. SANA report, 21 June, and CIS, *op. cit.*, p.14.
39. *Black Review*, 1974-75, p.25.
40. *Loc. cit*
41. *Loc. cit.*
42. *SRRSA*, 1974, p.205, and 1976, p.251.
43. *Black Review*, 1974-5, p.25.
44. *Natal Mercury*, 18 June, quoted in *Black Review*, 1975-76, p.100.
45. T. Motapanyane, *op. cit.*, p.57.
46. UCT workshop on the Revolt of 1976.
47. 'Amandla: the story of the SSRC', reprinted in *Z*, Vol. 2, No.5, n.d., p.7.
48. *Ibid*, p.10.
49. SANA, April/May/June Bulletin.
50. 'The story of the SSRC', *op. cit.*, p.1. The account in this article
    contains some serious errors. I have tried to avoid the more obvious
    misstatements.
51. The *Financial Mail*, 16 April 1971, stated that 55 per cent of Soweto's
    population was under 20 years, 16 percent were under 4 years.
52. See 'The story of the SSRC', p.5, on the lack of democracy.
53. This was implicit in many of the SSRC leaflets. It was made more
    explicitly (although ambiguously) in their leaflet dated 7 September
    1976. This will be discussed below.
54. SANA, 18 June.
55. Horst Kleinschmidt, (1976), *Black Parents Association*, (mimeo). This
    was a confidential document at the time. Similar material has now been
    printed elsewhere.
56. *Ibid.*
57. *Ibid.*
58. T. Motapanyane, *op. cit.*, p.58.
59. *SRRSA*, 1976, p.26.
60. H. Kleinschmidt, *op. cit.*, p.2.
61. *SRRSA*, 1977, p.33. Over R100,000 was paid to families in need.
62. *SRRSA*, 1976, p.67.
63. T. Motapanyane, *op. cit.*, p.52.
64. *Ibid.*, pp.53-4.
65. *Amandla-Matla*, newsletter of the ANC, Vol. 5, No.1, n.d.

66. *Ibid.*
67. As for example 'Death to the murderous oppressors! Our brothers and sisters will be avenged!' and 'People of South Africa — the African National Congress calls on you. Amandla Soweto.'
68. Other issues raised in the issue of *Amandla-Matla* are highly contentious. They will be discussed in a later chapter.
69. There were some disclosures about SSRC members who were in the ANC and also of contacts between leaders of the SSRC and the external wing of the ANC, at the trial of the 'Pretoria 12' in 1977-78. See in particular testimony relating to Naledi Tsiki, a former member of the executive of the SSRC, and Elias Masinga, one-time vice-president of SASM in the Transvaal. Both were amongst the accused in the dock. Accounts from *Rand Daily Mail,* June 1977 to March 1978.
70. This account was taken from reports of the trial of PAC members in the *Rand Daily Mail,* 10 March 1978 and 17 March 1978. Six of the 18 accused were said to have participated in YARM in Kagiso.

11. The Revolt Takes Shape

In the first eight weeks of the Revolt in Soweto, there were two periods of intense confrontation with the police. The first extended over the initial three days, from June 16 to 19, and the second for three or four days, starting on 4 August. These constituted peaks, in which the youth inflicted maximum damage on buildings and vehicles. Police violence was also at its height. The intervening period was less violent, but the township remained tense and there were innumerable small incidents which were no longer newsworthy and were not always reported in the press: stone-throwing, random police shooting (particularly of youth wearing school uniforms), occasional road blocks, or overturned vehicles. There were also events which did make the headlines: the anger at the government's announcement on 1 July banning the planned mass burial of victims of the shooting, and the indignation when it was learnt that many children, some as young as eight, were being kept in police cells.

Nevertheless Soweto was quiet over the period which coincided with the closure of the schools from 17 June till 22 July, and Joan Hoffman caught the atmosphere that others had noted when she went back to Jabulani High School on 23 July:

> I drove to the school, past buildings black and gutted, beerhalls with shattered windows, clinics that looked as though people had jumped on the roofs. The weird, creepy silence deepened as I went further into Soweto . . . a few people looked at me strangely, wondering. On the way out I saw a small boy bending or pretending to pick up a stone, but a woman shouted and he stopped. At school there were only a few students . . . [1]

During those long winter weeks when the children kept indoors, partly for warmth's sake, but also to avoid the cruising police cars, there had been changes in social customs which were not described in the newspapers, but which were more dramatic than many of the violent episodes that were remarked upon. The most important of these changes occurred at the funerals of the young victims of police violence.

The Funeral Ceremonies

One of the first acts of the Black Parents Association was to arrange for the funeral of the young people killed in June, and plans were afoot for a mass burial. When the Minister of Police banned the funeral arrangements there was deep resentment in Soweto. The 'private' funerals which would have to take place were inappropriate to the common tragedy that affected the entire population.

The feeling that the bereavements concerned a wider public than those traditionally involved in funerals was ultimately to affect the way people reacted to death and to conduct at the graveside. Youth, who had been traditionally excluded from funerals, now attended and even took a leading part, in the process displacing the married women who would otherwise have been the main mourners. This revolution in behaviour was profound and occurred at one of the most important ceremonies in the cycle of life and death. All traditional practices concerning women's place in the cycle of life, beliefs about entry into the 'other world', and concepts of pollution (associated with handling of the corpse) were challenged and new practices established.[2] This reversal of roles at funerals between married women and youth was more than an adjustment, radical as that was, in traditional practice. It was also a reversal in social status and corresponded to the reversal that had taken place in political practice. Only 27 years before, in 1949, when the Congress Youth League had had their programme accepted in the teeth of opposition from the established ANC leadership, they had to find 'esteemed elders' who would accept office in the organisation pledged to uphold the new *Programme of Action*.[3] In 1976 political leadership fell to the youth almost by default, and they did not feel obliged to defer to adults.

The funerals became events at which the reversal of social custom coincided with the fact that the victims (at least initially) were all young. The adults mourned children, the youth mourned lost comrades. The adults wept and the youth grieved too, but they swept away the tears and vowed vengeance.

There were adults present, many of them neither related nor close kin — and this too was a departure in practice — and they too were expressing political, and not only social, solidarity. They too thought or spoke of vengeance. The new atmosphere percolated through to close kin and parents. They not only accepted the changes in traditional practice, but also the political stance of the audience. Funerals were no longer seen only as rites of passage in which the departed were entering the other world, but also as gatherings at which there could be an affirmation of the demand for a new South Africa. Dr. Harriet Ngubane records that when she revisited Soweto in July 1977:

> I myself saw . . . a woman, whose child had been shot and killed by the police, standing erect at the graveside shouting slogans meaning 'We shall

overcome', 'Power is ours', etc. Only a few years ago she would have been sitting there in the traditional manner, covered and hardly visible. [4]

In July 1976, the youth gave the clenched fist salute, and participated in funeral rites. A year later they were leading the entire group in salutes and chants at the grave: priest, relations and friends. This took place not only at funerals of those who had died at the hands of the police. All deaths in the townships were seen in political terms. Malnutrition, disease, quarrels and gang fights were all attributed to apartheid, and every death was blamed on the government and its pernicious policy. Dr. Ngubane records that, when she offered her condolences to a man who had lost his 20 year old son, shot by the police, he had replied: 'It could have been anyone's child'. [5] That too constituted a radical change in approach; a change that will not be easily reversed in the years to come.

The police were aware of the use to which funerals were being put by the youth, and knew that the grief at the graveside was mingled with fervent hopes for radical change. They were not prepared to stand aside and were always to be found in the vicinity of any burial. As a consequence of these confrontations at burials, stones were thrown and shots fired, and all too often there were new martyrs at the end of the day. It was a macabre game, in which the police seemed determined to show that they were the true servants of death.

Back to School?

The government made a number of tactical retreats during July. The regulation on the medium of instruction was rescinded on 6 July by the Minister of Bantu Education, M.C. Botha. On 18 July Joseph Peele and Abner Letlape, the members of the Meadowlands Tswana School Board, dismissed in February, were reinstated, and it was announced that the regional director of education and one of the circuit inspectors would be transferred from the Soweto area. [6]

The students had won a victory and they were aware that it was only because of their resolute actions that the government had been forced to withdraw. But the victory was limited because nothing had changed in the schools and nothing had been altered in the country. The question of Afrikaans tuition — even though it had been a real issue — was relatively unimportant. It had been a convenient point around which the school pupils had rallied and, having united and paid a fearsome price in lives and injuries, they were not going to be satisfied with this restricted concession. It was the whole of Bantu Education that had to go, and that, henceforth, was to be the students' slogan.

When it was announced that the schools would be reopened on 22 July the school pupils saw little reason for returning. The heavy police patrols and the presence of Hippos indicated that nothing had altered. After an uneasy weekend, some of the youth gathered at the schools on Monday the 26th, but drifted away during the morning, congregating at street corners and jeering at the police who stood by.

The SSRC was caught in a dilemma. Their president had called for a return to school. Not because he necessarily wanted a 'return to normal', but because,

> The schools were the focal point of SSRC activities, and while students were scattered through the townships in their homes and in the streets it was impossible to get any sort of programme of action going. In the schools, it was another matter. The SSRC had more or less free entry ... [7]

The SSRC could not, however, tell the students their reason for wanting the schools opened again and the statements that were made only added to the existing confusion without securing the return that Mashinini had called for. When the BPA backed the SSRC alongside the school principals and the hated Urban Bantu Council, the students felt deserted!

This must call into question the wisdom of calling for a return to school and does indicate that the SSRC was out of touch with the mood of the youth. The first tentative move to secure the reopening of schools on 26 July received little support and even the teachers were undecided. Classes often failed to start even when children had assembled in the classrooms. [8]

There were larger numbers at school on 27 July, but reports were received that a school at Mamelodi (Pretoria) had been burnt and that the same had happened at a farm school in Irene (Pretoria district). That evening six schools and a youth club in Soweto were damaged by fire and, over the next 10 days, some 50 schools were damaged or destroyed in the Transvaal, Natal and the OFS; [9] the Cape schools were only to join the revolt the following month.

The SSRC, seemingly persuaded that they were correct, were unable to sense the mood in the schools and streets and continued to call for a return to the classroom and also condemned the burning. In the surrounding townships, particularly at Alexandra and Thembisa, there were fresh outbursts as the month drew to a close. Buses were being stoned at Alexandra and pupils were marching to the police station in Thembisa in protest against a police assault on a pupil during interrogation.

If the SSRC had not altered course at this stage, they would have lost the credibility already attained. An opportunity came on 1 August when the Minister allowed the first public gathering since 16 June. The UBC called the meeting and UBC members, together with school principals, appealed for an end to the burnings and a return to school. The students barracked and, according to some accounts, broke up the meeting. That afternoon the BPA held a meeting at the Regina Mundi church and Mashinini, in his first public appearance, called on each school to send two delegates to a meeting of the SSRC. He still endorsed the 'return to school' appeal. [10]

The authorities were alarmed at this move to extend the SSRC and it seems likely that it was this which led to police raids on the schools in search of the leadership. Despite a promise made by the Minister that the police would be kept away from school premises during school hours (reported at the meeting on 1 August), there were large-scale raids on 3 August, students were interrogated and some arrests made. This provocation led to clashes with the police and shots were fired. Thereafter the schools emptied and pupils poured out into the streets. [11] That ended the calls for a resumption of lessons and the boycott returned — first to Soweto and Thembisa, and then to the rest of the country, bringing in the Cape in the process.

The March on Johannesburg

On Wednesday, 4 August, the students were out in the streets in their school uniforms and, in the first instance, tried to persuade the adults not to go to work. A stretch of the railway line to Johannesburg had been damaged overnight and trains to the city were cancelled. Buses that raced through the township were stoned by the youth.

Organised by the SSRC, the students then joined with many of the adults who had stayed at home that day and marched in a column towards Johannesburg. Pictures from the air showed them marching round obstacles, pressing forward in their desire to get to the police headquarters at John Vorster Square to present their demand that the detained students be released. The entire township seemed to have concentrated on the one objective — to press on and present themselves in the city centre.

Joan Hoffman, coming into Soweto in the early morning, saw the immensity of the operation that day:

> When I turned on to the Soweto highway . . . I began to realize that something was wrong, because there wasn't a single car coming out. It was as though the road had been rubbed clean. Then I saw two Putco buses, a few taxis, but still no cars, when normally they would be bumper to bumper into town. The road stretched wide in the early light, the whole world empty and silent. [12]

Watching at another exit, one of her friends said: 'They were like ants, and like ants they [the children] just kept going.'[13]

The marchers, carrying a huge banner that read, 'We are not fighting, don't shoot', were halted by a cordon of police. The students aimed to get to the city centre, but there was no move to break through the line of police blocking them. Moreover, the leadership, in the front ranks of the marchers, had a firm control over the students. It was stalemate — the police unyielding and the students stationary and unwilling, in fact unable, to go back.

Once again there was shooting and twelve fell, three of the students dead. Three other students were seriously injured when teargas canisters were shot at them.

There were over 20,000 people in the column which now swung back, the orderliness shattered in the haste to get under cover. That afternoon buildings were burning again in Soweto, including the houses of two black policemen.

The events of 4 August inaugurated a new phase in the Revolt of 1976. In the wake of the shooting at the road block, violence returned to Soweto and to the rest of the country. The fact that on the same day there had also been shooting in Thembisa when students marched to the local police station to demand the release of a student who had been detained, only reinforced the indignation felt everywhere at police terror.

However, a second and more important factor had entered the struggle. The students had appealed to the workers to stay-at-home and, with the assistance of some of their fellows who had organised the disruption of transport, they had ensured that at least 60 per cent of the African work force stayed away from the city. The employers called it 'student intimidation' or explained the withdrawal of labour by reference to the trains. Few sought to explain the obvious support that the workers gave the students that day.

The extent of their success in stopping workers going to town seemed to have persuaded the youth that they could paralyse the economy and that they only had to issue the call for the factories to grind to a halt. Student Power, they thought, could be extended to Workers' Power, and (presumably) their demands would be met. The enormity of their mistake was only to become apparent later with the failure of the November stay-at-home.

They did not stop to reflect that Wednesday — and probably they could not stop in their tracks then. On Thursday 5 August they again called on the workers to stay-at-home and they set up road blocks to reinforce their call. But the workers saw no purpose in losing another day's pay and ignored the call. In Alexandra, where the students appeared to be more determined, there were some clashes with workers. Inevitably the government felt this to be a heaven-sent opportunity for dividing the township and they gave their blessings to workers who wanted to carry knobkerries (knob-headed batons) as protection against 'agitators' and 'intimidators'!

The students never really learned how and when they could call on the working class to join them against the authorities. But the workers did do so on 4 August and would again on several occasions. Sometimes they joined the students — but there were times when the workers ignored their call. The factors which helped determine these responses will be discussed in Chapter Thirteen.

The events in Soweto had taken on a new momentum and were not easily stopped. On Friday attempts were again made to stop workers leaving Soweto, and again the students failed. It is not certain whether the SSRC was in control at the time. If they were, they had not understood the feelings of the workers or, alternatively, they had lost the ability to command and their opinions were not heeded. Marches were organised in the township, both on Thursday and on Friday, and on both occasions there were casualties. It seems that the police were prepared to shoot at any student or group of students on the streets.

The SSRC was faced with another problem — small but vital. Until now, students had been summoned to appear at demonstrations in uniform. This helped advertise the action as being student operated, and student led. It also helped keep the push-outs in the background, because they were so markedly different in dress, although the extent to which this exclusion was deliberately planned is unknown. Wearing school uniforms had also helped bind the demonstrators together, but in so doing a new factor had been introduced. The police treated students as public enemies and any person found in the streets in a uniform was a target for cruising police cars. Henceforth students had to be advised not to appear in school clothes.

Nation-wide Response

On 5 August there was violence in Cape Town. Students at the University of the Western Cape, who had started a boycott of lectures on 2 August were angered when the whites-only staff association dissociated themselves from the student action. On 4 August 800 students clashed with police when they demonstrated outside their campus and on 5 August the administration buildings on the campus were burnt down. The initial boycott had been only partially connected with the events in the Transvaal, but everyone connected the latest events with the clashes in the north, and local demands were seen to merge with the nation-wide conflict.

It was in the Transvaal that the response to the new Soweto events was most marked. On 6 August a beerhall was fired at Brakpan; there was stoning for the first time at Dobsonville (near Roodepoort); students clashed with police at Kagiso during a march protesting against the detention of a student. Two schools went up in flames in GaRankuwa; three schools were destroyed in Mhluzi (Middleburg). And in Johannesburg the third White was killed when Africans in a truck ran down a traffic warden. [14]

The marching, burning and stoning did not stop through August and into September. New communities were drawn into the protest movement in every corner of the country. The schools were prime targets, but so were buildings belonging to the Bantu Affairs Administration Boards, beerhalls, liquor stores and buses. In mid-August the students also protested at the visit of Henry Kissinger, US Secretary of State at the time, to South Africa, and their slogans scrawled on banners received world-wide publicity. 'Kissinger, your visit to Azania is bullshit. Even animals are angry.'

By this time the Revolt had also taken off in the Cape — with two separate foci, Cape Town and Port Elizabeth-East London, from which it raged across both Western and Eastern Cape. It extended to outlying towns in the Northern Cape, to Kimberley and to Upington, and it took in towns across the Cape where the largest group was Coloured and not African. New social forces entered the revolt when Coloured-African unity was seen to be effective in the streets of the main urban centres of the South.

References

1. J. Hoffman, *op. cit.*, pp.52-3.
2. See Harriet Ngubane, (1977), *Body and Mind in Zulu Medicine,* (Academic Press), pp.80-5.
3. See Karis and Carter, Vol.4, *op. cit.*, p.98.
4. Harriet Ngubane, (1978), 'The politics of death in Soweto', (mimeo), p.6.
5. *Ibid.*, p.7.
6. *SRRSA*, 1976, pp.61-2.
7. 'The story of the SSRC', *Z*, Vol.2, No.5, p.4.
8. *SRRSA*, 1976, p.63.
9. CIS, *op. cit.*, pp.15-6.
10. 'The story of the SSRC', *Z*, Vol.2, No.5, p.2.
11. CIS, *op.cit.*, p.53.
12. J. Hoffman, *op.cit.*, p.53.
13. *Loc. cit.*
14. *X-Ray*, July-August 1977.

12. The Cape Province Explodes

The Witwatersrand is built over the gold mines which provided the base for the massive investments that poured into South Africa and consequently led to the industrialisation of the region which is by far the most technologically developed area in the country. The Southern Transvaal, which includes the Witwatersrand and the industrial complex that stretches down to the Vaal River, contains a quarter of the country's population and the largest concentration of African workers. Inevitably it has been the centre of some of the most bitterly fought struggles in both factory and township, and many of the national campaigns called by the ANC in the fifties received their strongest support in and around this industrial complex.

Other urban centres, particularly in the Eastern Cape, have on occasion been the scenes of campaigns which have surpassed the Transvaal in initiative, imagination and daring. The peculiar conditions which led the inhabitants of each locality to participate have to be sought in the social composition of each town and its environs, and the meaning of each campaign for the persons involved must be determined. Only then will there be any understanding, for example, of the widespread success of the Defiance Campaign of 1952 in the Eastern Cape, of the concentration of strikes in Durban in 1973, or of the massive response to the Soweto Revolt in Cape Town in August 1976. By the same token such a study will reveal the reasons for the relative quiescence of the Natal population through the Revolt of 1976-77.

In this study it has not been possible to investigate the conditions of many urban centres during the Revolt and, at most, it has been possible to indicate some of the factors which help explain outbursts of activity in some regions. Any detailed examination would only lengthen the book without necessarily throwing further light on the factors which led to the explosion in South Africa. Nevertheless the situation in the Cape is so significantly different from that of the Southern Transvaal that it is necessary to look briefly at some of the factors which influenced the two black populations in the period preceding, and during, the second half of 1976.

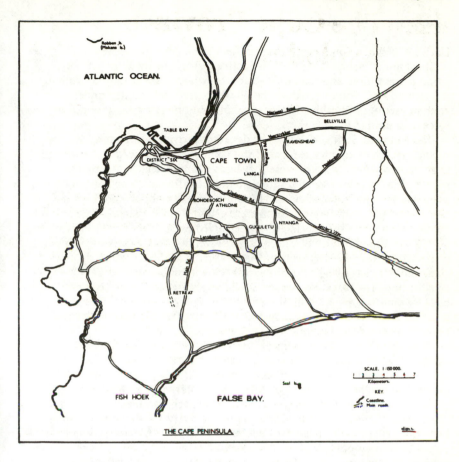

THE CAPE PENINSULA.

215

The Shaping of Cape Society

Until 1910, when South Africa was unified, the country consisted of four political units, each with its own distinctive history, its own unique population composition, and economic structures which were already profoundly different. The Union effected by the Whites placed the country under a common set of political institutions, established one army and one police force, and unified fiscal control.

The Union of South Africa was designed to provide white political hegemony. The economic control of the country did not need to be written into the new constitution because that had already been decided by the nature of investment from both foreign and local financiers and entrepreneurs. But the land question and the provision of labour were kept in mind when the political institutions were established. Parliament, the government, and the provincial councils were reserved exclusively for Whites.

The pre-Union history of the colonies prevented the drafters of the final constitution from disenfranchising the Coloureds in the Cape and the few thousand Africans who had qualified for the vote under the old Cape constitution. The black vote was devalued in 1930 when white (but not black) women were placed on the voters roll. The African voters were removed from the common roll in 1936 and, in 1956, the Coloureds also lost the vote after a five year constitutional wrangle.

The Cape Coloured community, it was once said, was a 'statutory category' and not a race or a nation. [1] Defined as the people who do not look like or are not accepted as being white or African, they are those who are generally lighter skinned than Africans, but darker than Whites.

This ethnic ambiguity has created profound social problems for them. Their total number in South Africa is approximately 2.4 million, but an unknown number has in the past moved into the white community, where skin colour made that possible. The advantages of 'passing for white' made many sections of this community deeply conscious of colour, and efforts by political movements to overcome these prejudices were not very successful.

The overwhelming majority of the coloured people have always resided in the Cape and, with approximately 1.9 million in that Province, they outnumber the Whites by some half-million; and with over 730,000 in Cape Town (and districts), they are the largest population group in South Africa's legislative capital.

Although a large proportion of the coloured people are in severe financial straits, they are legally less discriminated against than Africans. The areas they live in are not fenced in, as are the townships — although the housing position is often no better than that of the African areas and a large number have been forced, due to the lack of accommodation, to live in squatter camps. They have some right to own property and to trade within designated suburbs known as Group Areas. Certain skilled trades are open to them and they have the legal right to trade union organisation and to strike. Their wages, consequently, tend to be at least marginally better than that of the

African and the facilities in schools are also comparatively of a higher standard.

The advantages brought by a lighter pigmentation were, however, limited and over the years the privileges were whittled away. The vote went in 1956; the Group Areas Act of 1950 was enforced, and Coloureds were moved out of districts that they had occupied for centuries; segregation was enforced in university education; and a multitude of laws were introduced to control this 'in-between' category of persons. To make them fit the apartheid laws, they were declared a nation, but a nation without a 'Homeland', without a language (most speak Afrikaans), and without a separate economy.

The one 'gift' presented to them in 1955, they would gladly dispense with. It was announced in that year that the African peoples would be removed from the Western Cape and that all work done by Blacks (that is, unskilled work) would ultimately be performed by Coloureds!

The 'Eiselen' Line

One of the Nationalist Party's plans for the country was that all Africans should be removed from the area west of the Eiselen Line (which extended almost due north from a point on the coast, just west of Port Elizabeth to the OFS border near Colesburg). According to their calculations all the necessary unskilled labour could be performed by Coloureds, and the African population could be transferred to the Transkei and Ciskei and directed from there to other labour centres.

The policy was outlined by Dr. W.W.M. Eiselen, Secretary for Native Affairs, in a paper presented to the pro-government South African Bureau of Racial Affairs (SABRA) in 1955.

In that year there were said to be 178,000 Africans in the Western Cape, 65,000 of whom were in Cape Town. It was this group of people of whom Dr. Eiselen said:

Briefly and concisely put, our Native policy regarding the Western Province aims at ultimate elimination of the Natives from this region. It should take place gradually, so as not to lead to harmful dislocation of industry. It is a long-term policy which makes provision for the following stages:
(a.) Removal of foreign Natives and freezing of the present situation so far as Native families are concerned, coupled with limited importation of single migrant workers to meet the most urgent needs.
(b.) Removal of Protectorate [Basutoland, Bechuanaland, and Swaziland] Natives and reduction of the number of Native families, with gradual replacement of migrant labourers who return to the reserves, not by new migrants, but by Coloured workers.
(c.) The screening of the Native population and classifying them in two groups: 1. Natives who have remained Bantu and who in time can be moved back to the reserves, where they can play an important role in the

building up of an urban economy; [and] 2. Natives who have established
relationships with Coloured women and who in all but colour belong to
the Coloured community . . . should obtain citizenship within the
Coloured community . . . [2]

With consummate care, Dr. Eiselen laid down the conditions that would
govern Africans who would be allowed in temporarily, if 'absolutely
necessary', as single male migrants. Of those that would be allowed to remain
he said:

The legally admitted remainder are to be housed in good rented quarters
for families and single workers. Because Natives in this Coloured area
should not enjoy the same residential privileges as Coloureds, they are not
allowed – in contrast with the practice elsewhere – to buy or build
houses. It is hoped and expected that the Native population will not grow,
but steadily decrease. [3]

As a first step, the government announced that no more funds would be
available for erecting family houses in Langa, Cape Town's only African
township at the time. Instead, only hostels for single male migrants would
be erected. All families then living in Langa would be moved elsewhere. [4]
A second township, designed to hold 8,000, was set up at Nyanga. All
squatters in the Cape Peninsula were to be rounded up and taken to this
sandy wasteland. There they would be screened and those who satisfied the
authorities that they were in the Western Cape legally, would be allowed to
erect shacks on plots measuring 27 feet by 14 feet. The rental for these
would be £1 per month. All other squatters would be 'repatriated'. [5] Families
were to be settled in the region later named Guguletu. Residents living in
shanties in and around Cape Town were moved to shacks and pre-fabricated
dwellings, prior to more permanent buildings being built.
    At the end of 1973, just 22 years after the ultimate removal of Africans
had been decreed, their number in Cape Town had all but doubled. The
actual number of Africans in the city was not known and had never been
known, and the number of squatters alone was over 50,000. [6] The official
figures for the townships is given in Table Ten.

Table 10
The African Population Statistics of Cape Town, December 1973 [7]

Population Category	Langa	Nyanga	Guguletu
Men: 16 years and over	24,969	10,358	15,573
Women: 16 years and over	2,371	2,851	11,981
Children under 16 years	3,738	3,886	25,286
Total	31,078	17,095	52,840
No. of adult men in single quarters	23,627	8,123	4,333

Despite the government's plan to stop the flow of Africans into Cape Town and the Western Cape, their numbers grew steadily and in 1967 new plans were produced to reduce the African population by five per cent per year. Consequent upon this, further housing for Africans was frozen. Thereafter, the pressure on housing facilities in the townships became unbearable and the squatter camps grew even larger. [8]

The Eiselen Line did not achieve what the government said it aimed to do, but it did lead to the increased immiseration of both black communities. There were insufficient jobs for the Coloureds in Cape Town and the Western Cape. Large numbers were unemployed and thousands accepted any work that was available. The housing situation was intolerable and some 200,000 Blacks lived in squatter camps. In one account of the plight of these people, a reporter said:

The picture for Coloureds is . . . appalling . . . There are approximately 22,400 structures scattered across the Cape Peninsula housing 120,000 people.

They are the poorest members of society . . . they have very little schooling — Standard 2 is quite common, Standard 4 quite an achievement; the men work as labourers or do unskilled work, so are paid low wages — R20 per week is average . . .

Some are shack dwellers because they have been evicted from local authority housing . . . others have moved out of townships because of . . . violence, lack of social cohesion, cold damp dwellings. Some have been forced out . . . because of the Group Areas Act or road-development demolitions . . . [9]

In these camps they were often joined by Africans — by families that refused to sleep in single-sex barracks; by people who could not find any accommodation in the overcrowded townships; by men (and their families) who had no permits to be in town; and by many who found that a shanty was preferable to a house under the control of township administrators.

The Schools in Cape Town

Until 1963 the bulk of coloured education was in the hands of state aided mission institutions. The advantages, and the disadvantages, noted in the discussion of mission education for Africans were also apparent in the coloured schools — but by 1963 nobody relished government control in the schools. The disadvantages outweighed any advantages that might come.

There were some 347,730 coloured children at school by 1963, the vast majority being in the Cape. Nevertheless 95 per cent were in the primary schools and most left school after three or four years. It was estimated that 60 to 100 thousand children of school-going age were on the streets and little hope was held out that there would be places for them in the classrooms.

There were two basic changes after 1963. The missionaries (who controlled 72 per cent of the schools) were required to have their institutions approved by the Department of Coloured Affairs which assumed overall control of the schools; and teachers would have to adhere to an approved syllabus. The teachers, who had always played a prominent part in radical political movements in the Cape, were to be tightly controlled under the Act. They could not belong to, or further the aims of, any political organisation, nor encourage resistance to the laws of the state. They could not criticise any department or office of the state, except at the meeting of an approved teachers' organisation. [10]

The Act did not lead to an improvement in education. The quality of the teaching provided was reflected in the sum of money spent per year on the pupils. Against an average of R605 spent on each white child, R125 was spent on each coloured youth at school. That, in turn, was luxurious when compared with the R40 per year for each African child at school. [11]

Compulsory education was only introduced for Coloureds as from 1974 and would not be fully implemented until 1979 for children aged from 7 to 13 years. There was also little change in the structure of the schools and by 1976, of 655,347 at school, 68 per cent were in the lower primary classes and 85 per cent in the primary schools as a whole. Those in the upper forms were a tiny minority – only 4.5 per cent of all school-going youth being in the top three forms [12] and only a tiny fraction would ever obtain a university entrance pass.

Comparisons can be invidious, but it must be noted that the African schools in Cape Town were not only inferior to their coloured counterparts, but were also inferior to African schools elsewhere in the country. Because of the declared intention of removing the African population, there was little new building (except for that provided by TEACH), and an estimated 75 per cent of the children who managed to graduate from primary schools could not be accommodated in secondary schools. [13] They had to seek places in the Reserves, and as those were boarding-schools, very few could afford the fees – at some R300 per year. These were not so much push-outs, as left-outs!

In a lecture delivered in September 1976 at UCT, Dr. Margaret Ellsworth described the conditions in some local schools.

> Most classrooms are bare shells with very little or no equipment, no electricity, and often no desks. Three schools . . . have electricity . . . It is significant that many of the better-equipped schools are erected by TEACH.
> Langa High School, founded 30 years ago, has a block of four classrooms, still in use, which was condemned as unsafe *twenty* years ago . . .[14]

The rest of her account is familiar. Insufficient material resources, no audio-visual equipment, no teachers (or equipment) for instruction in physics, a shortage of textbooks, or textbooks in the wrong language, and so on.

Later that year, a more comprehensive document was issued after school pupils had been consulted. The usual run of complaints, important as they were, need not detain us here. But one point was central to the dissatisfaction at the time and indicates that the chaos experienced in the Transvaal was also being felt in Cape Town, and undoubtedly throughout the country. Under the heading school facilities, the pupils indicated:

> Immediate provision is urgently required to accommodate present Form I scholars in 1977. The present situation is that 1,806 Form I's will have to fit into classrooms which are already overfull with 982 Form II's. (2 litres of milk simply will not fit into a one litre bottle.) [15]

'Coloureds are Black, too'

Adam Small, head of the department of philosophy at the University of the Western Cape (UWC), when invited to read a paper at the conference on Black Theology, said:

> When I was invited to speak here, I was invited as a black, and immediately made a point of this. I was not invited as a non-black in the way that I used to be and still am invited, as a non-white . . .
> We have come, and we are coming, to recognise ourselves as black, and at least a part of our task is, and will be, to unfetter every man who is not white from whiteness . . . [16]

It is doubtful whether Adam Small got very far in the 'unfettering' of the coloured community. His message was far too intellectual and never came to grips with the problems faced by the coloured people. After declaring that Blacks would 'live without apology, or as if apologising', and that we are not 'beggars for life', he continued:

> Protest will therefore play a role in our future actions, but we will realise that protesting is a form of begging, and we cannot beg. Protest will be a secondary form of expression for us. Our primary form of expression will be the repeated manifestation of our blackness, time and time again . . .
> It must be clear to anyone who knows the meaning of culture that blackness is for us a supremely cultural fact. It is in this South African context, the consciousness that we have tremendous resources of the soul at our disposal out of which to grow strong in every sense . . . [17]

Looked at in the context of the problems facing the coloured population at the time, there was a strange air of unreality in these words. The squatters, if they heard these sentiments and if they knew what Adam Small meant, would have found the passage completely irrelevant to their lives. The speech was apolitical, if not anti-political, and the equation of protest with begging could have no meaning for men and women who existed in dire need. Nor in fact could the students, who were so enamoured of black consciousness, have known how to interpret these words of their lecturer — and one of their champions!

The students however, did seem to absorb this strange talk of 'culture' and 'soul', taking in all the ambiguities and contradictions of Small and other proponents of black consciousness. They sought out the one overwhelming point that Small did make as he concluded:

> Our blackness — black consciousness — is not so much a matter of severing contacts so much as it is a matter of a certain historical necessity . . . [the fact that blacks] have a will to survive the fury of our time.
>
> If therefore we reject apartheid it is for a much profounder reason than that we want *integration*; for we do not want integration, we reject it. We want to survive as men, and if we do not insist on our blackness we are not going to make it . . . [18]

More than anything else, the appeal to blackness was taken up by students at UWC. They flocked to join SASO and their leader on the campus in 1973, Henry Isaacs, was also the national president of the South African Student Organisation. The coloured students were militant and they were always amongst the first to support their peers on other campuses, as already described in Chapter Four. They were also the first group in Cape Town to take action in support of the pupils of Soweto.

The conflict between students and the administration at UWC had been building up over some period. The students resented the high ratio of white to coloured staff — 18 Coloureds in an establishment of 119 lecturers and professors; and they resented the fact that Dr. Ismail Mohamed had not had his appointment as Professor of Mathematics confirmed by the council, although his competence was not in doubt and he would have been the first coloured professor.

The students were angry on many accounts, not least of which was their complaint that the education they were receiving was inferior to that provided at the white institutions.

Their complaints were not restricted to campus affairs and they were also deeply aware of conditions in the ghettos. They had been reared and educated in these slum areas and their parents still lived there. They knew only too well the poverty that surrounded the coloured people and they knew that their own economic horizons were bounded by apartheid. They were, furthermore, caught up in the wrangling that surrounded the Coloured Persons Representative Council (CPRC, or sometimes CRC), established in 1968 to replace all previous forms of coloured representation in the now all-white assemblies.

Coloureds and Apartheid Politics

The first election to the CPRC took place in 1969. Forty members of the Council were to be elected and 20 would be nominated by the government after the elections were completed.

There were three main political tendencies in 1969 and they showed a continuity with political groups that had existed in the early post-war period. There were, firstly, the boycotters led by intellectuals in the late sixties, as they had been in the fifties. The hard core of the movement that called for a boycott of 'dummy' institutions in the 1940's and 1950's had been members of the Teachers League of South Africa. They had resolutely opposed the Coloured Affairs Commission set up by the Smuts government in 1943 and had committed themselves to fight against the establishment of a Coloured Affairs Department. The name they chose for their political movement was the anti-Coloured Affairs Department (anti-CAD).

Dr. M.G. Whisson, in a study prepared for Spro-Cas in 1970, claimed that the boycotters were the heirs to the Non-European Unity Movement and its main Cape components, the Anti-CAD and TLSA. Of the boycotters in 1969, Dr. Whisson claimed:

> While the actual membership of organisations of boycotters is probably very small outside the TLSA, being numbered in hundreds rather than thousands, the influence of the movement has been much wider. It has been led by men revered as intellectual leaders among the coloured people; many of them have been banned at one time or another and many more have left the country for more congenial places. Through the schools the tradition of boycott, the ideology and the language have all been maintained. [19]

The second group consisted of a number of parties that declared in favour of the government and its apartheid politics. Many of them were openly racist and they hoped to gain votes on an anti-African platform. They failed to win the elections, but in 1969 gained a majority in the CPRC by being handed all the nominated places. In the 1975 elections they lost heavily at the polls and could not have formed an executive even if they had been given all the nominated seats.

The third group consisted of parties who claimed to be anti-government and anti-apartheid, but nonetheless maintained that they could use the elections (and hopefully seats in the CPRC) to secure a public platform for their views. Although there were a number of small groups which nominated candidates for the Coloured Council, none secured seats at the elections. The only group with sufficient support to oppose the pro-apartheid members on the Council were candidates who stood in the election as members of the Labour Party.

The Labour Party had been kept out of control of the CPRC after the 1969 election and their leaders declared that they would make the council unworkable if they ever gained control of the Executive. [20] This failed to satisfy all their members and in particular the leading members of their junior section, the Labour Youth Organisation. The leadership was criticised for working inside one of the government created institutions and there were some demands that the Labour Party identify more closely with the Black Consciousness Movement.

The polarisation inside the Labour Party became most obvious at the conference held in 1973. Sonny Leon, the party leader, was obviously attracted to the stance adopted by Gatsha Buthelezi, and invited him to speak at the opening session. The youth supported the SASO position and forced through a resolution allowing them to open the Labour Youth Organisation to youth of all races. That proved to be only a stepping stone to the split that had to come, and the most radical spokesman, Don Mattera, resigned shortly after the conference and joined the BPC. [21] Shortly thereafter he was banned by the government.

During electioneering in 1975, anti-CPRC groups were formed – AFRO (or anti-CPRC front) in the north and ACROM (anti-CPRC committee) in the Cape. Their members declared that they would not form a political party and would not nominate candidates. Both groups called for a total boycott of the elections and their leaflets carried the slogan: 'Don't vote for apartheid – Don't vote for the CRC.' [22]

A spokesman for ACROM said that its members ' . . . see themselves as the vanguard of Black Renaissance. They have taken upon themselves the duty of politicizing the people and making them aware of the values of Black Consciousness.' [23] The group's greatest strength in the Cape seemed to be at UWC and in some of the schools, although it had too short a life to gather together many members. During the election period of 1975 it was reported that students of the Alexander Sinton High School in Athlone (Cape Town) demonstrated against their school-hall being used as a polling station for elections to the CPRC. They distributed leaflets issued by ACROM and were dispersed, with some show of violence, by police who had been summoned to the hall. [24] Not unexpectedly, students at the Alexander Sinton were in the fore-front of the Cape Town revolt in August 1976.

The Theron Commission

The Labour Party won an overall victory in the 1975 elections and, despite past declarations, the leadership decided to use the Council to press their demands for full citizenship for the coloured people. When the new Council convened in September 1975, students picketed the entrance to the assembly hall and were subsequently dispersed by police. [25]

The Labour Party was able to block all normal business on the grounds that the Prime Minister had not given satisfactory replies to their demands for integrating the Coloureds into the political institutions of the country. For several months the Labour Party seemed to have won a signal victory, but they got no support from the students who denounced 'integration', and their own weakness was exposed when the government revoked the appointment of Leon as Chairman of the CPRC Executive and appointed a nominated member to that post.

While this wrangling continued in the Council Chamber, a government appointed Commission of Inquiry Relating to the Coloured Population Group, under the chairmanship of Professor Erika Theron (a sociologist at Stellenbosch University) was touring the country hearing evidence. The Commission had been instructed to inquire into factors obstructing the development of the coloured people and to make recommendations on how such development could be further promoted.

It was quite clear from government statements that the Commission was not to formulate any new guidelines for policy towards the Coloureds and that proposed reforms should be made inside existing apartheid structures. The Labour Party, consequently, had denounced the Commission because they could not accept that the coloured people were a separate population group from whom full citizenship rights were excluded.[26]

The Commission report was tabled on 18 June 1976, two days after the Soweto Revolt had begun. Contrary to Labour Party expectations, the report recommended that Coloureds be given direct representation in Parliament, the Provincial Councils and in local authorities. This was rejected in a government white paper. The Commission added that the Immorality Act and the Prohibition of Mixed Marriages Act should be repealed. This too was rejected by the government.

The Commission also made a large number of other proposals. They urged that all universities be opened to Coloureds; that compulsory education up to the age of 15 years be instituted; that job reservation be removed, opening all work opportunities to Coloureds; and that many other barriers to coloured advancement be removed. These recommendations were not specifically rejected in the government white paper, but neither were they endorsed.

In July Mr. Leon claimed that Coloured disillusionment with the government had boiled over when the political recommendations were rejected,[27] but the extent to which his view reflected opinion is subject to some doubt. There must have been resentment at the government's reaffirmation of their apartheid policy for the Coloureds, and a few students and intellectuals who had spoken out against integration might have felt that personal ambitions would not now be fulfilled. Nonetheless, they had spoken and continued to speak against forging any ties with the Whites, and they still espoused a black alliance. It is hard to see how this squared with 'disillusionment boiling over'.

The final word on the Theron Commission report came on 10 September 1976 when the President of the Senate, Marais Viljoen, opened the session of the CPRC. Labour Party members boycotted the session and staged a demonstration in support of their demand that their national chairman, Rev. Alan Hendrickse (at that time detained) be released. Senator Viljoen announced a number of concessions which were directed at pleasing, and so winning the support of, the wealthier section of the coloured people. The new concessions consisted of:

    the right to open industries in any area;
    the right to trade outside the Group Areas;
    the right to proper consulting room facilities in district surgeon offices;
    better seating at arts and science conferences (!) and in courts of law;
    representation on housing planning committees;
    more extensive legislative and executive powers for the CPRC;
    removal of some points of friction in eating and rest facilities (e.g. on the motorways);
    a better ranking structure in the prison services; and
    representation on the committees of mixed trade unions – subject to this being justified by the membership.[28]

These new 'rights' were offered a month after the Revolt had swept through the Cape Province. More concessions, or more appropriate concessions, might have helped cool the situation in the Cape which had reached boiling point at the time. But the government clearly had no intention of 'cooling' the Coloured people. All evidence pointed to an avowed intention in the government ranks of subduing and repressing the opposition. Concessions might even have been counterproductive to government plans!

Cape Schools Join the Revolt

The school students in Cape Town reacted to the news they heard of events in Soweto. A teacher at one of the Coloured schools was later to write: 'We haven't done much by way of teaching since the Soweto riots first began. Kids were restless, tense and confused.'[29] There is no similar record of what the African children thought, but it is known that they were aware of the extra police patrols that were set up in the townships following June 16. After the first shootings in Cape Town, a teacher at one of the schools recounted:

    . . . pupils from Fezeka and I.D. Mkize [Secondary Schools in Guguletu Township] used their schools at night for studying because these schools had electricity. During the Soweto unrest the police surrounded these schools so that the pupils could not use them properly. . . . They were stopped from studying at night.[30]

There were some incidents within a week of the first Soweto massacre: on 24 June the principal's office at Hlargisi Primary School in Nyanga was burnt out and on the following day the riot squad was on standby at Langa when a crowd threatened officials of the Bantu Administration. On 27 June there were further arson attacks at the Langa post-office and at Zimosa school. The police officer in command issued a statement saying that the events had no connection with events in Soweto.[31]

July was vacation time in South Africa, and schools reassembled just before August. On 2 August students at UWC boycotted classes (as described in Chapter Eleven); on 6 August the Hewat Teacher Training College in Athlone was set alight in solidarity with the UWC boycotters; on the 8th, fire destroyed classrooms and the principal's office at Struis Bay (east of Cape Town), and on 10 August there was increased activity — another unsuccessful attempt to burn down buildings at Hewat, a prefabricated building that was part of the Peninsula College for Advanced Technical Education was gutted, and there were three explosions at Die Goeiehoop (Goodhope) Primary School in Cape Town.

Sometime in early August African pupils had also decided that some demonstration in sympathy with Soweto was necessary. The pupils of Langa, Nyanga and Guguletu were in communication and it was decided to march together on Wednesday 11 August.

Reports from several sources seem to indicate that the decision had not been widely circulated and that plans were vague. Themba Nolutshungu, a youth organiser with the South African Institute of Race Relations reported that pupils at Langa High School met on the sports fields in the early morning.

> Speaker after speaker could be seen gesticulating, obviously striving to hammer a point home. A distinct feature of the meeting was the fact that participation in the actual discussion was neither confined to nor monopolised by a recognised clique.[32]

They refused to enter the school and after congregating marched out on to the streets bearing placards that declared solidarity with the students of Soweto.

At another school, this time in Guguletu, a teacher described the scene as follows:

> The students marched towards our school singing softly, *Nkosi Sikelel'i-Afrika.* It was really touching when they sang. They were marching quietly around the school to the parade ground where the school conducts its prayers. Two girls came forward and spoke to a teacher, saying: 'Good morning, sir. We have come to ask permission to get together and pray for Soweto.' They were directed to the principal. . . .'[33]

They did not get the required permission, but the pupils at the school just left the building and the teachers let them go. The atmosphere, according to the teacher was 'extraordinary. Nobody could speak.'

The students planned to converge, but the students of Guguletu and Nyanga were dispersed by police with tear gas at least twice, and then finally confronted and told to disperse within eight minutes. They stood firm and were then showered with gas, and 25 to 30 were arrested.

Each attack by the police had left them even more resolute and, in one instance, pupils of a school that had been undecided joined the demonstrators after they witnessed the police in action.[34]

After the arrests, the youth re-formed and followed the police to the Guguletu police station and demanded the release of their fellow demonstrators. Bottles of water were passed around and faces doused as a protection against gas. Eventually volunteers met the police and secured the release of the detainees.[35]

The pupils of Langa had in the meanwhile marched through the streets of their township, followed by their teachers who 'were determined to see to it that the demonstration remained orderly'. They were, in turn, followed by riot police, and the entire procession was surrounded by the crowd that had gathered at the school and grew as the group passed through the township. It appears that it was persons in the surrounding crowd who hurled abuse at the police and also started throwing stones at the first bottlestore that was passed. At that stage the students turned round and returned to their school. The stoning then stopped.[36]

The students had gone out of their way to maintain the peace, but the crowds that had gathered were not as restrained. At some stage after the school pupils had stopped marching, the stoning started and the police were quick to respond with gas and with bullets. That unleashed the terror that Soweto had experienced in June. Administrative blocks in the townships were burnt first, then shops and bottlestores. When workers arrived home they joined the demonstrators and more buildings went up in smoke. Some residents blamed the *tsotsis* and even tried to organise vigilante groups — but they were dissuaded by other residents.

The shooting carried on well into the night and that day 33 persons were killed and an unknown number injured, according to the Cape Town Commissioner of Police.[37] What was not explained was the fact that the majority of those killed were children, but whether these were part of the group of push-outs or not, is not clear.

Rioting reached a new peak on 12 August. At Langa and Guguletu attempts were made to stop workers leaving for work and riot squad cars that arrived to stop this action were attacked and damaged. Police fired at the crowd through the mesh windows of the wrecked cars.[38]

In the streets young children (some described as *tsotsis*) stopped all cars and cried out 'donate, donate', in their demand for petrol to make 'Molotov cocktails'. Cars were only allowed to proceed if the driver gave the Black Power salute and hooted in support.[39]

Later that morning students of the Langa High School marched to the local police station to demand the release of fellow students detained since the demonstration. Shots were fired and one of the students, Xolile Mosi, was killed. The students retreated to their school grounds and stood congregated outside the buildings. Two police helicopters hovered above them and dropped tear gas canisters. The entire student body of Langa High, together with pupils from other schools, again marched to the police station, carrying banners: 'We are not fighting. We have just come to release our people.' While one pupil, carrying a white flag, went in to negotiate the release of the arrested, his fellow students stood outside singing hymns. All that happened, however, after three-quarters of an hour, was the appearance of six policemen wth a demand that the demonstrators supply the names of those who had been detained.

In Nyanga, students and others gathered at a road block and were met by a line of police. Dogs were turned on the crowd, tear gas was thrown and, after the crowd responded with stones, the police fired. Three bodies were removed after the demonstrators retreated. On the night of 12 August, any administrative buildings, beerhalls, bottlestores or shops that had not yet been gutted were destroyed. Some R2,000,000 worth of damage was done in 36 hours of fighting.

Students in Cape Town also marched on 12 August. The University of Cape Town provided one group that marched towards the centre of town, giving the Black Power salute to passing Blacks until stopped by the police. Seventy-three students were arrested. Six hundred coloured students also marched from the Bellville Training College and clashed with baton wielding police. And at the UWC a poster parade was broken up by police and banner bearers arrested. The messages on the posters were quite specific: 'Sorry Soweto'; 'Kruger is a pig'; 'The revolution is coming'.[40] The storeroom at the Modderdam High School in Bonteheuwel was set alight.

On Monday 14 August there were more reports of arson in the African townships and on 16 August pupils at the Alexander Sinton High School and the Belgravia High School boycotted classes. One of the slogans of the time in the townships was: 'Once we return to our desks — our cause is lost'. The coloured students concurred.

Separate, Yet Together

For over a month, first the youth, and then the adults, in the coloured townships boycotted, demonstrated and faced police terror. And during that same month, the youth and residents of Langa, Nyanga and Guguletu protested, demonstrated and fought with the police. Two detachments of rebels faced the same central authority, had the same basic demands, and knew that they were allies in the same fight. Youth of both communities even managed to penetrate to the centre of the city in order to demonstrate — but the moves were not co-ordinated and took place on successive days. The physical separation of the two communities, each tied to their respective ghettos, prevented joint action and probably militated against the smooth functioning of a joint committee, described below.

Each community was aware of what was happening in the other townships and events in one centre evoked sympathetic action in the other. In fact, the process was made more complex by the fact that Cape Town was not an island divorced from events elsewhere in the country. They responded to events in the Eastern Cape, where a new focus of revolt had been established in Port Elizabeth and East London (as described later in this chapter); and to events in the North, in Soweto and elsewhere.

On Monday 16 August, 500 students at UWC marched to the Bellville Magistrate's Court where 15 students were appearing on a number of charges arising from recent events. The crowd swelled to 1,000 and were forcibly moved by riot police. The rest of the week was relatively quiet. There was a fire at Arcadia High School in Bonteheuwel on 17 August and a boycott of classes at Somerset West after permission to hold a prayer meeting in sympathy with 'Blacks who have died' was refused.

Two events, not necessarily unrelated, but with different roots, led to the next stage of the Cape revolt. On 22 August the funeral of Xolile Mosi was scheduled to take place in Langa. The magistrate of Wynberg had ordered that the funeral be restricted to parents and close relatives. Mosi's fellow students wanted a mass funeral procession and defied the ban. There was, inevitably, a clash at the graveside and the crowd was dispersed with tear gas. The youth retreated to the school grounds. Yet again they were met by police and once more were saturated with gas. The next day there was a demonstration at Guguletu, called to commemorate the death of another young pupil, Mvuseleli Tleko, aged thirteen. A large crowd gathered and stones were thrown at a bus. Tear gas and a baton charge were used to disperse them.

The second event occurred in nearby Bonteheuwel. Students at the three high schools organised a demonstration 'in sympathy with Soweto' on Monday 23 August to coincide with the first day of a general strike called by the SSRC in Johannesburg. The demonstration at one of the schools, the Modderdam High School, was broken up by the riot squad and the next day none of the Bonteheuwel High School students would attend classes. They called for peaceful demonstrations in the school grounds. There had in fact been a transformation over the past few days. On 20 August F.A. Osmany, a reporter, wrote in the *Muslim News* that after interviewing coloured youth he had found:

Students are emphasising that they are boycotting classes because they want to make people aware of the situation, and that they also want to bring to the notice of everybody what is happening at the University of the Western Cape and at Black schools, and also of the oppression and suffering in South Africa.

We want people to know we are not trying to hamper our own education or disrupt anything. We merely want to voice our dissatisfaction of the educational system.

On 23 August, a statement by the pupils of Athlone High School condemned police brutality, inferior education, segregation laws and the plight of detainees. And they added: 'We wish the people to know that we are prepared to sacrifice everything, our carefully planned careers and aspirations, for the ensurance of a better and more just future.'[41] The students who issued that statement might have been a bit ahead of their fellow students elsewhere, but others would come to the same position within the coming days.

The police had also changed their tactics. They seemed determined now to move into the schools, seek a confrontation and break the spirit of the youth. A letter by two schoolteachers, written to the London *Guardian* describes the position at coloured schools from 24 August. Other reports give similar accounts of events in the coloured townships. Their account reads:

> On August 24 . . . pupils of Bonteheuwel High School held a peaceful demonstration in the school grounds. They carried placards expressing sympathy with fellow scholars in African areas. The atmosphere of the demonstration was jovial rather than aggressive.
>
> The Riot Squad arrived in mesh-protected vehicles; they were wearing camouflage battle dress and were armed with shotguns, rifles, and teargas guns. Immediately the principal asked them to leave . . . They ordered him to stand aside. The commanding officer ordered his men to line up and, without warning, tear gas was fired at the children. They were then baton charged.[42]

The children fled but only the boys managed to climb the school fence. The girls, trapped in the grounds, were beaten up by the police. A crowd of protesting parents who gathered in the area were forced to flee from the returning Riot Squad. 'Fleeing was the only defence the people had against the guns of the Riot Squad; stone throwing their only means of expressing their anger and pain.'[43]

For three days the unequal fight continued. The police set up ambushes to draw the crowds into the streets and then peppered them with buckshot. Many were left severely wounded or dead. On Wednesday 30 August about 600 students from five secondary schools decided to march to Bonteheuwel. On the way they were confronted by four riot squad vans. A reporter on the *Muslim News* described what happened:

> Some students appealed for calm as they did not want to provoke police action. Meanwhile a member of the riot squad read out something to the students which was incomprehensible.
>
> According to some students on the scene the riot squad aimed tear gas canisters at the students before the order to disperse was given. One student said, 'They did not release the tear gas to disperse us but were aiming the canisters to hurt us.' . . .
>
> When the tear gas took effect among the students the riot squad batoncharged them. There was general panic as students fled in all directions.[44]

The reporter then added that local residents offered the students sanctuary, but the police fired into the backyards in order to 'flush' the students out.

Blacks Invade the White City

Through August the pattern of the North had been repeated in Cape Town. All the fighting had taken place in the Black areas and the Whites continued in their enclaves, undisturbed and seemingly unperturbed by the events that flowed past them. The march to Bonteheuwel showed quite clearly that the action had to be taken into the White centre, and the school pupils at that stage still thought in terms of marching and demonstrating. In fact, as their objective was publicity, that was one of the few means open to them.

On Wednesday 1 September pupils of the schools of Langa, Nyanga and Guguletu arrived at Cape Town railway station without any prior notice or publicity and then marched through the central business district of the city. Unhindered and unmolested, they carried their placards: 'Away with apartheid'; 'Equal education'; 'We want our Robben Island Prisoners'. They then marched, 2,000 strong, back to the station and returned home.[45]

Coloured students had also reached the end of a road and, after the most recent confrontation with the police who were intent on destroying the Revolt, sought a new peaceful way of presenting their demands. The African demonstration on 1 September seemed to point a way and on the following day they too streamed into the city.

The police had been caught off guard when the Africans marched through the city, but the next day they were ready, and they descended on the marchers with an unprecedented ferocity. The city centre was sealed off and the police closed in on the youth and the white onlookers amongst whom they were caught. Tear gas in the streets seeped into the buildings forcing shopkeepers, clerks, attendants and the public into the streets where they were subjected to more gas and to riot sticks.[46]

The youth, however, were far from cowed. Despite the drubbing they received that day, they came back into the centre of the city again on 3 September. Once again the police sealed off the city centre and only police vans were allowed in, hurling gas cylinders into crowds or into the streets at random.

As men and women came streaming out of gas filled buildings, the riot police in battle dress marched abreast, guns at the ready and firing buckshot into the ethnically mixed crowd. As people fled, they were beaten by police wielding batons and an assortment of staves and metal piping, and arrested.

Those who escaped got into the coloured areas, only to find the riot vehicles waiting, ready with more gas, buckshot and bullets. The police were out in force in the coloured districts that day. The teachers who wrote to the London *Guardian* gave their account of events there:

> The children of Trafalgar were standing in the playground watching tear gas being fired in the city below. A police car stopped in the road outside and a policeman jumped out and baton charged a boy of nine or ten. As the police pulled off the watching pupils booed. Immediately the car stopped and, without warning, policemen fired tear gas.

The children fled but later tied posters to the school fence saying: 'We want rights not riots'; 'Give us Justice'. Almost immediately two riot cars arrived, and fired tear gas, birdshot and bullets at the fleeing children. 'A bleeding boy fell to the ground. The principal ran forward to help him, but was ordered back.' The letter continued with an account of children throwing stones. The police burst into the school, guns at the ready, and beat up a teacher and children in the classrooms.

The pattern was repeated in other schools. At the Alexander Sinton High School, not only students but bystanders were shot. A youth who had polio-myelitis was hospitalised after being beaten up and was said to be permanently crippled. Other children had broken limbs after jumping through windows to escape the police who poured tear gas into crowded classrooms.[47] 'Instead of crushing the Coloured youth, . . . all hell broke loose in the [Cape] Peninsula. The kids at the high school refused to attend classes.'[48]

The Cape Town revolt had passed the point where intimidation could force the youth off the streets. Despite all the reports – of shootings, of savaging by dogs, or of gassing – the children were still out in the streets. Their mood was one of determination and yet, as they marched, they chanted: 'No violence, no violence'. To no avail: the riot squad charged again and again. The chant in the streets changed: 'We are not afraid to die. We shall sacrifice.'[49] And again the response was tear gas, riot sticks and buckshot.

That weekend (4-5 September), the youth were out in the coloured townships. They had stood all that they could bear. Schools, libraries and a magistrates court were set alight. On Monday there were few pupils at school and the pupils were dismissed for a week. On Tuesday the revolt was in full swing from the suburbs of Cape Town through to Stellenbosch and Somerset West, some 30 miles away. They fought in the city centres and they fought in the suburbs – destroying vehicles and ducking the police charges. By far the biggest battle occurred in the Coloured slum of Ravensmead where the inhabitants set up a road block of flaming tyres and threw petrol bombs at police vans. For two days they held off the police and brought the industries of the area, only 12 miles from Cape Town, to a halt.[50]

The demonstrators in the Cape then moved for the first time into the exclusive all-white suburbs, stoned vehicles and shop fronts, removed goods and set buildings alight, and in Fish Hoek threw petrol bombs into houses.

Urged on by the government, white vigilante groups had already come into existence to protect white schools and property, and to organise counter attacks on bands of black youth in the neighbourhood. Large cinemas converted into rifle ranges were packed and gunsmiths were besieged by a clientele that cleared the shelves. One indication of the mood of the day came from a report which the press were not prepared to print. Students at Stellenbosch, the premier Afrikaans medium university, were apparently enrolled into local Commando groups and joined nightly patrols, armed with FN guns. They were said to have participated in shooting-raids on black youth 'suspected of stone throwing'.[51]

Was There a Cape Town Leadership?

In his report of events in the Cape Town townships on 11-13 August, Themba Nolutshungu quoted Kittman Fresi of the Black Mamba People's Movement as saying:

> The people were waiting for us to direct the course of events and organise all the forces that were related to this commotion. . . . Our policy was to stay put, watch, analyse, come up with a historical document, and later on submit a questionnaire to the public. We would not stick our neck out for an unscrupulous bunch. But the audacity of the students is something worth taking note of. The adults have to listen to the youth. The best they can do is to take orders.[52]

This statement by Mr. Fresi had a familiar ring about it. It came out of the tradition of small left groups that flourished for brief periods in Cape Town. They analysed endlessly, wrote their historical documents, but always 'stayed put'. Submitting questionnaires was a new departure and what the Black Mambas hoped to achieve by so doing was not recorded. It seems, however, that this time the Black Mambas, and presumably other groups too, decided to 'listen to the youth' and to 'take orders'.

There is unfortunately a dearth of information on the groups that existed in the townships. Some were responsible for leaflets which appeared on the streets, and called for action or supported the stay-at-homes and so on. But they maintained anonymity and there is nothing on the many leaflets issued in August and September to indicate which group or groups were involved.

Many of the adults remembered the events of 1960 and the stories of that time must have been handed down to the children. Some undoubtedly belonged to clandestine groups and it was known, at least from the trial of David and Sue Rabkin and Jeremy Cronin, that there were ANC and Communist Party groups active in the Western Cape.[53]

Direct evidence is, understandably, difficult to obtain, but it is hard to believe that there were no groups in the townships. The memories were too vivid to allow for their disappearance. A teacher, talking to Lindy Wilson in mid-August would only say: 'You must salute to Black power and most people are excited by this Black power, even though they know people are dying. It's after 16 years of being bottled up and afraid. Adults have not forgotten 1960.'[54]

Some of the youth were also involved in political groups. A few had joined the Western Cape Youth Organisation, the local section of the National Youth Organisation (NAYO). Some had contacts with SASM. The slogans found on a classroom blackboard at the Roman Catholic school in Nyanga on 12 August indicated political awareness:

Cape Town Comrades. Mdantsane [East London] Comrades. Soweto Comrades. Maputo Comrades.

All these Comrades must unite.
No racism
No colonialism
Equality [55]

But the politically orientated students were probably in a tiny minority and most of the demands expressed in August and issued as statements (or chalked on placards) were related to better schooling and teaching, more equipment and playing fields, and improved job opportunities for school leavers.[56] Students at Langa High made a statement on 23 August, which included some of the earliest political demands:

> We want our fellow students who have been detained to be released, and other detainees, regardless of colour.
> Equal job, equal pay. Free education.
> We will never attend classes unless these demands are fulfilled, and the South African government will experience daily rioting if the above mentioned demands are not fulfilled.[57]

A large number of leaflets appeared in the streets. Some were produced by pupils of particular schools and bore their names. Others were produced anonymously. They carried complaints about conditions in the schools and also about police brutality. On 30 August a leaflet drawn up by students at three Bonteheuwel schools listed their grievances:

> the system of apartheid and Coloured education;
> lack of compulsory education;
> lack of sports ground facilities;
> general behaviour of the police during the unrest in Black areas;
> police interference with demonstrations in school grounds;
> the taking into custody of fellow students;
> the attitude of White teachers on the staff;
> the inconvenience allowance paid to White teachers — seen as an insult.[58]

An anonymous leaflet commenced: 'We the students of the Cape Peninsula declare that: We identify with the struggle for a basic human society.' The Bantu, Coloured and Indian Affairs Departments were condemned, and three demands were made: free and equal education for all; equal wages and work according to merit; and an end to influx control. There was no call to stage any particular action and the leaflet concluded: 'Students you have an important role to play in the change. All oppressed people must stand up now and be counted. So unite now.'

Although there were signs of co-ordination in the African areas and also signs of some centralising body in the Coloured suburbs, there were no names attached to most of the calls for action. Even a call for a strike in mid-September (which will be discussed in Chapter Thirteen) appeared anonymously and, equally anonymously, was supported by a variety of groups. One leaflet expressing solidarity called for 'Workers Power and Peoples Power' and must have been the product of one of the many small groups tucked away in one of the communities.

At the end of October a body calling itself the United Students Front declared its existence. It was stated that a group of African, Indian and Coloured pupils from schools in the Cape Peninsula had formed this body three months previously. Their aim was to 'politically educate and unite the Black oppressed masses', and one of their proposals was that no examinations be written until the government took active steps to remedy their grievances.[59] If this committee was responsible for any of the events of the past three months, it had not only kept a low public profile, but had also only had a limited effect on the student body. There were few signs that the coloured students and African students had planned jointly, and only limited evidence that events even inside each of the two main population groups had been co-ordinated.

There can be little doubt that committees had to protect themselves and that a certain degree of anonymity was desirable — but committees which never declared themselves and never published under their name stood in danger of remaining unrecognised amongst the people.

The roots of the conflict were partly local and could be found in conditions in the suburbs and townships of Cape Town, and part of the struggle stemmed from attempts by the central government to implement an apartheid system that the population found obnoxious. Explanations of events as shattering as those of 1976, however, require more than a set of objective conditions that are oppressive. There had to be the will to struggle and the organisation to maintain that action once it had started.

There were, as has been shown above, some organisations that tried to provide leadership, even if evidence of their existence has been hard to find. At times this was overcome by students following a lead suggested by activities in the Transvaal. Having once moved into demonstrations, the logic of events suggested new tactics and new methods. This in turn became known through press accounts to the SSRC in Soweto (and elsewhere), and the tactic was applied locally. Students in Cape Town helped initiate the marches into the city centres — or at least showed the way. In like fashion Soweto students often suggested to other communities what the next step might be. After a while, therefore, a description of events in only one region becomes one-dimensional and the dynamics of the struggle are left unexplored.

The events of Cape Town were merged in the national struggle in September and, although local conditions laid a stamp on the actual mechanics with which plans were executed, it was the national pattern which became important.

Other Centres of the Revolt[60]

In describing the peculiar social conditions in Cape Town, and claiming that the particular ethnic composition, the poor housing, and so on were contributory factors which led to the spread of the Revolt into the Western Cape, there is an obvious danger that the Capital city might be seen as a unique case. If, indeed, only the region around Cape Town had caught fire that August, there would have been good reason for seeking out factors which differentiated it from all other towns in the Cape and, obviously, Natal and the OFS.

Although there are only some newspaper accounts and sparse reports in the annual surveys already cited, it is clear that more detailed accounts will show that few urban centres were left unaffected by the Revolt. It also seems clear that the Revolt in each town started in the local school or schools, and then spread out into the townships and suburbs of the town. It also seems that every tactic evolved in Soweto and Cape Town was repeated in some form in most of the big centres. How far any one centre was influenced by events in Johannesburg or Cape Town is not known, but the timing does indicate that local populations learned from what had happened elsewhere.

Because local conditions were so very different, there were obviously unique factors which entered into and altered the course of events in every town. Local variations were also affected by the presence of persons with particular political affiliations, by the existence in a town of an active political body or community association, and pressing local or regional problems. Too little is known about the history of the many small communities to be able to place the episodes that have been reported in perspective and none of the leaflets or other material produced by local leaders has become available. There is little, consequently, which would help provide further understanding of events in most of the outlying regions.

There was a spate of incidents immediately after the opening of the schools on 22 July. Within a few days a secondary school at Tugela Ferry was burnt down and a school library damaged at Vryheid, both in Natal.[61] On 9 August the Bantu Administration Board complex at Pinetown was destroyed by fire and at least five other schools set alight that month, and students at Ohlango High School (KwaMashu, Durban) staged a march in mid-September and held a protest rally at the sports stadium. As a result 285 students were arrested and the township was sealed off by police. Shortly after this event, 'mysterious' veld fires were reported in Natal; probably the first since the early 1960's when these had been part of the sabotage campaigns of the time.

Events in the Eastern Cape indicate that the Revolt there was protracted and bitter. The first incidents in the townships were reported on 7 August in New Brighton (Port Elizabeth) and on 9 August in Mdantsane (near East London). That is, a few days before the students marched in Cape Town.

There were very few days in August in which the press did not carry stories of incidents of the Revolt in the main townships of the Eastern Cape: fires at schools, libraries, administration buildings, bottlestores and beerhalls;

marches, boycotts, freedom songs, road blocks and confrontations with riot police. The dead, the injured, and the closing of all schools — all these items appeared. There were also accounts of attempts by African townships to join together in demonstrations and of coloured and African students planning to march together, but being frustrated by police intervention.

There were demonstrations of sympathy with Soweto; marches in protest against the detention of Rev. Hendrickse (national chairman of the Labour Party) in Uitenhage, his hometown, and at Graaf Reinet; marches and freedom songs at Zwelitsha (near Kingwilliamstown) after the death in detention of Mapetha Mohapi of the BPC; and there was a march of 500 students through the streets of Lady Frere (Transkei) in protest against the proposed 'independence' in October. Cars were overturned and set alight, telephone wires were pulled down, and eventually about 300 were arrested by the police.

Marches of 300 to 500 were common. On 18 August the crowd rapidly grew to 4,000 when residents of Port Elizabeth's townships joined the students of KwaZakele High School who tried to march to the local Wolfson Stadium. The march was followed later in the day by attempts by approximately 1,000 residents of the three townships, New Brighton, KwaZakele and Zwide, to march to the main administration buildings. The police scattered the crowd by means of tear gas, but they regrouped, set up road blocks and stoned vehicles. All transport into the townships was stopped and the police sent in reinforcements. Bottlestores, a bank, post office and an administration office block were destroyed. At least eight Blacks were killed and 20 injured.

On the same Wednesday, 18 August, students at Mdantsane announced a boycott of classes until a detained student was released. The youth gathered in the streets and cars were stoned until the police arrived with tear gas. All post-primary schools were henceforth closed by the Ciskei Education Department.

Towns with previous histories of struggle or strife, and towns which had never before experienced such conflicts, were the scenes of these clashes. Port Elizabeth and Mdantsane, Lady Frere, Uitenhage, Genadendal, Graaf Reinet, Idutywa, Stutterheim, in the Eastern Cape, Transkei and Ciskei, were all the scenes of major incidents. Other smaller towns did not warrant a notice in the press, already filled with news from the Transvaal and the Western Cape and, when they could be squeezed in, Kimberley, Upington (both in the Northern Cape), and Bloemfontein and Kroonstad in the OFS.

The accumulated anger over oppression, the urgent desire for freedom, the frustration caused by slum housing, bad transport, and hunger, the hatred of officialdom and the police, were all fed into the Revolt. What needs to be explained is not why the communities entered the Revolt, but why some regions witnessed such little action in those opening months and indeed throughout the long Revolt.

Although Natal seemed to be relatively quiet, there was actually far more action than appeared from the scattered news items in the provincial press. There were demonstrations, strikes and acts of arson in many of the towns, led in the main by school students. But the number of secondary schools and the number of African youth in the secondary schools in the urban centres outside the Southern Transvaal and the Eastern Cape was minuscule.

Although there were local conditions which make generalisations difficult, there was a direct correlation between the concentration of secondary schools in a region and the extent of local participation in the Revolt. In parts of the Cape, where African secondary schooling was not extensive, the combined coloured and African school participation more than made up for the low numbers of African students.

In keeping with the policies laid down by Dr. Verwoerd when he first introduced Bantu Education in 1954, the bulk of African secondary education had been moved to the Reserves. In March 1975, when the intake into African secondary schools had already been doubled, the proportion of pupils who received their education in the Reserves was 70 per cent. 221,827 youth received their secondary education in the Reserves while only 96,741 were accommodated in the 'white' urban centres.[62] The vast majority of these were in schools in the Southern Transvaal and the Eastern Cape. Few townships in the Northern Cape, the Orange Free State or Natal could boast more than one secondary school and, where they had been established, the annual intake was usually small. This obviously acted as a damper on the extent of activity such students could undertake — and there was seldom any follow-up to an initial demonstration or strike.

The heavy concentration of schools in the Reserves did, however, stimulate the Revolt there. Widespread activity took place in BophutuTswana, in Basotho Qua-Qua and to a lesser degree in Lebowa. The schools in the Ciskei and the adjoining areas of the Eastern Cape were deeply involved after August. Only KwaZulu and the Transkei remained areas of comparative quiet.

Any attempt here to describe conditions in these latter two areas in detail would go outside the scope of this book. It must suffice to state that the Transkei had been governed under emergency laws since 1960 and that all opposition to the regime had been summarily dealt with. A strike in August 1960 by 1,300 workers for higher wages followed an alleged assault by a white foreman on a black woman. All the workers were dismissed after the police had been summoned.[63] In the field of constitutional politics there were equally draconian measures to silence any opposition. Between 25 and 27 July, nine leaders of the opposition Democratic Party were placed in detention and at least eight more were incarcerated during August.[64] The fact that there were student demonstrations at Idutywa and elsewhere bears testimony to the courage of the students, but there were obviously severe limitations on the Transkeian students which prevented them playing a prominent role in the events of 1976.

The situation in KwaZulu was rendered more complex by the strong control maintained by Gatsha Buthelezi. In his territory there was little opportunity for an opposition force to be established partly because of the continual surveillance of any group which might emerge to support the King in his political intrigues, and partly because Buthelezi's populist appeal attracted many of the youth. This did not prevent some of the students demonstrating, particularly as the target was not Buthelezi but the South African government's Bantu Education Department. Of even greater importance, was the widespread support Buthelezi had built up amongst the workers in Durban and its environs. Throughout the Revolt the Chief appealed for an end to all violence, for a return to school, for a disciplined black community, and at the same time let it be known that students who embarked on militant action would be speedily dealt with. The workers saw no reason for taking action and the students were unable to move. In the event Buthelezi, who had been seen as a possible embarrassment to the regime, proved to be a valuable asset to the government forces.

The pattern of events in July and August did not yet allow some of these trends to manifest themselves. The students seemed to carry everything before them and they were confident that they could give the lead in the months to come. There were already signs that they were going to introduce new tactics, at least in the main centres, and once again the initiative would come from Soweto. The other towns would follow.

References

1. Maurice Hommel, a coloured teacher, quoted in *SRRSA*, 1954-5, p.4.
2. W.W.M. Eiselen, (1955), *The Native in the Western Cape*, (SABRA, Stellenbosch), pp.15-6.
3. *Ibid.*, p.11.
4. L.B. Lee-Warden, (1957), 'The crime of Langa', *Africa South*, Vol. 1, No. 3, April-June 1957.
5. *Loc.cit.*
6. The official estimate, reprinted in *Financial Mail*, 9 July 1976, was 20,000. In only one camp, that of Modderdam, where the official figure was approximately 2,000, the actual number was over 10,000.
7. The Minister of Bantu Administration and Development, quoted in *SRRSA*, 1974, p.67.
8. See 'Background to squatting', *Reality*, July 1977, pp.16-8.
9. *Muslim News*, Vol. 16, No. 12, 23 July 1976.
10. *SRRSA*, 1963, pp.229-30.
11. *SRRSA*, 1976, p.341.
12. *Ibid.*
13. Dr. Margaret Ellsworth, (1976), 'African Education in the Cape', compiled from notes taken at her talk on 16 September 1976, and printed in *Z*, Vol. 1, No. 2, October 1976.
14. *Loc.cit.*
15. A list drawn up by the Trustees of the Bantu School Fund after consultation with pupils of 13 African schools. This was mimeographed under the heading 'Recommendations from the pupils of the Cape Town Bantu schools' and dated 5 September 1976.
16. Adam Small, (1971), 'Blackness versus nihilism: black racism rejected',

in Basil Moore, (Ed.), (1973), *op.cit.*, pp.11-2.

17. *Ibid.*, pp.15-6.
18. *Ibid.*, p.17.
19. M.G. Whisson, (1971), 'The Coloured community', in Peter Randall, (Ed.), *South Africa's Minorities*, Spro-Cas occasional publications, No. 2. p.56.
20. *Black Review*, 1973, p.48.
21. *Ibid.*, pp.46-50.
22. *Black Review*, 1974-5, pp.66-7.
23. *Ibid.*, p.132.
24. *Ibid.*, p.69.
25. *SRRSA*, 1975, p.19.
26. *SRRSA*, 1973, p.13.
27. *Rand Daily Mail*, 29 July 1976, quoted in *SRRSA*, 1976, p.15.
28. The *Star*, 11 September 1976.
29. Letter from a teacher to a friend in Britain, printed in the London *Guardian*, 7 December 1976.
30. Lindy Wilson, (1976), 'Cape Township riots — some African accounts', *South African Outlook,* August 1976.
31. Victor Norton, (1976), *Preliminary chronology of events in Cape Town in the unrest following the Soweto riots,* Cape Town, September 1976, (mimeo).
32. Themba Nolutshungu, (1976), 'Inside Langa and Guguletu', *South African Outlook*, August 1976.
33. L. Wilson, *op.cit.*
34. *Loc.cit.*
35. See the accounts by both L. Wilson and T. Nolutshungu.
36. T. Nolutshungu, *op.cit.*
37. *SRRSA*, 1976, p.72.
38. V. Norton, *op.cit.*
39. L. Wilson, *op.cit.*
40. V. Norton, *op.cit.*
41. CIS, *op.cit.*, p.27.
42. Letter from two teachers to the London *Guardian*, 1 November 1976.
43. *Ibid.*
44. *Muslim News*, Vol. 16, No. 16, 3 September 1976.
45. CIS, *op.cit.*, pp.29-30.
46. *Ibid.*, pp.30-1.
47. As reference 42. See also *Muslim News*, 24 September 1976.
48. As reference 29.
49. *Ibid.*
50. V. Norton, *op.cit.*
51. UCT workshop on Revolt of 1976.
52. T. Nolutshungu, *op.cit.*
53. See report of trial, *SRRSA*, 1976, pp.138-9.
54. L. Wilson, *op.cit.*
55. T. Nolutshungu, *op.cit.*
56. As reference 15.
57. Quoted in CIS, *op.cit.*, p.20.
58. V. Norton, *op.cit.* The inconvenience allowance was condemned by the school pupils and students at UWC. The school principals, and the

Rector of UWC denied any knowledge of it.
59. *SRRSA*, 1976, p.79.
60. I must thank Nick Barker for his summary of newspaper items used in this section.
61. *Black Review*, 1975-6, p.101. No other account, to date, mentions the earlier events quoted here.
62. The Minister of Bantu Education, replying to questions in parliament, quoted in *SRRSA*, 1976, p.330.
63. SANA Bulletin, No. 2, September 1976.
64. *SRRSA*, 1976, pp.242-3.

13. New Tactics in the Revolt

Reaction Takes the Offensive

After the first attempted march on Johannesburg on 4 August, and the partial stay-at-home which kept at least 60 per cent of the labour force away from work, the SSRC was forced on to the defensive. There were large-scale arrests, and the committee members never spent two days at the same place.[1] On 11 August the Minister of Police, J. Kruger, introduced 'indefinite preventative detention' to break the Revolt.

There were signs of an unholy alliance emerging against the youth. The government was determined to smash all organisations that opposed their apartheid plans. Kruger told a Nationalist audience on 21 August: 'He knows his place and, if not, I'll tell him. The Blacks always say "We shall overcome", but I say we shall overcome.'[2]

In Soweto the Urban Bantu Council was busy organising vigilante groups. In the court action brought by Winnie Mandela on 15 August, and mentioned in Chapter Ten, it was claimed that the government had given this body permission to set up a 'Home Guard' which would attack the homes of members of the Black Parents Association when trouble occurred. A police officer who was at the meeting, apparently assured those present that no one would be prosecuted for carrying weapons and that the vigilante groups would have police co-operation.[3]

From further information, it appears that the police also sought the co-operation of the makeshift tribal courts known as *makgotla* which had the support of the UBC. These 'courts' dealt with minor criminal cases, family disputes and a range of misdemeanours. Those found guilty by the *makgotla* officials were publicly flogged. The courts had no legal standing, but were not prohibited by the government. The youth were known to despise these tribal institutions, and there was little love lost between them and the 'court' officials. Nevertheless, the *makgotla* remained neutral throughout the Revolt.

The police also sought support amongst migrant workers, some of whom had turned on the youth on 4 August when called upon to strike. These labourers, largely isolated from the more permanent inhabitants of Soweto, had few local roots. They had no contact with the students and no knowledge of their problems. The slogans of the Revolt were meaningless to them, and they were more likely to find the closing of the schools incomprehensible. Education, for many of them, was still the prized object they had failèd to attain.[4] The unemployed youth, on the other hand, were (or appeared to be) the *tsotsis* they hated and feared as pay-day predators. The migrant worker, furthermore, would tend to be amongst the first to resent action that led to an absence from work. Their pay was low and their presence in town was designed to secure the maximum possible return before their contracts expired. A strike which would not lead to direct pay increases — and which could even lead to dismissal — was not readily acceptable.

The Zulu migrants also had a background of strife which they brought with them into the urban areas.[5] The police seemed to have had information which allowed them to manipulate the residents at one of the hostels, Mzimhlope, in Soweto. It was only the Zulus at this one hostel who seemed to be vulnerable, and other hostels, where comparable numbers of Zulu lived, were not similarly penetrated by police agents. The Zulus at Mzimhlope, furthermore, numbered only 1,630 (out of a total of 10,300 men who had their abode there) and were only one of five approximately equal ethnic groups.[6] The group was, however, quite large enough for the nefarious plot the police were preparing, and during August they waited their opportunity to employ these men against the students.

Chief Gatsha Buthelezi stepped into the murky waters on 10 August, when he issued a statement calling 'for the establishment of vigilante groups to protect Black property against political action'.[7] The newspaper report on his statement continued: 'Appalled by the destruction of African schools and educational equipment, the chief warned Black radicals that they might soon be confronted by a backlash from the responsible elements of the Black community.' He was also said to have expressed dismay at 'the powerlessness and inaction' of the government.[8]

When eventually a stay-at-home was called on the weekend 21-22 August, other upholders of 'law and order' made statements in similar terms. Major-General Geldenhuys warned: 'Agitators who attempt to enforce a work stay-away in Soweto will experience a backlash from law abiding citizens in the townships. People in Soweto are getting sick of these people, and because of this the police are not worried.[9] And on the second day of the strike, Col. Visser warned: 'Go to work and disregard the groups of young intimidators telling people not to go to work. People must go to work and just thrash the children stopping them.'[10] The message was clear — and groups at Mzimhlope Hostel were indeed being prepared to 'thrash the children'; it also seemed clear that the Major-General had been misinformed: workers in Soweto were not 'sick of these people', and had in fact responded to the call for a three day strike!

Azikhwelwa Madoda! (Stay at Home!)

Azikhwelwa Madoda! The call to stay-at-home was slipped under the doors of houses in Soweto by the students. The leaflet was brought out under the name of the ANC, signifying a degree of co-operation with the SSRC which fluctuated during the months to come, but was always present in 1976. It also stressed a continuity with the stay-at-homes in the 1950's called by the ANC, and now, once again, called by the same movement from the political underground.

On 23 August there was an 80 per cent response to the joint SSRC/ANC call. Some factories ran on skeleton staffs; others were closed down. The young pickets who gathered at Soweto railway station had little to do and there were no taxis or buses inside the township. Only police-protected buses, on the outskirts of Soweto, were available for the small pockets of men who ignored the taunts of the young.

Many of those who chose to work were migrants, but only from some hostels. Reports from other hostels indicated that they fully supported the strike. There was no sign of the much heralded backlash, despite some skirmishes when the men returned that evening. The SSRC and ANC had scored a major victory, even though SSRC President, Tsietsi Mashinini had to flee the country the day the strike began. His statement from exile that the ANC was 'extinct internally' and that 'as far as the struggle is concerned they are not doing anything'[11] was incomprehensible and only devalued the work, done jointly, in preparing for the strike.

On the afternoon of the second day of the strike, the long heralded event occurred. The Minister, the UBC, the Major-General and Chief Buthelezi could not all be wrong. Armed hostel dwellers, (carrying sticks, assegais and long bladed knives) charged through the streets of Soweto, flanked by police Hippos. When the youth tried to halt the hostel dwellers, they were fired at by police, and the 'backlash' continued in a path of destruction.

The myth spread, and is probably still believed by many, that the Zulus were on the rampage. The fact that it was a tiny minority of one hostel that acted this way has been obscured by the real damage inflicted by a group of men, protected by the police and, according to available evidence, fed by them with marijuana and urged to kill the 'troublemakers'.[12]

A second myth appeared in the wake of the first story, to the effect that it was Buthelezi who persuaded the hostel dwellers that their action had been misguided. Buthelezi had been informed by the Minister that he would not be allowed into the hostel. But the Chief ignored the ban and addressed the men of Mzimhlope and, strangely, the authorities did nothing. He later made a statement accusing the police of having staged the whole affair. Kruger warned the press not to publish the account, but the *Sunday Tribune* printed it in full. Again nothing was done. Gibson Thula, Buthelezi's urban representative, was also warned to stay away. He defied the ban and spoke to the hostel workers. He later made the claim that not only Zulus were involved in the fighting and killing.[13] No one accepted Mr. Thula's account, but that was of little consequence. He, too, was not apprehended for defying the ban.

Even if all the bans were bluffs, and the Inkatha leaders, by ignoring the government's statements, showed them to be hollow, the story as told conceals the fact that students, hostel dwellers and other parties met, and a reconciliation was arrived at without Buthelezi's intervention. The question that needs to be asked is why this elaborate charade was staged, and what was being concealed in the process?

Friday, 27 August, was the third day of the strike. Despite the attempt by the police to produce a backlash the previous day, the strike held firm. Although there were reports from some factories that workers had reported for duty, other establishments stated that there were even fewer workers than before. The government, however, continued its provocative line and claimed that law abiding Blacks would put a stop to the students' actions. The Minister of Police, for example, stated: 'People are allowed to protect themselves against physical intimidation. The situation will calm itself once people realise there is a strong backlash.'[14]

The stay-at-home proved to be a valuable step; it provided fresh impetus to the struggle throughout the country, and the Cape students, as previously described, declared their solidarity by staying away from classes. In towns big and small across the Cape, there were demonstrations, stonings and burning buildings. Riot police were airlifted from the Rand to Cape Town and the concerted move to smash the coloured students was begun with unprecedented ferocity. The success of the strike was not, however, complete. There was an attempt to get the workers of Mamelodi (Pretoria) also to stay at home, but the call seems to have been ignored despite the fact that the school boycott movement in Pretoria had commenced with industrial action. There was also a call for a stay-at-home in Port Elizabeth at the end of August, but this too seems to have gone unheeded.

In the flush of the victory in Soweto, these failures were overlooked, and the students did not heed the fact that the workers would not necessarily respond to every summons, and that there had to be good grounds for staying away from work. This was to be underlined for many families, on Friday 27 August, when many firms paid for only two days labour. There was little food on Soweto tables that weekend.

In the light of the obvious hardship following the solidarity displayed that week, the leaflet that was put out, claiming that the real losers were the bosses, was not very convincing: 'Well, that we will lose these wages is a fact but we should not cry over them. We have to rejoice over the fact that while we lost these wages, we dealt the Racist Regime and Factory Owners a heavy blow — They Lost Their Profits.'[15]

To Return or Not to Return to School

In the first week of September the students in Soweto and Cape Town were under pressure to return to school from parents, from teachers, and from official and unofficial bodies. The SSRC used the issue to produce a general statement addressed to 'all residents of Soweto, hostels, Reef and Pretoria'. In an eight point message they called for Black (African) unity and urged that all in-fighting should cease. Two of the points were directed against 'false leaders' and 'political opportunists', and a third point admonished: 'We say to all black students, residents and hostel inmates: You know your true leaders. Listen to your leaders. Support your leaders. Follow your leaders.'

Point seven was a restatement, said the SSRC, of their demands to the government that all students and black leaders be released; that Bantu Education be 'scraped off'; that apartheid be abolished; and that the government consult with the parents and black leaders to end the crisis.

The final point was addressed to all school students. They were told that they had to return to school and the teachers were to start teaching 'and stop wasting time discussing about us and not with us'.[16]

The Cape Town students had no need at that stage to appeal for unity, nor had they been confronted in August by weapon wielding migrant workers. That time would come, but there was not yet such a problem. There was no clearly declared leadership, and no counter-leaders, and the students did not have to address themselves to the kinds of problems the SSRC faced in Soweto. But they did have to provide a lead on the issue of school attendance.

A leaflet was issued 'From the African scholars of Cape Town' and commenced with the slogan that had been popularised: 'Once we return to our desks — the cause is lost.' This set the whole tone of their declaration and determined their approach to the boycott. They claimed:

> Even if the natural scholar-leaders were to return to school now their friends would not agree. The leaders would be regarded as traitors to the whole school community and would be victimised.
> It is the whole system of Bantu Education which is at issue — no less. The schools represent a rejected system which offers an education so poor as to be practically valueless.
> Violence is likely to break out again and continue if nothing is done. In the Homelands many schools have already been burned down because authority would not listen. Schools in the Cape may not be spared in the future.

The following conditions were set down for returning to school:

> Release of detained scholars — 'parole prior to standing trial is acceptable'; police to stay out of schools unless requested by a principal; re-establishment of communications between the students and government authorities, with security guarantees for representatives of the students; real changes in the educational system; and adjustment to the end of year examinations with extra tuition to allow candidates the possibility of passing.[17]

The leaflet was addressed in part to the government and in part to the African students. The central demand was that Bantu Education be scrapped and that was indeed central to the demand of every African student in the country. But in the Cape Town context more had to be said, and the African students obviously had not found a means of raising slogans that would apply equally to themselves and to their allies in the coloured schools. The inability to bridge the gulf, created by the system of apartheid, underlined the difficulty of building a real co-ordinating committee that could represent all black students.

The final demand also introduced a note of equivocation that was not in keeping with the militant stance of the document. By raising the issue of extra tuition for the end of the year examinations, the students indicated that they were thinking of returning to school and that the entire issue could be over before December. This could indicate supreme confidence in their power to win their demands or, alternatively, give notice that they could not stay out indefinitely and did not wish to spoil their chances at the examinations.

The Soweto appeal to return to school was unrealistic — even if it was only a tactical move to restore an organisational base for the SSRC. There was no response from the majority of students, and the schools stayed closed. In view of police tactics at the time, it was hardly conceivable that the youth would go back. The riot squads were out in force in the townships, and neither homes nor schools were safe from their raids. To have gone back to classes in the circumstances would have been an admission of defeat — and this was precisely what government spokesmen were demanding in their public statements.

On 8 September Vorster addressed a Nationalist Party meeting in Bloemfontein. He maintained that he would never hold talks on the question of one man, one vote. The only way that he knew for governing South Africa was 'by the policy and principles of the Nationalist Party'. He assured his audience that law and order would be restored immediately and that, if this could not be done by existing methods, other steps would be taken. Mr. Kruger also spoke to the meeting. His message was direct. Every White had to protect his own property and, if he had to kill in the process, that was justified.

The Nationalist Party members got the message — and so too did the black students.

Legality and Illegality in Soweto

From August through to December the schools of Soweto hardly functioned. There were occasions when a clutch of youth attended formal lessons, and large numbers would often come to the school premises in order to avoid being picked up by the police when off the school precincts. Jabulani school, being a technical secondary school, functioned more 'normally'. Yet even there, the timetable was only sometimes adhered to, the formal syllabus mostly forgotten. Attendance fluctuated. Joan Hoffman's account captures the atmosphere of all Soweto, refracted through the eyes of a (white) teacher at Jabulani.

From August to November we continued to teach on days when we felt able to get in and open the school. On some days classes were fairly well attended, although many other schools were almost deserted. On other days only a few pupils might arrive. Sometimes all of them would disappear at about ten-thirty, because of some message of danger or news of a meeting, which they seldom imparted to us.

. . . Sometimes we read stories . . . It was soothing to read about pretty, soft things, magic, troubles which ended happily in any case. For the students it might be a way of avoiding the recurring inner debate about which course to take: to boycott school and lose hard work done so far, for the sake of solidarity and a dream to gain; or to attend, and be a sell-out in one's own eyes or the eyes of others.[18]

The SSRC, through this entire period, was called upon to provide leadership in the schools on a large number of issues. If Joan Hoffman's pupils did not arrive, or suddenly disappeared, it was invariably in answer to a call from the student leaders. They helped organise stay-at-homes, they were on the picket lines, they marched to Johannesburg, they demonstrated against Henry Kissinger's visit to South Africa on his arrival — and at Jabulani that Friday, 17 September, two pupils lay dead after police fired at them.[19] Eventually they had to provide a lead on the most contentious of all issues, that of the end of the year examinations. The SSRC called for a complete boycott and were faced with the problem of persuading thousands of students who were concerned about their futures and did not want to waste a year. Khotso Seatlholo, SSRC president from September till mid-January, toured the schools and urged, successfully, that the examinations be ignored.[20]

The SSRC campaigned tirelessly from the end of August, when the students called for a stay-at-home and received massive support, right through to Christmas. New campaigns were launched at frequent intervals. Taken together, the list of events displayed an ability to organise on a level not previously surpassed.

13-15 Sept:	Third stay-at-home.
17 Sept:	Anti-Kissinger demonstrations.
23 Sept:	Second march into centre of Johannesburg.
Early Oct:	Intensive anti-drink campaign.
17 Oct:	Mass turn-out at funeral of Dumsani Mbatha.
24 Oct:	Mass turn-out at funeral of Jacob Mashabane.
27 Oct:	Shebeens ordered to close down.
	Campaign starts to stop celebration of Christmas festivities.
End Oct:	'Operation Clean-Up' to remove refuse from Soweto.
1 Nov:	Final year examination boycotted.
	Stay-at-home called . . . but flops.

To this list must be added the extensive activity before 26 October to expose the farce of 'independence' for the Transkei; and the many small incidents that took place, involving only small groups of students or residents.

Many of these campaigns teetered on the edge of illegality. Others were organised in open defiance of one or other of the many regulations governing black behaviour, and this was to be demonstrated two years later when students held in detention for protracted periods were charged with sedition — the sentence for which can be death.[21]

Each one of these demonstrations extended the authority of the SSRC, and each success made them more confident. In a statement on behalf of the SSRC on 29 October, Khotso Seatlholo said that:

> We have the full right to stand up erect and reject the whole system of apartheid. We cannot accept it as our fathers did. We are not carbon copies of our fathers. Where they failed, we will succeed. The mistakes they made will never be repeated. They carried the struggle up to where they could. We are very grateful to them. But now the struggle is ours. The ball of liberation is in our hands. The Black student will stand up fearlessly and take arms against a political system. . . .We shall rise up and destroy a political ideology that is designed to keep us in a perpetual state of oppression and subserviency.[22]

The statement was defiant, but unfair. Their fathers had not accepted the system, and had fought against the government and against the bosses in campaign after campaign. Throughout the fifties and well into the sixties there had been stay-at-homes, a defiance campaign, bus boycotts, strikes, anti-pass campaigns (particularly by the women), and militant struggles in the Reserves. Mobile police squads had been rushed to Zeerust and Sekhukune-land (in the Northern Transvaal) and the areas had been sealed off in order to stamp out rebellions. The women of Natal had battled with police. And in the Transkei there had been a serious revolt which was only quelled after troops were moved in, men slaughtered, and a state of emergency declared which still operates today.

Mistakes were made, but it was a tradition of struggle that the youth were heir to, and they did their fathers and mothers less than justice in their sweeping condemnation. Nor were the youth exempt from mistakes. They made many, and it was only by making mistakes that they could possibly learn. A more modest stand might have stood them in better stead.

Nevertheless, their defiant statement did carry a message of hope, and for that it should be welcomed. Their campaigns had been impressive and they had succeeded where few would have imagined they could. Their bravery, too, had become the hallmark of the Revolt. They had sacrificed lives for a cause that inspired more and more to join them, and this was expressed in Seatlholo's words in his statement of 29 October: 'The struggle for my freedom will go on until each and every one of us drops dead. This is a vow that the Black youth have taken over the dead bodies, and written with the Blood of their wounded brothers.'

These were words charged with emotion, and did express the sentiments of the time, and they expressed a pledge to secure the changes that so many youth had died for. But there was a danger that emotion would take over from real considerations. The Revolt was not flowing to victory at the end of October, and it was necessary to be realistic about the balance of forces in the country. In fact the youth had miscalculated, and were in error in calling for a five day stay-at-home — as the SSRC did in this statement. They also had to be realistic about their achievements to date. What they had managed did not yet amount to a taking up of 'arms against a political system' as Seatlholo claimed. The students had demonstrated, and in so doing claimed results that had not been achieved. John Berger's analysis of the relation between ambitions and demonstrations is more than apposite to the Soweto Revolt:

> Demonstrations express political ambitions before the political means necessary to realize them have been created. Demonstrations predict the realization of their own ambitions and thus may contribute to that realization, but they cannot themselves achieve them.[23]

If the SSRC leaders, on the other hand, were serious in their contention that they would rise up and destroy apartheid, they had another task on hand: 'The crucial question which revolutionaries must decide in any given historical situation is whether or not further symbolic rehearsals are necessary. The next stage is training in tactics and strategy for the performance itself.'[24]

The problem in Soweto, and even more pointedly in the rest of the country, was to ask who and where the 'revolutionaries' were. There was no doubt that by October the SSRC were already seeking alternative methods of struggle, despite an avowal that they were in favour of non-violence. Nevertheless they were still only the Soweto Students Representative Council and received their mandate from school pupils, and not from the township. They had transcended this narrow base by showing that they had the ability to call out the entire population, but they still rested on a narrow social base and could lose their mass following at any time. If they were to act as a 'revolutionary' leadership, they would have to transform themselves and cease acting as an exclusively school body.

There was an obvious change in both tone and activity from October to December and, although the details are not available, this was partly the result of contacts with the underground ANC. Some information on this contact has now become available because of disclosures made by state witnesses at trials in South Africa. Despite a reluctance to use such evidence (which is subject to tailoring by the Special Branch in order to secure convictions), it does seem that, in essence, the facts are correct.

At an early stage of the Revolt some leading members of the SSRC were taken to Swaziland in order to meet Moses Mobhida, a leading member of the ANC in exile. The ANC offered assistance and co-operation and wanted close contact with SASM. It is not clear how this contact was to be maintained, nor what the role of ANC members in the SSRC was to be. Tebello Motapanyane was at the time secretary-general of SASM and also a member of the ANC. And Elias Masinga (one of the *Pretoria Twelve* on trial in 1977 for allegedly furthering the aims of the ANC, but found not guilty) was a leading member of the SASM and, despite his denials of the charges in court, he was probably sympathetic to the ANC.

Naledi Tsiki, also one of the *Pretoria Twelve*, received a 14 year sentence after being found guilty, and he was closely associated with the SSRC, at least close enough to the President, Khotso Seatlholo, to meet him just before Christmas 1976, together with two other members of the executive, and demonstrate a machine gun and grenades. He urged the President to affiliate to the ANC, said state witness T.N.A. Mthenjane, but that apparently was rejected.[25]

The SSRC had been in receipt of explosives and training in their use well before December. Some time at the end of September or beginning of October, Seatlholo and Micky Tsagae (also a member of the SSRC) established an urban guerrilla group which became known as the Suicide Squad. This group was led by Paul Mafgliso Elliot Langa, and probably worked with the ANC. It seems to have collapsed when Langa was arrested.

The Suicide Squad was not the only group known to have been interested in such action. The trial of two young men in November 1977 affords some (limited) information about an organisation known as the South African Freedom Organisation (SAFO) which planned or was actually engaged in sabotage between June and December 1976. It was claimed in court that SAFO aimed to throttle the country's economy by preventing Blacks getting to work and by destroying power supplies to the trains.[26]

At the trial of Mafgliso Langa in July-August 1977, it was claimed that the Suicide Squad was responsible for several explosions in Soweto. On 24 October 1976 the Jabulani police station was badly damaged by the Squad. The next day part of the railway line between Mzimhlope and New Canada stations was damaged by a blast. The Squad also used explosives at the Pelican Night Club, where liquor was being sold despite the SSRC (and ANC) call for an end to such transactions. In a further, unexplained, set of actions, Langa and others were said to have abducted three leading members of SAFO and exploded dynamite in the vicinity of some of its members in order to intimidate them.[27]

SAFO trained people in the manufacture and use of bombs, and was also said to have recruited youth for military training outside South Africa. That would seem to indicate that they were linked with an external, exile organisation. It is not clear whether the Suicide Squad also had direct links, in this case with the ANC, and also recruited youth for such training. But it does seem most probable, despite Seatlholo's refusal to countenance affiliation to the ANC, that the formation of an urban guerrilla force led to direct links with the external movement.

The demise of the Suicide Squad led to the abandonment, at that time, of an urban guerrilla force. The SSRC returned, whether by necessity or otherwise, to methods of non-violent political activity. Whether they believed all along that the youth had to be involved simultaneously in 'legal' (that is non-violent) politics and in clandestine violence, is not known. But one fact was clear: the leadership had decided that demonstrations had to continue.

The September Stay-at-Homes

In September it still seemed to the SSRC, and particularly to the newly elected President, that all options were still open. There could be legal demonstrations and there could be violence. The legal demonstrations would keep the name of the SSRC before the public, and the acts of sabotage would allow the body to find the most promising cadres for further, as yet uncharted activity. In September, furthermore, the student bodies in Johannesburg, Pretoria and the Cape were still testing their own strengths, as well as that of the state. They, therefore, sought means of demonstrating their *own* power, and looked to methods whereby this could be achieved.

At the time, the strike at the Armourplate Safety Glass factory in Springs, described in Chapter Eight, was still in its infancy. It was an event of great importance and raised the entire question of the recognition of African trade unions. It is possible that, at some stage in the long ten-week strike, some students made reference to the bitter struggle that was taking place there, but there are no comments on it in the material to hand. In general the actual strikes that took place were not often mentioned by the students.

Yet there is evidence that they, or at least part of the student body, were aware of the importance of the workers in the struggle to change South Africa. In a leaflet entitled *The black students' message to their beloved parents* issued after the August stay-at-home, education was described as a means to secure 'a more efficient black labour force to be exploited by those in power'. Throughout the leaflet, which was exceptional in where it laid its stress, the workers were seen as the pivot of the liberation struggle. In the words of the black students:

> The students believe that South Africa is what it is, and has been built by the blood, sweat and broken bodies of the oppressed and exploited Black workers, it is a well known fact that the Blacks carry the economy of this country on their shoulders. All the sky-scrapers, super highways, etc., are built on our undistributed wages.
> It is because of these facts that the students realise that in any liberatory struggle, the power for change lies with the workers.

This was by far the most explicit statement on the role of the black worker. Yet even here there was no mention of the actual strikes going on in the country, no expression of solidarity with workers currently involved in struggles in the factories. It was as if the recognition of the importance of the workers in any struggle remained a theoretical construct that could not be made concrete. And if that is the case, it could only be because the young students were not able to make organisational contact with the real flesh-and-blood workers in industry.

The SSRC decided on a three day stay-at-home, commencing on 13 September. The leaflet addressed to 'beloved parents', foreshadowing the call, had a special appeal to 'our parents in the hostels'. They described the men as 'our parents . . . [who] are victims of the notorious migrant labour system', and appealed for a united stand against injustices. The SSRC also held large-scale meetings with hostel dwellers on Sunday, September 5, to inform them about the intended strike and enlist their support. The township was then informed in a leaflet addressed to parents (co-operate with us); workers (stay away from work); and hostels (do not fight!). The strike was not aimed overtly at industry and was obviously designed to build township solidarity. The call was: 'This will be a proof that you are crying with us over those cruelly killed by police and those detained all over the country in various prisons without trial.' The SSRC then listed five 'objections': to shooting by the police; to arrests and detentions; to murders in detention; to a train accident in Benoni; and to 'the cutting down of our parents' wages who have stayed away from work in sympathy with their killed sons and daughters'. A special leaflet to taxis urged them not to transport anybody except nurses. It also requested assistance in informing 'hostel people' about the strike.

Soweto stayed at home on Monday the 13th and only nurses and a few workers queued for buses and taxes. There were also massive stay-aways along the Witwatersrand and an attempted strike in Alexandra. At the latter township police made house-by-house raids, pulling out adult males and children and either ordering them to report for work or school, or arresting them. Some 800 spent that day in the police cells and many of them were endorsed out of Johannesburg — that is, were sent back to the Reserves.

On the next day, the 14th, there were more workers in the factories. The threat of lost wages was enough to force some of them to leave the township and report for work. The pickets therefore had a harder task and there was shooting by the police, at the railway stations and in the streets, to stop any 'interference' with those who waited for transport.

That night the skirmishes were particularly fierce, as strikers confronted those who had worked. Once again there was a large police contingent present, and they protected the strike breakers. The *World* estimated the number of dead for the two days at 16 — all shot by police.

Despite, or perhaps because of, police terror, the strike held firm on the third day, and it was estimated that half a million were on strike that day.

Wednesday, 15 September, was a remarkable day in the political annals of black South Africa. In addition to the Transvaal, some 200,000 coloured workers, representing about 80 per cent of the work force in Cape Town, stayed at home in response to a call for a two-day abstention on 15 and 16 September, and a large (but not usually mentioned) proportion of African workers also stayed in the Cape Town townships.

There was no acknowledged leadership in Cape Town, and a number of leaflets, from obviously different sources, appeared in the streets calling for the strike. One leaflet headed only 'Strike' called for the rejection of all government sponsored black institutions. The thrust of the appeal was not to mourning (as in Soweto), but was more political in content.

The racists do not spare their bullets. Their guns try to cut down our

march for freedom. But the march to freedom must not end. Reject all concessions that the racists grant us. Concessions are crumbs. . . .
   All black people suffer alike. Get rid of apartheid. . . .

A second leaflet, also of unknown origin, and without any indication of who produced it, called on workers (specifically) to strike in protest 'against a slave system', and declared that the 'rulers' would never allow 'fundamental changes'. The group that issued the call then stated: 'Workers are compelled in defence and in pursuit of a better life to call into being worker organizations in the locations and in the factories.' It then proposed that the slogan around which the 'exploited' should rally was: 'Workers Power and Peoples Power'.
   This leaflet went further than the Soweto students' *Message to their beloved parents*. It not only recognised the central role that the black workers would be called upon to take, but also raised for the first time the possibility of (black) 'workers power'. Without any further indication of the response to the leaflet, and with no indication of how widely it was distributed, it is not possible to appraise the impact of the slogan. There are no known reactions from workers and the slogan does not appear to have been raised again in the months that followed. The sentiment and the slogan therefore appear to have been a possible portent of the future when, conceivably, they will be a rallying call to which the workers will respond.

The Workers Stay at Home

The response from the workers to the strike call was remarkable. From samples taken by students at UCT, 75 per cent stayed away on Wednesday in Cape Town, and 80 to 85 per cent on Thursday. The clothing industry, staffed mainly by coloured women, was all but closed down. Some 90 per cent of the women stayed away. In Langa and Nyanga, one of the most notable features was the strong solidarity shown by the large work force of migrant labourers.[28]
   A number of one-day strikes were called in smaller Cape towns. Most of them were highly successful, and concided with the end of the Cape Town stay-at-home on 16 September.
   By Thursday, in the Transvaal, the workers were all at work, even though some of the youth tried to get the action extended beyond the 15th. In the Cape the strike was terminated, as planned, on the Thursday.
   Then the workers of Thembisa were summoned to down tools for three days from 20 to 22 September. Many of the Thembisa workers had once lived in Alexandra township, but had been forcibly moved because they worked on the East Rand at Isando, Kempton Park, the airport, or other East Rand towns. They seem to have taken with them the militancy for which Alexandra was famous. The leaflet was issued by an unknown group, but there were indications of political influences at work, and that the students at Thembisa

were in contact with the Soweto students and possibly with the ANC. The leaflet they issued consisted largely of portions taken from the one that appeared in August in Soweto, (then produced by the ANC), and extracts from other leaflets used in Soweto in September. This leaflet, more than others, caught the spirit of the time, and warrants reproduction in full. The fact that it also referred to some strikes (in 1974 and early 1976) is also of interest. (The errors have not been corrected, and provide some indication of the lack of resources available to the leaders in the townships.)

AZIKWELWA E THEMBISA
AZIKWELWA ! ! ! From MONDAY to WEDNESDAY,
20th-22nd Sept.

The people of South Africa are going into the third phase of their struggle against the oppressors namely OPERATION AZIKHWELWA !!

The racists in our last demonstration — called by the cynics a riot lost millions of rands as a result of the people not going to work. Thus they thought of immediately breaking the student-worker alliance. They immediately called on workers to carry knobkieries and swords to murder their own children — who are protesting for a right course.

Parent workers, you should take note of the fact that if you go to work, you will be inviting Vorster to slaughter us your children as he has already done. In Soweto and Alexandra, Vorster and his gangsters, have already claimed that this week's shootings were made to protect parents from their own children. You will be giving Vorster a pretext for murdering us, if you go to work. Please do not allow Vorster to instigate you to murder your own child. Let him do this dirty and murderous job without making you a scape-goat! We want to avoid further shootings — and this can be done by you keeping at home without being stopped.

We want to write exams, but we are not so selfish to write even if our brothers are being killed at John Vorster Square. Parents, you should rejoice for having given birth to this type of a child. A child who prefers to fight it out with the oppressors rather than to be submerged in drunkenness, frustration, and thugery. A child who prefers to die from a bullet rather than to swallow a poisonous education which relegates him and his parents to a position of perpetual subordination. Aren't you proud of the soldiers of liberation you have given birth to? If you are proud, support them!! Do not go to work from MONDAY to WEDNESDAY!

Do not shiver and think that we have lost and wasted a year. This year will go down in history as the beginning of the end of THE OPPRESSIVE SYSTEM, the beginning of the end of the oppressive conditions of work in South Africa.

Vorster is already talking of home ownership for Blacks in Soweto and other Black Townships. This is a victory because we, the students, your children decided to shed their blood. Now for greater victories: the scrapping of BANTU EDUCATION, the release of prisoners detained during the demos., and the overthrowal of oppression. We the students: our parents to stay at home and not go to work from MONDAY.

Parent-workers, heed our CALL and stay away from work *like in*

Soweto and Alexandra. We the Black Society have nothing to loose from STAYING AWAY FROM WORK, but our chains!! Let our oppressor tremble! The people of South Africa are resolved in one word they will be crying: "Kruger, release our children!" "Kruger, we wont abort our children by going to work!"

Our slogan is: Away with Vorster, Down with oppression!!! POWER TO THE PEOPLE!!!!!! When have these criminals (Vorster) cared for you? Didn't he order for killing of twelf workers in Carltonville? Were not dogs called when in Croeses people went on strike? Were not pregnant women strangled and battered (beaten) by Vorster's police thugs at Heinemann Factory?

A Z I K H W E L W A   M A D O D A ! ! ! ! ! !

The workers stayed at home, and the industrial complex at Isando was empty on Monday 20 September. The strike remained firm on Tuesday, but by Wednesday most workers had returned to work. Nonetheless it was a remarkable performance and rounded off the tribute that the working class paid to the students for their role in the 1976 Revolt.

From the Thembisa leaflet, it would seem that the authors meant the stay-at-home to be part of a prolonged series of strikes that would, conceivably, bring South Africa to its knees. It was the 'third phase', presumably following the demonstration of 16 June and the attempted march on Johannesburg on 4 August.

The support given to the youth in the stay-at-home would have made any leadership euphoric. It seems to have blinded the SSRC to the many difficulties they had still to overcome, and it prevented them taking a long hard look at the tactics they were using. Unfortunately there were no other warning voices, because there had been few serious discussions of the tactics used in South Africa in the fifties. Some problems were technical, and with time could have been overcome. Other, more fundamental difficulties arose from the nature of the general strike, and its shortcomings as a revolutionary weapon.

The technical problems, some unique to South Africa, arose from the nature of housing in towns and in industry. The mines, railways, municipal services, power stations, hospitals and many industries maintained compounds at, or near, the places of work. Stay-at-homes, organised in townships, could not hope to win the support of these essential work forces. Thus, for example, the railway management could say that their services were not affected: '. . . fortunately, most of our non-White workers live in compounds outside Soweto'.[29] The other establishments that housed their own workers could say the same.

A second difficulty arose from the fact that the stay-at-homes were called by local township committees, and the dates chosen did not necessarily coincide. The police, therefore, could be moved from area to area in order to keep local populations under control. If, furthermore, residents from more than one township worked in a town, a failure to keep the workers of one of

257

these areas from getting to work weakened the strike. On 13 September, for example, the police moved into Alexandra township, where the student body was less well organised, and forced a sizeable number of workers to report for work.

Problems of the Political Strike

It was not entirely accidental that the first big successful strike (on August 23) was called jointly by the SSRC and ANC. It was the latter movement which used the stay-at-home extensively during the 1950's, with outstanding success on some occasions, and with equally disastrous failures. Far too little thought was given to the nature of the tactic, and the youth therefore adopted it uncritically. Some believed in 1976 what their fathers had thought in 1950-60: that a withdrawal of labour would lead to a collapse of the entire South African economy.[30] It was this belief which led some youth to think that the three-day strike in September should be extended indefinitely, and there were rumours that a three-week strike would be called at a later date.

The townships, with their large concentrations of workers, were obviously easy centres for organisation and directed action. But they were also a source of weakness. In an analysis of the strikes of the 1950's it was suggested that there were inherent difficulties involved in asking the population to remain in the townships.

> Firstly, the people of the townships cannot stay home indefinitely. To do so is to starve. Even if food is stored in advance the families cannot hold out for long because of the presence of the children, the aged and the sick. The township can be sealed off and starved out only too effectively by small detachments of the army and the police. But far worse, the army and police showed in Langa and Nyanga [in 1960 as in 1976!] that they could go from house to house, drag the inhabitants out, beat them up and force them to work.
>
> Secondly, by staying in the townships, the worker surrenders all initiative. He cuts himself [or herself] off from fellow-workers in other townships. He divides himself from his allies in the rural areas, and he surrenders the entire economic centre to his enemies.[31]

There were occasions, although obviously not during stay-at-homes, when the youth did carry the struggle into the commercial centre of the enemy's city. That was an important move and in Johannesburg, as will be described below, the Whites were horrified by the 'invasion'. No attempt was, however, made to mobilise the working class for a similar sortie into the industrial areas.

The relationship between the working class and the youth was complex. Most of the younger generation had been born into working class families. They were aware of the problems facing their parents, and they faced the same hardships. However, by virtue of their status as school pupils, particularly in the upper forms, they had distanced themselves from their parents — whether consciously or otherwise. They had already begun to view the world differently, and were unable to place working class demands at the centre of their campaigning. Their closeness to the workers (in many cases their intimacy) led them to talk of a student-worker alliance, but it was a one-sided relationship, and there was a peculiar inability to see that they could not make endless demands on the workers leading to sacrifices which brought no returns.

There was one mitigating factor. The students could not be expected to organise the workers: and any pretensions on their part that they could do so would have been rebuffed. The township, furthermore, was not the place for industrial organisation. And, in so far as some workers belonged to legal trade unions, there was no evidence that union officials encouraged any positive action to assist the students in the long months of the Revolt.

There are indeed two foci of possible organisation. One inside the townships, and the other in the factories and shops, mines and railways, and so on. The students dominated the townships in 1976. A limited number of unions existed in industry. There seemed to be no way in which organisation in the residential area could establish real links with bodies in the industrial field, and that did militate against political and economic demands fortifying and buttressing each other. As a result, the students overlooked the important strikes that were occurring in the factories, and the workers (together with union leaders) did not link their demands to events in the townships.

The stay-at-home, therefore, must be viewed as a method of demonstration and not as a means for radically altering society. What Berger said about demonstrations in general was also expressed by socialists in their debates on the general strike at the beginning of the twentieth century. The conclusions reached then are still valid today·

> The general strike is only a means of organising the working class and calling them to struggle against their enemy, the state. But a strike itself cannot solve the problem, because it tires the worker sooner than it does the enemy, and this sooner or later forces the worker to return to the factories.
>
> The general strike has its greatest importance only when it is the beginning of the fight between the workers and the capitalists: that is, only when it is the opening move in the revolutionary rising of the worker. Only when such action wins over part of the army to the worker can the worker think of winning his struggle . . .
>
> The general strike leads to the organisation of both sides, and shows how prepared the ruling class is to break the organisation of the workers. It shows what force will have to be used in order for victory to be won in the struggle. It shows how much blood the state is prepared to shed in order to keep the power . . .[32]

There was little need to question the state's readiness to shed blood in 1976. The continued provocation from the police — the shooting without

warning, with every intention of killing; the use of the hostel dwellers to cut
down anyone in their path; the rapidity with which armoured cars were
brought into Soweto; and the speed with which police were deployed – all
indicated that the state had been preparing for insurrection for some time.
For years, recruits to the army, and these were exclusively white, had been
drilled in mock battles in urban uprisings, and mobile police units had been
prepared for similar events. Even if the police terror was not planned for
16 June, there can be little doubt that, in the aftermath of the Soweto rioting
that day, the police were ordered to go into the townships and schools, and
shoot to kill.

This did not mean that there were no situations in which the workers
should have been called upon to embark on a general strike. This would have
been a powerful weapon if used at the appropriate time, and if backed by
other means of struggle. It did, however, mean that it was a tactic that had to
be used sparingly.

The SSRC, however, had nobody to warn them of the difficulties involved
in calling the workers out too often. In August, and again in mid-September,
they had only to summons the workers to stay-at-home, and they were
followed. At the end of October they called once again for a close down of
industry, but on this occasion they were badly out of touch with the mood in
the townships. The call they issued from Soweto was for a national stoppage
– even though their contact with other townships was tenuous or non-
existent. They also called for a full five-day strike from Monday 1 November,
and the only slogan they offered was: 'Blacks are going into mourning for
their dead.' In a press statement this was supplemented with demands that
the government resign; that all political detainees be freed; and that there be
consultation with black parents leading to 'settlement and peace'.[33]

The strike call and the demands made were unrealistic. Families did not
mourn for the dead by starving – and that would have been the consequence
of a whole week's stoppage. Nor could workers be expected to respond again
and again when the strikes achieved nothing. The call was ignored.

On 1 November, examinations were due to begin, and these were boycotted. The students had not been defeated and they meant to continue the
struggle. But after 1 November it became clear that the momentum of the
Revolt had ebbed, and that in future the main slogans would be restricted to
demands relating to the schools and education. Even when the Soweto
students took up township issues, as they did in 1977, there was a direct
connection between the new campaigns and school issues or, in the case of
rent increases, between these increases and student actions during the Revolt
in June and July 1976.

The other campaigns, and the increased police terror in 1976, also
indicated that changes were necessary. The pinnacle had been reached in the
September stay-at-home, and the overwhelming response from the workers
seemed to open the future for even greater assaults on the state. The fact that
the Revolt had lost momentum was concealed by successes in other
campaigns, and few seemed to note that the victories were only symbolic and

brought no tangible concessions. Perhaps it was no accident that the largest gatherings and demonstrations were at the funerals of men who had died while in the hands of the police. The people mourned, but grieving could not topple a police state.

References

1. The story of the SSRC, *op.cit.*, p.4.
2. CIS, *op.cit.*, p.16.
3. Testimony from a witness, cited in CIS, *ibid.*, p.25.
4. Reports from Nqutu and surrounding districts, from which the men came, indicate that the local inhabitants could not understand the closing of the schools. (Conversation with Elaine Unterhalter, who spent some time in the region in 1977.)
5. The reports were always imprecise. Thus the *Star*, 13 November 1975, carried reports of two Zulus shot in a hostel room in Soweto. The report also claimed that the men came from the Tugela Ferry district where there was a longstanding feud between Mthembu and Mchunu clansmen. It was also reported that the bitter faction fighting in Natal in December 1976 was a spill-over from differences over events in August. (Conversation with Elaine Unterhalter.)
6. *Rand Daily Mail*, 27 August 1976.
7. *Cape Times*, 10 August 1976.
8. *Ibid.*
9. CIS, *op.cit.*, p.22.
10. *Ibid.*
11. Quoted in Callinicos and Rogers, *op.cit.*, p.163.
12. See the evidence collected together in CIS, *op.cit.*, pp.24-5.
13. *Rand Daily Mail*, 27 August 1976.
14. CIS, *op.cit.*, p.24.
15. 'Soweto Invaded: why we should remain united and not rest', anonymous leaflet undated but post August strikes.
16. SSRC leaflet, 7 September 1976.
17. From the African Scholars of Cape Town, 5 September 1976.
18. J. Hoffman, *op.cit.*, pp.56-7.
19. CIS, *op.cit.*, p.41. Six students died and 35 were wounded that day.
20. The story of the SSRC, *op.cit.*, pp.6-7.
21. I have not had the opportunity of reading any of the evidence presented at the trial of students, still in progress at time of writing.
22. Printed in *Pro Veritate*, November 1976, under title 'A Soweto student speaks'.
23. J. Berger, *op.cit.*, p.249.
24. *Ibid.*, p.250.
25. Reports in newspapers of 16 July 1977.
26. *Rand Daily Mail*, 24 November 1977.
27. Reports in newspapers, 6 July–18 August 1977.
28. UCT workshop on the Revolt of 1976.

29. *Financial Mail*, 17 September 1976.
30. Socialist League of Africa (1960), 'South Africa: ten years of the stay-at-home' (mimeo). Reprinted in *International Socialist*, Summer 1961.
31. *Ibid.*
32. *Die Neue Zeit*, quoted in *ibid.*
33. Seatlholo, *op.cit.*

14. The Revolt Winds Down

The March on Johannesburg

The mid-September stay-at-home was a remarkable show of solidarity which took in communities right across South Africa. It raised morale and gave many communities the will to participate further in open battle with the government. The political success was not, however, matched by any real achievement in either factories or homes. The workers had sacrificed three days' pay, and some had been fired, and there was much hard thinking on the Friday when the pay envelope came half empty.

Indeed it is hard to see how it could have been other than grim. The stay-at-home had not been launched in order to improve conditions in the worker's household. Strikes of finite duration, announced at the inception as being for a limited period, cannot win any betterment for workers. Nor had any of the SSRC demands been pitched at securing concessions from the employers.

When the strike was first called, the SSRC listed five objections. The first three were complaints about the oppressive methods employed by the police. The fourth referred to a train accident. The final objection was to the deduction of wages after the August strike. The response from most employers could have been predicted beforehand. They deducted wages for days not worked.

It seems from the tone of the leaflets which appeared soon after pay day, that the students felt the need to reassure the population. They announced a new stage – the 'fourth in series', at the same time as Thembisa was announcing the 'third phase of the struggle'. The leaflet, issued in Soweto, spoke enthusiastically of events in Cape Town and welcomed the coloured people to the common struggle. The main thrust of the document was to call on Soweto to emulate the students' demonstration in the city centre.

In their argument, the authors of the leaflet stated that it was necessary to keep the local police and soldiers busy in order to prevent them being posted elsewhere, and urged that it was not the time to retreat. To return to school would be a betrayal of the nation's cause. The comments were both bitter and defiant:

Already his (Vorster's) police thugs are demanding passes at gun-point,
already rents have gone higher . . . .

If we profess to be leaders the first and indispensible character is:
Independent thought and moral courage. If we are still looking for
favours . . . [to be recognised] as matriculants, it simply means that we are
not independent but servants of the system like Gatsha Buthelezi . . . .

Education is in itself good but the first school for an oppressed people
is a revolution.

At about 8.00 a.m. on Thursday 23 September, some 1,500 school pupils
met at the central Johannesburg station. Many more had set out that morning
but had been stopped along the way by police who were out in force. The
city centre was about to fill as they started their march through Eloff Street,
the main commercial district of the city. They were joined by sympathetic
black workers, and marched behind banners calling for the release of all
detainees.

The riot police arrived within a very short time with dogs, and converged
on the marchers. Every Black in the area, whether in the demonstration or
not, was attacked, and many Whites in the crowd that soon gathered went to
the assistance of the police. One youth who tried to slip away was run down
by a motorist who accelerated to reach him. Those who were caught were
bundled into police vans and taken into detention. These included at least
three children under 14 years of age and two (white) students of the
University of the Witwatersrand. More than 800 ended the day in police cells,
and by 9.30 a.m. the demonstration was over. [1]

There had been no shooting in Eloff Street, and only batons were used. In
Soweto there was less restraint. The police moved through selected areas,
shooting at anyone trying to escape their net. Alexandra township was also
sealed off and police moved through the area, arresting people. At the Mara
Higher Primary school, children fled when they saw an advancing police car.
The police drove in pursuit and shot at the children, killing at least one, and
wounding several. [2]

The 'fourth stage' had not been very fruitful, the disruption of the city
centre had been minimal, and the students had suffered at the hands of the
police. They did not venture into the city again and, except for funerals, did
not gather in large numbers. They also changed tack, and initiated a campaign
against Christmas festivities, linking this with their stand against alcohol.

Alcohol and the Christmas Season

The campaign against alcohol, and raids on bottlestores, beerhalls and
shebeens, commenced soon after the Revolt started. Within days of the
shooting on 16 June, the streets ran with wine, sherry, brandy and beer as
the township supplies were destroyed. And on the day the youth of Langa,
Nyanga and Guguletu first marched, the bottlestores were attacked in

Cape Town.

The shebeens were not closed completely, however, and in mid-August a leaflet, claiming to be 'The voice of the ANC', called on the shebeens to close from the 23rd onwards. The publication was crude and called on Blacks to kill the Whites and burn their buildings. The crudity of style and sentiment renders the leaflet suspect, and it is not at all certain that the ANC was responsible for its production. Nonetheless it was circulated in Soweto, and the call to close these pot-houses was read by a large audience.

Prior to 1962, Africans were not legally entitled to buy any alcoholic drink except for traditionally brewed beer. When the Liquor Amendment Act was passed, there were mixed feelings in the townships. There were many who supported the new act because they could now purchase their wines and brandies without facing arrest and prosecution. But there were many people who opposed the new law. The women who relied on sales of their own (illegal) home brews complained, and so did religious groups who favoured prohibition. More surprising, perhaps, was the fact that when a poll was conducted in Cape Town, 79 per cent of the Africans opposed the introduction of the new legislation.

The political movements had always kept clear of the controversy although individuals had condemned the sale of alcohol in their private capacities. From exile, Ranwedzi Nengwekhulu maintained that:

> One of the things that used to worry [members of the BPC] for quite a long time was the number of bottle stores in Soweto. You have more bottle stores than clinics and more police stations than clinics. Every railway station, and in Soweto you have more than 20 railway stations, had a bottle store. When our parents leave work with their pay, which is very meagre, they immediately buy liquor and then they go home without money . . . . If you go to Soweto you will find that every small location has a bottle store and a big beer hall. But since the 16th of June bottle stores no longer function because the first targets were bottle stores . . . . Then, there are the places we call 'shebeens' where they illegally sell liquor. The government has been trying for the past fifty years to stamp them out but they could not succeed. Now nobody sells liquor because the students have appealed to them . . . . [3]

It is not possible to ascertain from press reports what the non-student youth thought. There was at least one section which looted and drank the liquor during the many raids, and it is possible that the move to declare the township 'dry' was a reflection of the tensions between the school youth and the unemployed. On the other hand Ranwedzi Nengwekhulu's contention that even 'alcoholics found the courage to destroy the institution they knew was destroying them' was confirmed by other sources. [4]

Campaigns against alcohol grew stronger as the weeks went by. At the end of September graffiti in the streets of Soweto and Cape Town townships read: 'Less liquor, more education!'; 'Away with boozers'; 'No more liquor till next year. Please we need sympathy.'

Even at this stage the youth noted the need for concessions to the hostel dwellers. These single-sex groups were heavy drinkers, and it would not be easy to convince them to abstain. On 11 October a ban on liquor was declared, and in Soweto the shebeen owners formed an association in order to co-operate with the youth. Here at least the ban was complete. In Cape Town, however, because of the high percentage of migratory 'single' men, the shebeen owners felt they had more to lose and they opposed the ban strenuously.

In the earlier phase of the struggle in Cape Town a large number of shebeens (one estimate claimed over 100) were destroyed, and a number of the bottlestores were gutted. The shebeen owners were able to find allies amongst a section of the migrants, some of whom had been antagonistic to the youth from early August when the first marches took place. These they mobilised to protect their premises, and the police brought in reinforcements from amongst migrant workers in the smaller towns. The students made several attempts to approach these men, obviously prepared for, and ready to go on the rampage. The police, who were standing by, intervened and drove the students away with tear gas. [5]

Fighting in Cape Town was particularly severe, and the migrants capped with white *doeks* (head cloths) killed or maimed many African youth. On 6 December, long after the clashes had started, the Transkei 'consul' to Cape Town, Chief Dumalisi, addressed more than 4,000 residents of Nyanga and urged them to stop the internecine fighting. [6] Egged on by the police, however, there was no end to the bitter struggle and on 31 December student leaders were still urging the migrants to stop drinking. They demanded: 'Show you are with us if you want to enjoy the privileges of a just society.' [7]

At the end of October the SSRC called for a 'period of mourning for the dead'. It called for a boycott of Christmas festivities; a stop to Christmas shopping; and a continuation of the ban on alcohol. The campaign involved a pledge of solidarity with all those detained and tortured; a call for the release of all political prisoners and an expression of sympathy with all who had lost pay in the September stay-at-home. Through November and December the youth campaigned around the boycott of shopping and won the co-operation of the Soweto population. But their success in the north was not repeated in Cape Town, and by late December there were daily assaults on the township population by the now familiar white-doeked hostel dwellers.

The Ministers Fraternal of Langa, Guguletu and Nyanga, representing the major denominations of the Cape Town region, drew up a report on the events during the Christmas weekend. [8] They made a series of allegations which they supported by eye-witness accounts of men and women who were at scenes of violence. They claimed that:

1. It was the riot police who made possible the appalling killings and burnings of the Christmas weekend in Nyanga, and that if they had chosen, they could have prevented any serious clash.
2. The riot police or a significant section of them encouraged and

instigated certain immigrants to attack.
3. Certain migrants were deceived into thinking that they would be stopped from going to work.
4. Some were told to arm themselves to avoid attack when this was not intended.
5. Riot police actually assisted with the attacks — shooting at residents — preventing them from protecting their families and houses.
6. Some riot police actually encouraged the migrants to kill some of the residents by pointing out the wounded on the ground.
7. Petrol bombs were used in attacks. Some were trained, by certain people in authority, on how to make and use petrol bombs. [9]

The report, which was sent to every Member of Parliament, was banned in South Africa on the grounds that it was harmful to race relations and the welfare of the state. This led the Rev. D.P.H. Russell to draw up a memorandum for M.P.s in which he added further eyewitness accounts substantiating the accusations of the Ministers Fraternal. The only response of the police was to demand the names of three of the witnesses quoted in the document. For refusing to supply this information, David Russell was sentenced to three months imprisonment. [10]

Despite police harassment and brutality, the campaign against Christmas celebrations was successful. Many small white traders in Johannesburg suffered considerable losses, and the morale in the townships was high. In one respect, however, the Revolt was over. The school year closed for the long summer vacation and this, at least temporarily, shifted the focus away from the schools. The students were dispersed and their school base was not available. The year had ended with few taking the examinations, and very few would accept the school's offer that they write the supplementary examinations in the New Year. The Coloured youth in the Cape had already ended their boycott of classes, and the vacation provided time for a cooling off period before the new academic year commenced. The memory of the alliance of August-September was still strong, but the basis for joint campaigning was past.

The year also came to an end with an ever increasing onslaught by the police. House to house searches and arrests continued, leading to an exodus of children who fled to relatives, rural areas, or across the borders. The number detained rose, and the courts meted out sentences of caning, or of imprisonment. The political life of any new community leader was painfully short, and new leaders were picked up in successive swoops. Even leaders of black movements which had not been involved in overt activities during the Revolt were suppressed. In the closing weeks of November and through December, 27 trade unionists and members of the university wages commissions were banned, and so removed from any further industrial organisation.

Divided Counsel on Examinations

Despite all the harassment, 1976 closed with the students in good spirits. The boycott of Christmas festivities had been successful, and the ANC leaflet of 16 December which called for more recruits to the military arm of Congress, Umkhonto we Sizwe, praised the youth: 'To all of you we say: Forward brave fighters! Forward brothers and sisters! Maintain your revolutionary unity and fighting spirit. Together we will raise the struggle to more glorious heights . . . ' [11]

The student leaders, in Soweto as elsewhere, faced a difficult problem in the New Year. The schools were opened earlier than usual, on 5 January in Soweto and Cape Town. This was done in order to prepare candidates for the Junior Certificate (third form) and matriculation examinations which had been deferred from 1976 till mid-February. Other classes would hold internal examinations in order to allow for the promotion of successful candidates. The new school year would commence after all the tests were completed.

There was confusion amongst the students. Some wanted to write the examinations and thus avoid wasting a year. Others stated categorically that they would not return to school until Bantu Education was scrapped. In every township they turned to their local SRC for guidance, and these bodies, which had been established in most areas in 1976, were divided in their counsel. In Cape Town the decision was to boycott — and on 10 January 1977 six schools were badly damaged by fire in Langa and Nyanga, to prevent any breaking of the ban.

In Soweto, however, a series of contradictory statements were issued by the SSRC. Their first statement called for a complete boycott of the schools until all detained pupils were released, and also until black youth received the same educational facilities as Whites.[12] The SSRC then reversed its stand, and in a statement published in the press stated:

> We are requesting all students and their parents to ensure that every child reports for school tomorrow morning. We warn our colleagues and their parents that these people who speak about the continuation of the boycott are speaking for themselves and do not represent the recognised school body.
>
> We therefore appeal to all students to ignore them because they are nothing but trouble shooters trying to exploit the situation for their own ends. [13]

The SSRC was not alone in calling for a return to school. Albert Mahlangu, speaking on behalf of ASSECA, called on the youth to return; the teachers had, in the majority of cases, reported to the schools for duty; and a body calling itself the Soweto Union, led by a former detainee L.M. Mathabathe, also urged parents to send their children to school.[14]

The senior students were not convinced. At Orlando High School some 60 (out of a student intake of 900) arrived at school, many over an hour late.

Some 90 (out of 800) arrived at the Morris Isaacson School. Nor was the situation any different elsewhere. On 6 January attendance was marginally better, and on Friday the 7th it seemed as if the boycott might be ending, at least at some of the schools.

But even as students drifted back to school in Soweto, the old problems were asserting themselves, and new difficulties were raised. There was a severe shortage of teachers at some schools, and one establishment was reported to have a staff of seven, who were required to supervise twelve classes. The staff shortage was chronic and had been exacerbated by the sacking of teachers who had shown their sympathies for the students too openly in 1976. Punitive action was also taken against some students accused of having taken leading roles in the demonstrations, and this heightened tensions in the classrooms.

It was also announced by the universities that they would be unable to accept students who wrote their matriculation examinations in mid-February, because they would arrive long after lectures had commenced. There was already division amongst the students on whether to accept or boycott the proposed examinations, and the debate on this issue now raged more fiercely.

The first pronouncement from the SSRC on examinations was in line with the stand in 1976: namely, that they could not write while fellow students were in detention. Opinions in the schools were divided on this issue, and students of schools which had been in the forefront of the Revolt, the Morris Isaacson and Naledi High Schools, stated that they would write. It appears, from subsequent reports, that the SSRC was split on the issue, and that the only way to maintain the unity of the body was to compromise. On 19 January it was announced that individual students could decide for themselves whether they should enter for the examinations. [15]

Conditions in the schools became even more unsettled as news came in from other townships. Unlike Soweto, it had been announced that secondary schools in Alexandra and Pretoria (amongst others) would commence on 2 February, and that there would not be examinations at those centres because some had written in November last. Those who had failed to attend would have to repeat the school year. The Pretoria primary schools were scheduled to open on 18 January, but, one week earlier on 11 January, it had been announced that all children wishing to register at the Mamelodi High School would have to produce residence permits issued by the local Superintendent's office before being accepted. The ostensible reason for this was that there was congestion in the school and that it was necessary to exclude children who had no right of residence. This started a wave of protests which led to a boycott of all Mamelodi schools at the beginning of February. A few days later Atteridgeville pupils decided to follow the Mamelodi example.

By 8 February the dispute over examinations had become a major issue in Soweto. There were renewed demands that Bantu Education be scrapped and that equal education be instituted. Groups of youth moved from school to school and disrupted class tests. The police moved their forces to protect schools, and used tear gas to disperse angry students. The situation grew ugly as groups of students faced each other, and those writing tests stoned the disrupters. At Orlando, Naledi, Musi, Meadowlands and Madibane books were burnt, and cars or delivery vans found near the schools were destroyed. Some schools were damaged and furniture was smashed. [16] A large crowd collected in Meadowlands and police used gas to disperse 4,000 youth. Shots were fired and many were injured.

Nevertheless the examinations were proceeded with, and a large number did attend and write. The police patrolled all school areas and they had instructions to arrest any youth not in school during school hours. [17]

In Cape Town there was a return to schools before the scheduled examinations, but only after a warning that youth not at school by 4 March, or absent without good cause for more than four days, would be excluded permanently. Pupils having returned, all tests were written with very little disruption.

The SSRC Abolishes the UBC

In mid-February 1977 the SSRC was in disarray. In fact it seemed to have been in crisis ever since Khotso Seatlholo was shot by police in mid-January, and had to slip across the border. Daniel Sechaba Montsitsi and his executive were immediately caught in the middle of the crisis over examinations and were not able to find a solution.

Problems in the schools kept them busy. The fourth formers who were repeating the year complained when successful Junior Certificate students entered their classes. The older youth found themselves having to accommodate groups who had been their juniors, and there was also a disparity, in levels of knowledge, between youth in their second year in the same form, and the newcomers. Yet there was nothing the SSRC could do to placate the disaffected.

The BPC emerged as an organisation in late March, after months of apparent inactivity. They called upon all people to observe a week of mourning for those who had died in Sharpeville (1960), in detention, and in Soweto and elsewhere in 1976. The population was asked to wear mourning during the week and to abstain from all festivities. They also had a message for the Church:

> We call upon all the churches in this country to respond positively and co-operate with the spirit expressed in this message. We believe that the true Christian gospel supports the struggle for human dignity. We say the true Christian must ask himself, 'What shall I tell the Lord on the day of reckoning? Shall I say I have not been able to put my hand in the effort to endorse God's image in the black man, as much as in the white man?

The week was to culminate in a march and a meeting in Orlando.

There was a moderate response and the week passed with no incidents.

On the 27th, however, the march was light-hearted 'until a group of soccer-dress clad policemen interfered with the crowd, after which the mood turned ugly'. [18] Over 20 students were detained and pressmen reported seeing children assaulted while being arrested.

It was only in late April that the SSRC seemed to emerge from a long period of relative inactivity. The occasion was the announcement by the West Rand Bantu Administration Board, the government appointed body that managed the affairs of Soweto (amongst others), that from 1 May site rentals were to be raised by 84 per cent — from R6.25 per month to R11.50. There were similar announcements in other townships, and in many cases the increases were in the region of 100 per cent.

The students were brought into the campaign against the increase in rents from the inception. They were naturally angry, as were the residents as a whole, at having to find more money for their houses. Ever increasing inflation, set against low wages, left every family in dire poverty. The announcement of the increases also took no account of the many families who had lost breadwinners during the nine month long Revolt, nor of the widespread feeling of deprivation that accompanied the death or injury of members of the household.

There was another reason for the students to be incensed. It was stated that rents had to be raised because of the loss of revenue from beerhalls that had been gutted during the Revolt. What had seemed to be a triumph for the population was being turned into an excuse to exact more money from each householder. That was unbearable!

The SSRC moved on to the offensive and warned the Administration Board not to 'repeat the mistake made by certain officials of Bantu Education' in 1976. On 23 April there was a large public meeting in Soweto, and resolutions were passed not to pay the rent increase and to suspend the Urban Bantu Council. [19]

The SSRC, the members of which had long opposed any government created institutions, had always clashed with the UBC. Now they had additional reason for anger. The rent increases had been known to the Council members since February, and they had approved the new rates in March without informing the public. It also transpired that other UBCs (at Kagiso, Dobsonville and Mohlakeng) had also approved the rent increases during March. On 27 April thousands of students demonstrated in Soweto and, following a discussion with the police officer in control, were given permission to march to the Council Chamber.

The march did not end peacefully. Sections of the crowd stoned the Council building and were dispersed by the police with gas. In retaliation vehicles were stoned and two beerhalls set alight, and this led to shooting and arrests.

The demonstration produced results: the rent increase was suspended. The SSRC had reasserted its position as the only effective organised body in the township and, for the first time, had assumed the role of a political organisation. The student body had been acting politically for approximately one year, but until April 1977, every campaign had been related to the schools, to the educational system, or to the fate of arrested students. The slogans had inevitably taken in wider issues because Bantu Education was part of the total system of apartheid. In the many demonstrations concerned with events in the schools — starting with the fight against Afrikaans medium instruction — the main banners carried demands directly related to education or to the demonstration itself. But as Tebello Motapanyane said in an interview, other slogans had included: 'It happened in Angola — why not here?'; 'For freedom we are going to lay down our lives.'; 'Release all political detainees.' [20] But the central campaign in every instance had been related to school issues.

Having embarked on the rent campaign, it was not possible to stop with the suspension of the increase. The UBC itself had to go because they had acted as a government agency and agreed to the increase without consulting or even informing the residents.

The SSRC sent two of their members to interview the UBC, and when they were arrested in the Council Chamber without protest from the Councillors, the students forced the resignation of the UBC which took place at the beginning of June.

The collapse of the Council was so unexpected and so rapid that it seemed to many that the SSRC must have applied some secret pressures, and threatened the members with dire consequences if they did not comply. There was, however, little need for force. The SSRC was the only acknowledged body in the township, and it had the support of the vast majority of the population. The Councillors resigned because they recognised that whatever powers they had previously seemed to exercise had been taken from them.

Yet, even in victory, the SSRC was foiled. The government had already decided to replace all UBCs by Community Councils which would fall directly under the Minister of Bantu Affairs and receive powers delegated to them directly from the Minister. It was also announced that the rentals would still be increased, but in three stages, commencing December 1977.

On 3 June Sechaba Montsitsi issued a statement on behalf of the SSRC, calling on the population of Soweto to form their own representative body to replace the UBC, and to reject all government instituted bodies. [21] When Dr. Nthato Harrison Motlana of the Black Parents Association summoned a meeting to form such an organisation, representatives of the SSRC, SASO and BPC were present. Also in attendance were representatives of the Black Unity Front, which consisted of Inkatha, the Labour Party and like-minded organisations.

The new body that was launched was called the Soweto Local Authority Interim Committee or, more popularly, the Committee of Ten. Dr. Motlana was the chairman, and the other nine members included two members of the BPC, one member of the CI, a former member of the UBC, the chairman of the Soweto Traders Association, the former organiser of the National African Federated Chambers of Commerce, and the principal of the Morris Isaacson High School. The Committee was instructed to investigate ways in which

Soweto should be run. [22]

Within three weeks a blue-print for the future was produced. Soweto, it was stated, should become an autonomous modern city, governed by an elected council of 50 members. To provide the required facilities, the sum of R5,000 million would, it was envisaged, be spent over a five-year period. The money, said the Committee, would be raised from rates and taxes, fines, fees, charges for electricity and licences, and from loans raised at the Organisation of African Unity, the International Monetary Fund, and other international institutions.

Even if all the huge financial difficulties obviously involved could somehow be transcended, the project was still politically dangerous. It accepted segregation — provided that the segregation was made less onerous. That is, if an updated, modernised township was erected, and if Blacks could govern the area, the Committee of Ten and its supporters in the Black Consciousness Movement were prepared to accept the situation. There was little to differentiate this preparedness to take control of an urban segregated area, and Buthelezi's acceptance of a base in the Reserves. Buthelezi demanded land consolidation and sought foreign investment. The Committee of Ten would no doubt also negotiate the boundaries of Soweto and needed foreign capital. Buthelezi said that he would use the Reserves in order to gain a base from which to propagate his ideas. It was perhaps no coincidence that, in the heady days following the publication of the Committee's plan for Soweto, there was talk in the township of establishing an urban base from which the anti-apartheid struggle could be waged.

Even if it were objected that the Soweto Committee differed appreciably from Buthelezi in their appraisal of events in South Africa, they would have been saddled with an urban Bantustan if the government had accepted their plan. They were only saved from endless embarrassment by the rejection of the plan by the government. But not before they had themselves master-minded a scheme for making residential areas part of a segregated South Africa.

The First Commemoration of June 16

On 3 June the UBC had collapsed and the students announced that they were planning to commemorate the dead during the week 13 to 19 June. During that period shebeens were to be closed. On the 16th and 17th all shops in the township were to be kept shut, and there would be a stay-at-home. Students at the black universities also announced plans for commemorating the events of 1976, and school student bodies in other parts of the country also made plans for demonstrations.

The commemorations in Soweto actually started in late May when scholars at individual schools celebrated events that had preceded the June 16 demonstration. On 25 May pupils of the Belle Higher Primary School held their own meeting, and as the days went by the celebrations were taken up by other schools. Some of the meetings took place without further incident; others were accompanied by stonings of official cars. Shots were fired by police, and youth were arrested, so that Soweto was in a high state of tension well before 13 June.

On 10 June Sechaba Montsitsi and 17 members of the SSRC were arrested and only two seem to have escaped the police net. One of them, Trofomo Sono, became the new President and the newly selected executive proceeded with plans for the commemoration.

Tension in the country was building up, and this was heightened when three young urban guerrillas made a machine gun attack on premises opposite John Vorster Square in Johannesburg and, on 15 June a portion of the railway line between Umlazi and Durban was blown up.

On Friday the 10th, students at Turfloop boycotted classes and continued the stay-away on the 13th. There was a complete boycott of schools on 13 June and the township was sealed off by road blocks set up by the students. That evening there was stone throwing in both Pretoria townships and in New Brighton, Port Elizabeth. The schools in Soweto were empty, and about 40 per cent of the work force responded to the stay-at-home appeal. The shebeens stayed closed throughout the week.

On 16 June an audience of some 6,000 gathered in the Regina Mundi Cathedral to commemorate the dead. But the meeting was not allowed to proceed peacefully. The police fired a salvo of tear gas canisters into the church and forced the audience out. In other sections of the township police also fired tear gas into any crowd that collected, and doused several houses to flush the occupants out.

The biggest action on the 16th was in the Eastern Cape, where the main storm centre was at Uitenhage near Port Elizabeth. Eleven students were arrested during demonstrations, and in the reaction to police provocation schools, liquor stores, shops and administration buildings were put to the flame. For two days the youth were out in the streets, defying the police and replying to the shootings with stones and rocks. Once again, the events of Soweto the year before were being repeated. Over two days 10 were reported dead, 32 wounded, and 280 arrested.

Some students drifted back to school on Monday 20 June, but on the 23rd nobody attended in Soweto. Pupils marched through the streets protesting against the educational system, and against the continued detentions of Montsitsi and other leaders. They intended marching to Johannesburg to join a group at John Vorster Square police station who were holding a vigil for those who had been arrested. Once again the students were stopped. Police barred the way to Johannesburg, and the crowd was dispersed with gas. In Johannesburg, 146 of those standing outside the police station were arrested after they had been assaulted by baton wielding policemen. In Soweto, youth stoned vehicles and came into conflict with the police. At least one was killed that day and many were wounded. It seemed as if the cycle of demonstrations and shootings was to continue without anyone being able to stand up and call for a new approach to the struggle.

Just five days later the youth of Mamelodi and of Atteridgeville tried the same tactic, and met with the same response from the police. They too were dispersed by a barrage of tear gas canisters and guns.

SASM Politics in 1977

The SSRC venture into the political field had met with a success that was beyond the expectations of most people. A committee drawn from the schools of Soweto had brought down a government instituted body, the UBC, and appeared as the foremost political group in the community. Nonetheless, the mandate that the SSRC carried was to represent the interests of the students generally, and to press their demands for better facilities in the schools.

The SSRC had therefore to determine what they would do in the future, and decide whether they, as an organisation, could continue to act on general issues. Chris Wood, writing from Gaberone, gave this appraisal of the body:

> Being a school students' movement Black education is still the dominant issue for it; as Mr. Sono said on July 1, 'If it is death, we must die, if that is how Bantu Education must be scrapped. I say this with conviction and all students have that conviction.' But being Black all issues concerning Blacks are of equal concern to it.
>
> Approximately 650 of their fellow students have been killed by police bullets, thousands more wounded or beaten by police batons. Thousands have been detained, imprisoned and tortured and yet they have not been intimidated or cowed into submission. They have the initiative and they mean to keep it. [23]

Trofomo Sono had a few days previously made another statement which supplemented this 'do or die' declaration. On 27 June he reportedly said: 'We still maintain that our aims are not to overthrow the Government but to see Bantu Education driven to hell.' [24]

In one important sense, Chris Wood was correct. The SSRC had taken the initiative over the issue of rents — and they were not likely to surrender it. But it must be questioned whether they had the initiative in the broader strategy of the period. The government had moved its police around the country and had killed, maimed, arrested and detained at will. The ranks of the student movement had been sorely weakened, and to the numbers given by Wood, must be added the hundreds that had fled the country. The initiative that was in the hands of the students, was deceptive. Furthermore, to suggest that they would all die to get rid of the educational system, made good journalistic copy, but poor politics. The problem was to save lives and to protect personnel as far as was possible while conducting the struggle against the government. Mr. Sono eventually fled South Africa, and in so doing he was correct. To have offered his life as a sacrifice or even to risk arrest would at that stage have been pointless.

The more general statement, that the aim of the SSRC was not to over-throw the government but to destroy Bantu Education, raises problems that do not seem to have been thought out during the entire period of the Revolt. Assuming that the government could be forced into scrapping Bantu Education, and eventually providing universal compulsory education with 'equal' facilities for every boy and girl at school, without itself being toppled, little or nothing would have been altered in the country at large. How were African youth expected to achieve educational parity with white children if they lived in Soweto (even the revamped Soweto they seemed to support)? And if they achieved this parity, how were they supposed to compete for jobs as long as apartheid continued? What, furthermore, was supposed to happen to the youth who would be educated in the Reserves? How could they ever emerge as equals from these glorified rural slums?

By refusing to confront the problems of a class society, the SSRC spokes-men ignored the problem that confronts educationalists in every class society: namely, that offering equal educational facilities to every child does not lead to equal scholastic attainment, nor does it offer equal opportunity, in either higher education or employment.

But perhaps Mr. Sono did not really mean what he said. As long as he was in public office, and working openly, he could not confess to the aim of overthrowing the government. The movement to which he adhered was to meet shortly in conference in Soweto and its viewpoints would be presented to the membership for endorsement.

SASM had its annual general meeting in early July and adopted a set of general standpoints. These were listed as:

the rejection of all government created bodies;
religions should be made more indigenous and should promote the black struggle;
workers should participate fully in the liberation of the country;
wages should be determined by ability;
black professional people should seek to serve their community; and
foreign investment was condemned because it promoted apartheid. [25]

This set of six points is all that appeared in the daily press, and the annual Survey of Race Relations adds no further details. On the basis of such scanty information it is not possible to examine, in any depth, the opinions held by student leaders in that crucial period before the police moved in to smash their organisation.

The points listed consist of a set of political (and social) principles, and only one of them led to immediate action or, to be more exact, to the continuation of action already initiated. That is, the rejection of all govern-ment instituted bodies. This kept alive the struggle against Buthelezi and men of his ilk, and also served notice that the students would continue their campaign to force official (black) bodies to resign.

276

The rejection of foreign investment was in line with the stand taken by all anti-government bodies and added nothing new. On the other hand, the adoption of a standpoint on religion, deeply entrenched in the attitudes of members of SASO/BPC and BCP, was new to the school pupils' organisation.

The attitude to the role of the workers was, if anything, far more diffuse than the viewpoint expressed in September 1976 when students had stated that, in any liberation struggle, 'the power for change lies with the workers'. In July 1977, the workers seem only to have been called upon to 'participate fully in the liberation', and the centrality of their role in overthrowing the apartheid state was no longer underlined. Even the point on professional people was vague. They were rebuked, as indeed they needed to be, for not always seeking to serve their community. What had to be faced clearly – the role of intellectuals in the struggle – was thereby fudged, and the class issues which were posed so sharply when the Revolt was at its height, seem to have been blunted in this closing stage of the struggle.

At the beginning of July the SSRC had issued an ultimatum to members of the 26 school boards in Soweto, demanding their immediate resignation. After a short delay a number of boards resigned *en bloc*, and by the end of the month 10 boards had ceased to function. The others followed in August. The student leaders in Alexandra, Atteridgeville and Mamelodi seemed to have made the same demands following the conference and to have secured the required resignations. [26]

There was no news of similar action elsewhere in the country, although that could have been the result of poor reporting facilities. In August, it was announced that 17 members of the Port Elizabeth SASM had been arrested.

The Police Move In

Through August and September the policy of repression was pursued by the police. Schools were raided, students were arrested; and, as a result, boycotts deepened in Soweto, Guguletu, Atteridgeville, East London, Healdtown, etc. Even Jabulani, once condemned as 'unreliable', faced police fire and added to the toll of dead.

On 24 August the government announced that the 40 post-primary schools in Soweto would cease to be regarded as Community Schools. They would be reopened as Government High Schools, and all students would be required to re-register by 5 September. The students reacted by calling on the teachers to resign, and within a short time some 475 had responded positively. They claimed, after resigning, that the government takeover was arrogant and unacceptable and that continued service under Bantu Education brought them into general disrepute.

Both students and teachers were now out, and the boycott spread to Kwa Thema (Springs), to Alexandra, and to primary schools in Atteridgeville. Then on 17 September the news of the murder of Steve Biko burst on the country. In a wave of revulsion the schools emptied throughout the land.

The focus moved first to Vendaland and BophutaTswana, and then to Port Elizabeth, Uitenhage, Kingwilliamstown, and in October there were riots in towns throughout the Eastern Cape, and in towns small and large in every province. In every case the police used guns and gas, batons and dogs, to disperse the crowds. Hundreds of youth were thrown into prison cells and summary trials speeded up in order to get sentences passed.

By the end of the month it was reported that:

In Soweto there would be no matriculation examinations for the second year running.
In Venda all 357 schools were closed and over 100,000 youth sent home.
In Port Elizabeth all 39,000 youth were out of school.
In Kingwilliamstown, Cradock and Grahamstown the schools were almost all empty.
In Pietersburg five secondary schools were shut.
The schools of Atteridgeville were all closed.
In Soweto the boycott covered the higher primary and all secondary schools.
One-third of Turfloop's students had walked out over student rights.

Other areas were affected in varying degrees, and only in the Transkei and KwaZulu were the schools functioning normally. [27]

In August Sono, last declared president of the SSRC, fled to Botswana after some 20 SSRC members has been arrested. Thereafter the SSRC announced that it would be led by a secret committee of six. It continued to direct student activities, but could no longer rely on the publicity it had used so effectively since 16 June, and its work was considerably hampered.

Eventually the government moved on 19 October to outlaw 17 African organisations (most of which could be described as bodies belonging to the Black Consciousness Movement) and the Christian Institute. The *World*, the *Weekend World* and *Pro Veritate* were also banned as were several individuals. At least 42 people were detained. All the funds and property belonging to these organisations were confiscated, and this included a mobile clinic, a clothing factory and a boutique (all owned by the BCP and associated organisations). The total assets taken over by the state amounted to approximately one million Rand.

The government intention was to end the Revolt, and in this it succeeded. The initial response in the schools was to intensify the struggle, but that was the last spasm of a struggle that had been ground down by brute force, and by an inability to find new techniques of struggle. The students had 'rehearsed' too often without being able to move beyond demonstration.

In the New Year (1978) the return to school was not smooth, and it took several months before classes filled up. There was still sporadic unrest and students were quick to challenge teachers who tried to impose tight discipline in the classroom. Nevertheless the Soweto Students' League, which replaced the SSRC, altered course early in the 1978 school year. At first they urged a complete boycott of the state schools. But they reversed this stand and called for a return to classes, and this time the students tended to agree with them. The classrooms began to fill.

On 22 March the youth mourned the death of Robert Sobukwe (original founder of the PAC), and those that attended his funeral forced Gatsha Buthelezi to leave, but not before his bodyguard had fired into the air. Despite the undoubted appeal Sobukwe's name and martyrdom evoked, this did not unleash the reaction that had been so marked in September when Biko was buried.

The Revolt was not over. It could not be over as long as apartheid reigned. But the phase that had opened up on June 16 1976 was closed.

References

1. Craig Williamson, for *SANA*, 26 September 1976.
2. CIS, *op.cit.*, p.56.
3. R. Nengwekhulu, *op.cit.* See also Barney Makhatle quoted in CIS, *op.cit.*, p.56.
4. The CIS report, p.57, includes a remark from a 'regular drinker' who said 'What the kids are doing is right. They had to force a ban on shebeens because we lacked the willpower to do it.'
5. *Ibid.*, p.56.
6. *X-Ray*, July-August 1977.
7. *Ibid.*
8. American Episcopal Church, Catholic Church, Church of the Province of South Africa (Anglican), Methodist Church of South Africa, Moravian Church, Presbyterian Church of Africa, United Congregational Church of South Africa.
9. The Ministers Fraternal of Langa, Guguletu and Nyanga, (1976), *Role of Riot Police in the Burnings and Killings,* (Nyanga), (mimeo).
10. D.P.H. Russell, (1977), *The Riot Police and the Suppression of Truth: memorandum prepared for Members of Parliament,* (Cape Town), (mimeo).
11. 'December 16th is a historic day in the Freedom struggle.' A leaflet commemorating Heroes Day.
12. *SRRSA*, 1977, p.56.
13. *The World*, 4 January 1977.
14. P. Laurence reporting in the London *Guardian*, 5 January 1977.
15. Interview with President of SSRC, Daniel Sechaba Montsitsi, *Weekend World,* 27 February 1977.
16. *Rand Daily Mail* and *World*, 10 February 1977.
17. See P. Laurence, *Guardian,* 10 February 1977.
18. *SANA* report, May 1977/2.
19. *SRRSA*, 1977, p.401.
20. *The New Africa*, December 1977, p.1188.
21. *SANA* report, July 1977/4.
22. *SRRSA*, 1977, pp.402-5.

23. *Ibid.* See also the interview with Sono by Thami Mazwai, *World*, 1 July 1977.
24. *Ibid.*
25. *SRRSA*, 1977, p.32.
26. *SRRSA*, 1977, p.450, and CIS, (1978), *Buying Time in South Africa*, p.52.
27. 'Crisis in the schools', *Financial Mail*, 4 November 1977.

PART 3
Black Consciousness and the Struggle in S. Africa

15. Anatomy of the Revolt

Origins

On 16 June 1976, following the demonstration of school youth organised by the committee which was to become known as the Soweto Students Representative Council, the police fired at the unarmed crowd and precipitated the events which engulfed South Africa during the next 18 months.

By all previous experience in South Africa — or at least since the massacre of the religious sect known as the Israelites at Bulhoek (near Queenstown) in 1921, and extending to Sharpeville in 1960 — the short sharp burst of rifle shot should have struck terror into the hearts of the black population. After a few weeks of mourning, the populace should have returned to the life that the government was mapping out for them, and accepted their lot under the apartheid regime.

We cannot yet prove that this was the way the government planned events although there is some evidence to show that that was the case. By the time the Revolt spread to the Cape, there can be little doubt about the government's provocative use of riot police to destroy the spirit of the schoolchildren.

It can be said with certainty that the government intelligence forces were aware of the deep ferment in the country, and it is hard to believe that they had not planned some counter-action. Through their battery of informers they knew of the turmoil in the classrooms, and they also had information about the activity of the South African Student Movement. They were more than aware of the disruption in factories and mines since 1973 (although they seemed quite unprepared for the outbreak of the strikes); and they knew that the bus boycotts of East London, Newcastle and Kwa Thema could have been the prelude to an even larger boycott following the increase in fares from June 16, 1976.

Irrespective of government plans or machinations, there was deep-rooted discontent in the country, and this expressed itself in the strikes, boycotts and riots that had shaken industry and local black communities since 1972. From the Durban docks through to the Coronation Brick and Tile, and then to the Frame Textile Group constituted, geographically, a series of short jumps. Politically these were great leaps forward, and first the workers, and then the students and intellectuals, achieved a new consciousness of the strength they wielded in the country. The workers of Durban were followed by groups in the Eastern Cape and the Transvaal, and then by the mine workers. For the first time in over a decade, the working class showed that they had recovered from the massive defeats of the early 1960's and were prepared to take action to better their conditions.

During this period of ever growing strife, the black university students were also organising and making their discontent known. The origin of their struggle was embedded in the general discontent that affected the entire black population. They were sensitive to the social maladies that riddled South Africa and they were affected by the waves of discontent that expressed themselves in worker and community struggles. However, being students, they expressed the discontent in their own unique fashion. In some respects they were ahead of the black populace, and voiced political aspirations that had been stilled by the bannings of the ANC and PAC. They dreamed of a 'new man' who would assert his individuality and demand his just desserts. They felt that the task of 'liberation' could only be fulfilled by Blacks and that the (predominantly) white liberal voice was ineffectual. They severed their ties with the white student body and coined the phrase, 'Black man, you are on your own.'

Intellectually the black university students took the cause of national liberation to be their goal, but in practice they tended to concentrate on their own problems on the campus. The net result was that, while they claimed that they were bringing 'consciousness' to the masses, they lagged far behind the workers and, except for the indignation they expressed over the shootings at the Carltonville mine, showed little interest in the industrial strikes or the bus boycotts. The growth of consciousness amongst the workers, restricted as it was to economic and trade union demands, bypassed the students, busy in their soul-searching and quest for 'personal identity'.

Although the students' newfound awareness was, at least in part, a product of the stirrings in the townships, they were curiously insensitive to the broader struggles around them. As a result, in 1972-73, and through to 1976, they failed to seek common ground with the workers. Neither in their writings, nor in their activities, are there any indications that the black students involved themselves in any of the many workers' struggles up and down the country.

The university students, not unlike their peers elsewhere in the world, were disaffected. They too were aware of the barbarous war in Viet Nam and Cambodia. Of more immediate consequence, however, they followed events in Mozambique, Angola and Zimbabwe. These wars were also their wars, and they longed for the liberation they saw coming through Frelimo and (to a lesser degree) through the MPLA. They were somewhat confused on the issue of Zimbabwe and praised Bishop Muzorewa: but there too they looked to African liberation.

They faced hostile campus administrations, wedded to the apartheid ideal, and were in constant conflict with institutions that were designed to turn out second-class products. They formed their own black organisation and saw themselves as the leaders of a black move to liberation that would remove discrimination and allow them to take their 'rightful' place in the country. Their dreams were embodied in the slogan at Turfloop, which the government Commission of Inquiry was most concerned about, after the Viva Frelimo rally: 'Vacancies. Government of Azania. Majors, Lieutenants, Captains. Duties: To train and lead 50 million Blacks. Apply: SASO, BPC before the reach of the 4th Century of racist oppression.' [1] To be officers, not rank and file. To train, not to be trained. Such were the dreams of this small, relatively privileged group.

In any other country their class position would be assured. No matter who their parents were, this would be the petty bourgeoisie. They would aspire to the comforts of lucrative careers. Some would enter the government. The road would be open to office in the civil service and in the universities. In South Africa, being such a small select group, the passage to such employment would have been even more assured if it had not been for the racial barriers ordained by apartheid.

The students were angry. They hated the constraints on their lives, and they saw these reproduced on the campuses. All their efforts at school, and now at the university, seemed to lead to a dead end. Their hopes that they could escape the poverty of their kin through education had turned sour — or had been considerably dampened by the limited opportunities they now saw as being open to them. Nonetheless their petty bourgeois aspirations coloured their entire outlook. They looked inwards to their own problems. They sought 'awareness', 'self-identity', 'liberation from psychological oppression', and some mythical 'black value-system'. In contrast, the workers sought group solidarity and fought to improve their standard of living, and the wordy statements that emanated from the Black Consciousness Movement were meaningless to most of them: few, if any, of the pretentious statements coming from these young 'leaders' had any bearing on their lives. Both hated the white oppressor. But the young intellectual interpreted the discrimination in racial terms; the worker offered no interpretation, but knew that it was the factory boss and the host of supervisors, mostly white, who barred his way to better living conditions. The differences in understanding might not have been so very great, but the approach led the one group to endless philosophising, while the working class tackled the real problem of exploitation and embarked on extended strike action.

The limitations inherent in the workers' actions need to be stressed. They wanted higher wages (and lower transport costs) and there was little effort to go beyond this elemental form of struggle. To transcend these demands required a conscious political organisation that could demonstrate the link between low wages and the system of exploitation, and there was no such body in the country — or if it did exist, it did not get the ear of the worker. SASO/BPC did not have that understanding, and made little effort to reach the workers. There was, consequently, no possibility of the economic struggle being linked to the Revolt that erupted in 1976. Throughout 1976-77, continued strikes and some local community struggles, including at least one extended bus boycott in Kimberley,[2] were apparently ignored by the survivors of SASO/BPC (so sorely decimated by police action).

The school pupils to whom the mantle of leadership passed, altered their approach to the working class as the struggle gathered momentum. To be more exact, their verbal pronouncements changed and became more radical from July through to September. Later pronouncements, however, never matched the statements of mid-September, proclaiming the centrality of the workers in securing change in the country.

When the demonstration of 16 June was first planned, the students thought only of their own resources. Experience brought them rapidly to the realisation that they depended on the assistance provided by their parents and by all the workers in the township. By August they had called the workers out on a political strike, and they faced the wrath of the men of Mzimhlope Hostel who were turned against them. This made them even more aware of the need to win the confidence of the worker, and by mid-September they saw the importance of the workers in the struggle for radical change.

The recognition did not, unfortunately, lead to any changes in the central organisation of the Revolt. The students did not, or could not, enlarge their committees, and they rejected an invitation to join the ANC — although their theoretical advance was partly due to the contact they had made with the external wing of Congress. The students called upon the workers for support, gave them theoretical recognition of their role, but did not give sufficient prominence to working class demands in their slogans or campaigns. Nor did they take up the industrial strikes as they emerged, showing in fact the gulf between themselves and the men on the factory floor.

Ultimately, when the Revolt had passed its peak, the students turned inwards again, and the slogans seemed concerned largely with education and the schools. The central role previously ascribed to the workers was replaced by the call to the worker to 'participate fully' in future struggles.

The sudden emergence of the school pupils as a mobilising body in the townships took the Black Consciousness Movement by surprise. Although SASM (in particular) used some of the black consciousness phraseology, they owed no allegiance to SASO. But they did use the same language as SASO/BPC. Motapanyane, asked if SASM was an offshoot of SASO, answered as follows: 'It is not correct to say that SASM was an offshoot of SASO . . . we did not have in mind to copy what SASO was doing. But many ideas that we used to project, like black consciousness for instance, SASO was also preaching.' Asked, furthermore, how far the school pupils were affected by the atmosphere created by SASO/BPC he replied:

> Black consciousness as a concept did play a role in sensitizing the students . . . We did not, however, believe that black consciousness on its own would lead us to liberation. It was a useful tool to sensitize students who were not as politically aware as they should have been. [3]

Some of the leading members of SASM were in contact with the clandestine ANC, and that body, too, found it expedient to work within the framework of the Black Consciousness Movement. The youth at school, therefore, acquired the language of black consciousness from all their political contacts. (The same applies, obviously, to the groups of youth who were in contact with the PAC. The latter movement, even more than the ANC, were inclined to accept the ideas of black consciousness uncritically.)

The students at school, particularly in the urban townships, were much closer to the community than were their seniors in the universities. Their aspirations were also lower. Some did hope to get to the universities, but most would seek employment when they left school. Their futures were very much less bright than those of their fellows in higher education. They would have to find employment locally in commerce or industry, and except for some clerical posts they were not particularly well trained for any occupation.

Their disadvantages were legion. White youth with similar (and even inferior) education would take many of the jobs they aspired to. There was, furthermore, a prejudice against employing those who emerged from the upper forms, because they would not be compliant enough. In the parlance of Whites, they would be 'too cheeky'. Prospects for employment, which had begun to improve in the late sixties when South Africa faced a shortage of skilled and semi-skilled personnel, were once again poor in the light of the severe depression after 1973.

The school pupils also faced problems in the schools which led to a growth of militancy on their part. The language of black consciousness might have 'sensitized' some of them, but it was the reorganisation of the secondary schools which led to the growth of political groupings. The chaotic conditions following the quadrupling of numbers allowed to enter the secondary schools was completely disruptive. Students forced to repeat the year, a lack of staff, shortage of accommodation, and packed classrooms, were not conducive to ordinary lessons being given, or being received.

The introduction of Afrikaans medium instruction was the final straw, and the schools became the centre of new disturbances. The events of 1976 were the latest in a long history of school boycotts and strikes which extends from 1920 through to the 1960's, and although it would be stretching credibility to speak of a continuity in the many episodes, there were common features which contributed to the periodic flare-ups. There was the heavy-handed paternalism and the shortage of resources, and there was, also, the disjunction between what pupils were taught and their experiences in daily life. The prejudices, if not the lies, they encountered in their textbooks, could only lead to disenchantment with the schooling they received, and their successes at school ran counter to the officially held myth that they were not capable of such attainment.

Traditions of struggle are rarely established in schools because of students' transience, and each event had the mark of uniqueness. Yet each demonstration, and every riot, had in the past prepared an increasing number of young men and women for the existing political movements. In 1975-76 there were no such open movements to turn to, and this group of young people had themselves to become the political leaders of their community, while conducting the struggle in the schools. It was a role they were forced to adopt, and their inexperience allowed them to take some daring and surprisingly successful actions. But it also led to glaring errors, the first and foremost being their inability to establish a student-worker alliance, despite the claim made in the Thembisa leaflet.

Motapanyane, in the interview he gave, was not questioned about the effect on scholars of the strikes and bus boycotts. Nor did he introduce the issue himself. There is little reason to doubt that many pupils were affected by these events, and that their militancy was the natural outcome of the wider struggle, as well as of their discontent with conditions in the schools. Their perspectives, however, were shaped by their personal aspirations and, low as these were, they still hoped to secure better situations than the less fortunate push-outs. If they faced the prospect of unemployment, they were not brought closer to this large lumpen element. In fact, they desired more than ever to distance themselves from this class of youth. There is no way of knowing how many of these students wanted radical change in May 1976. Their hopes were probably very limited: they wanted the schools to function, they hoped they would halt the introduction of Afrikaans, and they also wanted jobs when they completed their schooling. Some undoubtedy went further, and wanted better education, without the distortions and open racism of Bantu Education. But very few spoke of unsegregated schooling, and nobody seems to have raised fundamental questions about the nature of education provided in South Africa. They wanted, at most, to receive tuition that would make them equals (in achievement) to their white peers. This was a radical demand in the South African circumstances, but not revolutionary.

The bourgeois framework that the black students had been introduced to in the schools was the same as that given to every South African child. It was designed to make products for a capitalist society — but for the Blacks, education for capitalism involved inferiority. The black youths' demand, therefore, was not for a change in the educational system — only that it should cease being of a lower standard. And on that basis they were prepared to demonstrate and strike. It was only after the first clashes with the police, in May 1976, that their demands became more radical, and after 16 June small concessions would no longer satisfy their newfound aspirations. The entire system of Bantu Education had to go and, with it, much more had to be changed in the country. As long as the students were successful, their expectations soared and ever larger sections were radicalised. When the forces of the state seemed too great to counter, they cut their demands, and spoke only about schools and the education they hoped to receive. In the period of radicalisation they were able to transcend their one time petty bourgeois expectations. When success no longer seemed feasible many turned their attention again to future careers and job opportunities despite their increased understanding and radicalisation.

Consciousness and the Revolt

Preceding the Revolt, there had been considerable publicity for the proponents of 'black consciousness' and, although members of SASO in exile were careful to say that they had not initiated the conflict, they nonetheless asserted that they had prepared the ground for revolt by propagating their ideas. Ranwedzi Nengwekhulu, one time 'permanent organiser' of SASO, addressing the assembly of the IUEF in Geneva, gave this assessment:

> Although the Black Consciousness Movement is supposed to be responsible for what is going on in the country, it is not responsible in the sense that it *organised* the students to do what they have been doing. It has been responsible in the sense that it has popularized the whole idea of Black consciousness around the country, mainly through SASO, BPC and SASM. One could say that it started almost spontaneously in the sense that people have been fed up with the situation in the country for a long time but one thing we have always suffered from, being South African Blacks, is a lack of ideology around which people could rally in order to fight for some kind of ideals. [4]

Fact and fantasy are mixed in this statement. The Black Consciousness Movement had not organised SASM, nor was it the school pupils who had spread or popularised the ideas of the Black Consciousness Movement. Nengwekhulu was also incorrect when he said that the Revolt started spontaneously. The history of events in the country, at least since 1973, and the sequence of events in Soweto schools for nearly six months, indicates that this was not the case. Unless there had been students prepared to organise the demonstration, and prepared to urge that they stand firm in the face of police provocation, the events of June 16 could not have initiated a Revolt; and, if it had not been for the many groupings in the township, ready to support the youth in the months that followed, the Revolt would have collapsed within a few weeks. To ignore this background and say of the Revolt that it was 'spontaneous' is quite untrue.

He was, furthermore, wrong when he claimed that black consciousness had been propagated 'around the country' and that SASO/BPC had supplied the ideology which Blacks had previously lacked. The extent to which the ideology had spread remains questionable, and it is yet to be shown that black consciousness adequately provided the ideology that was lacking.

Later in his address, Nengwekhulu claimed that the level of 'political consciousness' was higher in Soweto than elsewhere because the BPC had their office there and because SASM was centred there. The presence of SASM was indeed crucial. Without them the initiative taken by the pupils of Naledi and Orlando would have remained isolated incidents. But the political awareness of the school student leaders came from many sources, and the Black Consciousness Movement was not necessarily in the forefront of these influences.

The simplistic approach in this account by Nengwekhulu was shown in his claim that the large strike wave was centred in Durban in 1970 [an incorrect date] because SASO had its head office there. How SASO affected the strike when (as Foszia Fisher was quoted as saying in Chapter Seven) they had no contact with, and no influence on the workers, is incomprehensible.

But the Black Consciousness Movement, by virtue of its name, and because of the publicity it received, has raised afresh the problem of 'consciousness' in South Africa. We have to ask, then, what consciousness means, and how populations acquire this mysterious ingredient. Even more crucially, the question is one of changing perceptions (or, again, consciousness), and the way in which such perceptions alter under conditions of political stress.

The problem has two distinct dimensions. Firstly there is the development of a political ideology which is usually maintained and propagated by small groups of people. Their understanding of the problems of the country, and the solutions they advance, provide a measure of 'consciousness'. The extent to which they are able to strip away surface phenomena and get to the root of the problems of their society, will ultimately help determine the role they will play, if and when there is revolutionary change in the country. Their final effectiveness will depend on the extent of mass support they can win during periods of transformation.

Secondly there is the problem of raising the 'consciousness' of the people, or of classes in the population. This is not achieved through study, and is not primarily the result of an accretion of understanding. To conceive of consciousness as some kind of linear process, leading to ever increasing understanding (whatever that might mean) is unreal. Social processes do not work in this simple fashion.

It was this problem of the way the masses came to revolutionary action that led Trotsky to an understanding of the social dynamics of revolution and can throw some light on our own problem. The passage quoted refers to the Russian Revolution, but has more general application:

> The point is that society does not change its institutions as need arises, the way a mechanic changes his instruments. On the contrary, society actually takes the institutions which hang upon it as given once for all. For decades the oppositional criticism is nothing more than a safety valve for mass dissatisfaction, a condition of the stability of the social structure . . . Entirely exceptional conditions, independent of the will of persons or parties, are necessary in order to tear off from discontent the fetters of conservatism, and bring the masses to insurrection.
>
> The swift changes of mass views and moods in an epoch of revolution thus derive, not from the flexibility and mobility of man's mind, but just the opposite, from its deep conservatism. The chronic lag of ideas and relations behind new objective conditions, right up to the moment when the latter crash over people in the form of a catastrophe, is what creates in a period of revolution that leaping movement of ideas and passions which seems to the police mind a mere result of the activities of 'demagogues'.
>
> The masses go into a revolution not with a prepared plan of social

reconstruction, but with a sharp feeling that they cannot endure the old regime. Only the guiding layers of a class have a political programme, and even this still requires the test of events, and the approval of the masses. [5]

Trotsky then outlined the process of change *during* a revolution, where once again there are jumps of consciousness which are ever leftwards as long as there are no objective obstacles. Thereafter there is a reaction. Disappointments lead to the growth of indifference, and with this the growth of counter-revolutionary forces.

The situation in South Africa was not revolutionary, and there was never any possibility of overthrowing the regime. Nonetheless the dynamics of group or class consciousness described above are applicable both to processes during the Revolt — the changed attitude to funerals being only one example of the 'leaping movement of ideas' — and the lengthy period of political inertia which preceded the Revolt.

It is when the masses enter into the historic process in order to change society that parties and leaders acquire an increased importance.

They constitute not an independent, but nevertheless a very important element in the process. Without a guiding organisation the energy of the masses would dissipate like steam not enclosed in a piston-box. But nevertheless what moves things is not the piston or the box, but the steam.[6]

The central point, in this set of observations by Trotsky, was that the understanding that came to large groups of men and women in society was 'independent of the will of persons and parties'. Only when conditions were propitious would the innate conservatism be overcome, and people would move to insurrection. Then, and only then, would parties act as guides to large sections of society, and move outside the narrow group activities to which they had previously been confined.

When the masses burst through the constraints that had bound them, they would, in varying degrees, be receptive to the messages offered them by political organisations. But they were not passive receptacles for the programmes of any and every group. In many cases the masses created their own organisations that were far in advance of the established parties, and created new institutions to meet their new political needs. It was the political parties that tended to lag behind in consciousness at these stages. In the Revolt of 1976, it was the school pupils who were pushed to the fore by the events in Soweto, Cape Town and elsewhere, and they were able to take up the challenge where the Black Consciousness Movement faltered and was left behind. And it was during the height of the Revolt that the clandestine ANC, in particular, was able to join the students in organising some of the most important activities of the Revolt.

All that was still to come when SASO/BPC first raised the matter of consciousness. In none of their writings did they recognise that the development of consciousness would follow paths that were independent of their will, or of the will of any of the participants.

What they did do had its own importance in the early 1970's, and this will be discussed below. It is necessary, however, to separate out the intellectual climate which they helped create from the factors which led to June 1976.

To believe, as members of SASO seemed to believe, that consciousness would be raised by their going out to the communities and injecting a new value system — through their clinics, or through other projects — is reminiscent of the early populists in Russia who thought they would bring enlightenment to the peasants. The Russian populists failed, not because they lacked sincerity, but because the peasants were steeped in the life they knew and were not going to be radicalised by words or by good deeds. Yet it was these very peasants who would rise up two decades later and help destroy the greatest despotism in Europe.

Conditions in South Africa cannot be compared with those in Russia in the nineteenth century. The young studens who wanted to take the message of liberation into the towns and villages in the 1970's came with a different message, and used different techniques. Their basic approach to the problem, however, was remarkably similar. They were going to liberate people from the 'psychological oppression' that kept them quiescent; they were going to bring back 'black culture', let people 'rediscover their history', bring the message of a god that would liberate, and in fact let each black man and woman discover anew their 'personal identity'.

The clearest exposition of this approach to personal renascence was produced by Drake Koka, one of the founding fathers of the BPC. In a short document entitled 'On black consciousness and black solidarity', he stated:

> Through the philosophy of Black Consciousness Black people could be led onto the road of *self-discovery*. . . This would eventually lead to the *self-assertion* of the Black man's inner pride, of the 'I' in him and thus strengthen him to accept or reject with confidence certain things that are being done for him or on his behalf . . . he will develop an attitude of self-reliance . . . The self-realisation develops in the Black man a yearning to *create and to take the initiative in doing things.*
>
> As soon as Blacks become conscious of themselves as a people and identify themselves with their fellow Blacks and see their potentials in the social, political, economic and cultural spheres of the community of which they are part, they would be able to determine their destiny.[7]

Koka, founder and Secretary-General of the Black Allied Workers Union, said that that organisation would have been used '. . . to cultivate the workers at grass roots level. They had to be made aware of their potentials and significance in the job situation.'[8]

The process of making people aware of their potential, and of building 'self-reliance' was called 'conscientisation'. Again, in the words of Koka:

Conscientisation is the process through which people are made conscious of themselves as persons, their culture and their socio-economic conditions, their political position and their spiritual awareness. The avenues or methods to be used would be through a person to person contact, group discussions, lectures, leadership courses, public rallies, schools, community development programmes, theatre, art, music, attire and every conceivable platform where the message could be carried across to large numbers of people.[9]

The programme of 'conscientisation' would be advanced, said Koka, through ASSECA (to encourage Blacks 'to see to the education of their children'); the African Housewives League ('to make Black mothers realise and appreciate their positions as married women thus becoming responsible wives and mothers'); BAWU ('for creating awareness amongst workers'); SASO and SASM; BPC ('the training ground for worthy future rulers of any [*sic*] country'); IDAMASA and AICA ('where the Black man would be made aware of his spiritual values'); the BCP ('to make the Black Community aware of their social needs such as health centres, creches, home crafts etc.'); and finally the Peoples Experimental Theatre which would reach the people through drama 'and other cultural fields'.

The concept that Koka used was so wide that it is difficult to see where it coincides with the 'raising of consciousness' used by politicians. The programme that he outlined, consisted of a mixed bag of social welfare, social responsibility, and liberal do-gooding. The programme for women can only be called reactionary, and the political content of the entire set of proposals is (or was) of little relevance to the black workers.

In so far as SASO/BPC performed a political task, their work led to the formation of small groups of intellectuals, mainly on the university campuses, who undoubtedly absorbed and espoused the ideas of the Black Consciousness Movement. They acquired an 'awareness' through the groups they joined, and in this sense SASO/BPC raised the consciousness of a minute section of the black population.

The establishment of a group with a political orientation was no mean feat in the 1970's in South Africa. Despite all our criticisms, the work of Koka, Tiro, Biko, Pityana, Nengwekhulu and their comrades, locked in confrontation with the government almost from the inception, was a significant factor in two respects. Firstly, it allowed them to organise groups on the black campuses, and it brought them together with clerics, writers, journalists and other intellectuals, into an organisation that developed a distinctive identity. Through their language, songs, meetings and writings they generated a corporate spirit, and that gave them an internal strength. This did not make them a homogeneous group. There were differences at all levels, and we have not investigated these closely, because their unity was more prominent than the issues that seemed at times to divide them internally.

The second factor was equally important. In the words of Fanon (quoted in Chapter Seven) they made 'the people dream dreams'. Or at least, they did manage to get their message through to some groups of people who were seeking a political message and were already dreaming dreams. Precisely how they reached their audience has still to be explored. Some were undoubtedly influenced at gatherings. Others were won at the community projects that were successful, and there were also persons who were already seeking a political solution and welcomed an organisation that expressed some of their longings. But the biggest response to the Black Consciousness Movement probably stemmed from their courageous showing in the court cases — of the SASO/BPC Nine and of the NAYO Seven.

There were, however, significant social groups that they never reached. At one end of the class spectrum, amongst the traders who had grown relatively rich, and a section of the established professional group, they won few converts, although S.M. Motsuenyane, president of the National African Federated Chamber of Commerce, climbed on the bandwaggon at one stage. They were also actively opposed by men who worked in government-created institutions, both in the towns and in the Reserves.

Nor did the Black Consciousness Movement seem to have had any impact on the vast rural population — either in the Reserves or on the farms, and even parties that opposed the Homelands' ministries, but participated in elections to the local assemblies, were repulsed when they made some tentative moves towards the Black Consciousness Movement. It seems that the opposition spokesmen from Lebowa and BophutaTswana who were expelled from the Black Renaissance Convention, at the insistence of members of SASO (see Chapter Seven), had originally been invited to attend by these same men.[10]

Likewise, there were few indications that the Black Consciousness Movement won much support from the working class and very little, if any, from those organised in trade unions. Yet it might have been supposed that a movement wishing to build up grass-root support could not overlook this class.

The attitude to workers and to workers' organisations was stated explicitly by Biko. The first occasion arose in 1976 when he was called by the defence to testify on behalf of the SASO Nine. Donald Woods who reprints excerpts from the abridged court record says that Biko was called as 'the foremost proponent' of black consciousness. The following appears in his answers to state prosecutor, K. Attwell:

> *Attwell:* The military expert also suggested that the most productive sphere in which the blacks in this country could work toward change was the black worker sphere, do you agree with that statement?
> *Biko:* If you are talking about fundamental change perhaps it is a possibility, but I think there are other spheres which lend themselves to easier use. Take the field of sport for instance, which I think is in the vital interests of society also in that it foreshadows attitudes in other areas. I think the country now is at a stage where considerable pressure can be applied fruitfully in the sphere of sport.
> *Attwell:* But in what sphere in your opinion can the blacks exert the most pressure and be most effective?
> *Biko:* I am telling you now, sport.

. . . . .

   Attwell: So you would not agree that the black worker sphere is in fact the main sphere in which blacks can be most effective.
   Biko: Not now, certainly.[11]

Biko was ambivalent on the matter of 'fundamental change'. Even in that case it was only a possibility. In the short run, the workers were not the force that Biko looked to. He was to repeat his attitude in January 1977 when he met with Bruce Haigh of the Australian Embassy in South Africa. Woods reprints Haigh's account, in which the following was stated:

> Given the present attitude of the Nationalist government, Biko felt the prospect for peaceful change in South Africa was not good. He believed, however, that protests and boycotts had helped to some extent, and he cited the sport policy adopted by most countries towards South Africa as an example. Despite National party statements he believed they were sensitive to outside pressure, although a lot more was needed before they would consider making the basic changes necessary to remove the system of apartheid.[12]

Biko had told Woods, it appears, that he had liked Bruce Haigh and had 'been completely candid with him'. He appeared to have discussed many issues with Haigh, but there is no record of any statement that the workers would be considered as a force in any way. He was certain that sport was the answer, as he said in his court appearance, because:

> I think unless white people in this country are illogical, if you are going to mix on the sports fields and mix fully, as is eventually going to happen, then you have to think about other areas of your activity, you have to think about cinemas, you have to think about shows and dancing and so on, you have to think about political rights. It is a snowball effect, and the outside world is merely tackling this to bring to the minds of white South Africa that we have got to think about change, and change is an irreversible process, because I believe in history moving in a direction which is logical to a logical end.[13]

Black Consciousness as an Ideology

Black consciousness, as a composite set of political, legal, religious, social and philosophical ideas, or in other words as an ideology, was used both to organise groups and to define the nature of the struggle in the country. It is these ideas to which we must address ourselves next.

   From the inception of such an investigation there is a basic difficulty, because the many persons who made statements about black consciousness differed on many points. It is in the nature of broad, umbrella concepts that they attract diverse groups who offer their own interpretations of what the concept means. *Being* black, *acting* black, and *thinking* black, seemed to be the basic requirements — provided, that is, that there was agreement on the acts and the thoughts. Biko, for example, stated:

> I must state categorically that there is no such thing as a Black policeman. Any Black man who props the system up actively has lost the right to being considered part of the Black world . . . They are the extensions of the enemy into our ranks. [14]

Members of political parties in the Homelands, both in the governing group, and in opposition inside the Assemblies; members of Coloured and Indian groups who participated in elections to their respective Councils; members of groups who participated in elections to any urban councils; and many others disowned for some reason, were not black. Being black was a state of mind, and not a colour, was the claim and, by exclusion, this narrowed the field down. Nevertheless, there *was* a colour barrier. Not all Blacks might be 'Black', but no Whites could be 'Black', although Beyers Naudé (said Boesak) almost made the grade. Donald Woods seems to have believed that he too had almost succeeded.

Precisely what had to be *thought* (in order to qualify as Black) was a bit harder to define. In the aftermath of 16 June, Rachidi, as previously quoted, equated black consciousness with 'gut reaction, not lofty philosophy', [15] and claimed that out of the events, a new child was being shaped. At one level this observation was unexceptionable: the experiences of the youth following 16 June were bound to raise consciousness, and few who emerged from the events of those days could ever be the same again. But the initial 'gut reaction' could not be called 'consciousness'. Much more had to be learnt before the experience of that day, brave as it was, could be so described.

There were many diverse social groups drawn into the events that followed the shooting. There was rioting, arson, looting, and two Whites killed. Some of these activities were undoubtedly gut reactions, but some were carried out by *tsotsis* who sought personal gain at the expense of the local community. To call this 'black consciousness', without distinction, would make a mockery of all political processes, and the description need not detain us much further. The practical problem posed by the *tsotsis* was faced by the leaders of the SSRC and, on one occasion at least, the President, Sono, made a public statement declaring war on 'thugs', and apologised in the name of the student body to car owners and taxi drivers for all the stoning. He also found it necessary to apologise to the populace for some of the disturbances at funerals. [16]

Gut reaction, it would appear, was not always considered as part of black consciousness. It could work to the detriment of the main groups engaged in the struggle.

Black consciousness has been defined by SASO and BPC members in many statements, manifestos and newsletters. These definitions are central to the concept as it was used, but none of the many words caught the anger that helped shape the ideas. The fury of the youth was reflected in the poetry, rather than in the formal statements. Some of this verse was included as evidence against the SASO/BPC Nine:

When did the revolution/war begin?
It began the day the whiteman put his foot on the land.
It began when your forefathers were brought in chains to work the fields
They killed Chaka — it began
They killed Dingaan — it began
They incarcerated Sobukwe
                          Mandela
                          Sisulu — it began
Now it is on — the revolution
                          — because they killed Brother SHEZI
                          — because they muted our Leaders [17]

At times the bitterness crept into talks and there was always the feeling, in all that was said, that these young men and women had had enough. One declaration that caught the spirit of how they felt was voiced by Nyameko Pityana:

Many people would prefer to be colour-blind: to them skin pigmentation is merely an incident to creation. To us it is something much more fundamental: it is a synonym for subjection, an identification for the dis-inherited, the discarded people and the wretched of the earth. [18]

The definition of black consciousness, extracted from programmatic statements avoided the emotive tones, and contained some essential points. The major themes included a *liberation from psychological oppression,* the *building of a new awareness*, the establishment of a new *basic dignity*, the framing of a *new attitude of mind*, a *rediscovery of the history of the people*, and a *cultural revival.*

These seemed to be the major components of the doctrine, as enunciated by members of SASO and BPC. They marked black consciousness, in Koka's words, as an 'introspective' philosophy, as a road to 'self-discovery', and as a programme for self-realisation.

There were few attempts to build up a political doctrine, and the statements that were made periodically on race, colour, or on any of the structural problems in South Africa, were unfortunately very superficial. Before looking at these, it is necessary to establish the fact that there were two prongs to the slogans that are listed above. Firstly, there was the call to every Black to seek a new inner strength and assert his personal right to freedom. Secondly, there was an appeal to the past glories of the people: to the history and the culture that they had been deprived of by the white conquerors.

296

The first set of slogans sought to remove the barriers to black advancement, and to build up a new confidence. They looked to the problem of alienation and sought to build up a new corporate spirit of black solidarity. Much of it sounded like a course in group psycho-therapy, and not like a political programme, although many of the intellectuals they attracted turned their attention to political action.

The second group of slogans were not dissimilar to points made in most national movements. The appeal to the past, the search for national heroes, the search for a renascent culture, are part of the stock-in-trade of nationalist movements everywhere. In South Africa, however, such demands were riddled with contradictions which did not seem to have been considered. The heroes that were mentioned were invariably African (seldom Coloured or Indian), and most were drawn only from the Zulu and Xhosa tribal past. The content of the culture, on the other hand, was seldom discussed. In the fight against tribal separatism, there was no demand for the use of any of the African languages, and the literature, written and oral, of the African past received little attention.

Even stranger assertions were made by those Coloureds who espoused black consciousness. Adam Small spoke about coloured culture, but did not expand on what he meant. The commonest language in use by Coloureds was Afrikaans, the very language that had helped trigger off the Soweto Revolt. Their literature was scanty, and there was nothing 'national' in dress or in customs. The Indians — who did have a language, or languages, religions, and very distinctive customs — were ultimately divided from other Blacks, partly because of this separate 'culture'.

It was possible to build on some of the common traditions (mainly of struggle) between Indians and Africans, and it was possible to delve into stories of seventeenth century Khoisan heroines as Fatima Meer did at the Black Renaissance Convention, but this constituted very slender grounds for building a 'cultural revival', and even for 'rediscovering the history of a people'. These were tasks which, ironically, the leaders of the Homelands could advance, if they were so inclined.

Little was done in the few years of legal existence to put many of these slogans into effect. There was more talk about 'history' than actual writing of the subject, and more said about the need for a cultural revival than could be achieved. There is no way in which the success (or failure) of the attempts to free Africans from the burden of psychological oppression can be measured. If anything of the kind was achieved, it would still be necessary to indicate how this assisted in the 'liberation' of the black man.

It is my contention that, in all its outpourings, the Black Consciousness Movement was apolitical. In this respect they were very similar to some of the groups in the American civil rights movement of the 1960's. Irving Howe, at a New York forum in April 1965, described his impressions of Malcolm X, one of the greatest of the men to spring into prominence as a leader of Black American thought. Malcolm X had spoken to an enthusiastic audience on a Trotskyist platform in the USA just before he was murdered, and promised at one point to raise an army and march South. Howe's appraisal (harsh and polemical as it was) applies to some of Malcolm X's South African counterparts:

> For the Negroes in his audience, he offered the relief of articulating subterranean feelings of hatred, contempt, defiance, feelings that did not have to be held in check because there was a tacit compact that the talk about violence would remain talk . . .
> . . . Malcolm alone among the Negro spokesmen was authentic because . . . well, because finally he spoke for nothing but his rage, for no proposal, no plan, no program, just a sheer outpouring of anger and pain. And that they could understand.
> . . . Malcolm, intransigent in words and nihilistic in reality, never invoked the possibility or temptations of immediate struggle; he never posed the problems, confusions and risks of manoeuvre, compromise, retreat. Brilliantly Malcolm spoke for a rejection so complete it transformed him into an apolitical spectator. . .[19]

Black Consciousness and the Rejection of Class Analysis

The leaders of SASO/BPC did not offer any serious new thoughts on the question of racism and colour, and usually dismissed the question of class as being irrelevant. Pityana's approach was typical. His assertion, with little argument, was that colour was the central problem. This was followed by the arbitrary rejection of 'class' as a central factor, and then a lateral statement which allowed him to avoid the whole problem. In his *Power and social change in South Africa* he stated:

> My justification for using colour as a determinant for effectual meaningful social change is well spelt out by Sir Allen Burns in the book *Colour Prejudice:*
> As colour is the most obvious manifestation of race, it has been made the criterion by which men are judged, irrespective of their social or educational attainments. The light-skinned races have come to despise all those of a darker colour, and the dark-skinned peoples will no longer accept without protest their inferior position . . .
> I know some critics will differ with this thesis. They hold that the crux of the issue is not so much a colour question but one between the haves and have-nots. Some will even argue that it is basically a class struggle. I believe that a classless society will be created more easily among Blacks. There must be higher values to which all Blacks aspire . . .
> Black consciousness can then be seen as a stage preceding any invasion, any abolition, of the ego by desire.[20]

Pityana granted that some of his critics would argue that the central problem related to class and class struggle. He neither examined nor refuted the position, but moved to the assertion of black moral superiority. They would 'more easily' create a classless society, and the class struggle was removed by a sleight of hand. Precisely what the last sentence of the quotation meant is not clear, but presumably it equates classlessness with some control of the ego and of desire. Socialism and communism were not mentioned, and the desirable political state was left vague. The first stage was black consciousness, and all else would follow.

It seemed, however, that not 'all Blacks' (Pityana's phrase) aspired to higher values. There was a black middle class, said Mafika Pascal Gwala, editor of the 1973 *Black Review*, and an exponent of black consciousness. These were the leaders of the Homelands governments, the members of the Coloured and the Indian Councils, and those who owed their position to 'the white designers of Separatism'.[21] For Gwala, as for Biko, such people were not Blacks: they were 'non-whites'.

The rot, it seems, had gone further. There were black (or 'non-white') journalists who 'concentrate on coating the pill to make white lies more palatable'.[22] There were also many others:

> The purpose here today is to see to it that the intellectual decides whether to uphold superior status or is ready to phase himself out of the role of being carrier of a white official culture.
> It is here that we have to begin to accept and promote the truth that we cannot talk of Black Solidarity outside of class identity. Because as our black brother has put it, it is only the elite that are plagued by the problem of identity. Not the mass of the Black people. The common Black people have had no reason to worry about blackness. They never in the first place found themselves outside or above their context of being black. But the student, the intellectual, the theologian, are the ones who have to go through foreign education and assimilate foreign ethical values. Later when weighed against the reality of the black situation, this alienates them from their people.[23]

Mafika Gwala, although he spoke of Blacks, had Africans in mind. The majority of Coloureds and Indians had not found a basis for identification with Africans, and their intellectuals were still debating, painfully, about their identity as Blacks. It is not altogether certain whether Gwala's assertion about the common Black (African) people was correct. Many (or even most) were not plagued with the problem of identity, but not because they had achieved a class identity. They were black, and they knew they were black. They knew it because they were placed in that context in South Africa. Writing about this, Ezekiel (Zik) Mphahlele said:

> Having been born into the dark side of a segregated existence, I've never been encouraged to think anything except that I'm black. For three hundred years this has been drummed into our heads; first by cannon fire, then by acts of parliament, proclamations and regulations. Our minds have been so conditioned that a number of our responses have become reflex: everywhere, instinctively, we look around for separate public lavatories,

299

train coaches, platforms, hospitals. Instinctively, we make sure that
wherever we are, we have permits in the form of passes to stay in a
particular location, to work or look for work in a particular town, to leave
a particular farm, to leave a white man's farm, to look for work in a
district. . .[24]

The question of 'identity', where it was taken up, was the unique problem
of one section of the petty bourgeoisie, who sought a political role for themselves. Gwala was correct in stating that this group of petty bourgeois
intellectuals had to take a class position in solving the problem. They had in
part absorbed particular ethical values, and these were not necessarily foreign.
They were the all-pervading values of capitalism, and the students were
educated 'to fit into an environment, not change it', as Mphahlele said of his
own school experience.

Having seen, even if only partially, that the problem was one of class
identity, it was incumbent on Gwala to spell out the consequences, and
explain how 'class identity' fitted with 'black identity'. Blacks who did not
agree with Gwala had to be seen, not as 'non-whites', but as class enemies.
This would also require that those Whites who were not class enemies
(because they were prepared, as Gwala demanded, to forego their petty
bourgeois interests) be accepted as allies.

It was possible that Gwala, in his black consciousness role, was not really
talking about class identity, and was not prepared to think in terms of class
struggles. He certainly did not discuss the political situation in South Africa
in class terms, and that lessened the impact of what could have been a significant statement for those who sought a better understanding of the nature of
exploitation in South Africa.

The failure of Gwala to clarify the issue of class left the Black Consciousness Movement in limbo. There did not seem to be any consistency in the
way this problem was tackled in the few years left to SASO/BPC before they
were banned in October 1977. There were a few who sought to extend the
concept of class. Diliza Mji, President of SASO in 1977, stated in his address
to the annual congress that 'class interests will always affect the political outlook of people', and that students had to abandon 'middle-class interests' and
the corrupting influence of luxuries in the lives of African professional men.[25]

But Mji, and even Gwala, proved to be exceptions. The more common
view on the subject was to deny that class had any significance for the Blacks,
and clothe black aspirations in some mystique of black exclusiveness. Hlaku
Rachidi, President of BPC, made a statement at a press conference, following
the death of Biko. During the interview he expounded on the nature of black
consciousness.

Black consciousness is not a foreign concept. That is, it is neither
capitalism, communism nor western socialism — hence the ease with which
the people understand, accept and adapt themselves to it . . .
   Black Consciousness abhors and detests both capitalism and

communism with equal contempt. They are both foreign, imperialistic and bent on alienating the black man in his country of origin. They are both oppressive, one way or another.

Black Consciousness is founded on the conviction of blacks being an entity with a history and legacy of standards, political, social and economic; that the black man has an innate ability and capacity to learn, assimilate and adopt that which is good without alienating himself.[26]

There were, for Blacks (suitably defined to exclude 'non-whites' presumably), no class divisions and no class struggles. They aspired to a system they called black communalism, and would opt out of this wicked world of capitalism, communism, and Western socialism. The ideal system, adopted by the BPC as their programme, was to be: '. . . a modified version of the traditional African economic life-style which is being geared to meet the demands of a highly industrialised and modern economy.'[27] That is (as the programme explained), a highly centralised state, with nationalised transport, banks and industries; a state controlled trade union movement; and a private capitalist sector engaged in agriculture, commerce and industry.

The Black Consciousness Movement and Black Business

The BPC economic blueprint, which envisaged the setting up of a corporate state economy, looked to the future. It could only hope to achieve this end (if the black population accepted this as part of its aspirations), after the country had been 'liberated'. Until that was achieved, they had to shape their economic stake inside existing capitalist institutions. Pityane addressed himself to this problem and urged that they 'see themselves as a functional monolithic structure'. He urged: 'Work towards a self-sufficient political, social and economic unit. . . for a meaningful change to the *status quo*'.[28]

This was confusion of the very worst sort. There was no possibility of building any position of non-dependence in South Africa, and no way in which black workers, farm labourers, or people in the Reserves could build 'self-sufficient' economic units. What the independent political and social units were supposed to be was never disclosed. Nor was it clear how these self-sufficient units, or the sense of pride attained, was going to produce 'meaningful change to the *status quo*'.

S.M. Motsuenyane, President of the National African Federated Chamber of Commerce, also looked to black consciousness — but his aim was to build up African entrepreneurship. His goal was not economic self-sufficiency, but rather a 'shared-economy of partnership' with the Whites. He wanted to give the Blacks 'a real stake in the country's economy', and the right to contribute 'to the overall economic growth of the country'.[29] He spoke in the now familiar language of SASO/BPC: of a 'new intellectual and psychological climate', of 'the flowering of a new African personality', and of the 'overcoming of a pervasive sense of subjection, humiliation and inferiority. . .'

He continued:

> All of us ought therefore to be thankful for the new day of Black Consciousness . . . We have every reason to feel proud of what the Lord intended us to be: Human beings, no less than other men! We owe no man an apology for being created Black. Let us therefore echo the slogan of the times: Black is Beautiful![30]

Mr. Motsuenyane demanded higher wages for workers and their right to organise trade unions. But this was not entirely disinterested; he also protested against the fact that 70 to 80 per cent of black buying power was 'dissipated in the white area'. He wanted a higher African income, and he wanted the money to come his way. Hence he argued that:

> Something very urgent should be done to curb the steady flow of Black profits and investments into White areas. It is the Black people themselves who must take steps towards solving this problem. A project such as the Black Bank will help to keep our funds circulating among the African people themselves. The Black Bank alone is not enough. We are called upon to create as rapidly as we can our own Supermarkets, Chain Stores, Wholesalers, Factories, Insurance Companies and Building Societies etc. The Central Government should constantly be prevailed upon to open opportunities for Black Development even in the urban locations.[31]

This was followed by a seven point programme to achieve economic advancement. The sense of inferiority had to be overcome, African business ventures started, the Homelands developed agriculturally and industrially, more formal and technical education provided and black trade unions formed.

Steve Biko, who was always on the radical wing of the Black Consciousness Movement, also thought along these lines. He condemned 'capitalistic exploitative tendencies' and called for business co-operatives, but he wanted money spent by Blacks to stay within the community: 'We should think along such lines as the "buy black" campaign once suggested in Johannesburg and establish our own banks for the benefit of the community.'[32]

The African Bank, so desired by supporters of the Black Consciousness Movement was set up in November 1975. One year later it had branches in BophutaTswana, KwaZulu, Transkei and in Soweto. It had over 2,000 individual customers, and was able to provide personal loans and finance hire purchase transactions.[33] But the scope of its business was restricted by shortage of funds, and in the first six months of 1976 it was able to provide only five loans and handle an average of 25 hire purchase agreements per month. Even if its capital had been expanded ten-fold it is hard to see how this would have made any difference to the position of the country's black population. The BCP, in setting up small business enterprises in the Western Cape and elsewhere, did not raise their finances from this bank. Instead, they turned to the giant mining and finance group, the Anglo-American Corporation, for grants to fund some of their projects.

When eventually, in October 1977, the black consciousness groups were banned and their finances confiscated, the clinics and the businesses operated by the BCP were taken over by the government. These included several small manufacturing concerns, a trust fund to help former political prisoners re-establish themselves economically, and several small businesses, including a boutique in the Western Cape. The businesses were not run as co-operatives, but were directed by leading members of the BCP who received directors' salaries.[34]

The BCP had, by that time, spawned a considerable bureaucracy and a group of men and women who had a stake in the businesses that had been set up. The banning of their organisation ended their jobs, their salaries, and probably their business careers. Many were also detained and their futures jeopardised. As victims of state repression they earned widespread sympathy — but many had lost all contact with the people they had set out to 'uplift'. As a student critic said:

> The extent of the funds flowing into the organisations (which had proliferated) generated a bureaucracy, and a dependence. The ominous feature of organisations which have easy access to funds is that they lose contact with the people on whom they used to depend for legitimacy and material and moral support.[35]

The Petty Bourgeoisie: Urban and Rural

There was little doubt about the hostility shown by members of the black consciousness groups towards the leaders of the Homelands' governments. They were condemned again and again, and the whole policy of separatism was rejected unconditionally. The men who worked the system were condemned as 'parasites', 'collaborationists', and 'middle class separatists'.[36]

These appellations were in most cases apposite and, in the four volumes of *Black Review* that were published, references were repeatedly made to the venality of Homelands government leaders, to their ill-gotten riches, to their class snobbery, their three-star hotels and beauty salons, and so on.[37]

Most Homelands leaders did not bother to reply. They had the power they wanted, and they were prepared to lock up their opponents. Buthelezi of KwaZulu felt differently. He had his own political ambitions which extended beyond the borders of his fragmented reserve area, and was not prepared to concede the field to SASO or BPC. In fact he had contempt for these young persons and maintained that *he* was the proponent of black consciousness. He also sought to describe his black opponents in class terms and sought to use the writings of Marx, Engels and Lenin (as he understood them) to condemn the young intellectuals as petty bourgeois.

The occasion was, ironically, the opening ceremony of the Akulu Chemicals plant at Isithebe in KwaZulu. The finances had been supplied by

West Germany's Akzo Chemie, and Buthelezi justified the presence of foreign investments and assured his visitors that their investment would be safeguarded. He then chided his critics by citing Lenin. The issue that Buthelezi chose, was the attack on people who were against the spread of capitalist industries in the colonies, which alone would create the conditions for the oppressed people to struggle for their emancipation. Only small businessmen, and intellectuals without roots in the society, said Buthelezi, could oppose what Engels had called 'the revolutionising of all traditional relations by industry'.

Buthelezi quoted this, claiming that it was taken from a paper presented recently by a black journalist, and that he was offering it without comment.[38]

Over R3 million was invested in the new factory, and after two years of operation the total black work force employed in the plant would be 45. The total profits expected and the share thereof accruing to the KwaZulu government were not supplied. The government bureaucracy would expand, but the creation of the revolutionising proletariat — all 45 of them — would not make much impact on the local society.

Yet, leaving Buthelezi's sophistry aside, the description of the members of the Black Consciousness Movement as petty bourgeois was not entirely incorrect, not because they opposed foreign investments, but because many of them aspired to the positions in commerce and industry that they condemned in the Homelands leaders. Buthelezi (and to a greater extent Matanzima and other leaders) operated on a scale that the urban youth could never emulate. To a large extent, Buthelezi and company used their government appointed roles to enrich themselves. The BCP directors operated on a much smaller scale, and faced the danger of government expropriation. But their aspirations were not dissimilar. Under other conditions, they would compete, as did their peers in independent black African states, for control of the limited resources open to them. In South Africa, they competed from different positions and different geographic locations. The leaders of the Reserves used the apartheid structures to enrich themselves. The rural petty bourgeoisie used (white) state patronage; the urban petty bourgeoisie, under constant threat of removal to the Reserves, had to oppose the state and its controls.

From everything said by Buthelezi and his associates, the leaders of Inkatha saw themselves as leaders of a future 'internal settlement'. They wanted a peaceful handover to majority rule, with themselves as the rulers. But they also knew that, if the apartheid policy was made to work, their position in KwaZulu was assured. Either way, as they saw it, they would win.

The urban opposition, on the other hand, were totally opposed to the Homelands policy. Politically it was anathema. But economically it was also unacceptable, and their own futures were bound up with the fate of a unified larger South Africa.

In making such sweeping generalisations we are doing an injustice to many young men and women, who would be prepared to surrender their petty bourgeois status and work for a revolutionary transformation of the country.

The events of 1976-77 were a clear indication of the seriousness with which the youth, both urban and rural, were prepared to struggle. When eventually politics moved out of the realm of talk, and the struggle against apartheid was taken into the streets, Buthelezi and the other Reserve leaders stood up as the protectors of private property and of the *status quo*. Many of the more vocal Black Consciousness spokesmen retired into the background, but some found a place amongst the militant crowd: the tragedy at that stage was that the ideology they had espoused offered them no guidelines in the struggle they had spoken about for so long.

When the black consciousness organisations were banned, Inkatha remained intact. More than that, the moderate Committee of Ten obtained support from the Soweto branch of Inkatha, and it was also Inkatha's rejection of the elections to the Urban Bantu Council that allowed the boycott to go forward with such widespread support. Although the Homelands policy was still largely rejected, the failure in the past to discuss Buthelezi's political opportunism allowed his organisation to continue its career unimpeded. All the available literature, however, indicates that Buthelezi (with all his faults) would have been acceptable to the overwhelming majority of SASO and BPC, if only he had refused to accept office in the KwaZulu ministry.

The extent of co-operation between leading members of Inkatha and members of the Black Consciousness Movement has not always been clear. It would be incorrect, however, to believe that the organisations had no overlap of membership. Dr. Nyembezi, Inkatha's leading spokesman in Soweto, and H. Bhengu, also of Inkatha, were both members of the board of directors of the Black Community Programmes in 1977.[39] Since 1975, the BCP had been by far the most active body inside the Black Consciousness Movement, and was responsible for issuing *Black Review*, organised the Movement's clinic, the co-operatives and the trust fund for former political prisoners. Steve Biko and many prominent personalities in the black organisations were employed by BCP in one or other of their projects — that is, until they were banned or incarcerated. The appearance of Inkatha members on the Board of Directors of this key organisation made nonsense of the declaration that members of the Black Consciousness Movement would not work with collaborationist organisations, or their members.

The issue went far beyond 'collaboration' and working in government created institutions, and SASO/BPC members never seemed to understand that Buthelezi and his movement represented the newly emergent petty bourgeoisie in the Reserves. Buthelezi was not merely a man who worked in an apartheid body, but a man determined to protect the interests of his class. To claim that he could be supported if only he resigned from the KwaZulu government indicated that the Black Consciousness Movement had failed to understand the basic dynamic behind the Inkatha movement. This failure was no academic error, and in 1977 it was Buthelezi who was left with an impregnable base in Natal, with massive workers' support, a clean sweep in the KwaZulu election, and increasing support in the urban townships.

In order to undermine, if not oust him, it was necessary to go beyond the use of epithets. Describing the Bantustan leaders as 'middle class' was insufficient. Their place in the context of capitalism and of capitalist state relationships had to be explained. This the members of SASO/BPC/BCP were not prepared to do because that would have required an interpretation of South African politics in class terms, and not in terms of ethnicity, race, or colour.

That alone might have led some of the Black Consciousness Movement leaders to a new understanding of the nature of South Africa, and allowed them to avoid the confusion which only promoted the fortunes of Buthelezi. In the process they would, in the words of Cabral, have committed 'class suicide', and taken a clear class stand with the proletariat against discrimination and exploitation. This would not have appreciably affected the outcome of the Revolt, but it would have given them a new base to prepare for the struggle which must come.

References

1. W.G.E. Wolfson, *op.cit.*, p.28.
2. There is little information on this bus boycott. It started on 26 June 1977 and continued for over 3 weeks. See *SANA*, July 1977/4.
3. T. Motapanyane, *op.cit.*, p.51.
4. R. Nengwekhulu, *op.cit.*
5. Leon Trotsky, (1932), *The Russian Revolution*, (Gollancz), Preface.
6. *Loc.cit.*
7. Drake Koka, (1977), 'On black consciousness and black solidarity' (mimeo).
8. *Ibid.*
9. *Ibid.*
10. Personal communication from a leading delegate to the Black Renaissance Convention.
11. D. Woods, *op.cit.*, p.144.
12. *Ibid.*, pp.94-5.
13. *Ibid.*, p.144.
14. Frank Talk, (S. Biko), 'I write what I like: Fear – an important determinant in South African politics', reprinted in IEUF, *The New Terrorists, op.cit.*
15. *Black Review*, 1975-76, p.100.
16. Interview with the *World*, 6 July 1977.
17. Excerpt from 'Drum', reprinted in IUEF, *The New Terrorists op.cit.*, pp.34-47. Mtuli Shezi, vice-president of the BPC, was killed by whites who threw him in front of an on-coming train. For details, see *Black Review*, 1972, p.14.
18. N. Pityana, 'Power and social change in South Africa', *op.cit.*, p.174.
19. Irving Howe, 'New Styles in "Leftism" ', printed in *Dissent*, Summer 1965. Reprinted in Paul Jacob and Saul Landau, (1967), *The New*

Radicals, (Penguin), p.283.
20. N. Pityana, *op.cit.*, pp.180-1.
21. Mafika Pascal Gwala, (1976), 'Towards the practical manifestation of black consciousness', in T. Thoahlane, *op.cit.*, p.28.
22. *Ibid.*, p.31.
23. *Loc.cit.*
24. Ezekiel Mphahlele, (1962), *The African Image*, (Faber), p.68.
25. Presidential Address to 8th General Council of Students, printed in *SASO Bulletin*, Vol. 1, No. 1, June 1977.
26. Press conference, reported in the *World*, 16 September 1977.
27. Adopted at the Conference, meeting on 30-31 May 1976, and printed in *Pro Veritate*, June 1976. A slightly abbreviated version in *Black Review*, 1975-76 unfortunately contains errors.
28. N. Pityane, *op.cit.*, p.189.
29. 'Black consciousness and the economic position of the black man in South Africa', in *Black Renaissance, op.cit.*, p.51.
30. *Ibid.*, p.47.
31. *Ibid.*, p.51.
32. *Black Theology, op.cit.*, p.46. IDAMASA also played a central role in the talks that led to the establishment of the bank. See *Black Review, 1974-75*, p.137.
33. *SRRSA*, 1977, p.270.
34. See *Bulletin Two: a Journal of Student Critique*, (UCT, n.d.), p.19.
35. *Loc.cit.*
36. See, for example, M.P. Gwala, *op.cit.*, pp.28-9.
37. *Black Review*, 1975-76, pp.9-10, shows that the setting up of these hotels and beauty salons was part of deliberate government policy.
38. Address given at the opening of Akulu Chemicals (Pty) Ltd., 26 May 1977, (press handout).
39. See statement by G. Buthelezi, reported in *SRRSA*, 1977, p.37.

16. Black Consciousness in South African History

The Roots of Black Consciousness

Consciousness of being black, or at least of being different, has a history that stretches back through the centuries in Southern Africa. The existence, side by side, of conqueror and conquered, settler and native, master and man (or woman), slave owner and vassal, immediately introduces a knowledge of difference. The factor of colour only helps to stress the separation between interloper and victim. But the consciousness of being black (or brown, or yellow) was not the same as black consciousness. The first marked an obvious physiological difference, while the second introduced connotations of social or political awareness.

There would be little purpose in attempting to list those occasions on which 'consciousness' was seen to be raised. Any movement inside a community, ranging from the rallying of a tribe behind traditional institutions, through to the mobilisation of a large section of the population in a political organisation would have to be included. And the significance that each such move had for the community on a local or national plane would depend as much on conditions outside the will of the persons concerned, as on the effect of the organisations on their communities at the time.

Even a rough classification presents some difficulties. There were moves within tribes that aimed at restoring or replacing a chief; at retaining land or expanding land resources; at uniting the tribe or splitting it. There were moves to found local (and sectional) organisations to defend the interests of communities small and large: organisations of the Indian people by Mahatma Gandhi, or of the Coloured people by Dr. Abdurahman, and of the African people, in the Reserves, in the Provinces, and then nationally.

The organisations formed were not all ostensibly political, although most had political implications. There were the separatist churches, starting in the Cape in 1884, and there were industrial organisations commencing with the Industrial and Commercial Workers Union of Africa (ICU) in 1919 in Cape Town, and spreading to the four Provinces by 1923. There were also township groups which emerged to fight a particular regulation — involving part of or, at times, the entire local population. In many cases our knowledge of these bodies is shadowy, and it is not always possible even to trace the smaller groups that were merged together when such activity was conceived and planned.

And what is conceived so dimly in the urban townships has often been completely overlooked in the rural areas. The many revolts in the rural hinterland are only now being rediscovered by fresh research work. Only when much more is known will we be able to chart the ups and downs of consciousness in the larger communities of the country.

It was not only the revolts that marked upsurges of awareness. They were only those manifestations of stirrings most obvious in an area and most easily observed by the historian. The local separatist church, the chiliastic leader, the defiant chief, the stirrings against agricultural innovation leading to the overturning of dip-tanks, or the pulling up of survey pegs and the tearing down of fences all represent some awareness that, by being expressed, marked a change in the community.

The way by which these changes are subsequently described is of little interest to the people involved at the time. Their slogans and banners do not proclaim 'We are aware', but are far more prosaic and to the point. It is the prerogative of the social scientist to say, usually at a later date, that there was an 'awareness' or a growth of consciousness, and to add, dependent on his or her viewpoint, that it represented a growth of national, racial, colour, or class consciousness.

There are occasions, however, when the initiators of a new movement themselves use the language of 'awareness', and claim that a new 'identity' is being established. Members of Marxist movements debate the growth of 'trade union' or of proletarian and class consciousness, which they counterpose to petty bourgeois or bourgeois interests. Members of nationalist movements speak of national awareness or of identity — and deny the existence of class divisions inside an oppressed people. To ask whether this is or is not 'false consciousness', is to miss the point. What have to be sought are the class interests of the men and women who use these concepts, and these can usually be located by examining the activities they engage in, and charting the course of their organisational activities.

The most explicit statements on black awareness, from inside the national liberation movement, were those made by members of the Congress Youth League in the mid-1940's.[1] The CYL had had a long gestation. Groups of young African intellectuals, some of them graduates of the Anglican secondary school, St. Peters, in Johannesburg, others graduates of or expelled from Lovedale, Healdtown, Adams, Fort Hare and so on, had formed small ephemeral organisations in the late 1930's. Some of the individuals involved reappeared in the CYL when it was launched in 1944, were active in the revived ANC during the 1950's; and a few were even to reappear in the 1970's when the BPC was launched. William Nkomo, Menassah Moerane and Jordan Ngubane were all involved in associations of African youth prior to the second world war. During the early years of the war they were joined by a new generation of intellectuals — Oliver Tambo, Walter Sisulu (one of the few who had not been able to enter secondary school), Nelson Mandela, and the two men who were to lay their stamp on the future Youth League, Anton Muziwakhe Lembede and A.P. Mda.

The impetus for change in political thinking came from conditions inside South Africa in that period. When South Africa entered the war in September 1939, all African organisations were in a state of disarray. The ANC in each Province consisted of several factions who disputed amongst themselves and participated in little public activity. The All African Convention was all but dead, after its short spate of meetings and lobbying against the Native Bills of 1936-37. The African trade unions were practically defunct and were being slowly restarted in 1937-39, and the remnants of the old left movement were gathered together in the Non-European United Front. This was an anti-segregation and anti-war alliance, led by Dr. Dadoo and others, who were either members of or sympathetic to the Communist Party.

Both the ANC and the AAC supported the government in its war effort, and did not seem to be able to offer any effective opposition to the continued exploitation and discrimination of the black people. However, major structural changes brought about by an expanding economy, and the shortage of skilled and even unskilled workers, was accompanied by the turmoil in the towns and in the countryside, which led to new tensions in the country. The peasants in the Northern Transvaal were near revolt, and rumours of clashes in the Zoutpansberg filled Johannesburg. African trade unions, mainly in Johannesburg and along the Witwatersrand spread rapidly, and were involved in the longest and most sustained series of strikes that the country had ever known. Shops, municipal services, factories, and even power stations were affected. In some instances workers gained substantial advances: in others they were shot down, or the strike was broken by police action or, in the case of the power stations, by the use of coloured troops.

There were also protests in the townships, and longstanding discontent with the bus transport gave rise to the first of the great bus boycotts at Alexandra in 1943, and again in 1944. A new leadership appeared from amongst a number of men who were directly or indirectly associated with Hyman Basner, former Communist, and Native Representative in the Senate for the Transvaal and Orange Free State. These individuals were grouped together largely in the newly launched African Democratic Party, and it was this group, and not the ANC, which played the active role in Alexandra. In 1944, Sofosonko ('We shall all die') Mpanza, a member of the Orlando Advisory Board, led thousands of tenants from their overcrowded lodgings and started the first of the many shanty towns that were to galvanise the City Council into building new houses for the township. Once again, it was Basner and the ADP which gave this movement active support, while the ANC remained quiescent and stood aloof.

The young intellectuals, some already seeking a new leadership, gathered together in 1943 and resolved to form a pressure group that would reactivate the Congress. They were not homogeneous, and many different ideologies existed in the ranks of those who assembled together in the hopes of forming their own organisation inside the ANC. Lembede, who was to become their most prominent ideologue and spokesman was a passionate nationalist. He contributed the theory of 'Africanism', which included concepts that were later to be called African socialism throughout the continent; black exclusiveness and a call for self-awareness, very little different from the later black consciousness of the 1970's; and a virulent anti-Communism. A.P. Mda and others, mainly from the Eastern Cape, brought a passionate belief in the boycott tactic which they had learnt largely from the All African Convention and its main protagonist, I.B. Tabata. Mda also believed in the unity of *all* Blacks which Lembede dismissed as unattainable. These ideas were reinforced, supplemented, or at a later date amended, but they contained within them that core of ideas which set the black movements on the road to exclusive nationalism. The one major split that occurred inside the ANC (in 1959) revolved, programmatically, around the interpretation that should be given to the meaning of Lembede's 'Africanism', and the men who led the disaffected faction had all been active members of the CYL in the 1940's.

First the young men had to persuade Dr. Xuma, President of the ANC, that a youth section of the organisation should be established and, despite some misgivings on his part, it seems that he saw a Youth League as an invaluable lever against the new ADP, and in this he was correct. The ADP was never able to rally the youth to its side partly because of opposition from the Youth League, but also because their politics proved to be so inept. A formal resolution at the conference of the ANC in December 1943 led to the establishment of the CYL, and also of a Woman's Section which only flourished during the 1950's.

The youth group was always a small body which during the period 1943-49 contented itself with propagating its ideas and drawing up manifestos and declarations. But it eventually in 1949 secured the passage of a Programme of Action through the ANC annual conference. In the process the CYL were able to ensure that Dr. Xuma resigned from the presidency, and that a more pliant man took his place, so opening the parent body to their increased influence.

Before this happened, the CYL won a notable victory at Fort Hare by becoming the premier organisation there and removing the AAC as a potential threat to their political control. This they did by winning to their side a number of young men who were later to become part of the national leadership of the ANC. They recruited Godfrey Pitje, Robert Mangaliso Sobukwe (the first President of the PAC after the 1959 split), Joe Matthews (an erstwhile anti-Communist who was later to become a member of the Central Committee of the SACP, before being later expelled when he declared his support for Transkeian independence), Duma Nokwe, and others.

The Fort Hare section of the Youth League was always more active than others, partly because they were involved in student struggles, but also because their close association with the nurses of Lovedale involved them directly in the struggles of these trainees. Robert Sobukwe, presenting the address on behalf of the graduating class in October 1949, spoke about the struggle of the nurses, invoked the image (or was it spectre?) of Marcus

Garvey, and declared that freedom was on the way. His speech, then, was as dramatic as was that of O.R. Tiro nearly a quarter of a century later at Turfloop.

Despite the eclecticism in his ideas, the tenor of his speech was radical, and upset the authorities. He was not expelled because he had completed his course, but there can be little doubt that what he said did not assist him when he sought employment. For many years he taught in small provincial schools before he was appointed 'language assistant' (that is, second-class lecturer) at the University of the Witwatersrand. The address was long, but the spirit of his words can be demonstrated in some extracts:

> The trouble at the Hospital . . . should be viewed as part of a broad struggle and not as an isolated incident. I said last year that we should not fear victimisation . . . And we must pay the price. The Nurses have paid the price. I am truly grieved that the careers of so many of our women should have been ruined in this fashion. But the price of freedom is *blood, toil and tears*. . . .
>
> Education to us means service to Africa. In whatever branch of learning you are, you are there for Africa. You have a mission; we all have a mission. A nation to build we have, a God to glorify, a contribution clear to make towards the blessing of mankind . . . if you hear us talk of practical experience as a modifier of man's views, denounce us as traitors of Africa. . . .
>
> I wish to make it clear again that we are anti-nobody. We are pro-Africa. We breathe, we dream, we live Africa; because Africa and humanity are inseparable. . . . The future of the world lies with the oppressed and the Africans are the most oppressed people on earth. . . . We have been accused of blood-thirstiness because we preach 'non-collaboration'. I wish to state here tonight that that is the only course open to us. History has taught us that a group in power has never voluntarily relinquished its position. It has always been forced to do so.[2]

The Fort Hare branch, however, was exceptional in taking up the nurses' struggle. Except for isolated individuals who happened to be active members of a trade union, or the teachers organisation in the Transvaal, few Youth Leaguers became involved in practical organisational work or in the day-to-day struggles before 1950. They played little noticeable part in the organisation of the strike wave, the bus boycotts, the shanty towns, or the teachers' demonstrations for higher wages in the Transvaal. They seldom included reference to these events in their leaflets, manifestos, or articles. Only in August 1946, when some 70,000 workers on the Witwatersrand gold mines came out on strike in support of their claim for higher wages, and were brutally suppressed, did the CYL respond to the workers' struggle. They called for support for the strike — but they avoided mention of the African Mine Workers Union, led by Communists who were anathema to them.[3]

The general lack of activity had not gone by without comment. Jordan Ngubane, a member of the inner circle of the CYL at the time, and editor of the *Inkundla ya Bantu*, was scathing. He called on members of the CYL to

> . . . come down from the arid academic heights and settle down to
> practical work which, alone, will free the African. Let others do all the
> preaching and speaking, but the League must act; lead peaceful demon-
> strations, take part in protests against oppression, educate the people on
> how to fight oppression.
>
> [The community wants young people] whose only passion is to do
> more solid work and talk less; organise workers in factories; volunteer for
> night school work; preach the gospel of liberation through Congress on
> the farms, on the mines and in the locations.[4]

The same words could have been employed in the 1970's against the
members of SASO/BPC. The strikes, the bus boycotts, and the stirrings in the
townships helped generate the CYL, as it did the Black Consciousness Movement in the 1970's. But the youth never understood this. While political
unrest gave rise to the CYL and later to SASO/BPC, these groups, blinded by
their rhetoric, were to believe that they had themselves rekindled their people
through their own writings and speeches.

The Message of the CYL Leadership

Anton Lembede soon became the recognised spokesman of the CYL, and his
articles exerted considerable influence on this small group of intellectuals of
the time. In February 1945, a small mimeographed journal issued by the
short-lived African Youth League, *Inyaniso*, published an article by Lembede
entitled 'Some basic principles of African nationalism'. The six principles consisted of:

> *The philosophical basis:* [after rejecting communism and nazism] Man
> is body, mind and spirit with needs, desires and aspirations in all three
> elements of his nature. History is a record of humanity's striving for com-
> plete self-realisation.
> *The scientific basis:* Charles Darwin . . . pointed out the profound
> significance of the law of variation in Nature. . . . Each nation has thus its
> own peculiar character or make-up. Hence each nation has its own peculiar
> contribution to make towards the general progress and welfare of
> mankind. In other words each nation has its own divine mission. . . .
> *Historical basis:* We . . . [must] commemorate the glorious achieve-
> ments of our great heroes of the past, e.g. Shaka, Moshoeshoe, Hintsa,
> Sikhukhuni, Khama, Sobuza, and Mosilikazi, etc. . . .
> *Economic Basis:* The fundamental structure of Bantu society is
> socialistic. There was for instance no individual ownership of land in
> ancient Bantu society. . . . Land belonged virtually to the whole tribe and
> nominally to the King or Chief. Socialism then is our valuable legacy from
> our ancestors. Our task is to develop this socialism by the infusion of new

and modern socialistic ideas.

Democratic basis: In ancient Bantu Society, the worth of a man was not assessed by wealth. Any man could rise to any position. . . . In our Councils [or] Khotlas any citizen could take part in discussions, and if a man was being tried, anyone could ask questions and cross-examine the accused. The main point is the assessment of human value by moral and spiritual qualities. There is a legacy to be preserved and developed and highly treasured in our hearts.

Ethical basis: The ethical system of our forefathers was based on ancestor worship. People did certain things or refrained from doing certain things for fear of punishment by the spirits of dead ancestors. We must retain and preserve the belief in the immortality of our ancestors but our ethical system today has to be based on Christian morals since there is nothing better anywhere in the world. Morality is the soul of society. Decay and decline of morals brings about the decay and decline of society — so History teaches. It is only African nationalism or Africanism that can save the African people. Long live African Nationalism![5]

This piece, written in 1945, marked Lembede as being in advance of other nationalist thinkers in Africa. His ideas on cultural awakening, African communalism and African socialism, although not new, were only to be taken up a decade later by Senghor of Senegal, Nkrumah of Ghana and other leaders of African nationalist movements. Lembede was, in fact, following in the footsteps of the great nationalist leaders of the world. The myths he helped weave were in the tradition of the dreams spun by nationalists everywhere, and his roseate view of the past flowed from the deep feelings that a renascent African people would inherit the country.

Any criticism of Lembede, and of those who followed him later, must flow from an appraisal of the meaning of nationalism in South Africa, and that in turn would depend on the interpretation of the social and economic structures in the country. Lembede's views on this were made explicit in an article on the policy of the CYL which appeared in *Inkundla ya Bantu* in May 1946. He started his contribution with a stirring call to the African people:

The history of modern times is the history of nationalism. Nationalism has been tested in the people's struggles and the fires of battle and found to be the only effective weapon, the only antidote against foreign rule and modern imperialism . . .

All over the world nationalism is rising in revolt against foreign domination, conquest and oppression in India, in Indonesia, in Egypt, in Persia and several other countries . . .

A new spirit of African nationalism, or Africanism, is pervading through and stirring the African society. A young virile nation is in the process of birth and emergence. . . .[6]

There followed a list of seven 'cardinal principles' on which Lembede claimed African nationalism was based:

1. *Africa is a blackman's country* . . . .
2. *Africans are one.* Out of the heterogeneous tribes, there must emerge a homogeneous nation. The basis of national unity is the nationalistic feeling of the Africans, the feeling of being Africans irrespective of tribal connection, social status, educational attainment or economic class. . . .
3. *The leaders of the Africans will come out of their own loins.* No foreigner can ever be a true and genuine leader of the African people because no foreigner can ever truly and genuinely interpret the African spirit which is unique and peculiar to Africans only. Some foreigners Asiatic or European who pose as African leaders must be categorically denounced and rejected. An African must lead Africans. Africans must honour, venerate and find inspiration from African heroes of the past: Shaka, [and so on] . . . .
4. *Co-operation between Africans and other Non-Europeans on common problems and issues may be highly desirable.* But this occasional co-operation can only take place between Africans as a single unit and other Non-European groups as separate units. Non-European unity is a fantastic dream which has no foundation in reality.
5. *The divine destiny of the African people is National Freedom.* Unless Africans achieve national freedom as early as possible they will be confronted with the impending doom and imminent catastrophe of extermination. [Lembede then listed disease, infant mortality, moral and physical degeneration, loss of self-confidence, inferiority complex, frustration, idolisation of white men, foreign leaders and ideologies, and juvenile delinquency as a result of industrial and educational colour bars.] Now the panacea for all these ills is National Freedom. . . .
6. *Africans must aim at balanced progress or advancement.* . . . Our forces as it were, must march forward in a co-ordinated manner and in all theatres of the war, socially, educationally, culturally, morally, economically, and politically. . . .
7. *After national freedom, then socialism.* Africans are naturally socialistic as illustrated in their social practices and customs. The achievement of national liberation will therefore herald or usher in a new era, the era of African socialism. Our immediate task, however, is not socialism, but national liberation.
Our motto: *Freedom in Our Life Time.*[7]

The plans of the CYL were outlined in innumerable statements and articles in *Inkundla ya Bantu*, and in two manifestos issued by the executive committee. Lembede, in particular, was also frequently attacked in the columns of the Communist Party organ, *Inkululeko*, for anti-Communist statements he made at conferences and things he had reportedly been involved in.

The Youth League was avowedly anti-Communist, and also opposed to white liberals. Lembede publicly 'denounced all whites who pretend to, or pose as leaders of, the African people' at a Congress meeting in Orlando,[8] and the following year he moved a resolution at the conference of the Transvaal ANC, calling for the expulsion of all Communists from the ANC.[9] He also advocated the absorption of African trade unions into the ANC, in that way freeing them from 'foreign ideology disseminated by demented political demagogues and their agents'.[10] Joe Matthews, then one of the Fort Hare leaders, condemned the Communists for misunderstanding the nature of South African society, and warned Africans 'to be careful of these foreign theories that come with cut-and-dried solutions to our problems'.[11]

The attack on the CP was already embodied in the 'Basic policy' of the CYL in 1948. Under the heading 'Vendors of Foreign Method', it was declared that:

> There are certain groups which seek to impose on our struggle cut-and-dried formulae, which so far from clarifying the issues of our struggle, only serve to obscure the fundamental fact that we are oppressed not as a class, but as a people, as a nation. Such wholesale importation of methods and tactics which might have succeeded in other countries, like Europe, where conditions were different, might harm the cause of our people's freedom. . . .[12]

The bitter fight against the CP and the left was closely associated with CYL economic policy. Lembede's contribution to this subject consisted of his reaffirmation of the value of the communal system of land holding, which he hoped would be updated by 'the infusion' of new ideas. The 1948 CYL Manifesto called for the redistribution of the land to 'all nationalities in proportion to their numbers', and the application of scientific methods to agriculture. They also declared themselves in favour of 'the reclamation of denuded areas' (in the Reserves), at the very time when the peasants, throughout the country, were engaged in battle against the government rehabilitation scheme.[13]

The Manifesto continued by calling for the full industrialisation of the country 'in order to raise the level of civilisation [*sic*] and the standard of living of the workers; the abolition of industrial colour bars; and the full right to trade union organisation. The CYL also pledged itself to 'encourage business, trading and commercial enterprise among Africans', and to encourage co-operative saving, trading, etc. The overall policy was stated to be the ending of race domination and exploitation; to give all men and women 'an equal opportunity to improve their lot'; and to 'ensure a just and equitable distribution of wealth among the people of all nationalities'.[14]

An editorial in *Inkundla*, written by Ngubane, took the economic argument further. He was furious at the attack by the left on black capitalists, and argued:

> . . . while our leftists work for their millenium, let the African use the weapon of oppression against oppression. The Indians are doing that today . . .
> And, on the other hand, let the average African realise that the businessman in his own community is his surest friend and champion of his liberation. Let every African, therefore, support stores run by Africans. By

so doing they could be bringing national liberation nearer. . . Your
child cannot become a manager in a white or Indian firm, but he can rise
to the top in an African establishment. As a good African, why not
support it then.[15]

Ngubane, writing in the same issue of *Inkundla* under the pseudonym
'Twana', returned to the theme. The African businessman, he said, had the
responsibility of making a success so that he could employ more Africans. He
also stated that if Africans won the franchise on the morrow, they 'would be
in a very unhappy position without economic power. Economic power is the
dynamo that drives the political machine.'[16]

Economics and the Poverty of CYL Policy

There were few, if any, African economists in the 1940's and, except for
Govan Mbeki, there was no African in the ranks of the ANC who addressed
himself to problems of economic development during the 1950's. The few
articles that did appear referred to African purchasing power, or to the
impoverishment of the Reserves, and there were appeals to Africans to use
their 'economic muscle' by buying from black traders. This was generally
associated with the further observation that no African businessman
humiliated his customers by calling them insulting names.[17]

Nevertheless, the programme of the CYL, and more particularly its 1948
Manifesto, contained sections on the economy of the country. There they
recognised, as indeed they had to, that there had been profound changes in
the country which had been introduced by capitalism. Whatever they thought
about the capitalist system (and in fact the membership of the CYL usually
condemned capitalism on the grounds that it was incompatible with the
socialism their forefathers had once lived by), they still wanted more industrialisation and more technology. They also wanted African businessmen and,
if possible, African co-operative ventures.

The economic section of the programme, however, did not necessarily
intermesh with other parts of the CYL demands, and at times it seems as if
economic demands were divorced from other sections of the programme.
Alternatively, the framers of the programmes could not square their
ambitions for African business enterprises with their desire to present
nationalism as a goal that was uninfluenced by problems of economic interpretation. They were so insistent on their standpoint that Africans were
'nationally oppressed' and that the 'dynamism to make a successful struggle is
the creed of African Nationalism' that they closed their eyes to economic
realities.

It is thus, perhaps, not surprising to find in the 1948 Manifesto an attack
on tribalism, coupled with the following statement on nationalism:

Some people mistakenly believe that African Nationalism is a mere tribalist outlook. They fail to apprehend the fact that nationalism is firstly a higher development of a process that was already in progress when the white man arrived, and secondly that it is a continuation of the struggle of our fore-fathers against foreign invasion.[18]

Continuities can be established in the history of every people, and in that respect the statement says nothing exceptional. Insisting, however, that this was a development of a process already in progress before the white man came, even if at a 'higher' stage, is patently absurd. Whatever process was at work (presumably at the time of the great dispersion, or 'Mfecane', in the 1820's and 1830's), it was violently disrupted by the appearance of the Whites in the hinterland of South Africa and in Natal (as they named it). African tribes were conquered or dispossessed of their land, and the people were forced into restricted areas which later became the Reserves. Those allowed to stay on the newly acquired white farms learnt how to bargain with the farmers in order to gain whatever concessions they could, but were ultimately allowed to stay only as long as their services were required.

When, in the wake of the discovery of diamonds and gold, railways were built, and finance capital poured into the country, the reserve system was put to new use. The African subsistence economy, already much altered by white control, was 'conserved' in order to induce the men to go out to work in the mines and the new factories. The older racism, associated with slavery and the indentured system of forced labour, was replaced by new ideologies ('segregation' or 'trusteeship') designed to control a highly exploited prole-tariat. The Reserves and tribalism proved to be invaluable to capital. The poverty of these overcrowded areas, together with the need for cash, forced the young men to emigrate to the farms and (when required) to the towns. The Reserves did not consist exclusively of labourers or potential labourers, but the entire system was necessary for the social reproduction of the labour-ing class, and the discriminatory practices were therefore extended to cover the entire population. There had been some recognition of the anomalies created by this system in the thirties and forties, when an increasing number of clerks, teachers and professional men, and even some urbanised workers were given exemption passes to free them from some of the more onerous controls. However, the regulations which permitted this were withdrawn later by the Nationalist Party, and all Africans were apparently equally discrimi-nated against.

The response of the African people to discrimination altered with time, with place, and with class interest, but the centrality of land in oppression was an overwhelming factor which helped define African demands. Land, labour, and colour were intimately associated and all Africans saw themselves as oppressed even when, favoured by traditional status or by modern education, they had found means of accommodation to the existing power structure.

Discriminatory practices were expanded to meet new economic, social and political needs. But the government always defined the measures in racial terms, and the reaction from Blacks was inevitably framed in the same terms. It would indeed have been remarkable if a new law, heavily loaded with racial implications, was attacked in terms other than race. Whether consciously, or otherwise, the government (or was it the employers?) chose to confuse the issue by couching regulations in colour rather than in class terms.

The men who emerged as leaders of the African people often had a clearer perception of their class interests than has been recognised. They preferred to couch their statements in terms of colour and race, but more often than not they used this to conceal their class interests. What they stated privately has not often been published, and it is only in a few instances that research has turned up evidence to show how clearly class forces were perceived. One instance is quoted in a recent paper: Sol Plaatje, a founding member of, and leading official in, the ANC, was approached in 1918 by the General Secretary of De Beers diamond company with the urgent appeal that he stop the African workers from joining their white colleagues in strike action. In reply, Plaatje reported:

> I had to attend the Native Congress at Bloemfontein to prevent the spread among our people of the Johannesburg Socialist propaganda. . . . The ten Transvaal delegates came to the Congress with a concord and determination that was perfectly astounding to our customary native demeanour at Conferences. They spoke almost in unison, in short sentences, nearly all of which began and ended with the word 'strike'.
> . . . It was only late in the second day that we succeeded in satisfying the delegates to report, on getting to their homes that the Socialist method of pitting up black against white will land our people in serious disaster. . . [19]

Plaatje's contempt for men who spoke 'in short sentences' went side-by-side with a hatred of 'black bolsheviks'. This was repeated in the decades that followed and set the tone of many of the declarations of the black nationalist leaders. The economic roots of 'segregation' (as of 'apartheid' later) were generally ignored, and capitalism (local or international) seldom appeared in the lexicons of black leaders. It needed local tensions and the impact of world affairs to make the nationalist leaders transcend their narrow parochial ideas. It also needed some remarkable men to sweep aside the cant, and describe the struggles in terms of class, of capital, and of imperialism. At such times the entire conceptual framework was overturned, and new insight gained into the nature of oppression. South African Blacks had just witnessed the white electorate return the Nationalist Party to power, when Robert Sobukwe spoke at the Fort Hare 'Completers' Social' in 1949. Taking stock, he surveyed what was happening throughout Asia and (more tentatively) Africa, and electrified his audience with the words:

> We are witnessing today the disintegration of old empires, and the integration of new communities. We are seeing today the germination of

the seeds of decay inherent in Capitalism: we discern the first shoots of
the tree of Socialism. . . . We are witness today of cold and calculated
brutality and bestiality, the desperate attempts of a dying generation to
stay in power. We see also a new spirit of determination, a quiet confidence, the determination of a people to be free whatever the cost. We are
seeing within our own day *the second rape of Africa*; a determined effort
by imperialist powers to dig their claws still deeper into the flesh of the
squirming victim. But this time the imperialism we see is not the naked
brutal mercantile imperialism of the 17th and 18th centuries. It is a more
subtle one — financial and economic imperialism under the guise of a
tempting slogan, 'the development of backward areas and peoples'. At the
same time we see the rise of uncompromising 'Nationalism' in India,
Malaya, Indonesia, Burma, and Africa! The old order is changing ushering
in a new order.[20]

Sobukwe was echoing the sentiments that came from sections of the left in
the post-war era. The popular (radical) press was filled with accounts of constitutional advance in India; battles with the Dutch in Indonesia; new fighting
in Indochina; and successes of the Red Army in China. Stories also appeared
of massacres in Madagascar, riots in Algeria, and constitutional changes in the
Gold Coast, and the United Nations Trusteeship Council offered hope that
changes would also be wrought in the one-time mandated territories in Africa.
The anti-imperialist struggles in the colonies were seen as harbingers of change
in South Africa and, even if the current enthusiasm for Nehru, Sukarno,
Azikiwe and other nationalist leaders was naive and uncritical, this speech of
Robert Sobukwe took him giant steps beyond the writings of Lembede or the
CYL Manifesto of 1948.

There was still no analysis of segregation or apartheid in class terms, but
the enemies of African nationalism were seen to be capitalism and imperialism. Sobukwe poured scorn on the possibility of 'development' in Africa and
Asia as long as finance capital and imperialism dominated the world, and he
placed the destruction of capitalism on the order of the day.

The question of co-operating with Whites was also raised by Sobukwe, and
again he spoke the language of the radical. He condemned the missionaries as
a group that had in the past only helped divide the Africans and so prevented
unity against oppression. He also condemned the Liberals for doing the same
in the twentieth century, and he claimed that the missionaries had returned to
this, their role, in the subjugation of the Africans.

This was a remarkable speech, given the relative backwardness of theories
of racism in South Africa in 1949, and it seems today to be a landmark
amongst statements made by Youth Leaguers. But it was soon forgotten, and
no attempts were made, outside the left, to deepen the understanding of
apartheid. Sobukwe never again spoke in these terms, and in July 1949 he
was a co-signatory of the CYL's proposed Programme of Action, (together
with Rev. James Calata, Godfrey Pitje, G.B. Secenywa, and A.P. Mda). In this
the economic demands were confined to a call for the establishment of peoples
co-operatives and the incorporation of African trade unions into the ANC.[21]

The Programme of Action, finally endorsed by the ANC in December 1949 was even more nebulous. It called for the 'establishment of commercial, industrial, transport and other enterprises in both urban and rural areas'; and for the consolidation of trade unions to improve the standard of living of the workers.[22]

The ANC and the Programme of Action

The entire activity of the CYL during 1948-49 seemed to have been directed towards the formulation of a Programme of Action. This they then meant to introduce into the parent body, and in the process transform the politics of the liberation movement. By June 1949 A.P. Mda, in an article entitled 'Congress at the Crossroads', laid down a 10 point programme for any person that sought office in Congress. This included the rejection of the colour bar and the demand for the full vote, the acceptance of African nationalism and of the boycott weapon against the organs of political segregation.[23]

One month before the Programme was submitted to the annual conference of the ANC, Joe Matthews wrote ecstatically about its significance:

> This marks a remarkable stage in the development of African Nationalism. It means that the Africans are no more seeking a mere increase of rights within the present framework. We are not asking for a greater share to be given to the African in the running of the country. We are without apologies going to fight for a South Africa which will be ruled by the majority, i.e. by the Africans. . . . Congress would [now] cease to be a pro-African organisation intent on improving the lot of the people. It would become at once a revolutionary movement for the liberation of the African nation.

Matthews then added that the Programme of Action had two important aspects: '(1) it recognises the necessity for consensus and planned nation-building; (2) it is a programme of struggle.' And later in the same article he opined that: 'The nation-building aspect of the Nationalist Programme is probably the most important.'[24]

On the one hand, there was struggle. On the other hand, there was to be some form of nation-building. That presumably referred to those items in the Programme which called for the 'establishment of national centres of education' and of a 'national academy of arts and science', and for the uniting of 'the cultural with the educational and national struggle'.[25]

Drafts had already been published in the press, and did not seem to warrant such extravagant language. Dr. Xuma, who was invited by the CYL to stand in the elections in December for the Presidency, refused to discuss the matter with young men whom he dismissed as upstarts. In a published statement he wrote that he was not prepared to accept any pre-conditions for the elections, and he also informed the Youth Leaguers who visited him (Sisulu,

Mandela and Tambo) that, while he could accept their ideas on Africa for the Africans and on African Nationalism, he would not endorse the boycott weapon, on the grounds that it was divisive.[26] Dr. Xuma also stated that the CYL had nonetheless declared that they would vote for him because they knew where he stood. In the event, they only nominated and supported Dr. Moroka (who until then had not been a member of the ANC) at the last moment. But, said Dr. Xuma, the CYL 'strangely enough, supported me fully for the executive. This suggested political immaturity, confused thinking, and insincerity'.[27]

Dr. Xuma never understood the changes that took place. His castigation of the youth was not far off the mark. Many of them were immature and confused, but the mood in the country had changed and a new leadership was called for. The issue was not the boycott, which was never put into effective operation, nor even the slogan of 'Africa for the Africans'. There was widespread discontent in the country, and some movement had to place itself at the head of the populace and voice their demands. Whether the revamped ANC did this successfully or not, does not concern us here. It was seen to do so in 1949 and it did excite the imagination of tens of thousands of people in some of the campaigns that were organised through the 1950's. This gave the Programme of Action a distinctive place in the annals of the liberation struggles, and it derived a significance from those struggles which transcend the brevity of the document which was adopted with such acclaim at the ANC Conference of December 1949.

The central message of the Programme of Action was contained in its opening lines:

> The fundamental principles of the programme of action of the African National Congress are inspired by the desire to achieve National freedom. By National freedom we mean freedom from White domination and the attainment of political independence. This implies the rejection of the concept of segregation, apartheid, trusteeship, or White leadership which are all in one way or another motivated by the idea of White domination or domination of the White over the Blacks. Like all other people the African people claim the right of self-determination.[28]

There were few attempts to expand on the meaning of this passage, and little attention was paid to the claim for 'self-determination' or 'political independence'. The basic slogans around which all campaigns were conducted were 'Freedom in our lifetime' and an end to white domination. There was, indeed, a basic inconsistency between a call for self-determination and the one political demand that appeared in the document, namely: 'The right to direct representation in all the governing bodies of the country – national, provincial, and local, and we resolve to work for the abolition of all differential institutions or bodies specially created for Africans. . . .'[29]

The Programme of Action did not even evoke much action, and it was only after much bickering about a May Day demonstration organised by the

Communists in 1950, that a one day stay-at-home was called for 26 June. An anti-red campaign was started inside the ANC which involved many leading members of the CYL, and the issue was confused by claiming that the CP was led by whites. The matter of white leadership, condemned in the 1949 document, was taken up by the hard core of the CYL who claimed the mantle of Lembede, and it eventually led to their splitting the Congress movement in 1958.

In 1952 the ANC, together with the South African Indian Congress, prepared the ground for a campaign to secure the repeal on unjust legislation, and the Defiance Campaign was launched on June 26. Some 8,000 Congress volunteers were arrested before new draconian legislation brought the action to an end. Other ANC campaigns, in 1953-54, against the removal of the African township Sophiatown in Johannesburg and against the implementation of Bantu Education, proved ineffectual against a well entrenched government. In these circumstances a suggestion that a Congress of the People be summoned, at which the demands of the men and women of South Africa could be expressed, was taken up enthusiastically, and was organised for 25-26 June 1955. At the gathering a Freedom Charter was formulated, and replaced the Programme of Action as the central Congress document.

The Freedom Charter, adopted by the ANC in 1956 at a special conference after a long and bitter debate with the faction which called itself Africanist, explored problems that were never mentioned in the Programme of Action. It declared that the land would be redivided; that the banks, mines and industries would be transferred to the people as a whole; and that every person would have equal rights in a new, liberated South Africa.

But, in the process, something had been lost. Freedom from white domination, the key to the Programme of Action, was replaced by the more nebulous 'South Africa belongs to all who live in it, black and white. . .'. The earlier claim of the 'right to self-determination' which is the centre-piece of a *nationalist* programme, was expunged, and in its place there appeared the 'right of all the peoples of Africa to independence and self-government shall be recognised'. The Freedom Charter, furthermore, did not discuss tactics, and there was no parallel document to take up the issues of boycott and civil disobedience, which figured so prominently in the 1949 Programme.

The Africanists, organised around a paper of the same name, and strongly entrenched in Soweto, cried treason. They would have none of the formulation '. . . we, the people of South Africa, black and white, together — equals, countrymen and brothers. . . .' and they denied that South Africa belonged 'to all who live in it'. The nationalism that shaped the ANC, they claimed, depended on the Africans standing on their own, and liberating themselves.

The inspiration of the Africanists (and later the PAC) was, inevitably, Anton Lembede, the early CYL documents, and also Nkrumah of Ghana, who proclaimed the right of all African peoples to independence. The Programme of Action was held to contain the untarnished truth. The demand for self-determination and political independence, which had never been critically appraised, was taken up by the Africanists in their claim to be the true heirs to 1949.[30] The ANC on the other hand, without opening up the debate in order to examine the nature of exploitation, claimed to be both the heirs to the Programme of Action and the upholders of the Freedom Charter.

The dispute raged through the late 1950's, and the various movements of protest that emerged in the rural areas, and some in the towns, took second place to the internecine sniping between these two groups. The bus boycotts in Evaton in 1956 and in Alexandra in 1957 suffered as a result. The women's struggles in Zeerust, Sekhukuneland and Harding proceeded without ostensible assistance from either group. The PAC heaped abuse on the leaders of the ANC and brought up a full armoury of anti-Communist slogans. The ANC, in turn, cast scorn on the PAC and accused its leadership of being in the pay of the government or the CIA. There were few attempts to see what the Africanist programme involved, in class terms, outside of the ranks of the Communist Party and left groups in Cape Town and Johannesburg.[31]

By the time such articles or documents appeared the movements were in disarray, and both the ANC and the PAC had been banned. Nor can it be claimed, unfortunately, that many of these analyses were incisive. The applications of general class principles to South Africa were not made concrete. Class analysis of South Africa was based on dubious empirical data, and did not provide a sound theoretical base for describing the structure of the society, or for understanding the struggles of the time.

From Africanism to Black Consciousness

The youth of the late 1960's and early 1970's heard of the banned movement from their parents, from books (where these were available), and knew the names, and some of the ideas, of the former Congress leaders. The entire time period from the inception of the CYL to the formation of SASO was only 25 years, and Dr. Nkomo and Menassah Moerane were members of the groups that launched both the CYL and the BPC. Dr. Nkomo, in fact, was reported as telling an audience in 1971 that: 'There was a time when black people were apologetic in this country, but young men like Anton Lembede came and told the blacks that they should not be apologetic, and said this is your country.'[32]

The basic problems had remained unaltered over the 25 years, although the Reserves were even more impoverished and the women could barely supplement the pittances they received from their men in the towns. Many more Blacks were employed in industry, and a large number had become semi-skilled operatives. And because the Blacks were more militant, discrimination had become more marked and the level of political oppression had deepened.

The proponents of black consciousness ascribed their miserable conditions to colour, dismissing any mention of class oppression. This has already been documented in the pages above and need not detain us here.

There were two issues that did mark the later movement as being in some way different from the earlier groups. The first, and less significant, difference arose from the active interest shown by members of SASO/BPC in Black Theology. This close association between the members of SASO and Black Theology arose from a combination of factors, including their gestation period inside the UCM, and the influence that they felt from the black American experience. The BPC was also deeply impressed by what had happened in the US, and profoundly influenced by events inside the CI and the South African Council of Churches.

Members of the CYL, and particularly Lembede, Mda, Tambo, and many others, had been deeply religious. So too were Pityane, Biko, Koka and other leaders of SASO/BPC. Some of them were loyal members of established churches, while others spoke of a syncretist movement in which traditional African practices could be absorbed. There was no basic difference between many of the youth over the 25 year gap on the issue of religion, and the greater prominence given to the subject in the 1970's was partly due to black American influence.

The second major difference between the CYL and SASO/BPC arose on the issue of the Reserves. There was no 'Homelands' policy in 1945 and the CYL did not concern itself with the Reserves as a special political issue. In 1951 the Bantu Authorities Act was introduced, and the notion of having local, district and regional councils of chiefs was then condemned by the ANC as being unworkable, as well as undesirable. But during the 1960's the legislative assemblies were established in the Reserves and the issue of 'independence' was raised for the first time. No movement could ignore these new instruments of division, and the matter demanded political attention.

When, furthermore, Buthelezi of the KwaZulu region, and Leon of the Coloured Representative Council, together with opposition leaders of the Transkei and others, espoused their own brand of black consciousness, new tensions emerged. The leaders of SASO/BPC asserted their right to the title of Black Consciousness, and branded the opposition as traitors to the cause. Buthelezi was equally scornful of the youth. Symbolically the two sides clashed at Sobukwe's funeral, and Buthelezi was routed. The victory, however, was hollow because Buthelezi remained firmly entrenched, while his opponents were hounded by the police.

Biko could exorcise 'collaborators' by declaring them to be non-black, but they did not go away. No more than capitalism ceased to exist because Rachidi said that Blacks would have none of it, or class struggles disappeared because Pityane said Blacks were oppressed 'as a people, and not as a class'.

By 1976 the paradoxes in the movement had become clear, and the editor of *Black Review*, 1975-76, pointed to the strains. At one level he noted the existence of two 'variant attitudes':

> There are those who are taking Black consciousness as being chiefly of cultural interest;
> There were those who wanted to transform mere identity into positive

support for initiative towards defined socio-political change.[33]

On this issue he commented:

> There had been a danger of the intellectual groups succeeding in creating a reality that would only be available to themselves, a reality that, according to the more militant youth, would in effect be fictitious, since as one South African Students Movement member put it, 'a reality of pretending to be at least free in the ghetto'.[34]

This, however, was the smaller of the problems facing black consciousness. *Black Review*, edited from within the movement, stated:

> As the Black Consciousness organisations were almost succeeding to prise loose the grips of white liberal agencies in social welfare for Blacks, it was seen that the inner and outer contradictions of Black Consciousness were becoming more acute. The contradicitions of Black Consciousness had thrown focus on the nature of Black Consciousness as understood by those political groups operating on Separate Development platforms such as the CRC Labour Party, the Inkatha Cultural Liberation Movement led by KwaZulu's Chief Gatsha and the Transkeian opposition party, the Democratic Party, led by Mr. H.B. Ncokazi.

On the issue of Inkatha, the editor concluded: 'Until now the question of Inkatha's national claims has not been answered.'[35]

Unfortunately for the leaders of the BPC, the contradictions could not be resolved. Or at least not within the ideological framework which they had erected. As long as they saw the problem in colour terms, the leaders of Inkatha, or the Labour Party, Democratic Party, and so on, had as much claim to the title of black consciousness as did BPC. And in part BPC recognised this. They seldom criticised Buthelezi, or Leon, or Ncokazi, for the things they did. They did not criticise their campaigns or their activities: neither in the strikes, nor in the bus boycotts, nor in any of their many activities, except over the issues related directly to the Homelands policy and the associated matter of foreign investments. And yet, Buthelezi should have been taken to task for his role in many of these events. His behaviour during the long strike wave should have been criticised, his actions during the Soweto event condemned. To talk only of his 'working' the government institutions, bad as that was considered to be, was indicative of political myopia. But to criticise Buthelezi effectively, BPC would have had to evoke class analysis, and this they would not or could not, apparently, do.

Black Consciousness and Violence

The long record of events in the 1950's indicated that the CYL (and the CYL members who assumed leadership of both the ANC and the PAC) were opposed to violence. Despite every brutality perpetrated against themselves or their movements, they kept steadfastly to 'peaceful' methods. There was an irony involved in their holding so firmly to non-violence because every campaign they initiated led to, and they knew it would lead to, police violence. Few demonstrations or strikes ended without broken heads or lost lives.

And the more 'militant' the language, the less inclined were the movements involved to engage in any but non-violent means. The state insisted that this was a front and, in the many trials of the 1950's including the mammoth Treason Trial of 1956-61, it made every effort to demonstrate that the ANC was prepared to resort to violence. Yet, almost to a fault, the members of the ANC, despite some flippant talk, had eschewed violence. Only after the movements had been banned in 1960 did thoughts turn to other means of defeating the government and, starting in 1961, campaigns of sabotage were initiated in the country.

Most of the original internal movements were destroyed or severely crippled by mid-1964, but groups in exile continued training for, and talking of, incursions into South Africa and of eventual guerrilla warfare.

SASO/BPC leaders, in contrast, were resolutely opposed to the use of violent methods, and quite how they saw themselves overturning the government, is not certain. Some claims have been made that part of the leadership was considering the use of arms, but there is no firm evidence that this was the case, nor that any concrete steps were being taken in this direction. During the early life of SASO, when little was done off the campuses, the question remained academic. By the time the matter needed urgent attention, there was little left of the student body. The youth in the schools had to look to their own resources and find ways of countering police terror. In the process, early contacts with the external ANC, fully wedded to the need for sabotage and guerrilla war was readily accepted by the SSRC. (The same may perhaps be said of the youth at Kagiso and their contact with the PAC, and conceivably of other groups, about whom nothing is yet known.)

The Suicide Squad of the SSRC was established within three months of the first shooting, and was operative almost immediately. The experience of the external movement was, quite evidently, speedily transmitted to young men who had no previous training in, or experience of, such techniques. The first such attempt was smashed by police activity, and there was no early opportunity for a new group to be established inside Soweto. Instead, the external wing of the ANC prepared for and organised subsequent attacks on transport links.

It would seem that there is little likelihood in the future of any purely peaceful campaign being successful in the face of government intransigence, and political movements which hope to introduce radical changes will have to find military training and military support. Buthelezi, who has come to the same conclusion, but for other reasons, has asked the government to ensure that no guerrillas enter KwaZulu across its northern boundaries. He does not wish to entertain the idea of a clash with the government, and has nothing to gain from a victory of liberation movements that oppose his basic policy of working within apartheid institutions. His role, as he prefers to see it, is to wait in the wings until the government find it necessary to employ him for purposes of an internal settlement.

The ANC has the initiative in its hands now, in being the only movement with the capability of mounting some armed incursion. It also has the following and it has the goodwill of large parts of the population. Its leaders would be foolish to squander these possibilities, and need to take a careful look at the political, as well as the military, possibilities of attacking the state. In the process it is to be hoped that false claims will not be made. It was wrong to claim in 1976, and it would still be wrong to claim that: 'These racist murderers who were so eager to machine-gun unarmed kids and women took to their heels when they came face to face with armed freedom fighters of Umkhonto we Sizwe in Zimbabwe in 1967 and 1968.'[36] There is still much to be done before Umkhonto, or any other liberation force, is able to inflict defeat on the armed forces of Vorster/Botha.

Even more than a tempered approach to military incursion into the country, the political movements abroad need to refine their political analyses. Amilcar Cabral was only rephrasing a well known maxim when he declared that, '. . . if it is true that a revolution can fail even though it be based on perfectly conceived theories, nobody has yet made a successful revolution without a revolutionary theory.'[37]

This requires a hard look at the class forces amongst the Blacks of South Africa, their relation to one another and to the oppressors, their revolutionary (and counter-revolutionary) potentials, and the means by which they can be mobilised in the struggle which is not far off in South Africa. This was the first task that Cabral undertook in his own country, and no less can be expected in South Africa, where the forces opposing the liberation movement are so much more powerful than elsewhere in Africa, so well entrenched, and so well armed.

One of the stories told in the aftermath of the Revolt concerned a section of the school students in late 1976. This youth sought socialist literature and requested titles like Emile Burns' *What is socialism?* and Leontiev's *Political Economy*. These were books that circulated widely in CP circles before the passing of the Suppression of Communism Act in July 1950, and the youth would have heard the titles from their parents, or members of the ANC with whom they were in contact.

The books they were looking for would, if available, have been of little use to them, but it was the fact that they were searching for such texts that was significant. For over 25 years the government had banned all such literature, and there was very little socialist or Marxist literature available in the townships. Now, in the heat of a bitter struggle, the youth sought new answers to old problems. They were no longer content with simplistic answers which ascribed all the ills of society to skin colour. Their need, perceived then if only in part, was to understand the nature of capitalism, of state power, of imperialism, and above all, the nature of the class struggle.

In the months and years to come, the youth of South Africa will search increasingly for an understanding of these problems. They will confront these problems in their daily lives, but will have to search far and wide for literature to help them understand these phenomena. It will be the bounden duty of those who are at present in exile, to stretch out their hands and share with the young men and women in South Africa, on whom the brunt of the struggle must fall, an understanding of the forces they face. Only thus will the external wing of the liberation movement share fully with their comrades inside South Africa the task of transforming the country into the socialist world they desire together.

References

1. A fuller account of the war-time movements will appear in a forthcoming volume by the author.
2. The complete address is reprinted in Karis and Carter, *op.cit.*, Vol. 2, pp.331-6.
3. *Ibid.*, pp.318-9.
4. *Inkundla ya Bantu*, October 1945 (1).
5. Karis and Carter, Vol. 2, pp.314-6.
6. *Ibid.*, p.317.
7. *Ibid.*, pp.317-8.
8. *Inkundla ya Bantu*, 30 September 1944.
9. *Inkululeko*, October 1945.
10. *Inkululeko*, 22 September 1945.
11. *Inkundla ya Bantu*, 23 July 1949.
12. Karis and Carter, *op.cit.*, Vol. 2, p.330.
13. See, for example, I.B. Tabata, (1950), *The Awakening of a People*, (Peoples' Press), pp.89ff.
14. Karis and Carter, *op.cit.*, Vol. 2, pp.324-5.
15. *Inkundla ya Bantu*, 17 November 1944.
16. Jordan Ngubane wrote the editorials and also the columns under the names of Twana and Khanyise. He also drafted the first manifesto of the CYL together with Anton Lembede, according to P. Mda, writing in *Drum*, May 1954.
17. See, for example, Editorial in *Inkundla ya Bantu*, 5 March 1949.
18. 'Basic policy of Congress Youth League, manifesto issued by the National Executive Committee of the ANC Youth League, 1948', in Karis and Carter, *op.cit.*, pp.323-31.
19. Quoted in Brian Willans, (1977), ' "The gift of the century": Solomon Plaatje, De Beers and the old Kimberley tram shed, 1918-19', in *The Societies of Southern Africa in the 19th and 20th centuries*, Vol. 8, (Institute of Commonwealth Studies), pp.83-4.
20. Karis and Carter, *op.cit.*, Vol. 2, p.334.
21. *Inkundla ya Bantu*, 30 July 1949.
22. Karis and Carter, *op.cit.*, Vol. 2, p.338.
23. *Inkundla ya Bantu*, 11 June 1949.

24. *Inkundla ya Bantu*, 5 November 1949.
25. Karis and Carter, *op.cit.*, Vol. 2, p.337-8. The national academy was a project particularly dear to Anton Lembede.
26. Text of a public statement issued by Dr. Xuma, printed in the Cape Town *Guardian*, 23 March 1950.
27. *Loc.cit.*
28. The Freedom Charter is reprinted in Karis and Carter, *op.cit.*, Vol. 3, pp.205-8.
29. *Ibid.*
30. The Africanist case was stated by P. Nkutsoeu Raboroko, 'Congress and the Africanists: the Africanist case', in *Africa South*, Vol. 4, No. 3, April-June 1960.
31. See, for example, H.J. Simons, 'The Pan Africanists', *Fighting Talk*, Dec. 1960 and March 1961; B. Hirson, 'Ten years of the stay at home', *op.cit.*, and Democratic League, 'Lessons of the March days', (mimeo), Sept. 1960.
32. Quoted in *African Contemporary Record*, 1971-72, (Collings), 1972, B330.
33. *Black Review*, 1975-76, p.108.
34. *Loc.cit.*
35. *Loc.cit.*
36. *Amandla-Matla*, Vol. 5, No. 2.
37. Amilcar Cabral, (1971), *Revolution in Guinea*, (Stage One), p.75.

A South African Glossary

African: The majority black population of South Africa. Originally referred to in legislation and in literature as **Natives**, and later as **Bantu**. The size of the African population is uncertain, but estimates range between 17 and 25 million. They are not represented in the elected bodies of the Republic of South Africa, and may not vote for any of the White controlled institutions.

Afrikaans: The language spoken in South Africa by the Afrikaners (Whites of mainly Dutch and German extraction). It is the home language of some 65 per cent of the Whites, and of the majority of Coloureds. It is also the language most commonly used in the administrative services.

Bantu: A word originally used to describe the group of languages spoken by the African peoples of South Africa. Later used as a term to designate African people themselves.

Bantustans: See Reserves.

Black Consciousness Movement: A term used to designate the various groups which espoused the ideology of black consciousness in South Africa. There was no organisation that assumed this name, but the various groups which propagated black consciousness were often referred to collectively as the Black Consciousness Movement.

Boer: Literally farmer. The word 'boer' (plural, boere or boers) is often used as a collective noun for Afrikaners.

Chiefs: The traditional leaders of African clans and tribes were called 'chiefs'. The premier chief of an ethnic group was designated the Paramount Chief or, in the case of the Zulu, sometimes referred to as King (and occasionally as Prince).

Coloureds: The population of mixed ethnic origin, sometimes identified (legally) as persons of mixed blood, but also sometimes defined as that section of the population that is recognised as coloured by custom and by acceptance. The coloured population numbers some 2.4 million. Coloured men of the Cape and Natal enjoyed a limited franchise until 1956, when they were finally removed from the common roll.

Compounds: Barracks built near the mines, and near some municipal and industrial sites, to house the all-male African labour force.

Doek: A cloth, or head cloth, used by hostel dwellers in 1976 to distinguish themselves from other sections of the population.

Europeans: The Whites of South Africa. Their total number is approximately 4.3 million. They alone have the full franchise, and only they may own land and property in the 'white' region of the country, comprising some 87 per cent of the land surface.

Homelands: A euphemism used to describe the **Reserves**, in which nine (or latterly ten) African populations will exercise 'full' sovereignty. All Africans will, according to government plans, be attached to one of the homelands and will become citizens of those territories.

Indians: Descendants of indentured labourers brought from India from 1860 onwards to work on the Natal sugar plantations. Indians may not move freely between Provinces and are prohibited from entering the Orange Free State without permission. The majority still live in Natal. The Indian population is approximately 750,000.

Natives: The term most favoured by the government for the African people until altered by the Nationalist Party government to **Bantu**. There are separate administrative bodies employed to handle the large number of regulations and laws controlling the movements and activities of Africans. These were centralised by a department known successively as the Native Affairs Department, the Department of Bantu Affairs, the Department of Bantu Administration and Development, and since Soweto as the Department of Plural Relations.

Push-Outs: A term used in Soweto to describe the youth who were forced out of the schools. They were excluded from the educational system for a number of reasons. Either there was no accommodation for them, or they had failed an examination and were not allowed to proceed to the next class, or their parents could no longer afford to keep them at school.

The Rand: From 1910 to 1961, the South African currency was the pound, which was usually at par with the pound sterling. In 1961, a decimal currency was adopted, with the Rand as the basic unit. Two Rand was declared equal to £1 and each Rand was equal to 100 cents. In 1967 the pound sterling was devalued and the value of the Rand rose accordingly. In 1972, after the US administration suspended gold payments against dollars, the Rand was tied to the American currency, and this led to a *de facto* devaluation in terms of currencies that had been floated to higher parities. The value of the Rand oscillated between $1.40 and $1.50. In June 1975 the Rand was devalued from $1.49 to $1.42, and in September to $1.15. In February 1977 the pound sterling was quoted as equal to R1.4826.

Reserves: The land, constituting less than 13 per cent of South Africa's land surface, in which some Africans may own land under communal (and occasionally private) tenure, and keep livestock. The population in these areas is said to be between 8 and 10 million, and an increasing proportion of these people are landless. The Reserves have also been called, more recently, Bantustans or Homelands.

Schools: Until 1975 there was a 13 year school structure for Africans. Thereafter it was reduced to 12 years, by dropping the sixth standard which was unique to African institutions. There are four stages of education:

Lower Primary: Sub-standards A and B and Standards 1 and 2.

Higher Primary: Standards 3 to 5 (and previous to 1975, standard 6).

Junior secondary: Forms I to III.

Senior secondary (sometimes called High Schools): Forms IV and V.

Students: Youth at schools are called, interchangeably, pupils and students. The youth more usually referred to themselves as students.

Townships: Also called **locations**, they are areas reserved outside all towns, for the accommodation of Africans who worked in shops and factories of the neighbouring urban area or areas. Residence was only open to persons who could show that they were legally employed in the area, who had recognised business in the area, or were entitled to be present because of their profession or occupation. The limited leasehold rights, once available to a small group of Africans, had been stopped by the Nationalist government. A limited leasehold right for 30 years was granted after the Soweto Revolt.

Tsotsi: African youth in the townships, accused of being delinquent. The name was derived from the 'stovepipe' trousers that were once fashionable amongst these unemployed, and often delinquent, young men. (Their coloured counterparts were known as **Skollies**).

When Did It Happen?
A Chronology of Events

1799	First school for Africans opened.
1820	Lovedale Mission Station opened.
1834	Liberation of the slaves.
1841	First grant to mission schools in the Cape.
1853	Amamzimtoti Institute (Adams College) opened in Natal.
1854-61	Sir George Grey, Governor of the Cape.
1867	Discovery of Diamonds at Kimberley.
1886	Discovery of Gold on the Witwatersrand.
1910	Union of South Africa formed.
1912	ANC founded.
1916	Fort Hare University College founded.
1920	First recorded school strikes at Lovedale and Kilnerton.
1924	NUSAS founded.
1938-46	Strike wave at mission schools and Fort Hare.
1943-44	CYL founded.
1945	Fort Hare joins NUSAS.
1948	Pamphlet on Christian National Education published.
	Nationalist Party wins election and forms government.
1949	Robert Mangaliso Sobukwe delivers 'Completer's Social' address.
1950	Suppression of Communism Act passed.
1951	Bantu Authorities Act passed.
1953	Bantu Education Act passed.
1955	Boycott of schools in Southern Transvaal and Eastern Cape.
1957	Nursing Act Amendment Act passed.
1959	Extension of University Education Act passed.
1960	Shooting at Sharpeville and Langa-Nyanga. ANC and PAC banned.
1960-67	African university colleges demand right to join NUSAS.
1965	Christian Institute forms AICA.
1967	University Christian Movement launched.
	ASSECA started.
	Urban Training Project formed.

1968	UCT students strike over Archie Mafeje issue.
1969	Durban dock strike fails.
	SASO launched.
1970	African Students Movement (later SASM) formed.
	Gatsha Buthelezi becomes Chief Executive Officer of KwaZulu.
	Anglo American Corporation offer of money for Soweto classrooms vetoed.

1971	First steps to formation of BPC.
	Official price of gold raised from $35 to $46.5 per fine ounce.
	TEACH launched for black schools.
	Sales and Allied Workers Union started.
June	International Court of Justice ruling on Namibia.
Sept.	Durban workers threaten strike action and get wage increase.
Dec.	Ovambo workers strike.

1972	O.R. Tiro addresses Turfloop graduands and is expelled.
March	SASM launched.
June	PUTCO strike, in Johannesburg.
July	BPC formed.
Aug.	BAWU formed.
Oct.	Dockworkers strike, in Durban and Cape Town.
	Widespread university strikes and clashes with police.

1973	
Jan.-Feb.	70,000 workers in Durban-Pinetown-Hammarsdale on strike.
March	Strike at Tugela mills; B. Dladla involved.
June	NAYO formed.
Jul.-Sep.	Boycott of classes at UWC.
Aug.	Strikes in textile mills, Durban.
Sep. 11	Carltonville strike and shootings.

1974	Strikes spread to rest of country, and continue on mines.
	Inkatha Yenkululeko Yesizwe launched.
	Caetano government falls in Portugal.
Aug.	Schlebusch Commission reports on NUSAS.
	Entrance to African secondary schools doubled by lowering examination requirements.
Sep. 25	Viva Frelimo rallies called.

| 1975 | Trial of SASO 9. |
| | Trial of NAYO 7. |

Trials of ANC, SACP, and Okhela members.
Standard Six (exclusively in African schools) abolished.

Aug.	South African army enters Angola.
Oct.	Bus boycott, Newcastle.

1976

Feb.	Trouble at Thomas Mofolo school over Afrikaans medium instruction.
Mar.	Heinemann workers strike at Elandsfontein.
	Bus boycott at KwaThema.
	Buthelezi calls rally at Soweto.
Apr.-May	Strikes at several Soweto schools.
June 16	Demonstration called in Soweto.
June 18	Theron Commission reports.
June 18	Turfloop closed. Ngoye library destroyed.
June 21	Pretoria school pupils close schools.
June 22	Demonstrations in BophutaTswana.
July 15	All schools closed.
	School unrest throughout country.
Aug. 2	UWC boycott lectures.
Aug. 4	Soweto students try to march to Johannesburg.
Aug. 6-8	Schools burnt down in BophutaTswana.
Aug. 9	BophutaTswana Legislative Assembly buildings alight.
Aug. 11	Cape African schools demonstrate.
Aug. 16	Coloured students boycott classes in Cape Town.
Aug. 23	Stay-at-home in Soweto. Highly successful.
Sept. 1	African students march in Cape Town city centre.
Sept. 2-3	Coloured students also attempt marches in Cape Town city centre.
Sept. 6	10 week strike at Armourplate Glass Works begins.
Sept. 13-15	Stay-at-home in Soweto.
Sept. 15-16	Stay-at-home in Cape Town
Sept. 20-22	Stay-at-home in Thembisa.
Oct.	Campaign against all drink.
Oct. 24	'Suicide Squad' bombs Jabulani police station.
Oct. 27	Shebeens in Soweto ordered to close.
	Anti-Christmas celebrations announced.
Nov. 1-5	Five day stay-at-home fails to materialise.
	School examinations boycotted.

1977

Feb.-Mar.	Confusion over examination boycott.
Mar. 20-27	BPC calls Heroes Week.

April 23	Campaign against increased rents in Soweto.
June	Soweto UBC forced to resign.
June 15	Rail line in Natal blown up.
June 16	First anniversary of Soweto Revolt commemorated.
Sept. 17	Steve Biko murdered.
Oct. 19	17 African organisations and Christian Institute outlawed.

Bibliography

A. Books, Pamphlets, and Articles

Adler, T. (ed), (1977), *Perspectives on South Africa,* African Studies Institute, University of the Witwatersrand.

Beard, T.V.R., (1972), 'Background to student activities at the University College of Fort Hare', in H.W. van der Merwe and D. Welsh, (1972).

Bengu, S.M., (1975), 'The national cultural liberation movement', *Reality,* (September).

Berger, John, (1971), *Selected Essays and Articles: the Look of Things,* Penguin.

Berman, Myrtle, (c.1959), *The African Education Movement,* typescript, School of Oriental and African Studies Library.

Biko, Steve, (n.d.), 'I write what I please: Fear — an important determinant in South African politics', written under the pseudonym 'Frank Talk', reprinted by IUEF, (1976).
  (1972), 'White racism and black consciousness', in H.W. van der Merwe and D. Welsh, (1972).
  (1973), 'Black consciousness and the quest for a true humanity', in Basil Moore, (1973).

Boesak, Allan, (1977), *Farewell to Innocence: a Social-Ethical Study of Black Theology and Black Power,* Ravan Press, Johannesburg.

Burger, John, (Leo Marquard), (1943), *The Black Man's Burden,* Gollancz.

Buthelezi, Mangosuthu Gatsha, (1976), 'A message to South Africa from black South Africa', supplement to *Pro Veritate,* (March).
  (1977), 'Address: At the opening of Akulu Chemicals (Pty) Ltd, factory at Isithebe, 27 May 1977', press handout.
  and Beyers Naude, C.F., (1976), 'Statement on foreign investment in South Africa', (dated 10 March 1976).

Cabral, Amilcar, (1971), *Revolution in Guinea,* Stage One, London.

Callinicos, Alex and Rogers, John, (1977), *Southern Africa after Soweto,* Pluto, London.

Christian Institute of Southern Africa, (1976), *Detention and Detente in Southern Africa,* Johannesburg.

Coetzee, J.A. Grey, (1976), *Industrial Relations in South Africa,* Juta, Cape Town.

Cook, P.A.W., (1949), 'Native education', in E. Hellman, (1949).

Counter Information Service, (1977), *Black South Africa Explodes,* Russell Press.

(1978), *Buying Time in South Africa*, Russell Press.
Curtis, Neville and Keegan, Clive, (1972), 'The aspiration to a just society', in H.W. van der Merwe and D. Welsh, (1972).
Davis, David, (1974), 'How black workers are organising', *Anti-Apartheid News*, (October).
Dekker, L. Douwes, Hemson, D., Kane-Berman, J.S., Lever, J., and Schlemmer, L., (1975), 'Case studies in African labour action in South Africa and Namibia', in R. Sandbrook and R. Cohen, (1975).
Democratic League, (1960), 'Lessons of the March days', Cape Town, (September), (mimeo).
Desmond, Cosmas, (1971), *The Discarded People*, Penguin.
Education League, (n.d.), *Blueprint for Blackout*, Johannesburg.
Ehrenreich, Barbara and John, (1969), *Long March, Short Spring: the Student Uprising at Home and Abroad*, Modern Reader, New York.
Eiselen, W.W.M., (1955), *The Natives in the Western Cape*, SABRA, Stellenbosch.
Eisenberg, Pablo, (1962), 'Education in South Africa', in H. Kitchen, (1962).
Ellsworth, Margaret, (1976), 'African education in the Cape', (notes from a talk), *Z*, Vol. 1, No. 2, (October).
Fanon, Frantz, (1973), *The Wretched of the Earth*, Penguin.
Feit, Edward, (1962), *South Africa: the Dynamics of the African National Congress*, Oxford University Press.
First, Ruth, (1963), *South West Africa*, Penguin.
Fisher, Foszia, (1974), 'Class consciousness among colonized workers in South Africa', in T. Adler, (1977).
Gordon, D., (c.1951), 'Some impressions of the African intellectuals at Fort Hare', *Discussion*, Vol. 1, No. 2.
Gwala, Mafika Pascal, (1976), 'Towards the practical manifestations of black consciousness', in T. Thoahlane, (1976).
Hartshorne, K.B., (1953), *Native Education in the Union of South Africa*, (a summary of the report of the Commission on Native Education in South Africa, UG53, 1951), South African Institute of Race Relations.
Hellman, Ellen, (ed), (1949), *Handbook of Race Relations in South Africa*, Oxford University Press, Cape Town.
Hemson, David, (c.1977), 'Black trade unionism, industrial strikes, and mass struggle in South Africa', (mimeo).
Heppel, Alex, (1966), *South Africa: a Political and Economic History*, Pall Mall.
Hirson, Baruch, see Socialist League of Africa.
Hlongwane, Jane, (1976), 'Emergence of African unions in Johannesburg with reference to the Engineering union', in J.A. Grey Coetzee, (1976).
Hoffman, Joan, (1977), 'Fragment of a view', in *Quarry '77: New South African Writing*, Ravan Press.
Horner, D.B. (ed), (1975), *Labour Organisation and the African*, South African Institute of Race Relations.
Horrell, Muriel, (1963), *African Education: Some Origins and Development until 1953*, ibid.
(1964), *A Decade of Bantu Education*, ibid.
See also *Survey of Race Relations in South Africa*.
Houghton, D. Hobart, (1973), *The South African Economy*, Oxford

University Press, Cape Town.

Howe, Irving, (1965), 'New styles in "Leftism" ', *Dissent*, (Summer), reprinted in P. Jacobs and S. Landau, (1967), *The New Radicals*, Penguin.

Huddleston, Trevor (1957), *Naught for your Comfort*, Fontana.

Hurwitz, Nathan, (1964), *The Economics of Bantu Education in South Africa*, SAIRR.

Institute for Industrial Education, (1976), *The Durban Strikes, 1973*, Ravan.

International University Exchange Fund, (1976), *The New Terrorists: Documents from the SASO/BPC Trial*, Geneva.

Jabavu, D.D.T., (1920), *The Black Problem: Papers and Addresses on Various Native Problems*, Lovedale Press.

Jarrett-Kerr, Martin, (1960), *African Pulse*, Faith Press.

Kane-Berman, John, (1976), 'The Soweto upheavals, 16-22 June: a sociological and political analysis', (mimeo).

Karis, Tom and Carter, Gwendolen, (eds), (1971-1977), *From Protest to Challenge*, Vols. 1-4, Hoover Institute Press, Stanford, California.

Kirkwood, Mike, (1974), 'Conflict on the mines, 1974', *South African Labour Bulletin*, (Nov.-Dec.).

(1975), 'The mine worker's struggle', *ibid.*, (Jan.-Feb.).

Kitchen, H., (ed.), (1962), *The Educated African*, Heinemann.

Kleinschmidt, Horst, (1976), 'Black Parents Association', (mimeo).

Koka, Drake, (1977), 'On black consciousness and black solidarity', (mimeo).

Kotze, D.A., (1975), *African Politics in South Africa 1964-1974: Parties and Issues*, Hurst.

Lee-Warden, L.B. (1957), 'The crime of Langa', *Africa South*, Vol. 1, No. 3, (April-June).

Legum, Colin, (1976), *Vorster's Gamble for Africa: How the Search for Peace Failed*, Rex Collings.

Luxemburg, Rosa, (1970), *Rosa Luxemburg Speaks*, (edited by Mary-Alice Waters), Pathfinder.

McCann, Eamonn, (1974), *War and an Irish Town*, Penguin.

McConkey, W.G., (1971), 'A close look at Bantu education', *Reality*, Sept.

MacMillan, W.M., (1930), *Complex South Africa*, Faber.

Majeka, Nosipho, (Dora Taylor), (1952), *The Role of the Missionary in Conquest*, Society of Young Africa, Cape Town.

Malherbe, E.G., (1964), *Bantu Manpower and Education*, South African Institute of Race Relations.

Manganyi, N.C., (1973), *Being Black in the World*, Spro-Cas/Ravan.

Mare, Gerhard (Gerry), (1974), 'The East London strikes', *South African Labour Bulletin*, (August).

(1974a), 'The strikes in February 1973: insights from a research project just completed', in D.B. Horner, *op.cit.*

Ministers fraternal of Langa, Guguletu, and Nyanga, (1976), 'Role of riot police in the burnings and killings', Nyanga, Cape Town, Christmas.

Mkhatshwa, Smangaliso P., (1975), 'Putting the Black Renaissance Convention into correct perspective', *Reality*, (May).

Moore, Basil, (ed) (1973), *Black Theology: the South African Voice*, Hurst.

Motapanyane, Tebello, (1977), 'How June 16 demo was planned', *Sechaba*, Vol. 11(2).

Motsepe, C.A.R., (c.1950), 'Strikes in African institutions', printed article of unknown origin, found in Fabian Colonial Bureau papers, Oxford.

Motsuenyane, S.M., (1976), 'Black consciousness and the economic position of the black man in South Africa', in T. Thoalane, (1976).

Mphahlele, Ezekiel, (1962), *The African Image*, Faber.

(1962a), *Down Second Avenue*, Seven Seas.

Nengwekhulu, Ranwedzi Harry, (1976), 'Black consciousness movement of South Africa', International University Exchange Fund, Geneva.

Nettleton, Clive, (1972), 'Racial cleavage on the student left', in H.W. van der Merwe and D. Welsh, (1972).

Ngubane, Harriet, (1977), *Body and Mind in Zulu Medicine*, Academic Press.

(1978), 'The politics of death in Soweto', (mimeo).

Nkondo, G.M., (ed), (1977), *Turfloop Testimony: the Dilemma of a Black University in South Africa*, Ravan Press.

Nolutshungu, Themba, (1976), 'Inside Langa and Guguletu', *South African Outlook*, (August).

Norton, Victor, (1976), 'Preliminary chronology of events in Cape Town in the unrest following the Soweto riots', Cape Town, (mimeo).

Ntantala, Phyllis, (1960), 'The Abyss of Bantu Education', *Africa South*, Vol. 4, No. 2, (Jan.-March).

Nxasana, Harold and Fisher, Foszia, (1974), 'The labour situation in South Africa', in T. Thoalane, (1975).

Paton, David M., (ed), (1958), *Church and Race in South Africa*, SCM Press, London.

Pelzer, A.N., (ed), (1966), *Verwoerd Speaks: Speeches 1948-1966*, APB, Johannesburg.

Pityana, Nyameko Barney, (1972), 'Power and social change in South Africa', in H.W. van der Merwe and D. Welsh, (1972).

(1973), 'What is black consciousness', in B. Moore, *op.cit.*

Raboroko, P. Nkutsoeu, (1960), 'Congress and the Africanists: the Africanist case', *Africa South*, Vol. 4, No. 3, (April-June).

Randall, Peter, (ed), (1971), *South Africa's Minorities*, Spro-Cas Occasional Publications, No. 2,

Riekert, P.J., (1970), 'The economy of the Republic of South Africa, with special reference to Homeland and Border industrial development and the economies of Southern Africa', *Mercurius*, No. 10, (June), (Unisa, Pretoria).

Rogers, Howard, (1949), *Native Administration in the Union of South Africa*, (2nd edn revised by P.A. Linington), Government Printer, Pretoria.

Roux, Edward, (1949), *Time Longer Than Rope*, Gollancz.

Russell, David P.H., (1977), 'The riot police and the suppression of truth', Cape Town, (January), (mimeo).

Sandbrook, Richard and Robin Cohen, (eds), (1975), *The Development of an African Working Class: Studies in Class Formation and Action*, Longman.

Seatlholo, Khotso S., (1976), 'A Soweto student speaks', (Press release for the SSRC), *Pro Veritate*, (November).

Shepherd, R.H.W., (1971), *Lovedale, South Africa, 1824-1955*, Lovedale Press.

Sikakane, Joyce, (1977), *A Window on Soweto*, International Defence and Aid Fund.

Small, Adam, (1971), 'Blackness versus nihilism: black racism rejected', in B. Moore, (1973).

Socialist League of Africa, (B. Hirson), (1960), 'South Africa: ten years of the stay-at-home', (mimeo), reprinted in *International Socialist*, (Summer 1961).

(1961), 'South Africa: once again on the stay-at-home', *International Socialist*, (Autumn).

South African Institute of Race Relations, (1973), 'A view of the 1973 strikes', (20 November 1973), (mimeo), RR 151/73.

Spooner, F.P., (1960), *South African Predicament*, Cape.

Spro-Cas, (1972), *Apartheid and the Church.*

Suttner, Raymond, (1976), 'Why I will go to prison', UN Centre Against Apartheid, Notes and Documents No. 1/76, (January).

Tabata, I.B., (1950), *The Awakening of a People: the All African Convention*, Peoples Press, Johannesburg.

(1960), *Education for Barbarism*, Pall Mall.

Thoahlane, Thoahlane, (1975), *Black Renaissance: Papers from the Black Renaissance Convention*, Ravan Press.

Trotsky, Leon, (1932), *History of the Russian Revolution*, Gollancz.

Troup, Freda, (1976), *Forbidden Pastures: Education under Apartheid*, International Defence and Aid Fund.

van den Berghe, Pierre, (1976), *South Africa: a Study in Conflict*, University of California Press.

van der Merwe, Hendrik W, and Welsh, David, (1972), *Student Perspectives on South Africa*, David Philip, Cape Town.

Vigne, Randolph, (1973), *A Dwelling Place of our own: the Story of the Namibian Nation*, International Defence and Aid Fund.

Webster, Eddie, (n.d.) 'Consciousness and the problem of organisation: a case study of a sample of African workers in Durban', (mimeo).

Welsh, David, (1971), 'The growth of towns', in M. Wilson and L.M. Thomson, (1971).

Wentzel, Jill, (1977), 'Black United Front: an interview with Dr. Nyembezi and Mr. Mavuso, *Reality*, (July).

Whisson, M.G., (1971), 'The Coloured people', in P. Randall, (1971).

Willan, Brian, (1977), ' "The gift of the century"; Solomon Plaatje, De Beers and the old Kimberley tram shed, 1918-19', in *The Societies of Southern Africa in the 19th and 20th centuries*, Vol. 8., Institute of Commonwealth Studies, London.

Williams, Raymond, (1965), *The Long Revolution*, Penguin.

Wilson, Lindy, (1976), 'Cape township riots – some African accounts', *South African Outlook*, (August).

Wilson, Monica, and Thompson, Leonard, (eds), 1971, *The Oxford History of South Africa*, Vol. 2., Oxford University Press.

Wolfson, J.G.E., (1976), *Turmoil at Turfloop*, South African Institute of Race Relations.

Woods, Donald, (1978), *Biko*, Paddington Press.

B. Annual Reviews

Black Review, (Black Community Programmes).
1972, Khoapa, B.A., (ed).

1973, Gwala, Mafika Pascal, (ed).
1974-75, Mbanjwa, Thoko, (ed).
1975-76, Rambally, Asha, (ed).
Survey of Race Relations in South Africa (SRRSA), South African Institute of Race Relations.
1949-1970, Muriel Horrell, (ed).
1971, Muriel Horrell, Dudley Horner, John Kane-Berman, (eds).
1972, Muriel Horrell, Dudley Horner, John Kane-Berman, Robin Margo, (eds).
1973, Muriel Horrell, Dudley Horner, (eds).
1974, Muriel Horrell, Dudley Horner, Jane Hudson, (eds).
1975, Muriel Horrell, Tony Hodgson, (eds).
1976, Muriel Horrell, Tony Hodgson, Suzanne Blignaut, Sean Moroney, (eds).
1977, Loraine Gordon, Suzanne Blignaut, Sean Moroney, Carole Cooper, (eds).

C. Official Reports and Publications

Report of Inter-departmental committee of inquiry into riots on mines in the Republic of South Africa, (mimeo, n.d.).
Report of Native Economic Commission, 1930-32, UG 22, 1932.
Transvaal 1961-1971, (1971), Voortrekker Pers.

D. Collections of Papers

Luthuli papers, microfilm, Institute of Commonwealth Studies.
UCT workshop on the Revolt of 1976.

E. Taped Interviews

Alan Lipman, Professor of Architecture, Cardiff University.
James Phillips, former trade unionist.

F. Newspapers and Journals, South Africa

Africa South, Cape Town.
Amandla-Matla, (mimeo, n.d.).
Black Sash.
Bulletin of the UBJ, (Union of Black Journalists).
Bulletin two: a journal of student critique, University of Cape Town.
Discussion, Cape Town.
Eastern Province Herald.
Fighting Talk, Johannesburg.
Financial Mail, Johannesburg.
Guardian, Cape Town.

Ikhwezi Lomso, Natal.
Inkululeko, Johannesburg.
Inkundla ya Bantu, Natal.
Inyaniso, Johannesburg, (mimeo).
Liberation, Johannesburg.
Mercurius, Pretoria (Unisa).
Muslim News, Cape Town.
Pro Veritate, Johannesburg.
Race Relations News, Johannesburg.
Rand Daily Mail, Johannesburg.
Reality, Natal.
SASO Bulletin.
SASO Newsletter.
South African Labour Bulletin.
South African Outlook, Cape.
South African News Agency, (telex news).
The Star, Johannesburg.
Torch, Cape Town.
Vukani-Awake, (mimeo).
Z, University of Cape Town.

G. Newspapers and Journals, Britain

Africa Digest, London.
Anti-Apartheid News, London.
Guardian, London.
Namibia News, London.
Sechaba, (ANC), London.
X-Ray: Current Affairs in Southern Africa, The Africa Bureau, London.

H. Leaflets Issued During the Revolt

Leaflets issued in the name of:
    African National Congress, and Umkhonto we Sizwe.
    Black Allied Workers Union.
    Black Parents Association.
    Pupils of the Cape Town Bantu schools.
    Soweto Students Representative Council.
    Thembisa (students?).
    Anonymous.

Index

African National Congress, 6, 54, 64, 101, 327.
   Programme, 320-3.
   and Revolt, 199-201, 245, 251-2, 256, 268, 286, 290, 310, 327-8.
African nurses, 46, 60-1.
   in Strikes, 35, 61-2, 254, 311-2.
Angola, 8, 167-8.
ASSECA, 76-8, 109, 268, 292.

Bantu Education, 40-52, 55-6, 60-2, 77, 93-4, 239.
   Organised opposition, 47-52.
Bantu School Boards, 9, 99, 177, 208, 277.
Beerhalls and alcohol, 7, 183, 186, 189, 212, 249, 252, 264-7, 279
   ref. 4.
Berger, John, 180-3, 251, 259.
Biko, Steve, 78, 82, 114, 292, 325.
   Black consciousness, 110-11.
   Death, 277-8.
   On Workers, 293-4.
Black Community Programmes, 81, 85, 102, 110, 278, 302-5.
Black Consciousness, 7, 107, 110-11, 118, 127, 191, 196, 295-8, 325.
   Africanism, 309-25.
   'Black' defined, 72, 295-6, 299.
   Black theology, 73, 78, 325.
   and Class analysis, 298-300, 305-6, 319.
   and Communism, 109, 298-300, 311.
   and Economics, 293, 301-2.
   Tribal consciousness, 115, 118-9, 325-6.
Black Consciousness Movement, 5, 7, 107, 278, 331.
   'Black man, you are on your own', 69.
   and Revolt, 196, 288.
   see also under individual organisations.
Black Parents Association, 5, 196-8, 209, 243.
Black Peoples Convention, 7.
   Activities, 84, 292.
   Economic theories, 300-2.
   Founding of, 76, 82.
   Membership, 9, 107-9.
   Non-collaboration, 114, 305.
   and Revolt, 119, 270, 288.
   Trade unions, 127, 289; see also D. Koka.
   Trial of, 162-3, 293.
   Viva Frelimo rally, 84, 89-91, 160, 284.
   see also BCP and SASO.
Black schools, 332-3.
   Afrikaans medium, 99-100, 175-7.
   Cape schools, 219-21, 226-36, 247-9.
   Discrimination at, 100-1.
   Expansion in 1970s, 95-9, 150, 174.
   Industrial training in, 15-21.
   Mission control, 14-21, 26-9, 40-1, 45-6, 51-2, 55-6, 320.
   Numbers at, 15, 17, 20-1, 23-6, 62-3, 95, 98.
   in Reserves, 239.
   Strikes at, 8, 27, 30-2, 52, 56, 174-5.
   Whites at, 12-13, 17-18.
   see also Bantu education.

Black workers
and Black Consciousness Movement, 83, 87, 127-30, 156, 253,
284, 289, 293.
Migrant workers, 130-3, 140,
148-52, 218, 243-4, 255, 266.
and Revolt, 183, 189, 201, 211,
277-8.
Stay-at-home, 211, 230, 244-6,
253-63. *see also* Strikes.
Breytenbach, Breyten, 161.
Bus boycotts, 4, 153, 164-6, 282,
285, 310, 324.
Buthelezi, Dr. Manas, 197-8.
Buthelezi, Mongosuthu Gatsha, 52,
88, 114-6, 224, 239-40, 245, 273,
303-4, 327.
Black Consciousness, 115, 325.
Soweto rally, 168-72.
and Workers, 130, 135.
see also Inkatha.

Christian Institute, 79-81, 114, 272,
278.
Schlebusch Commission, 160.
Christian National Education, 41-3.
Churches
African Independent Churches,
76.
Christian Council, 79-80.
Dutch Reformed Church, 79.
Mr. Vorster and churches, 80-1.
Coloureds, 216 ff.
Anti-CAD, 223.
Coloured Persons Representative
Council, 222-5.
Theron Commission, 224-6.
Communist Party, 160-3, 199, 224,
310, 328.
see also Suttner.
Congress Youth League, 29, 34-5,
49, 53, 207, 310-8, 320-4, 327.
see also A.M. Lembede and
R.M. Sobukwe.
Consciousness, meaning of, 289-92,
294, 295, 308-9.
Curtis, Neville, 17-8, 66-7.

Demonstrations, 181-3.
see also J. Berger.

Dladla, Barney, 140-2.

Economy
Cost of living, 125.
Gold, 6, 124.
Growth rate, 94, 124.
Education
Financing of, 13-20, 22-5.
Inter-departmental Committee
report, 23-5.
see also Black schools.
Eiselen, Dr. W.W.M.
Commission of Enquiry, 43-4.
Eiselen Line, 217-9.
on Nursing, 60-1.

Fanon, Frantz, 112-3, 118, 292.

Grey, Sir George, 14-5.
Gwala, Mafika, 299-300.

Inkatha, 117-9, 245, 304-5.
see also Gatsha Buthelezi.
Inter-Denominational African
Ministers Association, 76, 81-2,
116, 292.
International University Exchange
Fund, 1, 85, 288.

Jabavu, J. Tengo, 21.
Jabavu, D.D.T., 16, 22, 27.

Koka, Drake, 82, 107, 109, 127-8,
291; and BAWU, 128-30, 291.

Labour Party, 88, 223-5, 325.
Lembede, Anton Muziwakhe, 310-6,
323, 325.
Leon, Sonny, *see* Labour Party.
Lovedale College, 14, 17-8, 21, 28-9,
30-2.
Lutuli, Martin, 20.

Mafeje affair, 67.
Majeko, Nosipho, 16, 27.
Malcolm X, 297-8.
Mandela, Nelson, 54, 64, 309, 322.
Mandela, Winnie Nomzamo, 3, 193,
196, 198, 243.
Mashinini, Tsitsi, 194, 209, 245.

Schlebusch Commission, 159-60.
Seathlolo, Khotso, 193, 249-52, 270.
Small, Adam, 88, 221-2.
Sobukwe, Robert Mangaliso, 35, 279, 311, 319-20, 325.
Sono, Trofomo, 193, 274-5, 278, 295.
South African Students Movement (Soweto Students Representative Council)
    June 16 demonstration, 180, 184-6.
    and NAYO, 103-4, 164.
    Oppose Afrikaans instruction, 177-8.
    Origins of, 102-5, 251, 282, 285, 288.
    Rents campaign, 270-2.
    Soweto Revolt, 191-5, 199-201, 209-12, 234, 243, 246-8, 251-4, 257, 260, 264-70, 275-9.
    Suicide Squad, 251-2.
South African Students Organisation, 7, 65, 71-3, 76, 81, 83, 85-6, 107–8, 113-6, 160, 283, 288, 291-3.
    see also BPC.
Soweto, 2, 3, 183-4.
Squatters, 218-9.
Strikes, 7.
    Armourplate Glass, 154-7, 253.
    Coronation Brick and Tile, 134-6.
    Dockworkers, 122-3.
    Durban-Pinetown, 133-9.
    East London, 151.
    Elandsfontein, 154.
    Legislation, 153.
    Mines, 88, 147-51.
    Ovambo workers, 130-3.
    Police action, 146-54.
    Political and economic strikes, 156-7.
    and the Revolt, 201, 253, 284.
    Textile workers, 134, 137-8.
    Transkei strike, 239.
    see also B. Dladla, Trade Unions, Black workers.
Student aspirations, 22, 27-30, 36, 40-1, 54, 64, 69-72, 83, 87, 90, 100, 103, 194, 235, 250, 253,

256-7, 276, 284-7, 333.
Suttner, Raymond, 160, 163.

TEACH, 97.
Tabata, I.B., 57 ref. 14, 62, 311.
Teachers, 47, 60, 62, 278.
Theron Commission, 224-6.
Tiro, Onkgopotse Ramothibi, 86, 292.
Trade Unions, 125, 218.
    Bannings, 142, 267.
    Garment workers, 125.
    Institute for Industrial Education, 126.
    Metal and Allied Workers, 142, 154.
    NUSAS, 126.
    Organisational forms, 126 142-3.
    and Strike wave, 139.
    Urban Training Project, 126-7.
    see also D. Koka.
Tsotsis, 4, 5, 194-5, 295, 333.

Urban Bantu Councils, 5,9,198, 209, 243, 270-1.
Universities
    Durban Medical School, 86, 187.
    Fort Hare, 28-9, 32-6, 52, 64-5, 68, 73, 86-8, 311-2.
    Ngoye, 64, 73, 116, 172, 187.
    Tribal Colleges, 53-4, 62-3, 74 ref. 11.
    Turfloop, 64, 86, 89-91, 187, 274.
    University of the Western Cape, 5, 87-9, 108, 222, 226-9.
    White Universities, 6, 33, 65-71, 87, 185, 229, 233.
University Christian Movement, 65, 70-1, 73, 82-3.

Verwoerd, Dr. H., 44-5, 49, 239.

Woods, Donald, 114-5, 295.

Xuma, Dr. A.B., 311, 321-2.

Zimbabwe, 8, 283.